WELTKULTUREN
MUSEUM

Country bin pull'em

LOOKING BACK TOGETHER

Edited by Matthias Claudius Hofmann,
Richard Kuba, Christina Henneke and
Isabel Kreuder

KERBER CULTURE

Content

Content

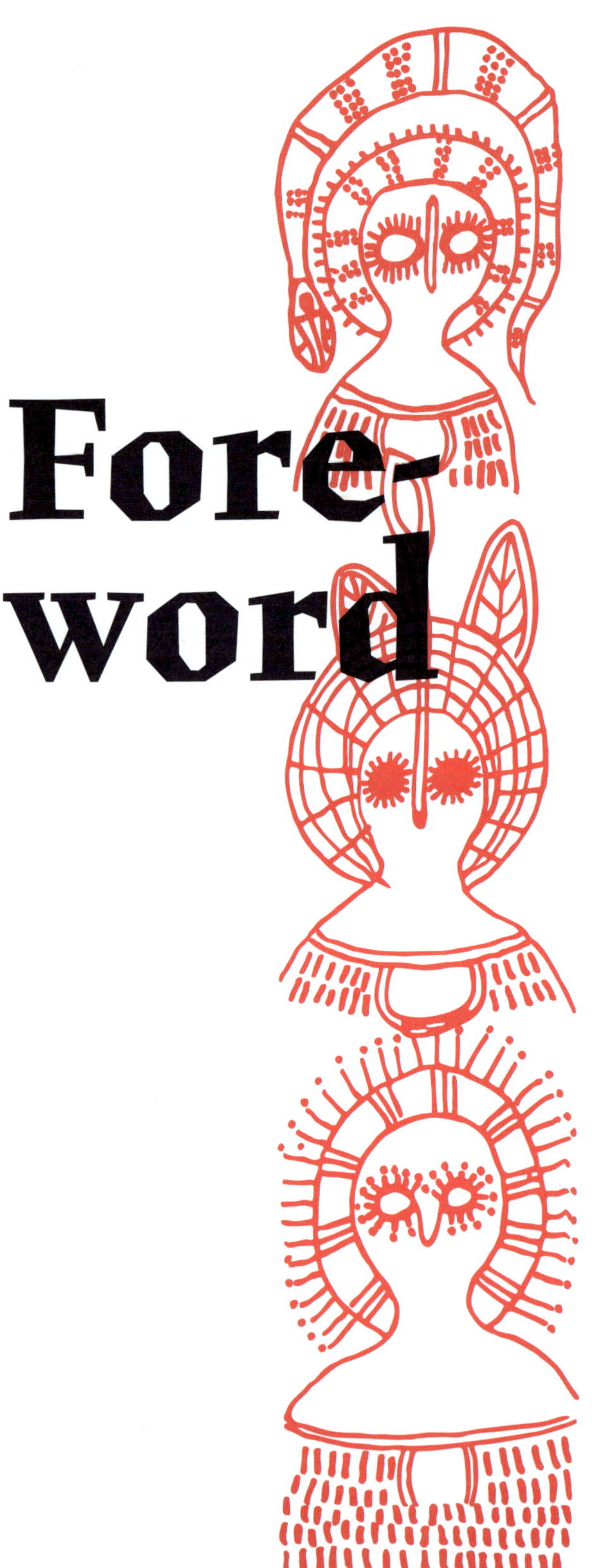

Fore-
word

Foreword from the *Wanjina Wunggurr* Aboriginal Corporations

As *Wanjina Wunggurr* Traditional Owners we are responsible to look after our Country, to keep practising our culture and to respect the knowledge from *Lalai* as our Law.

More than 80 years ago Frobenius Institute researchers and artists travelled to *Wanjina Wunggurr* Country and met our ancestors. They learned many things; they collected bush craft and made many different kinds of records, which they brought back to Frankfurt.

In 2023, four members of the *Wanjina Wunggurr* community travelled to Frankfurt to review these records and to create materials for the COUNTRY BIN PULL'EM exhibition. The exhibition has been co-curated as an invitation to the public to encounter some of these records and show that *Wanjina Wunggurr* Traditional Owners are still alive and their culture is strong.

Wilinggin Aboriginal Corporation,
Dambimangari Aboriginal Corporation,
Wunambal Gaambera Aboriginal Corporation

Welcoming Message from the Cultural Foundation of Hesse

**Looking back together,
looking forward together**

Dear reader,

at the Weltkulturen Museum in Frankfurt am Main – founded at the beginning of the twentieth century and Hesse's only ethnological museum – highly diverse cultures and world views are researched and presented to the general public, with its collection of over 60,000 objects telling many-voiced stories.

These inventories need to be continually examined and questioned with respect to their relevance and, of special importance today, their acquisition context which sometimes falls within the colonial period. Not least, an understanding for the diversity of the world's cultures and a view to our common history enable responsibility to be recognised and assumed. Such a reassessment process must be carried out with the participation of the Indigenous communities of origin – and requires both financial and personnel resources.

With the exhibition COUNTRY BIN PULL'EM. LOOKING BACK TOGETHER and the accompanying publication, the Weltkulturen Museum, under the curatorial direction of Matthias Claudius Hofmann, shows that such a joint re-evaluation, conducted on an equal footing, is possible and fruitful. The exhibition arose from a DFG-financed research project which was carried out by the Frobenius Institute under the direction of Richard Kuba together with the University of Western Australia, the Weltkulturen Museum, the Museum Fünf Kontinente, and above all, in close cooperation with the *Wanjina Wunggurr* people of Northwest Australia. The exhibition and catalogue build on this research, whereby every step was closely coordinated with the representatives of the *Wanjina Wunggurr* community and a special place was given to Indigenous perspectives on their own history and culture. This can be seen in the curatorial and artistic contributions of the Indigenous co-curators, both in the exhibition and the catalogue essays. The European museological and Indigenous perspectives enter into a dialogue of equals, resulting in a successful re-evaluation process and knowledge gain on both sides.

The catalogue COUNTRY BIN PULL'EM is a valuable addition to the intensely prepared exhibition. It summarizes the results in multifaceted contributions and thus presents an in-depth examination of the 1938 Frobenius Expedition to Northwest Australia from a variety of perspectives.

Such a multi-perspectival examination of the museum collection and the archives, which integrates different interests, holds surprises and new knowledge in store. We are happy to present a book that, even after the end of the exhibition at the Weltkulturen Museum, will be a pleasure to consult.

Colonial and post-colonial contexts must be re-assessed in a (self)critical, open-ended and just process, and contextualised with great expert knowledge and sensitivity. The Cultural Foundation of Hesse is happy to have made a contribution to this timely re-assessment of the collection history at the Weltkulturen Museum and the Frobenius Institute in Frankfurt. The scientific engagement with the collections and archives of ethnological institutions together with the communities of origin, as well as the sharing of the research results, form the basis for a responsible and transparent research practice and serve as an example for further projects of a similar nature.

Eva Claudia Scholtz
Executive Director of the Cultural Foundation of Hesse

Director's Foreword

The exhibition COUNTRY BIN PULL'EM and the publication of the same name are the product of a multi-year, intensive dialogue with the Indigenous community of the *Wanjina Wunggurr* in Northwest Australia. They reflect the research history of the Frobenius Expedition to Northwest Australia which set out from Frankfurt in 1938, and simultaneously illuminate the contemporary interpretations of the Indigenous cultural heritage. In a common effort, cultural heritage and Indigenous knowledge have been re-evaluated and made accessible – to the communities of origin in Australia, the exhibition public in Frankfurt and the international readership.

The exhibition shows historical works – monumental rock art copies, historic expedition photographs and ethnographic objects – together with contemporary works from Indigenous artists from Northwest Australia. The interplay between historical and new works reveals the creative appropriation of European research findings by the Australian project partners, and the aesthetic reflection on historical events and religious convictions bears witness to the deep connection between the *Wanjina Wunggurr* people and their Country, which continues to this day.

The multi-year, intensive exchange with the Indigenous Australians, the so-called Traditional Owners, is of inestimable value to the Weltkulturen Museum and the Frobenius Institute. The diverse feedback from the Indigenous communities and the cooperation-based exhibition praxis generate new perspectives on existing collections. The detailed written sources and archive materials evaluated during the course of the project illuminate historical acquisition contexts and open up new paths for provenance research. The cooperation with the Traditional Owners enables historical objects to be re-evaluated within a living cultural context.

During the course of the research project a relational archive-database was developed in cooperation with the Traditional Owners in which objects from the collection and archival material from the expedition, scattered over numerous locations, have been digitally collated and networked. After a decades-long hiatus, this living archive once again provides the Indigenous communities with access to this part of their cultural heritage, which can now be shared with the coming generations.

The exhibition and publication are the result of a multi-year, intensive cooperation between the Weltkulturen Museum, the Aboriginal Corporations Dambimangari, Wilinggin and Wunambal Gaambera, the Frobenius Institute at the Goethe University and the Centre for Rock Art Research of the University of Western Australia. The project was kindly initiated by the director of the Weltkulturen Museum at the time, Eva Ch. Raabe, and the head of the rock art archive at the Frobenius Institute, Richard Kuba.

I would like to thank all the Australian partners for their commitment, and especially the artists and co-curators Rona Charles, Leah Umbagai, Lloyd Nulgit and Pete O'Connor, who in preparation for the exhibition spent a long period as guests at the Weltkulturen Museum in 2023. A special thanks goes to Kim Doohan and Martin Porr for the continual support.

I am especially thankful to the curator Matthias Claudius Hofmann and the project assistant Isabel Kreuder for the sensitive, communication-intensive implementation of the research findings in a large exhibition project. For the scientific accompaniment of the project I would like to thank Christina Henneke and Richard Kuba.

I thank the editors Matthias Claudius Hofmann, Richard Kuba, Christina Henneke and Isabel Kreuder, as well as all the authors for their contributions to this book. I would also like to thank the Cultural Foundation of Hesse (Hessische Kulturstiftung) for their financial support of this publication.

I would like to thank the team from U9 for the graphic design of this exhibition and book, Jennifer Markwirth and Peter Steigerwald (Frobenius Institute) for the image processing and digitalisation and Wolfgang Günzel for the photographs. Furthermore, a heartfelt thanks to the museum team and everyone who contributed to the exhibition for their dedicated work.

Mona B. Suhrbier
Acting Director of the Weltkulturen Museum

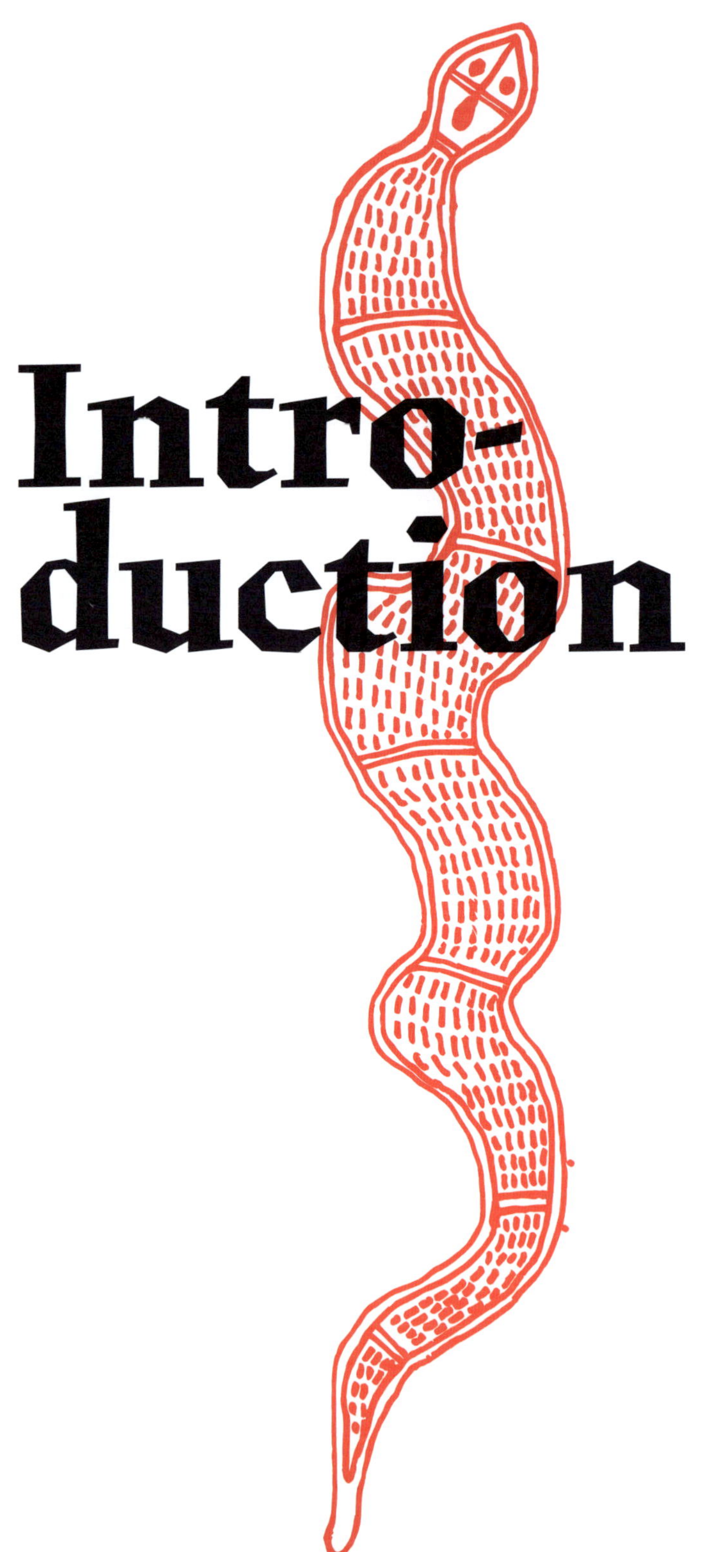

Intro-
duction

Looking Back Together

Matthias Claudius Hofmann and Richard Kuba

At the centre of this publication, as well as the exhibition of the same name, stands the Frobenius Expedition to Northwest Australia in 1938–39. This research and collection journey was conducted by the Frobenius Institute (the then Institute for Cultural Morphology) and the Weltkulturen Museum (formerly the Städtische Völkermuseum of the City of Frankfurt), which were managed in personal union at the time. The aim of the ethnographic expedition was to research the culture of the Ngarinyin, the Woddordda and the Wunambal – who are collectively referred to as the *Wanjina Wunggurr* community – in the Kimberley region of Northwest Australia. A special focus of the Frobenius Expedition were the rock paintings of the Kimberley region and their cultural meanings.

The Kimberley is among the very few regions in the world that provides such detailed insights into an Indigenous cultural tradition, of which the rock paintings of the *Wanjina Wunggurr* people form an integral part. A tradition that has even withstood the violent upheavals of European colonialism and the modern nation state. In 1938 the Frobenius Expedition, under the direction of Helmut Petri (1907–1986), embarked on the first attempt to produce a detailed and systematic ethnographic survey of the region, and in particular the rock paintings.

The research project
Richard Kuba

The Frankfurt exhibition COUNTRY BIN PULL'EM was preceded by another exhibition which was organised, more or less spontaneously, in the large, hot metal shed of the Wilinggin Aboriginal Corporation (WAC) in Derby. This served as a materials warehouse and garage for the large-engined, all-wheel-drive vehicles which the WAC rangers employed for their duties "on Country". On this day in June 2022 the heavy Land Cruisers were driven out, the shed swept and all materials moved aside in order to make room for the pictures.

Packages with large-format copies of rock paintings had been brought from Frankfurt[1]. Prints of copies which were made by two women artists from Frankfurt over eighty years ago on the territory of the Ngarinyin, who are now represented by the Wilinggin Aboriginal Corporation.

At the time the Ngarinyin, together with the Woddordda and Wunambal groups, who are closely related culturally, still lived "on Country", namely in the northwestern corner of the Australian continent which – to European eyes – was largely trackless. Almost everywhere in the world, the meaning of prehistoric rock paintings has been lost over the millennia as a result of the breaks in transmission and culture. However, in contrast, for many Australian Indigenous societies, this oldest form of visual communication has remained at the centre of their culture to this day. This is also the case with the three groups who consider themselves part of the *Wanjina Wunggurr* culture in the Kimberley region of Northwest Australia.

This tradition consists of images of powerful figures from the time when the world was created and the laws were decreed, such as the mouthless *Wanjinas*, the *Ungud* Snakes and Dumbi, the mythical owl. Their stories have been depicted on overhanging rocks everywhere in the Kimberley for millennia. They watch over the Country and its fertility. If one pays them due respect, then they give the hunters and gatherers what they need to live, protecting them from destructive forces, illness and injury, or the devastating violence of the seasonal tropical cyclones.[2]

In 1938, as the two women artists from Frankfurt travelled to the Kimberley with their male anthropologist colleagues to document the *Wanjina Wunggurr* culture, the local Indigenous communities already looked back on decades of often violent colonisation. In the extremely sparsely populated region there were a number of scattered cattle farms and mission stations, close to which many Indigenous Australians had settled.[3] However, the extremely important connection with the Country, its rock paintings, stone circles and countless stories and rituals, was still largely intact – an important reason why the Frankfurt researchers ventured their expedition.

A few years later, Japanese fighter planes also attacked the Kimberley, and after the war, when the economic situation and the provision of the isolated stations became increasingly difficult, almost the entire population moved further south, close to the small town of Derby. The members of the *Wanjina Wunggurr* communities now settled outside their Country, and it became increasingly difficult to visit the rock art sites, which were often hundreds of kilometres away. Returning on Country and refreshing the paintings so that they could continue to fulfil their protective and nurturing tasks became extremely difficult. The stories continued to live on in the respective families, however many people, especially the younger ones, had never seen the pictures. Even their precise location often fell into obscurity.

Consequently, the curiosity and enthusiasm of the Wilinggin Rangers was great when the life-sized, up to six meter long reproductions were unrolled, such that they immediately decided to hang them on the walls of the "Wilinggin shed" using improvised strings and rods. A number of the Elders were initially sceptical, as the Traditional Owners of the respective rock art sites should have been asked. However, the enthusiasm of the younger people overcame all reservations, and during the visit to the improvised exhibition a number of people were moved to sing the associated songs. Yornadaiyn (Donny) Woolagoodja, one of the most respected Elders, and a well-known artist who accompanied the setting up of the improvised exhibition, felt inspired to create a number of works.

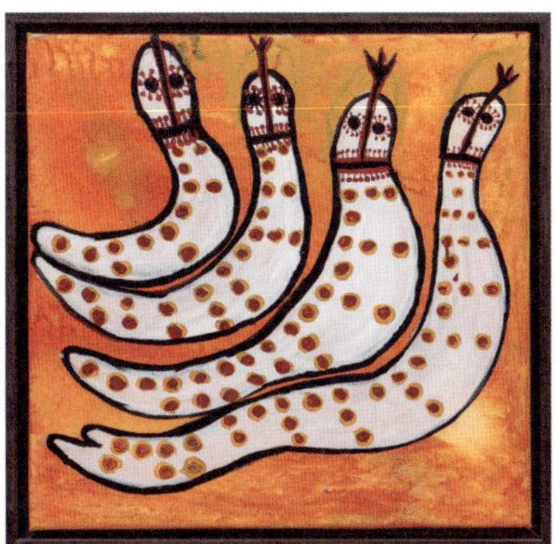

Fig. 1   Inspired by the exhibition in the Willinggin shed, in 2022 Yornadaiyn Woolagoodja produced this painting: *Ungud (snake)*. Acrylic on canvas, 45 x 45 cm. Collection: Weltkulturen Museum. Photo: Wolfgang Günzel, 2024

Fig. 2   Richard Kuba (left) and Kane Nenowat (right) are hanging the large-format copy of the Modum rock art painting. Photo: Kim Doohan, 2022

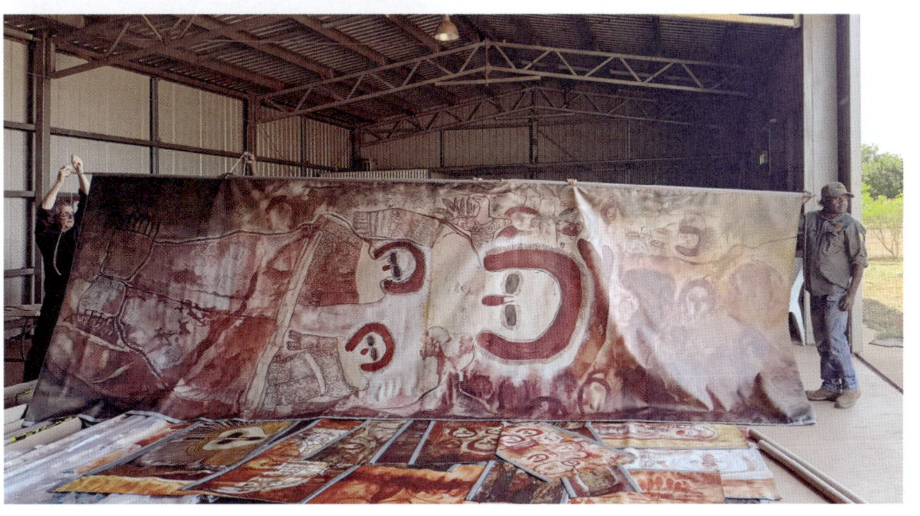

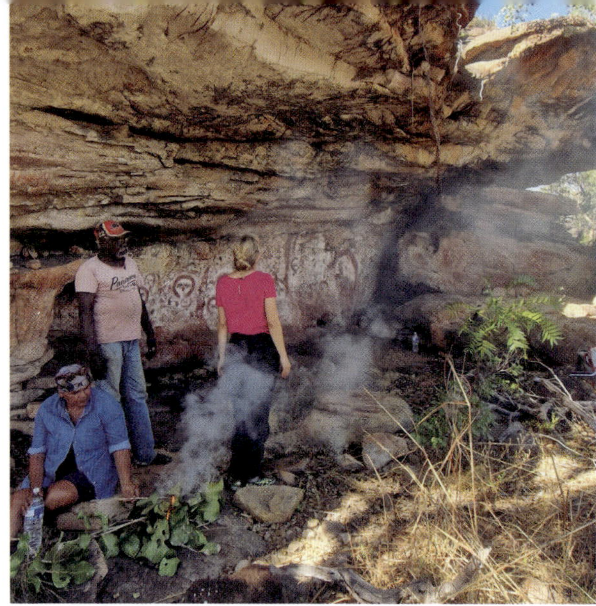

Fig. 3 *Smoking* (cleansing ritual) before visiting the Koralyi rock art site, July 2023. Photo: Richard Kuba

The question of what one is allowed to do, which rules are to be observed and what is actually forbidden, i.e. is to be kept secret, dominated many of the conversations around the repatriation project, whose result is the exhibition COUNTRY BIN PULL'EM, curated together with the Australian partners. It is a look back together at what took place at the end of the 1930s. Who did the researchers from Frankfurt have contact with at the time? What did the respective agency look like, and who could decide what? Back then, were the people who led the Frankfurt researchers to the rock art sites and interpreted them authorised persons, i.e. Traditional Owners? What value do the thousands of photographs, the hundreds of paintings and drawings that were produced at the time even have? Are there perhaps dangerous ritual objects amongst the collected objects in the Weltkulturen Museum?[4]

The initiative to recover the archival treasure originated from the *Wanjina Wunggurr* communities, however, the complexity associated with the return of stories, pictures and objects from a colonial context lends every trite call for a quick, general restitution – which is only "simple" at first glance – the character of a cheap apology stemming from postcolonial guilt.

Long before the current restitution debate the Frobenius Institute had already begun, in close cooperation with the scientists from the affected countries, as well as the local, i.e. Indigenous societies, to systematically transcribe and translate unpublished original sources, and in some cases to publish them. The initiative for such projects frequently came from representatives of the societies of origin. Throughout, the Institute processed its rich collections in the spirit of the "3-road strategy on the documentation and digital publication of collections from colonial contexts held in Germany" (access-transparency-cooperation), published in 2020. These three roads are not understood as part of a pre-established "top-down strategy", but as an open process. One road, especially as a means to share the historical picture collections, is the organisation of jointly curated exhibitions as well as the handing over of digital and analogue copies – as carried out, amongst other places, in 2008 in Ouagadougou (Burkina Faso), 2012 in Abuja, Ife, Makurdi, Minna and Yola (Nigeria), 2015 in Addis Ababa and Jinka (Ethiopia), 2017 in Dakar (Senegal), 2019 and 2021, again in Addis Ababa (Ethiopia) as well as 2022 in Derby (Australia). In an ethnologically informed, and culturally sensitive manner, the institute thus makes historical source material available to the people in the regions and countries in which it was produced over the course of the twentieth century. Here the photographs and drawings from the early twentieth century, with its dearth of images, play an important role, alongside the unpublished diaries, field notes and letters which often represent the earliest written sources from the region.

Fig. 4 Gerta Kleist and Agnes Schulz copying the Koralyi rock art site, July 1938. Collection: Frobenius Institute. Photo: Not stated

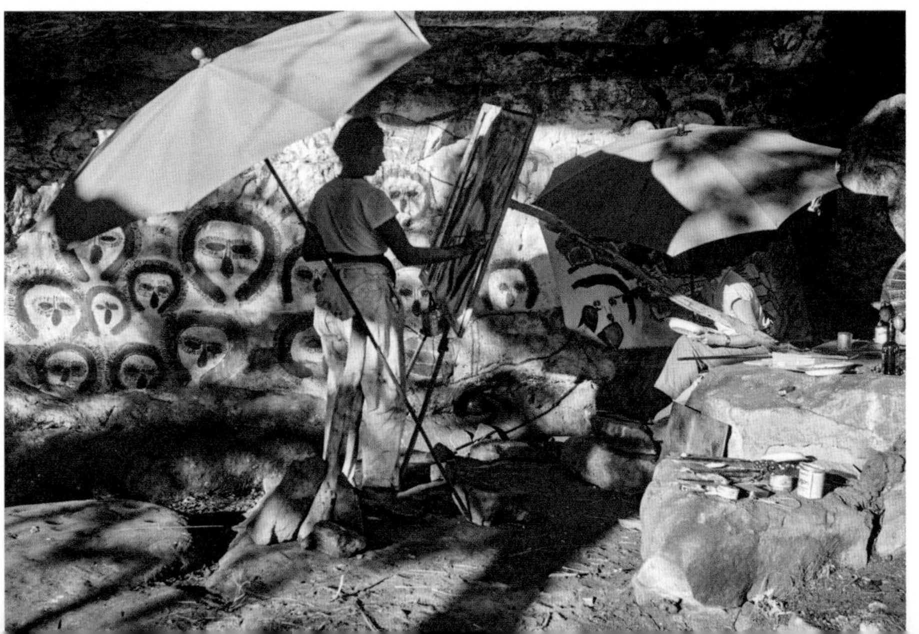

Introduction

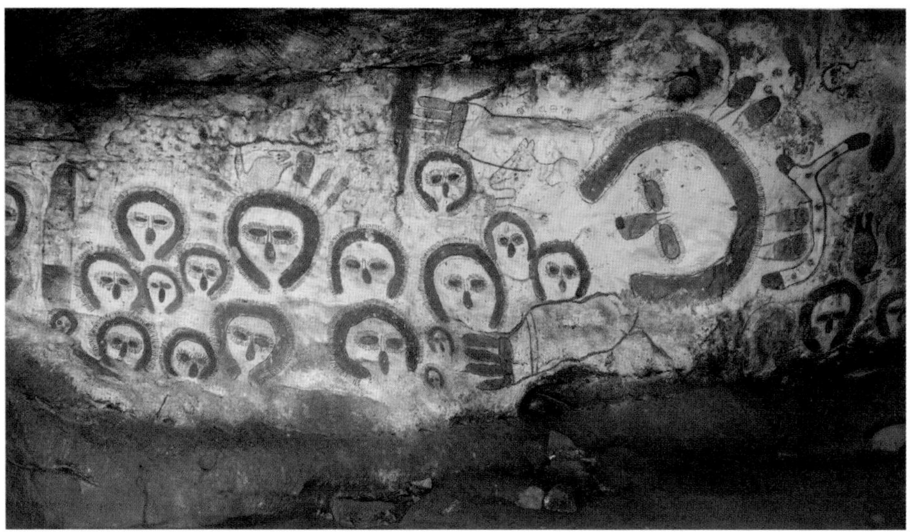

Fig. 5   The Koralyi rock art site, July 1938. Collection: Frobenius Institute. Photo: Not stated

"Paintings next to the head of the large reclining Wondjina. Three flying foxes are always depicted as if hanging from a tree. The reclining figure with the horizontal stripes is a Wondjina woman. Above it is a yellow crouching figure, a frequently shown posture for which we never received an explanation."

The subsequent opening up of the archives as part of a joint research undertaking profited enormously from the fact that the people from the countries of origin contributed their own ontologies and contexts of meaning, based on their local knowledge. The preconditions for this are long-term, trusting relations, as well as openness and sensitivity towards the sometimes problematic ethical contexts in which the documents were produced, as well as towards the specific local needs which the research is designed to serve (who's history?). The multi-perspectival and self-reflexive processing of the collections leads to an understanding on the manner in which they should be opened, published and used in future, and ultimately digitally repatriated in a responsible manner.

This constitutes a dynamic process from which both sides profit, and which is ultimately the source of the exhibition title COUNTRY BIN PULL'EM. This was Rona Gungnunda Charles's summary after the members of the German research project (Christina Henneke, Richard Kuba and Martin Porr), together with herself and

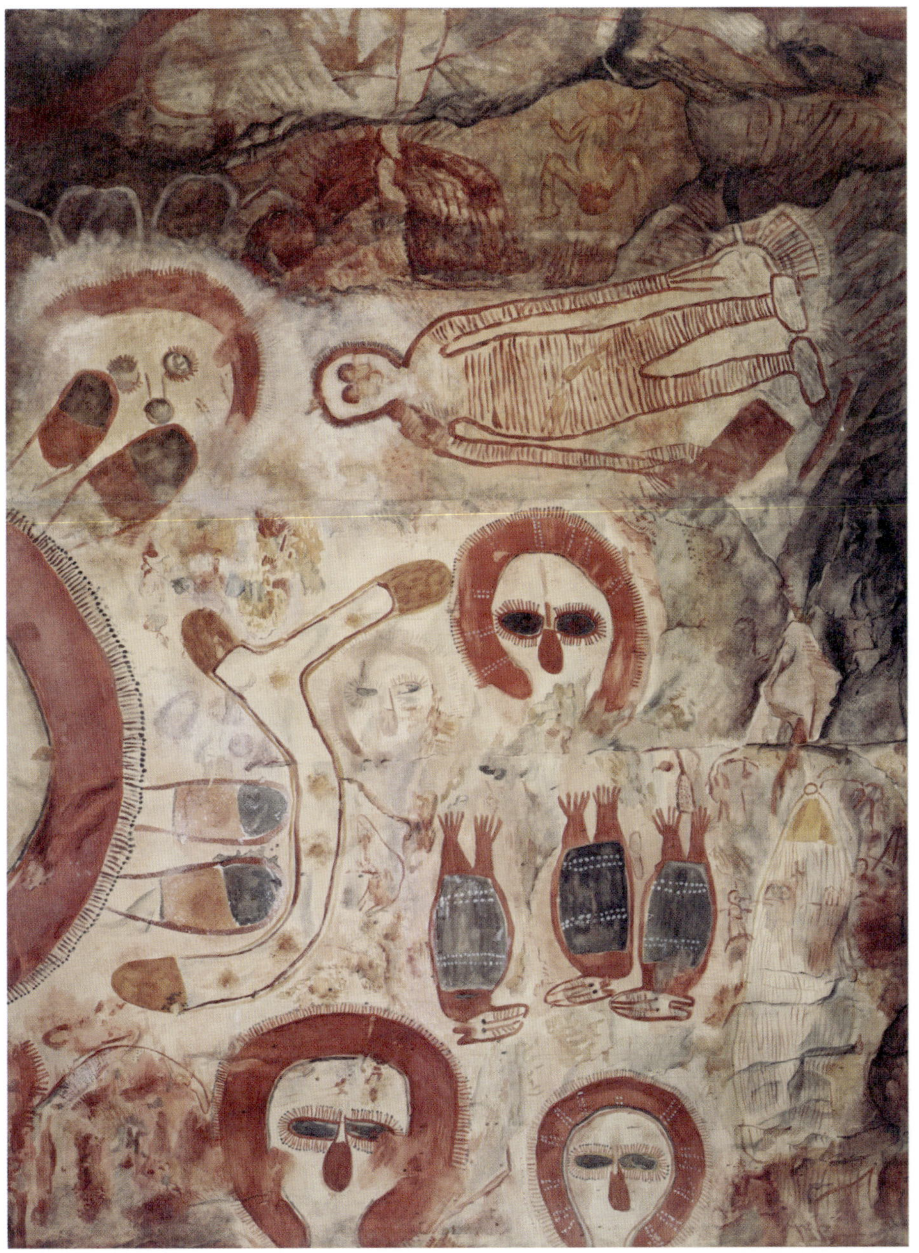

Fig. 6   Koralyi rock art site. Kimberley, Northwest Australia. Rock art copy by Gerta Kleist and Agnes Schulz, July 1938. Watercolour on paper. 181 x 245 cm. Collection: Frobenius Institute. Photo: Not stated

other Traditional Owners, spent eight days in July 2023 at the rock art sites of their ancestors. On location we placed the historical records and traditional stories side-by-side, in an attempt to gain an understanding through this juxtaposition. It was an inspiring research venture, and the magic of the rock art sites in the spectacular vastness of the landscape of west Kimberley, with its red rocks, deep ravines, clear streams and, following the rainy season, emerald green vegetation, captivated us all. On the way there the *Wanjinas* were already called and informed of our visit. In front of the rock paintings a small fire of spicy-smelling ironwood tree leaves was lit and everyone cleansed themselves in the smoke. Loud talking and exclamations were forbidden. The effect of the "Country" was almost physical and its agency was palpable. Rona's phrase "Country bin pull'em" – the Country drew them here, appeared quite apposite: It was not the initiative of the Frankfurt researchers that brought them to the Kimberley, but the Country that drew them and invited them. It was exactly the same with the material that lay hidden in the Frankfurt archives for eighty years, which was now returning – Country bin pull'em. Everything had to happen this way.

Notwithstanding all the difficulties that the Indigenous Australian communities had endured at the hands of Australia's majority society, both today and in the past, it was also important for our partners to emphasise that, despite everything, their traditional culture lives on. Thus it was necessary to refute the pessimistic conclusions of the Frankfurt researchers, as exemplified in their published books with titles such as *Sterbende Welt in Nordwest-Australien* (The Dying World in Northwest Australia) (Petri 1954) or *Fortschritt ins Nichts* (Progress into Nothingness) (Lommel 1968). This was not just countered by the traditional knowledge, which first lent the correct meaning to many of the records from Frankfurt. The artistic tradition also lives on, with the Indigenous communities bringing forth numerous artists who continue to develop the tradition of the rock paintings in acrylic paint on canvas. This is subject to a strict copyright: only those motifs are allowed which are derived from the respective family's own rock art site. It is generally extremely painful for the *Wanjina Wunggurr* communities to see how strangers make use of their motifs and how artists without a connection to the region employ *Wanjina* motifs. This motif first became well known when a gigantic enlargement of Namarali, an especially powerful *Wanjina* figure, was hoisted in the stadium during the opening of the 2000 Olympic Games in Sydney. This took place at the time with the express permission and participation of the Traditional Owner Yorna Woolagoodja. However, in recent years, the meeting of the commercial art market and the fascination for the traditions of the oldest living culture has resulted in outsiders attempting to appropriate the *Wanjinas* for their own commercial ends. In order to protect their culture and prevent misuse, the *Wanjina Wuggurr* communities have now registered the characteristic *Wanjina* head as a protected trademark.

Our partners were extremely critical of the English translations of the German publications which were issued by an Australian publisher over recent years without any consultation with the communities. Especially as a number of the illustrations depict ceremonies which are denoted as secret/sacred, and from their perspective are not for the eyes of the uninitiated and female persons. A "cleaned" version of one of these books can be seen in the exhibition.

The explosive political force that scientific interpretations can develop was shown a few years ago during the fierce controversy over the rock paintings known as *Gwion Gwion*, which earlier researchers termed "Bradshaw paintings". This refers to a style also widespread in the Kimberley, whose long-limbed, filigree figures clearly distinguish themselves from the *Wanjina* rock paintings, and which emerged around 12,000 years ago. It is thus around twice as old as the *Wanjina* tradition.[5] In the past Australian researchers had the presumption to state that these older rock paintings represented a culture completely different to that of the *Wanjina Wunggurr*, a culture who today's Indigenous people could have no knowledge of. Such a statement has an impact far beyond the confines of an academic debate. During the recognition of Indigenous land rights, the so-called "native title" negotiations, the close cultural connection of the communities to the Country has to be precisely demonstrated in a meticulous legal process. The *Wanjina Wunggurr* communities responded to this and have clarified their own version of the *Gwion* story and their deep connection to it in various publications.

These examples may help to throw some light on the complexity of the consultation process associated with the interpretation and repatriation of cultural materials, and not least, as experienced during the joint curation of the exhibition COUNTRY BIN PULL'EM. Who is actually speaking for whom and who said what and when? All this needs to be discussed, time and again, as broadly and patiently as possible, as "the" society of origin no more exists than "the" German society.

The joint exhibition
Matthias Claudius Hofmann

The collections compiled during the expedition are now divided between different institutions. After the separation of institute and museum in 1969, the collection of material culture remained in today's Weltkulturen Museum as part of the Oceania Collection. The Frobenius Institute houses the copies of the rock paintings completed in the Kimberley along with numerous historical and ethnographic photographs and watercolours which were produced by the artists Agnes Susanne Schulz (1892–1973) and Gerta Kleist (1911–1998) who accompanied the expedition. In addition, there are numerous unpublished written sources from the estates of the painters and researchers. A number of the objects collected in 1938 by the expedition member Andreas Lommel are now housed in the Museum Fünf Kontinente in Munich. Furthermore, there are around seventy recordings on wax cylinders in the Berlin Phonogram Archive which have not been scientifically evaluated until now.

Together, these collections provide a comprehensive picture of the Ngarinyin, Woddordda and Wunambal in the Kimberley around eighty five years ago. The joint examination and evaluation of the historical material, together with the *Wanjina Wunggurr* community, provide a unique insight into the continuities and transformations of the Indigenous cultures of Northwest Australia. Today, both in this publication and the exhibition COUNTRY BIN PULL'EM, the project partners take a look back. The focus is on the history of the Frankfurt Frobenius Expedition as well as contemporary Indigenous perspectives on the collections and the numerous documents and recordings generated during this research journey.

The beginnings of the project

The initial spark for the exhibition and the preceding research project was provided in 2010 by the visit of Martin Porr from the University of Western Australia to the depot of the Weltkulturen Museum. It was through his reading of Petri's expedition report *Sterbende Welt in Nordwest-Australien* (The Dying World in Northwest Australia) from 1954 that his attention was directed to the collections of the Frobenius Expedition. It is thanks to the efforts of Martin Porr that the contact between the communities of origin of the *Wanjina Wunggurr*-people, the Frobenius Institute as well as the Weltkulturen Museum was established. Furthermore, he provided the impulse for reuniting the collections divided between the institutions and evaluating them in a joint undertaking.

As early as 2015 the Australian ethnologist Kim Doohan, together with Leah Umbagai, and once again in 2017 with Leah Umbagai and Leonie Cheinmora, two Woddordda Traditional Owners, visited Frankfurt in order to study the collections of the two institutions. During the visit to the museum's Oceania depot and the institute's Rock Art Archive the idea of a joint exhibition was discussed with Martin Porr, Richard Kuba, Eva Ch. Raabe and Matthias Claudius Hofmann. However, it quickly became clear that an exhibition would have to be preceded by extensive research into the expedition and the collections acquired during its activities.

The research project was conducted under the direction of the Frobenius Institute and with generous support from the German Research Foundation (DFG) from March 2020 to March 2024. The results of the project have flowed both into this publication as well as the exhibition COUNTRY BIN PULL'EM.

As already indicated, the production of the catalogue and the planning of the exhibition repeatedly gave rise to questions concerning who was allowed to see which objects, photos etc. It is not permitted for certain objects or information considered secret/sacred to be seen by the uninitiated, only by initiated men. This not only excludes members of other cultures. Indigenous women are also not permitted to see certain objects, be involved in certain rituals or share in ritual knowledge. As a consequence, in November 2023, during an artists' residency for the purpose of exhibition planning, the traditional owners Lloyd Nulgit and Pete O'Connor inspected the collections in the museum and institute in order to assess which objects, i.e. photos, could be shown publically, and which fell into the category secret/sacred.

The English language publication of Petri's 1954 expedition report by the Australian publisher Hesperian Press, *The Dying World in Northwest Australia* (2011) – carried out without prior consultation with the communities – is also to be considered under this aspect as it contains illustrations and descriptions of ceremonies which are considered secret/sacred[6]. It is much to be welcomed that decades after the publication of the expedition report the scientific reception of the research

Fig. 7   Eva Ch. Raabe with Kim Doohan and Leah Umbagai in the Oceania depot of the Weltkulturen Museum. Photo: Martin Porr, 2015

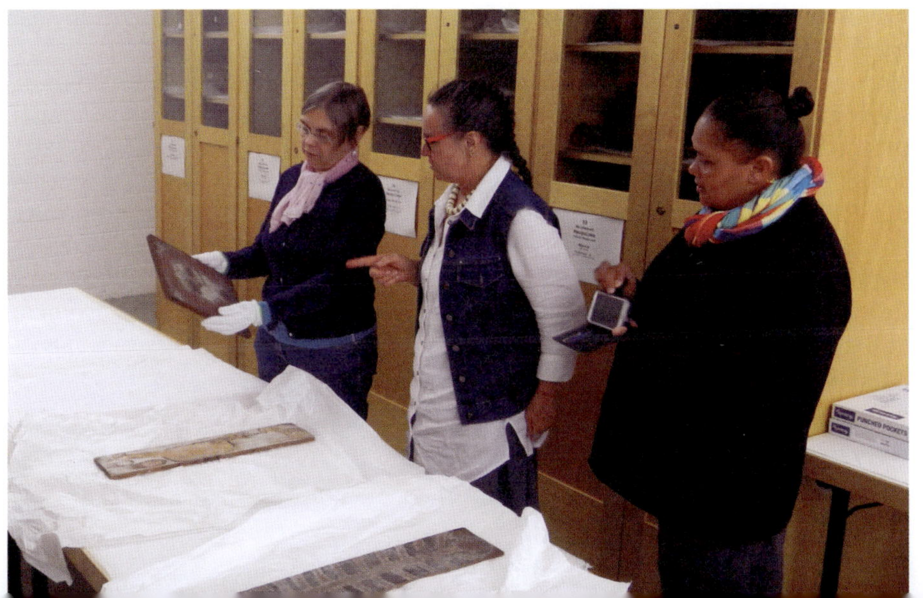

Introduction

results has now been made possible in the English speaking world as a result of the translation, and thus also in Australia.[7] However, an opportunity was also missed to develop a culturally 'unobjectionable' version of Petri's monograph together with the *Wanjina Wunggurr* community and publish it jointly.

The catalogue essays

The following catalogue essays provide insights into the history of the Frobenius Expedition to Northwest Australia as well as the culture and world view of the *Wanjina Wunggurr* people.

It begins with the essay from **Richard Kuba** on the history of the expedition which he places in the context of an over eighty years relationship between the *Wanjina Wunggurr* community and the Frankfurt institutions, from the end of the 1930s to the present. Today it is the exchange with the Indigenous communities that stands at the heart of this relationship, as the extensive ethnological archive compiled during the expedition should, above all, benefit those that it concerns the most: The *Wanjina Wunggurr* people. Furthermore, the 1938 expedition was one of the earliest comprehensive scientific surveys of the *Wanjina Wunggurr* culture, and thus is especially important to their descendants as a historical source.

This close cooperation with the *Wanjia Wunggurr* people was of fundamental importance for the exhibition and the accompanying publication. This also included consultations on the choice of rock art copies, paintings, ethnographic objects and photographs, as well as the granting of permission for the publication of cultural material and the checking of the texts. Ultimately, the goal of the exhibition and the catalogue was "looking back together". The voices of the Traditional Owners are therefore highly present, both in the exhibition and this catalogue.

This especially applies to the religion and world view of the *Wanjina Wunggurr*, which are also of central importance for an understanding of the rock art motifs. In their joint contribution **Kim Doohan,** together with **Rona Gungnunda Charles, Matthew Martin, Lloyd Nulgit, Pete O'Connor, John Rastus and Leah Umbagai** as representatives of the communities of origin, attempt to provide an introduction to the world view of the *Wanjina Wunggurr*. Here the focus is on the terms *Wanjina, Wunggurr* and *Lalai*, or *Larlan*. The latter refers to a mythical prehistory and concerns the world and its creation through the actions of powerful creator beings, the *Wanjina*, and the creative force *Wunggurr*, frequently in the form of a snake. They reinforce and cyclically repeat the creation events, making them non-linear and therefore always present. For the Traditional Owners this space-time continuum is not about conventional archaeological dating or a sequence of events. Instead it is about *Lalai*, the beginning of the world, which the countless rock paintings, as manifestations of the mythical prehistory, bear witness to.

This Indigenous perspective is followed by **Martin Porr's** essay on an archaeological classification of the rock art in the Kimberley region. The findings of such archaeological research cannot always be reconciled with the Indigenous knowledge systems; however, it can definitely enrich our understanding of the rock art as well as the history of the people in the Kimberley over the last 50,000 years.

"This is my grandfather who we have never seen in our life before."

Fig. 8   Rosilyn and Angelina Karadada with the photo and the drawing of their father Jack and his father produced by Agnes Schulz in 1938. Kalumburu. Photo: Christina Henneke, 2023

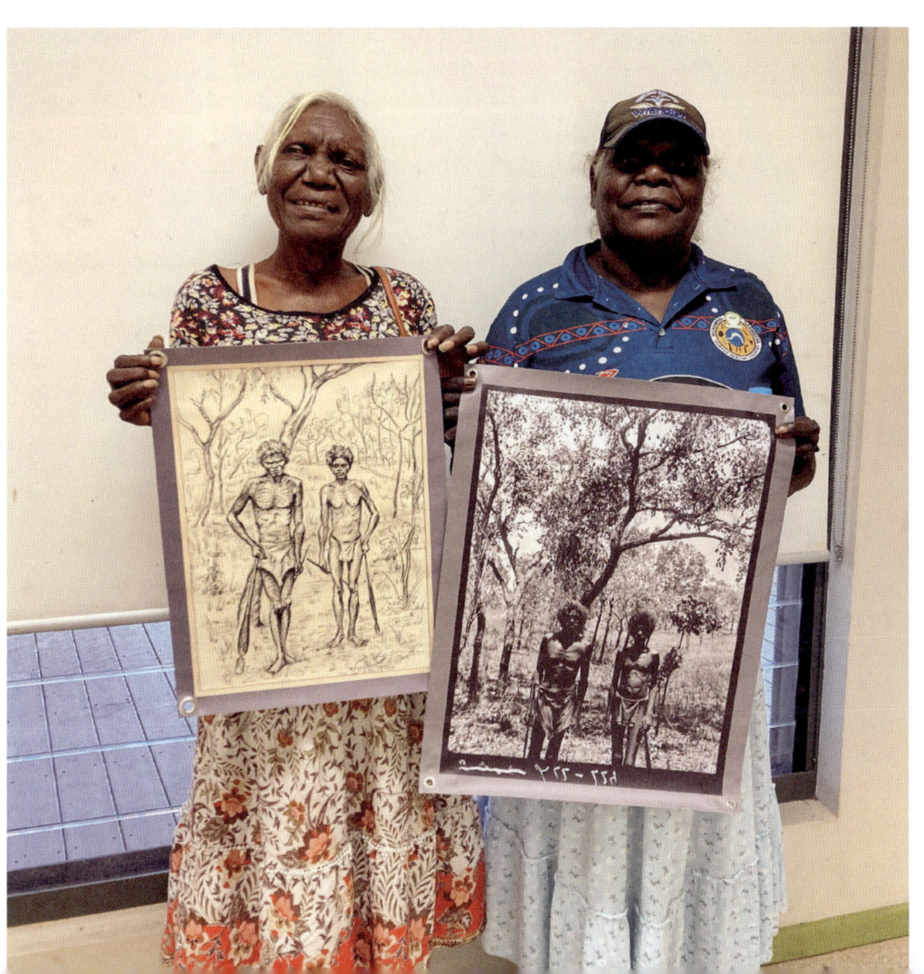

Anthony Redmond's contribution follows with an overview of the history of the Kimberley region from the 1930s, when the expedition visited the Kimberley, to the present. He focuses on a period when, in the second half of the twentieth century, the *Wanjina Wunggurr* people suffered crises and resettlements resulting from colonial influences, and since then have found themselves in a process of self-assertion and a struggle for land rights and the sovereignty of interpretation over their own culture.

In her essay, **Eva Ch. Raabe,** as longstanding curator of the Oceania collection and director of the Weltkulturen Museum, examines the museum's various Australia collections. In her report on the path of the objects to the museum, their documentation and their deployment in the work of the museum, she also provides am impression of the ethnomuseological history of the Australia collection in Frankfurt, at the same time tracing the history of the museum's development using the example of these regional collections.

Without doubt, an especially tragic aspect of the collections from Northwest Australia is that the vast majority of the objects were destroyed, along with the museum building, during the aerial bombardments in the Second World War. In his engagement with these war losses, **Matthias Claudius Hofmann** pursues the question of what one can still find out about the lost objects if one follows their traces in the archives of the Weltkulturen Museum and the diaries and research reports of the expedition members. What insights can we gain about the original collection as a whole and its reception? What does this collection tell us about the acquisition history of the objects as well as the relationships between the researchers and the Indigenous people?

Michaela Appel's contribution focuses on Andreas Lommel and Katharina Lommel, who returned to the Kimberley region in the late 1950s and continued the documentation of the rock paintings. On the basis of Lommel's biography one can also see how the ethnologist's relationship to the *Wanjina Wunggurr* people changed over the decades.

Recordings of musical practices in the Kimberley, especially from the first half of the twentieth century, are rare. However, during the Frobenius Expedition to Northwest Australia the expedition members also bought a phonograph in order to record speech samples and the songs and music of the *Wanjina Wunggurr* communities. Following their return the wax cylinder recordings were sent to the Berlin Phonogram Archive. Although the wax cylinders were copied onto audio tape in the 1960s, the recordings largely fell into obscurity. Although there were references to the audio recordings in the diaries and research reports, like the film recordings, they were assumed to have been lost, i.e. destroyed in the war. It was only by chance that the museum heard of their existence.[8] The ethnomusicologist **Sally Treloyn** examined these recordings for the first time since they were recorded in 1938 and subjected them to a systematic analysis. In her essay she provides an initial overview of the content and context of the "Frobenius – (Frankfurt) Expedition, W-Australia" recordings (cf. Ziegler 2006: 134–135).

Christina Henneke's report on her visit to the Maliba rock art site in July 2023, together with **Rona Gungnunda Charles and John Rastus,** uses the example of the "Rubbish Painting" to show how, through joint work, the archive material can be critically evaluated and knowledge of the archive sources both corrected and extended through cooperation between ethnologists and Traditional Owners. Following long discussions in front of the supposedly 'worthless' rock painting, the Traditional Owners uncovered the reason why, in 1938, the Ngarinyin Lorri probably tried to lure the expedition members away from the rock art site.

The artists' residency at the Weltkulturen Museum in 2023

In November 2023, in preparation for the exhibition, the four Traditional Owners Leah Umbagai and Pete O'Connor (Dambimangari Aboriginal Corporation) as well as Rona Gungnunda Charles and Lloyd Nulgit (Wilinggin Aboriginal Corporation), accompanied by the ethnologist Kim Doohan, attended an artists' residency at the Weltkulturen Museum. Through an engagement with the Frankfurt collections, they created artistic contributions for the exhibition. At the same time curatorial approaches were discussed and the first ideas for the content of the joint exhibition were agreed.

For this catalogue **Kim Doohan,** together with **Rona Gungnunda Charles and Pete O'Connor** compiled an overview of the residency which illustrates the engagement of the four Traditional Owners with the Frankfurt collections. At the same time it addresses the question of how one can convey to the museum public that the *Wanjina Wunggurr* people are precisely not a 'dying culture' that belongs to the past, as repeatedly intimated in the archive material and the resulting publications. Thus, they set out to decisively refute this and show that their culture is still alive and unbroken.

Here the revitalisation of the *Bulamana Junba* was of special interest to the four Traditional Owners. On the basis of photographs taken during the Frobenius Expedition this dance could be reconstructed and re-choreographed. At the time the *Bulamana Junba* addressed the dramatic turning point of colonial land seizure in the early twentieth century and the beginning of livestock breeding on large cattle farms. Since 2019 it has been regularly performed at festivals. **Rona Gungnunda**

Charles and Pete O'Connor were personally involved in the revitalisation project. Together with **Leah Umbagai and Lloyd Nulgit** they discuss their own experiences during the performances as well as the significance of the revitalisation of historical *Junba* for the *Wanjina Wunggurr* people, both today and for coming generations.

COUNTRY BIN PULL'EM

A further question that was the subject of controversy during the residency was the title of the exhibition. An initial idea was derived from Petri's expedition report *The Dying World in Northwest Australia*. The extremely pessimistic attitude expressed in this title was to serve as a reference and also be clearly contradicted. However, "looking back together" should not, once again, take the Western/scientific view as its starting point. A change of perspective was needed.

As during the visit to the rock art sites a few months earlier, Rona Gungnunda Charles suggested COUNTRY BIN PULL'EM: Today, just like eighty five years ago, the ensouled Country has drawn the German researchers to it. Accordingly, the relationship between the *Wanjina Wunggurr* people and the members of the expedition was initiated by the Country itself.

Endnotes:

1 These were faithful copies of the "original copies" produced in 1939 and 1954. These were generally executed using watercolours on paper and, after decades of inadequate storage, were in need of special restoration measures. The new copies, on robust Airtex material, were manufactured and presented within the framework of the research project "The German ethnographic expeditions to the Kimberley in Australia. Their importance for research history, digital repatriation and the joint interpretation of the indigenous cultural heritage." Thanks goes to the German Research Foundation (DFG) that largely financed the project directed by Richard Kuba (Frobenius Institute, Frankfurt a.M.) and Martin Porr (University of Western Australia, Perth). Further generous support was provided by the University of Western Australia.

2 See Kim Doohan et al., *The Country Owns Us* in this volume.

3 See Anthony Redmond, *When the Dreaming Becomes a Nightmare* in this volume.

4 See Richard Kuba, *An Eighty Year Relationship* and Christina Henneke et al., *"Rubbish" Painting* in this volume.

5 See Martin Porr, *The Archaeological Perspective* in this volume.

6 Neither the museum nor the Frobenius Institute were either consulted or informed prior to the publication of the translation.

7   Further essays from Petri and Schulz were reprinted in an anthology by Akerman and Pawsey (2015), also published in an English translation.

8   In this context, thanks is due to Vanessa von Gliszczynski who discovered references to the audio documents in the Berlin Phonogram Archive (cf. Ziegler 2006: 134–135) and established the contact between the archive and the research project.

References:

Akerman, Kim and Margaret Pawsey (eds). 2015: *Cologne to the Kimberley. Studies of Aboriginal Life in Northwest Australia by Five German Scholars in the First Half of the 20th Century.* Perth: Hesperian Press.

Lommel, Andreas. 1969: *Fortschritt ins Nichts. Die Modernisierung der Primitiven Australiens. Beschreibung und Definition eines psychischen Verfalls.* Zurich: Atlantis.

Petri, Helmut. 1954: *Die Sterbende Welt in Nordwest-Australien.* Braunschweig: Albert Limbach.

Petri, Helmut. 2011: *The Dying World in Northwest Australia.* With a foreword from Susan Bradley and an introduction from Kim Akerman. Perth: Hesperian Press.

Ziegler, Susanne. 2006: *Die Wachszylinder des Berliner Phonogramm-Archivs.* Berlin: Ethnologisches Museum, Staatliche Museen zu Berlin.

Introduction

An Eighty Year Relationship

Richard Kuba

Over ten years ago, on a cold January day, an Australian delegation visited the Frobenius Institute at the Goethe University Frankfurt. Mikailo McKenzie and Gordon Junior, Ngarinyin Traditional Owners from the Kimberley in Northwest Australia, boarded a plane, together with the anthropologist Heather Winter, in order to take a look at a treasure in Frankfurt: This consisted of around 2,400 photographs and 150 copies of rock paintings.[1]

Compiled in 1938 by the participants of the institute's 22nd expedition, the existence of this archive almost fell into obscurity for a whole generation. In distant Germany, pictures and stories, from a time extremely lacking in images, were preserved as if in a time capsule. Portraits of long-deceased grandfathers and great grandmothers, rock paintings that many Ngarinyin living today only know from stories, along with cultural records from the days when the Ngarinyin and their related Indigenous groups, the Worrorra and Wunambal, still lived on their ancestral lands and could cultivate their very special relationship to their Country, with all its myths and rituals, more intensely.

A short while later a further delegation announced their arrival, this time from the Worrorra. It was at this point that we realised that we were in possession of a very special archive and that it needed to be thoroughly researched. The question of who could have access to the material, and which cultural protocols had to be observed, was in urgent need of clarification. After all, quite a few of the photos showed highly secret ceremonies which, under no circumstances, were to be seen (for their own protection) by uninitiated eyes. To this day, the rock paintings still 'belong' to very specific families; only they can grant access and are allowed to artistically process the motifs.

This was the beginning of an adventurous research undertaking[2], during the course of which, together with our Australian partners, we tracked down lost archives across Germany, deciphered barely legible handwriting and translated it into English, repatriated pictures, both physically and digitally, and finally, gazed in wonder at the ancient originals at the hidden rock painting sites in Kimberley, almost 200 km from the next human settlement, and compared the different pools of knowledge: that around eighty years old from the world of paper, and that retold from generation to generation within the local families.[3]

There are prehistoric rock paintings throughout the world. In Europe we are familiar with the Ice Age cave painting sites, as fascinating as they are mysterious, such as Altamira, Lascaux or the Grotte Chauvet, first discovered in the 1990s, and whose paintings are up to 36,000 years old. On all continents prehistoric picture galleries, painted or carved on rocks, provide evidence of the astounding artistry and rich imagination of our earliest ancestors. In the vast majority of cases the

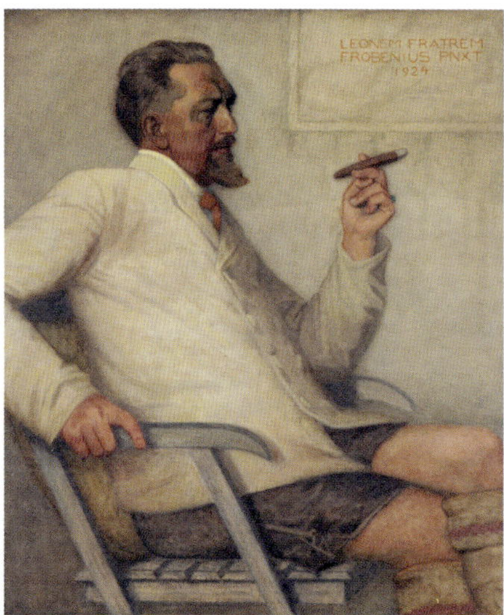

Fig. 1   Portrait of Leo Frobenius 1924, painted by his brother Hermann Frobenius (1871–1954). Oil on canvas. Collection: Frobenius Institute. Photo: not stated

hardware has been preserved but the software has disappeared: The stories and ideas which first gave meaning to the pictures have not survived the course of the millennia. Apart from a few exceptions: In many Indigenous Australian communities rock paintings are still at the centre of the cultural systems, as is the case in Kimberley, one of the most sparsely populated regions on earth.[4]

The backstory

But how did it come about that, of all people, it was German researchers that set out for the Kimberley shortly before the outbreak of World War II, and what makes the material that they collected so special?

Here it is worth taking a look at the history of the institute that sent the researchers, which at the time went under the name Forschungsinstitut für Kulturmorphologie (Institute for Cultural Morphology). Now named after its founder, the German ethnologist Leo Frobenius (1873–1938), it is the oldest German-speaking research institute in the field of cultural anthropology, whose beginnings stretch back to the end of the nineteenth century (fig. 1).

Admittedly Frobenius's interest was Africa, and he described himself as the first trained ethnologist to conduct field research in Africa (Frobenius 1925: 26). Time was crucial: "At the speed at which African culture, under the influence of European economic life, is now being destroyed, it is necessary to quickly and systematically explore its full extent". His first Africa expedition in 1904 took him to what was then Belgian Congo, and up until the outbreak of World War I he travelled almost uninterruptedly throughout West and North Africa. Driven by the "threat that peoples and entire cultural groups will melt under the heat of the European will to power", he saw "cultures rushing towards destruction" everywhere (Frobenius 1925: 21, 26).

Consequently, he felt the urgent need for a form of "rescue ethnography". For Frobenius, the collection of ethnographic objects was more of a means to finance the expensive expeditions, for which the researcher regularly hired painters and draughtsmen for the visual documentation of "dying Africa" (Frobenius 1923). This resulted in an enormous archive of fairy tales and myths, architecture and handicraft, masks, traditional costumes and cults. The older the more valuable.

The year 1912 marked a turning point when Frobenius received an audience with the German Kaiser, Wilhelm II. This led to a lifelong friendship between the two men (Franzen, Kohl and Recker 2012), resulting, amongst other things, in access to new sources of finance, removing Frobenius's reliance on collecting for German ethnological museums.

From then on, he was able to concentrate on the oldest and most primordial manifestation of African cultures, the prehistoric rock pictures. In his eyes the key to European Ice Age art was to be found in Africa. It was here that the tradition lived on after the Ice Age, and it is here that one could also find the myths that explain them (Kuba and Porr 2022). In 1913 he set off on his sixth "German Inner-African Research Expedition", together with three painters to Algeria. A purely photographic documentation was out of the question as "a drawing produced in a living process is in many cases more 'quintessential' than a mechanical photograph" (Frobenius 1937a: 21). In the craggy mountains of the Saharan Atlas the artists submitted the prehistoric carvings to canvas as accurately as possible, in monumental life-size pictures of up to ten metres in width. Including the rocky background, the cracks, erosions and defects. This established a completely new, previously unrivalled standard of rock art documentation.

Only weeks before the outbreak of World War I, the expedition returned with some 320 copies of rock pictures. It is the foundation for the world largest collection of rock picture copies. In and after the war expeditions were conducted to Eritrea and Egypt. However, the largest addition to the collection was made by the ninth expedition from 1928–30, which documented Southern Africa's extremely rich rock art tradition. For the first time, in addition to three ethnologists and a painter, Frobenius was also accompanied by three women painters, Elisabeth Mannsfeld, Maria Weyersberg and Agnes Schulz.

From now on Frobenius almost exclusively employed trained women artists for the copying of the rock pictures. He praised the "heroic services of the delicate natures", who in weeks-long work, "continually exposed to wind and rain, and often cut off from the rest of humanity for just as long, mastered such huge works" (Frobenius 1930: 84). Furthermore "over the course of the years they had learnt […] to convey the *spirituality* that gave rise to the works" (Frobenius 1937a: 21).

In the 1920s and 1930s a total of nearly two dozen men and women painters were employed at Frobenius's institute. While the male artists in particular continued their careers after leaving the institute, the women painters appear to have had a stronger identification with the institute and its charismatic director. Many of them were well-brought-up young ladies from bourgeois families. The unpublished diary of one of these women painters, Elisabeth "Katta" Krebs, not only bears witness to her sense of wonder at the fantastic play of light and shadow, colours and forms of the Saharan landscapes, but also tells of a wild and free life beyond the constraints of bourgeois society. The work at the Frankfurt institute promised variety, travel and adventure, and opened up completely new possibilities, especially for young women. As scientist or draughtswoman they had a strong position at the institute – to a great extent with equal rights – which was also given the title "little Amazon state" (Beer 2006; Stappert 2019). At least seven painters married members of the institute and thus also remained connected to it in this way. Painters such as Agnes Schulz, Maria Weyersberg and Elisabeth Pauli were amongst the most experienced women expedition members, who from the middle of the 1930s also led expeditions to European rock picture regions, to France, Scandinavia, Spain and Italy, and also produced their own scientific publications.

From the mid-1930s onwards the research focus extended beyond Africa. Prior to this Frobenius had completed his last Africa expedition in the eastern Sahara. He summarised the character of the expedition as follows: "Discipline amidst the greatest poverty, clarity of tasks, joy in life, happiness i.e. success" (Frobenius 1937a: vii). Sandstorms, injuries and car breakdowns, but also the gruff Prussian manner of the director, who was miserly with the food rations and for whom "an expedition is no life insurance" took him, but also his assistants, to the limit of their capabilities. Frobenius marketed the great Sahara expedition as his 12th and last expedition, "the scheduled completion of the exploration of the African continent". In fact Frobenius, now sixty years old, and whose health had become increasingly fragile over the preceding years, was concerned to hand over responsibility for future expeditions to the assistants who had trained under him.

Over the course of thirty years and a total of 12 DIAFEs (Deutsche Inner-Afrika Forschungs-Expeditionen – German Inner African Research Expeditions) Frobenius had acquired considerable know-how in the organisation and conduction of expeditions, had developed documentation standards and increasingly placed the "worldview", in particular as expressed in mythology and art, at the centre of his research interests (fig. 2).

At the same time he had established his personal idea of how foreign cultures are to be understood amongst his students. It was about "turning off one's own attitude and mentality to the extent that what is observed can become alive within us" (Frobenius 1929: 272). Frobenius, who was also guilty of racist statements typical for the time, repeatedly complained of the prejudices and blindness of Europeans. On the other hand, he claimed an openness which allowed him – in his opinion – to overcome his own projections and to apprehend the reality beyond egocentric subjectivity. Only so could the European gaze – shaped by rationalism and utilitarianism, and which merely saw foreign cultures as "curiosity cabinets" – be overcome so that these cultures could now serve as "our teachers" (Frobenius 1932: 68).

Thus the reality behind the facts tends to reveal itself to the sensitive artist as opposed to the rationally thinking scientist:

> *"Only they who are genuinely musical or really a lover of art [...] can have an idea of the sublime grand nature which finds immediate expression in the Ethiopians' language of customs, and the crudeness we must apply [...] in order to take measure of the fathomless richness of feeling with the millimetre-by-millimetre acquisition of our rational judgement"* (Frobenius 1929: 239).

Thus the ground had been laid for a new generation to continue the work. However, this required expanding the radius of action of his privately run institute that repeatedly faced the threat of financial ruin. The formula that he found for this in the mid-1930s was "Deutsche Umwelt" (German environment), abbreviated to DU (Schmidt-Leonhardt 1936), that can also be understood as a concession to the zeitgeist of the new political situation in the country (Kuba 2024).

While mainstream ethnology, institutionally, and in terms of content and personnel, largely integrated itself into the National Socialist system (Streck 2000: 9; Gingrich 2005: 123), Frobenius's cultural morphology tended to remain on the periphery. Nevertheless, Frobenius, who entertained great hopes on Hitler's assumption of office, was in a very comfortable position in the mid-1930s and, despite the growing ideological opposition of orthodox Nazi functionaries, was able to secure enough funds for his institute, enabling him to organise his last Africa expedition and send his assistants to European rock picture regions. Clearly one can argue that Frobenius's penchant for intuition, irrationalism, mysticism and his rejection of the 'West' (Marchand 1997) emerged from (and flowed into) a zeitgeist in the

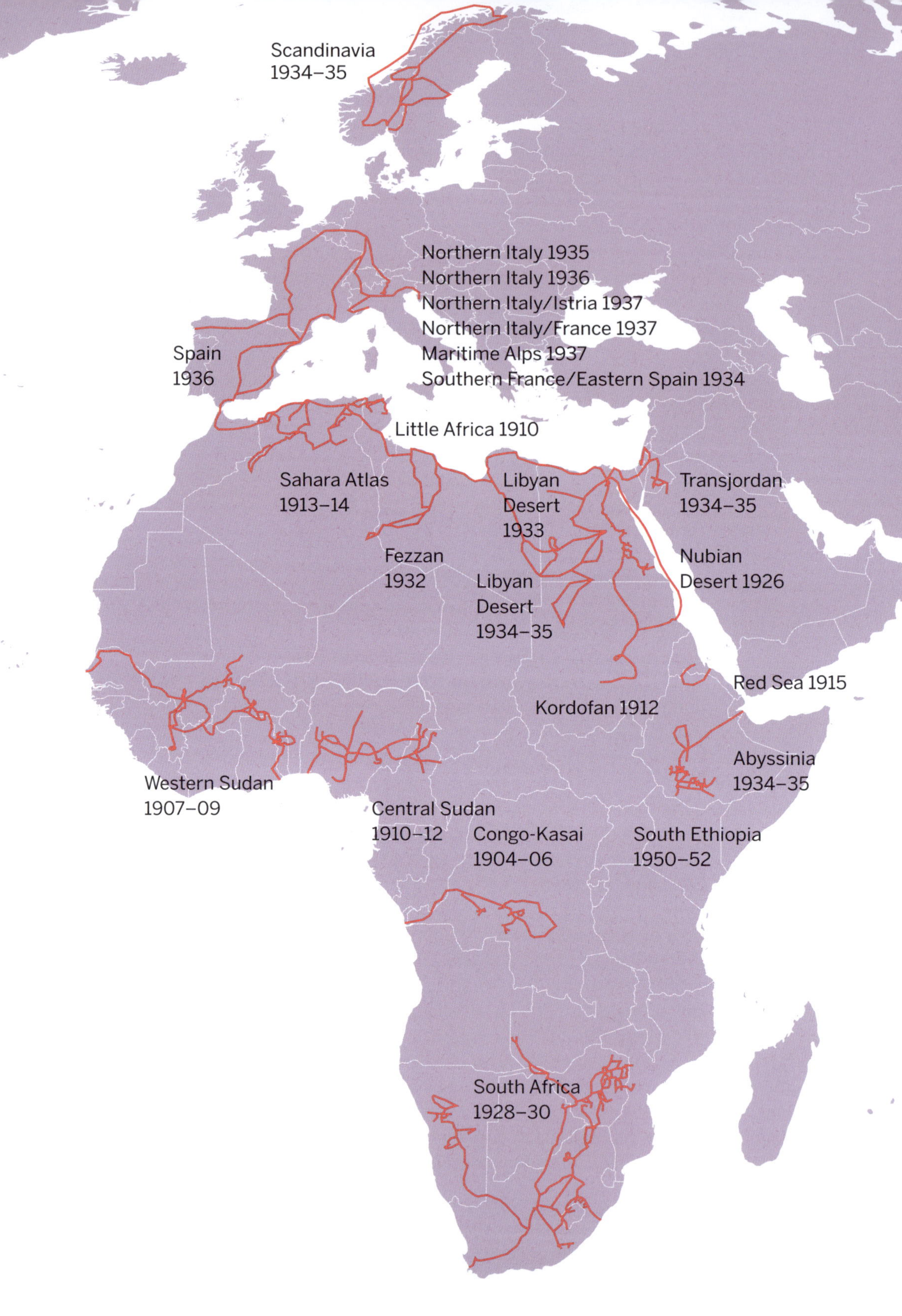

Scandinavia 1934–35
Northern Italy 1935
Northern Italy 1936
Northern Italy/Istria 1937
Northern Italy/France 1937
Maritime Alps 1937
Southern France/Eastern Spain 1934
Spain 1936
Little Africa 1910
Sahara Atlas 1913–14
Libyan Desert 1933
Transjordan 1934–35
Fezzan 1932
Nubian Desert 1926
Libyan Desert 1934–35
Red Sea 1915
Kordofan 1912
Western Sudan 1907–09
Abyssinia 1934–35
Central Sudan 1910–12
Congo-Kasai 1904–06
South Ethiopia 1950–52
South Africa 1928–30

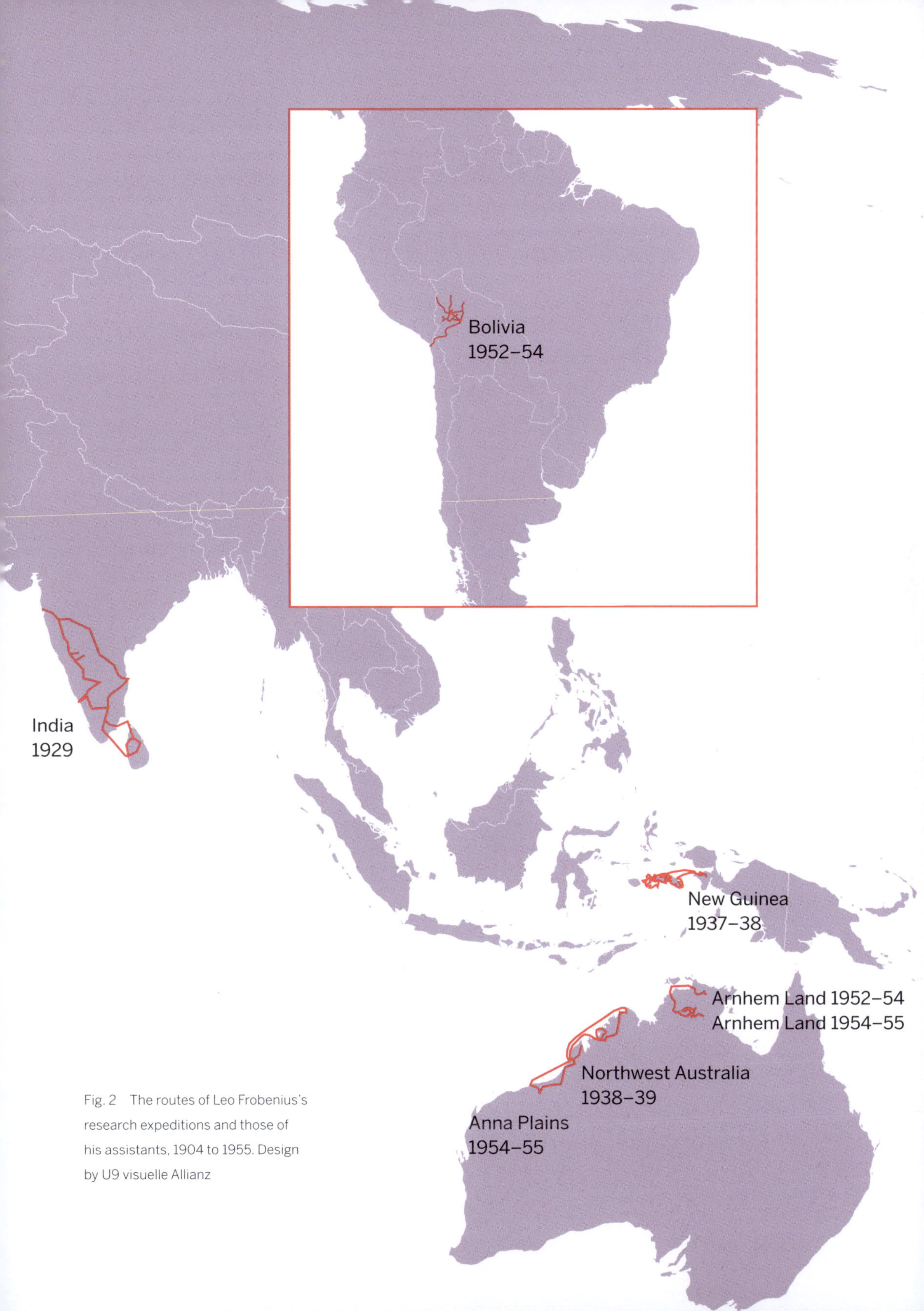

Fig. 2　The routes of Leo Frobenius's research expeditions and those of his assistants, 1904 to 1955. Design by U9 visuelle Allianz

period after World War I which also nourished the early Nazi ideology (Streck 2014: 164–69). However, his refusal to include race as a factor in his cultural theory increasingly strained relations with the regime. Thanks to the support of a network of friends within the Nazi hierarchy and the protection afforded by his popularity, together with the fact he was not perceived as a threat to the regime, he was never seriously endangered in the period before his death in August 1938. However, without the popular figure at its head, the "politically highly suspect" institute would increasingly encounter troubled waters (Geisenhainer 2005: 381).

To Australia

The inspiration for an expedition to Australia can be traced to the German missionary and ethnologist Carl Strehlow (1871–1922), who published a five-volume work on the central Australian Aranda and Loritja people (Strehlow 1907–1920). Frobenius put out the first feelers in the direction of Australia and Oceania as early as 1933, when, in a short foreword to the book *Kolun-Neuguinea. Drei Männer suchen Gold*, he wrote of the "longing for a journey to the Oceanian tropics together with the author" (Beinssen 1933). The intention was for the author, the German-Australian Ekkehard Beinssen, to establish the initial contact with Australia and assist in founding an outpost of the institute in Sydney (Beinssen-Hesse 2004: 158). Although this scheme, as well as the hope of mobilising Australian funding for a research expedition, did not come off, Frobenius stuck to his plans and in the last year of his life not only sent his assistants on an expedition to Seram and West Papua (1937–38) but also to the Kimberly in Northwest Australia.

This remote region of Australia was chosen, amongst other reasons, because it was home to "tribes who have been little effected by white civilisation", as noted by an Australian newspaper reporting on the arrival of the Germans (Western Australian 1938). The goal of the expedition was to "learn [something] of the material and spiritual cultures of the people of the Kimberley plateau in the past and present" (Fox 1937). The expedition was largely financed by the "Advertising Council of German Industry under the authorisation of the Ministry for Propaganda and the City of Frankfurt in the person of the Lord Mayor Krebs". A total of 1,140 Australian pounds, i.e. 10,000 reichsmark could be raised from "Berlin sources" (Frobenius 1937b).

In preparation a research permit had to be obtained, which was acquired in the name of the Städtische Völkermuseum, of which Frobenius became the director in 1935. For the Australian authorities it was henceforth known as the expedition of the Frankfurt "Peoples Museum". On 30 August 1937 the long awaited permit finally arrived, signed by the Chief Protector of Aboriginals in Western Australia,

Auber O. Neville (1875–1954), who was later known as 'Neville the devil' for his racist politics and his responsibility for the Stolen Generation. The conditions were listed as follows:

> 1) *"refrain from unduly interfering with or molesting the native peoples to be found on the native reserves;"*
>
> 2) *"abstain from obtaining or removing any ethnological specimens from such reserves […] probably a limited number of cultural objects, weapons, etc. might be acquired […];"*
>
> 3) *"refrain from taking photographs on native reserves, such being prohibited […] permission may be granted on condition that a print of every photograph taken on an native reserve is supplied to the Department"* (Premier's Department 1937).

Special negotiations were required for the institute's request to take two female members of the expedition to the "native reserve", as well as the wish to bring hunting rifles into the country for the purpose of hunting for food. Ultimately, both request were approved and after a six-week sea voyage the five expedition members arrived in Perth in Western Australia at the beginning of March 1938. The German party was led by the thirty-year-old ethnologist Helmut Petri (1907–1986), who everyone called Petrus, and who had been working at the institute in Frankfurt since 1935. He was assisted by the German-American Douglas C. Fox (1906–1979), journalist, adventurer and bon vivant. He had already participated in numerous Frobenius Expeditions as driver, logistician and photographer, and in 1937 organised the Institute's celebrated rock art exhibition at the Museum of Modern Art in New York. The ethnologist Andreas Lommel (1912–2005), who had just received his doctorate, also joined the party at short notice. While the male members of the expedition focused on ethnographic and prehistoric studies, the two women artists were responsible for the visual documentation, in particular the copying of the rock paintings: Agnes Susanne Schulz (1892–1973) known as "Asuschu", and sometimes also as the "Signora", was one of the institute's most experienced artists and already had ten years experience copying rock pictures in southern Africa, the Libyan Sahara, Scandinavia and Northern Italy. As the oldest she was highly respected, especially by the expedition leader Petri: "Schu made him so nervous" (Kleist 1938). Furthermore, she was clearly also responsible for the finances (Schulz 1938). Her younger artist colleague was Gerta Kleist (1911–1998) alias „Kleiklei", who, following a short documentation trip to Northern Italy, now embarked on her first major expedition outside Europe. Although less experienced, she was the only one to note the names of the people she portrayed (fig. 3).

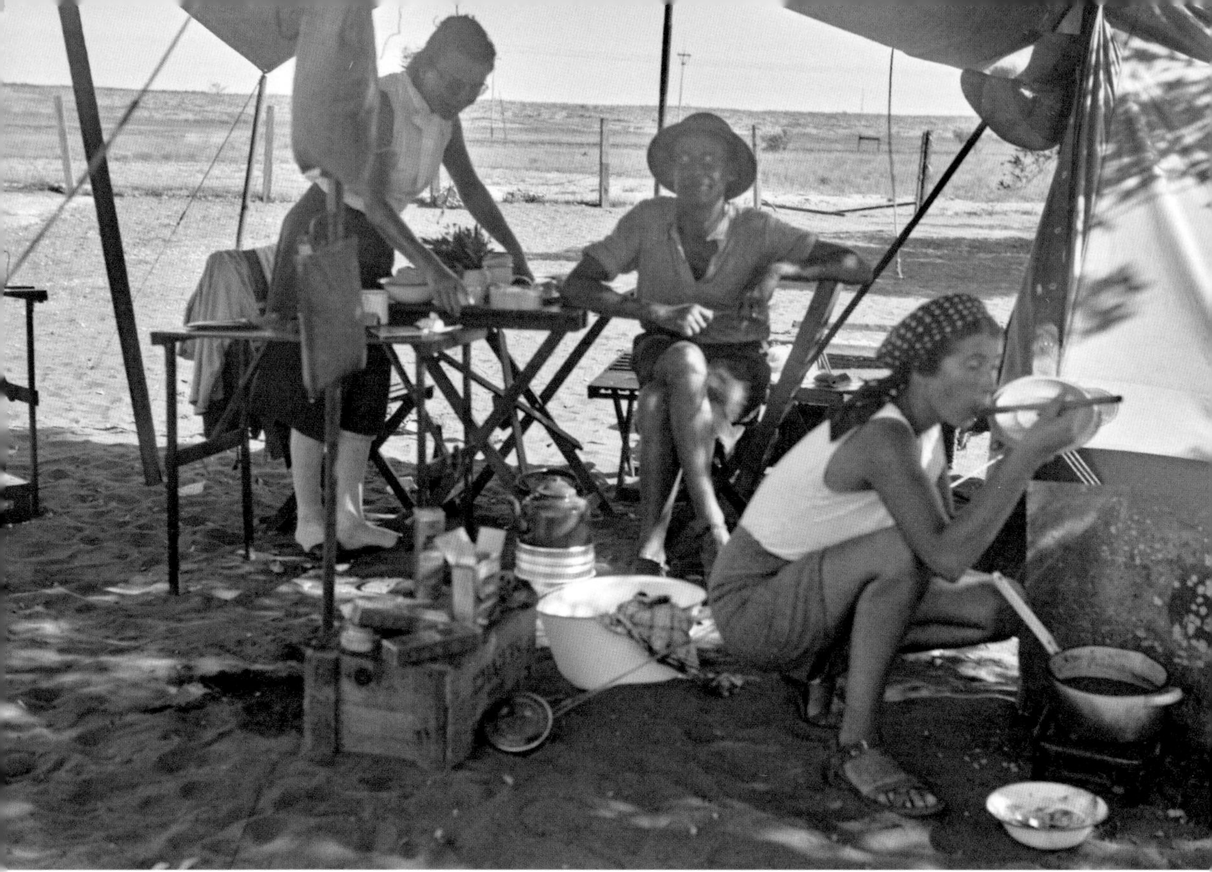

Fig. 3   Agnes Schulz, Gerta Kleist and Andreas
Lommel in the camp near Port Headland in April 1938.
Collection: Frobenius Institute. Photo: not stated

In the Kimberley

In Perth the Australian psychology student, Patrick Pentony, joined the party with the intention of researching the dreams of the Aboriginals for his bachelor thesis (Pentony 1938). The first leg of the journey was by liner to Broome located further north, the centre of pearl fishing, and from there three days travel on a small schooner in the direction of Walcott Inlet and the Government Aboriginal Station Munja. This was one of the "Feeding Stations" where, amongst other things, the Aboriginals received food rations in order to keep them off the land of the cattle breeders and prevent them spearing the cows. This was preceded by huge land theft and the often violent displacement of the Indigenous population from their ancestral land.[5] Munja, as well as the mission and trading stations subsequently visited further north, represented the expedition's essential logistical nodal points in an otherwise sparsely populated landscape almost devoid of tracks. Here one could hire mounts and pack animals (horses, donkeys, mules or camels), replenish provisions, send post and organise longer trips to the rock art sites or camps of the local population. These stations were run by white Australians, who, together with their families, lived largely isolated in the outback over many years, and were sometimes suspicious or even dismissive of the Germans, but sometimes also extremely welcoming.

In Munja the station director Harold Reid belonged to the first category and initially refused the travellers transport horses. However, more importantly, the team was assigned two Aboriginals who lived on the station named Paddy and Leggings. "The first more-or-less speaks English and can also be used as an interpreter, the latter hardly speaks English but is the more intelligent and also knows a great deal about his own people" (Petri 1938a: 3). Stone arrangements and "native camps" were visited in the surroundings, as well as the first rock painting sites which were copied by the two women artists.

In the following months the expedition members repeatedly divided up into smaller groups with different destinations. The women artists camped at especially rich rock painting sites, sometimes for weeks, accompanied by an Aboriginal guide and one of the male expedition members as "Lord Protector of ladies in the painter camp" (Petri 1938a: 11).

In September the women, together with Lommel, set off by boat to the isolated Presbyterian Mission Station Kunmunya to the north, with Petri and Fox travelling over land. The relationship to Reverend J.R.B Love (1889–1947), who had already been running the station for over ten years, proved to be extremely difficult. Love not only spoke the local Worrorra language, but in 1936 had also published an ethnographic study of the Worrorra, *Stone-Age Bushmen of Today*. From the beginning the reverend was sceptical of the possibilities of the German researchers, and even before the start of the exhibition wrote to Petri:

> *"I do not think you will get a working knowledge of any native language under three months' continuous work and association. This is the only thing that will make your work of real value, and, is, I should say, essential. Three months will not, I fear, enable you to discuss matters of belief with the aborigines. This could only be done after long years of association"* (Love 1938: 2).

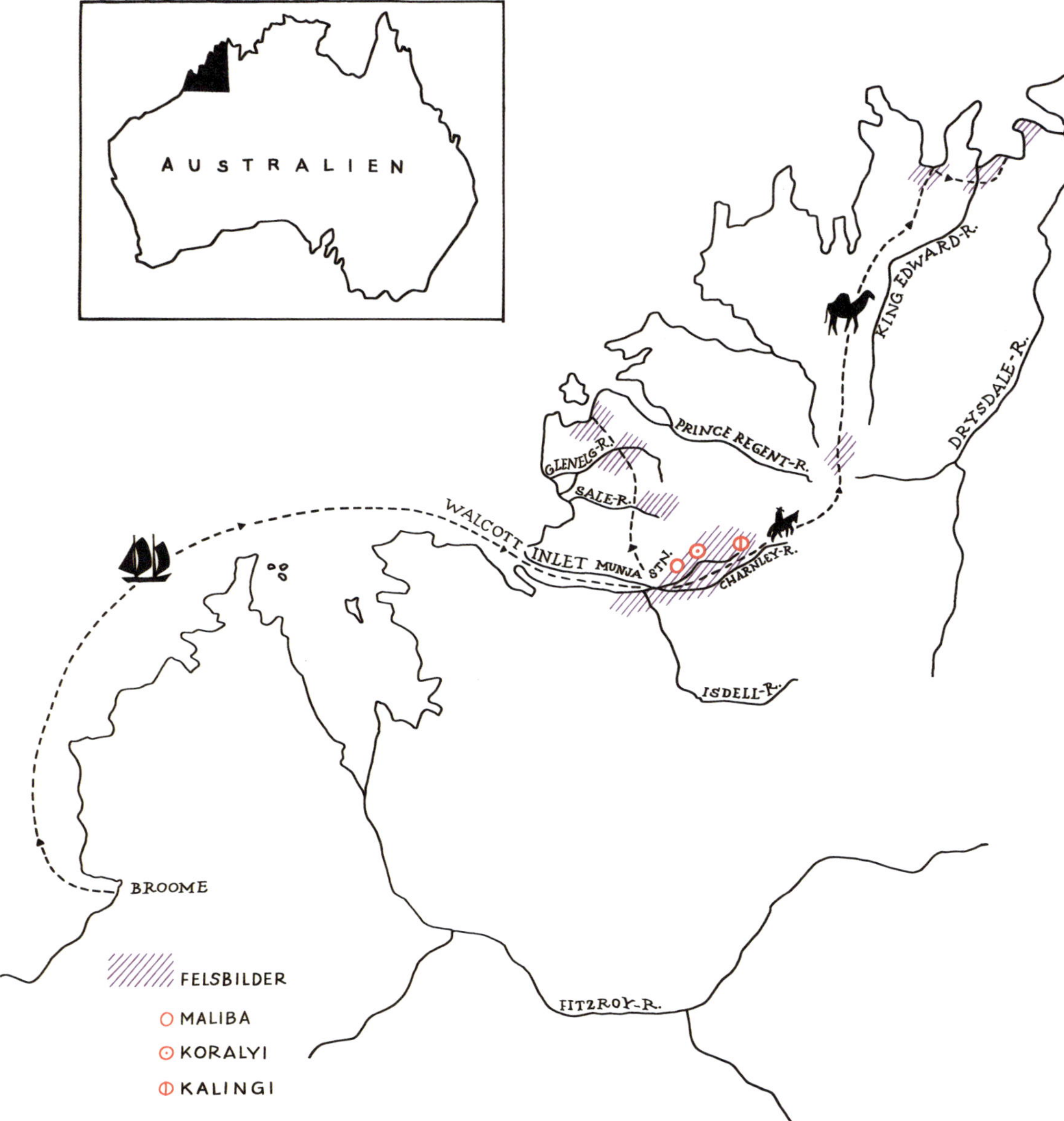

Fig. 4   Schematic map of the expedition route. Presumably drawn by Agnes Schulz, 1938. Collection: Frobenius Institute. Design by U9 visuelle Allianz

The visit to the isolated mission station also proved to be equally complicated. As Petri noted in his report:

"It has to be admitted that Mr. Love made an honest attempt to play the friendly host. However, as he is by nature stiff and a Presbyterian clergyman, and as he sees himself as dictator of the Kimberleys in general and personal owner of Kunmunya in particular, it is not easy to strike a freer conversational tone with him. This applies above all to the scientific field. He considers the Worora to be his personal reserve and he is not particularly happy about our presence in this country" (Petri 1938b: 13).

Petri traces this back to a deep-rooted hatred of the Germans on the part of this former ANZAC combatant[6]:

"He saw in us, under the pretext of ethnographic work, people on the lookout for a new colony for Germany. The fear of spies is a very widespread illness in Australia" (Petri 1938c: 1).

By way of confirmation, there is a confidential letter in the Australian State Records from a "Flying Doctor" who met the expedition members in Kunmunya, and addressed his concerns to the Australian ministry of the Interior:

"While there we met a party of three Germans, self-styled anthropologists, two women and a man. The man is a German Army Officer with army equipment and the women are very poor exponents of their supposed jobs. Also, wherever they go, trouble amongst the natives has followed. I think the Commonwealth Defence Department should investigate these customers more fully" (Collings 1938).

Admittedly, the reverend's fundamental opposition to the collection of ethnographic objects, which Petri can somewhat understand, is more important:

"In his opinion it represents a debasement of the native culture when one trades tobacco for the black's cultural property. Perhaps there is a certain justification in this standpoint. However, as we want to acquire a nice collection for our museum. I can't currently occupy myself with such lines of thought" (Petri 1938b: 14).

The women artists were especially disappointed that Reverend Love did not allow the visiting of rock art sites, or even their copying, "with reference to the feelings of the natives which were to be respected, and who would be insulted by the presence of women at such places" (Schulz 1939: 5). After a week in Kunmunya they moved on to a camp three days travel away and quickly set about making copies of the Jandara rock picture site, which, amongst other things, features a large crocodile (fig. 5). Here the proximity of the women to the rock paintings did not always prove to be in conformity with the cultural values of the Indigenous population, and was also punished – albeit only indirectly. Agnes Schulz wrote in her diary:

> *"On the evening before the decampment Klei-Klei scalded her foot. The natives said that she had been bitten by the crocodile because he didn't allow people to get so close to it, as we did when copying"* (Schulz 1939: 32).

However, Schulz's enthusiasm at the discovery of ever new rock paintings was not dampened by her colleague's mishap. She traced her receptiveness to them back to her teacher: "One often has the strong feeling that the immediate impressions of vivid reality are unique and irreplaceable, insofar as one is receptive and open to them – which, in this respect, we have Frobenius to thank!" (Schulz 1939: 32). Fox also sees himself as beholden to the institute's director: "As students of

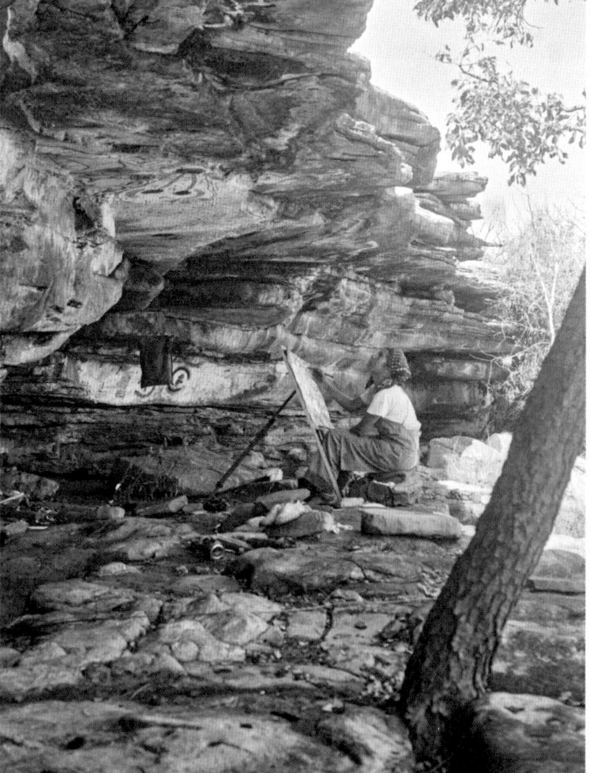

Fig. 5   Gerta Kleist in November 1938 while copying the large crocodile. Jandara, North Kimberley. Collection: Frobenius Institute. Photo: not stated

Frobenius we know only too well how the individual, spiritually and physically, is dependent on and influenced by the landscape; we know how closely spirit and environment are linked" (Fox 1939: 6).

Consequently, the expedition members are appropriately dejected when the news of Frobenius's death reaches them in August 1938. "The good mood was gone and the next days, which were filled with the preparations for our return to Munya and the onward journey to Drysdale, were very subdued. We decided to complete the expedition as the director had intended and planned it, but above all to comply with the instructions that we would receive from the institute" (Petri 1938b: 16).

Two researchers

Towards the end of the year the ladies returned to Perth, where, in January 1939, they exhibited their portraits and copies of the rock paintings in the hall of the Western Australian Museum housing the casts of antique statues (fig. 6). All of the German expedition members soon returned to their homeland with rich scientific spoils: around 2,400 photos, a total of 260 copies of rock paintings, landscape scenes and portraits, mainly watercolours, hundreds of collected objects, as well as audio recordings, reports, field notes and diaries. Shortly before the outbreak of World War II an exhibition was held at the Städtische Völkermuseum in Frankfurt, and soon after Lommel and Petri were conscripted into the army. They both survived the war and imprisonment, but it wasn't until the 1950s that they had the opportunity to process their material and each publish an ethnographic study. The majority of the objects collected were lost during the bombing of Frankfurt in 1944, as well as Petri's notes on the mythology and apparently around 360 meters of film material.

The two ethnologists selected different groups from the Kimberley as the focus of their research. Petri chose the Ngarinyin and Lommel the Wunambal who lived further north. During the research Petri complained of his younger colleague: "It would have been appropriate if he had also written to me about his research [...] however it is a recurring theme that Lommel doesn't believe that he needs to occupy himself with such things, and as before I don't know what he is actually doing" (Petri 1938d). In the coming decades they would continue to take completely different paths.[7]

Andreas Lommel was the first to publish with his slim volume *Die Unambal* in which he gave expression to his extremely pessimistic view of the cultural survival of the society he examined (Lommel 1952). In the same year Helmut Petri's voluminous post-doctoral thesis appeared *Der Australische Medizinmann* (Petri

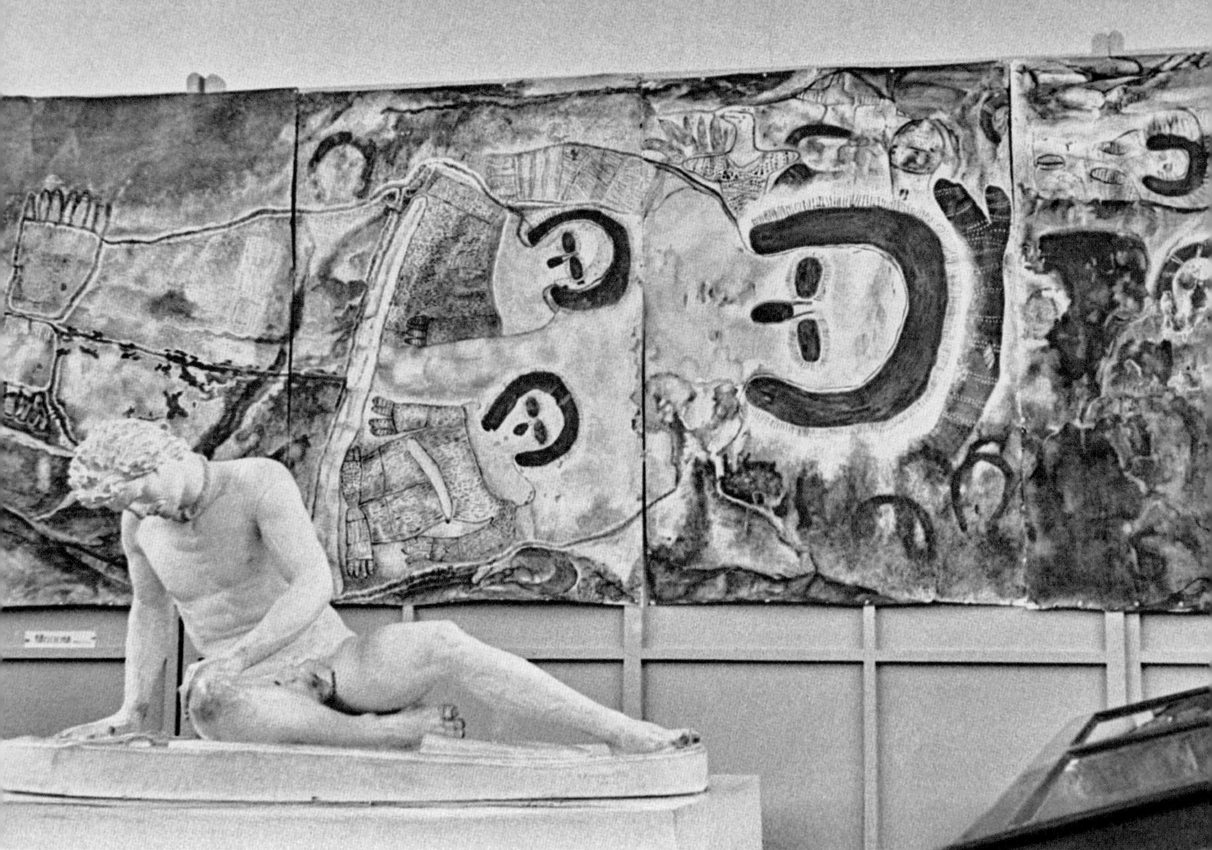

Fig. 6   Copy of the Modum rock painting by Gerta Kleist and Agnes Schulz in the hall of the Western Australian Museum housing the casts of antique statues, January 1939. Collection: Frobenius Institute. Photo: not stated

1952–53) and two year later *Sterbende Welt in Nordwest-Australien* (Petri 1954). While it is possible to discern a similarly pessimistic view in the latter title, which surely goes back to Frobenius, the works displayed significant differences. Petri displays a strong commitment to the wellbeing and promotion of surviving Aboriginal groups. He not only addresses the disappearing customs, but also shows the vitality of the Aboriginal cultures undergoing change.

Furthermore, the scientific standards of the two men differ. Lommel does not refer to relevant secondary sources. Neither does he refer to Petri, with whom he must have had the opportunity for detailed discussions on the long return journey. Furthermore, he does not give us any insights into the process of information gathering. In contrast, Petri is well versed in the secondary literature and refers to it in his argumentation. He also states that he discussed with Lommel and exchanged notes. Wherever relevant, we learn who his informants were and to what extent they agreed. The problems that the researcher was confronted with, and his relationship to the Indigenous people, are also described so that we can form an opinion of the quality of his research. Here, without doubt, Petri shows himself to be the more mature field researcher and scientist (Beinssen-Hesse 1991: 140; Kolig 2017: 390).

Ultimately, the two researchers represent completely different schools. Andreas Lommel, who was appointed the director of the Staatliches Museum für Völkerkunde in Munich (today: Museum Fünf Kontinente) in 1957, increasingly concentrated on making richly illustrated books on the art of the Indigenous Australians accessible to a broader public. Unfortunately, these books are marred by idiosyncratic and judgemental comments and an almost complete dependence on the short field research trips conducted in the thirties and fifties.[8] His concern was to present the Indigenous art to the German public as an aesthetic curiosity: Evidence of a culture which was irrevocably condemned to extinction, and therefore, in its contemporary, living manifestations, was not worthy of attention. Lommel's work from 1969 *Fortschritt ins Nichts: die Modernisierung der Primitiven Australiens. Beschreibung und Definition eines psychischen Verfalls* (Lommel 1969) played an important role in this. This publication decisively shaped the German perspective on Australia's Indigenous population. In contrast, Petri became a professor at the University of Cologne and continued to conduct scientific research and publish. In his review of the book from his former "junior research assistant" Petri commented sarcastically: "From an ethnological perspective [the observation] really proves to be an 'advance into nothing'. One forgives the great researcher's former 'companion' these unfriendly words" (Petri 1970: 236).

Epilogue

The expeditions of Frobenius, his male and female assistants and his successors have left behind extensive ethnographic archives. These should benefit those who have the greatest stake in them, namely those communities from which the material originally came. Consequently, for many years the Frobenius Institute has striven to open up visual and written sources and make them available in various formats. Exhibitions, publications and conferences have been realised with local partners in in Burkina Faso, Nigeria, Senegal and Ethiopia. In this respect, the cooperation with Australian partners is especially exciting, not least because the 1938 expedition represents one of the earliest comprehensive scientific studies of the *Wanjina Wunggurr* cultures.

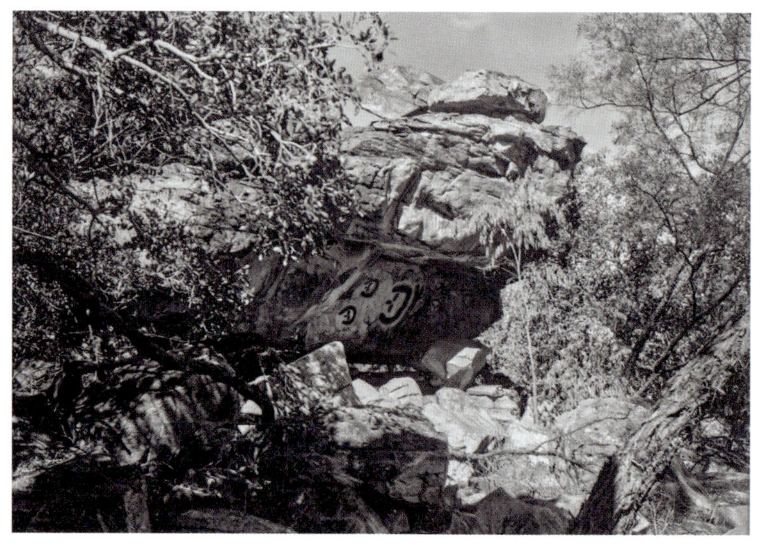

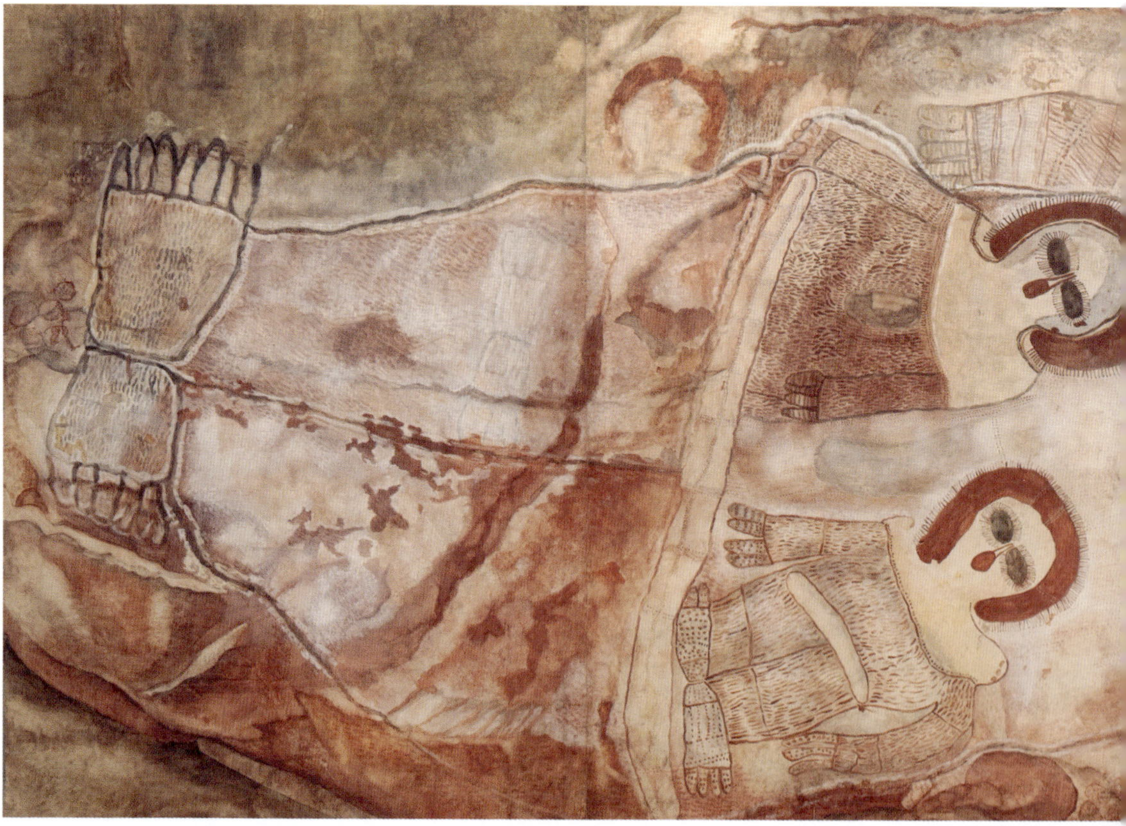

Fig. 7   View of the Modum rock art site, May 1938.
Collection: Frobenius Institute. Photo: Not stated

"Large reclining Wondjina with two small ones which are described as his children. The Wondjina heads to the right are the subjects of the large reclining Wondjina who sent up into the sky to make rain. He has to lie down because if he was to stand up there would be a flood and everything would be drowned."

Fig. 8   Modum rock art site. Kimberley, Northwest Australia. Rock art copy by Gerta Kleist and Agnes Schulz, May 1938. Watercolour on paper. 589 x 214 cm. Collection: Frobenius Institute. Photo: Wolfgang Günzel, 2024

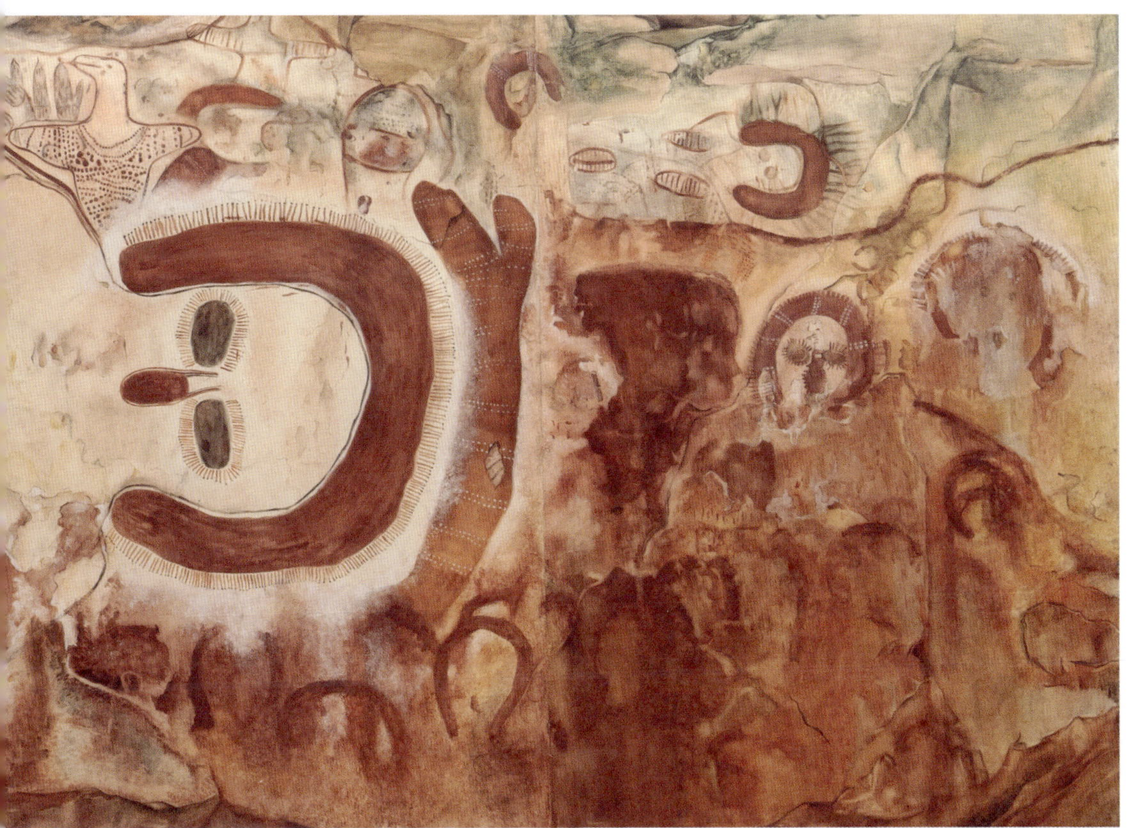

Since 2016 the Frobenius Institute has also presented copies of rock paintings from the expedition to Northwest Australia in a number of exhibitions. In each case our partners in the Kimberley, the Traditional Owners, on whose ancestral land the rock art sites are located, are asked for permission. In the exhibitions we were not only able to display the impressive copies of the rock paintings from Agnes Schulz and Gerta Kleist, but also present the corresponding letters of consent, and thus point to the continuing connection between the Indigenous communities in Kimberley and their Country.

However, the digital repatriation of the material required a more comprehensive project.[9] This included various reciprocal visits as well as the development of a relational database with all the sources, whereby the written material, frequently hand written, first needed to be deciphered, transcribed and translated into English. This has resulted in a comprehensive annotated information infrastructure which has first made the collaborative exhibition COUNTRY BIN PULL'EM possible, and placed the over eighty year relationship[10] between German researchers and the representatives of Indigenous groups in the Kimberley on a completely new, future-oriented basis.

Endnotes

1   The information concerning the Frobenius Institute originally came from Martin Porr, who as a German archaeologist teaches and researches at the University of Western Australia. Consequently, he was familiar with the largely German publications of the expedition members of the time and was the first person to make contact.

2   A very special thanks is due to the German Research Association (DFG) who largely financed the research project "The German ethnographic expeditions to the Kimberley in Australia. Their importance for research history, digital repatriation and the joint interpretation of the indigenous cultural heritage" (GZ: KU 2860/6–1) from 2020–24. The University of Western Australia also generously supported the project led by Dr. Richard Kuba and Ass. Prof Martin Porr.

3   See Martin Porr, *The Archeaological Perspective* and Christina Henneke, *"Rubbish" Painting* in this volume.

4   Around 40,000 people live on an area as large as Germany and Austria combined.

5   See Anthony Redmond, *When the Dreaming Becomes a Nightmare* in this volume.

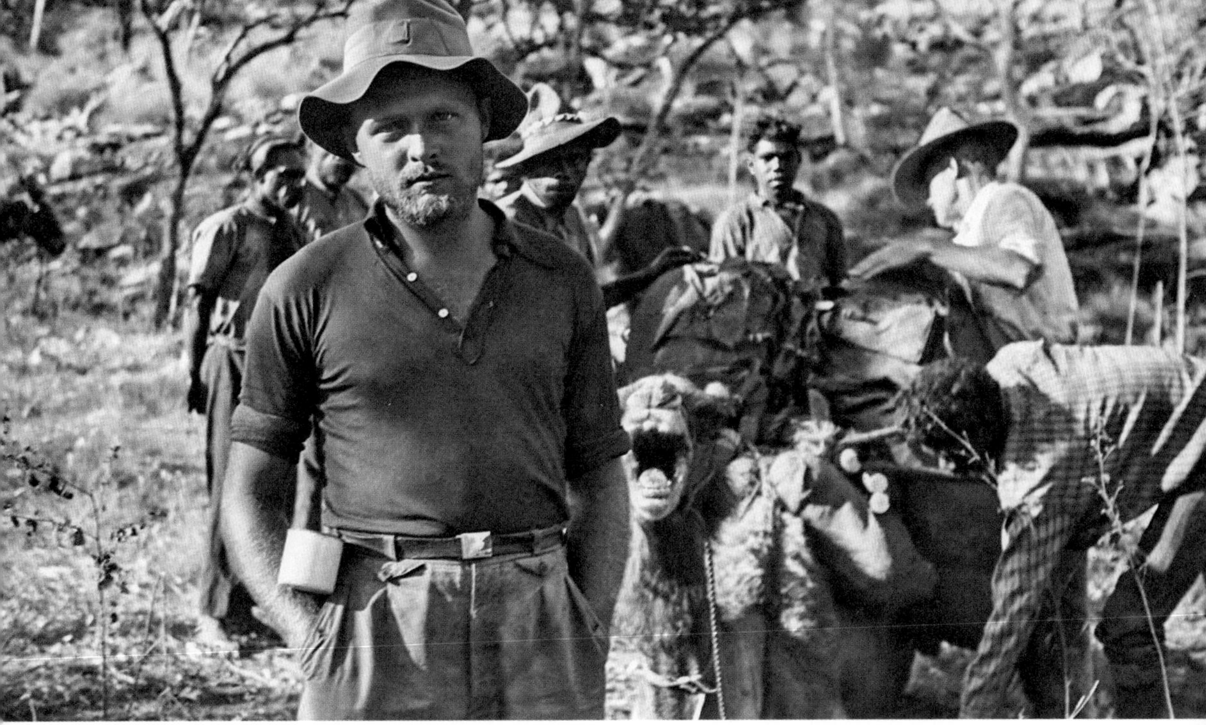

Fig. 9   Helmut Petri riding overland with camels to
Drysdale Mission (today Kalumburu), August 1938.
Collection: Frobenius Institute. Photo: Douglas Fox

6   ANZAC is the acronym for Australian and New
     Zealand Army Corps which during World War I
     fought on the side of the Entente against the
     German empire and its allies.

7   See Michaela Appel, *Andreas and Katharina
     Lommel* in this volume.

8   Following the war Petri, Lommel and Schulz
     made a further trip to Australia. Schulz under-
     took a solo research trip to the Arnhem Land in
     northern Australia, where, now sixty two years
     old, she copied rock paintings, isolated in the
     bush for months. In a diary entry from 1954
     she wrote of the Kimberley: "One can no longer
     pursue the undertaking that were possible for us
     in 1938. No one lives beyond the Leopold Ranges
     any more, and only very few natives" (Schulz
     1955: 7). However, in 1954–55 Lommel returned
     to the Kimberley for five months together with
     his wife, the former painter from the institute
     in Frankfurt, Katharina Marr. On the Gibb River
     cattle farm his wife produced huge, impressive
     copies of rock paintings. It would be Lommel's
     last field research. However, in contrast, Petri
     remained faithful to research and together with
     his wife, the ethnologist Gisela Petri-Odermann,
     undertook numerous further journeys to Western
     Australia through to the 1980s. However, he now
     concentrated on areas in the southern Kimberley.

9   „The German ethnographic expeditions to the
     Kimberley in Australia. Their importance for
     research history, digital repatriation and the joint
     interpretation of the indigenous cultural heritage"
     was financed by the German Research Associ-
     ation. In addition to the Frobenius Institute, the
     partners were the Weltkulturen Museum and the
     University of Western Australia, the Dambi-
     mangari AC, the Wilinggin AC and the Wunam-
     bal-Gaambera AC.

10   The title of this essay is a modified quote from
     Paul Lane, former General Manager of the Wiling-
     gin Aboriginal Corporation: "A partnership that
     began in the 1930s" (July 2022).

References:

Beer, Bettina. 2006: ‚Ein kleiner Amazonenstaat'.
Frühe Ethnologinnen und Ethnographinnen am
Institut für Kulturmorphologie (Frobenius-Institut).
In: Karl-Heinz Kohl and Editha Platte (eds): *Gestalter
und Gestalten.* Frankfurt am Main: Stroemfeld.
133–166.

Beinssen, Ekkehard. 1933: *Kolun-Neuguinea. Drei
Männer suchen Gold.* Berlin: Frundsberg.

Beinssen-Hesse, Silke. 2004: Leo Frobenius in the
Pacific? Plans for Founding a German Institute for the
Morphology of Culture in Sydney. In: Walter Veit (ed.):
*The Struggle for Souls and Science. Constructing
the Fifth Continent. German Missionaries and
Scientists in Australia.* Alice Springs: Northern
Territory Government. 152–182.

Beinssen-Hesse, Silke. 1991: The Study of Australian
Aboriginal Culture by German Anthropologists from
the Frobenius Institute. In: David Walker and Jürgen

Tampke (eds): *From Berlin to the Burdekin. The
German Contribution to the Developmemnt of
Australian Science, Exploration and the Arts.* Ken-
sington: New South Wales Univ. Press. 135–150.

Collings, J.W. 1938: *Letter to the Minister for the
Interior, Canberra, from 27.1.1939* (unpublished ar-
chive source). Perth: State Records Western Australia,
WA S2030-cons993 1937–39_0019.

Doohan, Kim et al. 2016: Produktion und Befugnis.
Über Präsentation, Repräsentation und die Zusam-
menarbeit mit den traditionellen Besitzern der Fels-
malereien der Kimberley-Region, Nordwestaustralien.
In: Karl-Heinz Kohl et al. (eds): *Kunst der Vorzeit.
Texte zu den Felsbildern der Sammlung Frobenius.*
Frankfurt: Frobenius Institute. 93–105.

Fox, Douglas C. 1939: *Megalithfunde der Australien-
Expedition* (unpublished archive source). Frankfurt
am Main: Archive of the Frobenius Institute, HP 029.

Fox, Douglas C. 1937. *Letter to Reverend Love from 7.7.1937* (unpublished archive source). Perth: State Records Western Australia, WA S2030-cons993 1937–39_0207.

Franzen, Christoph; Karl-Heinz Kohl and Marie-Louise Recker. 2012: *Der Kaiser und sein Forscher. Der Briefwechsel zwischen Wilhelm II und Leo Frobenius (1924–1938)*. Stuttgart: W. Kolhammer.

Frobenius, Leo. 1937a: *Ekade Ektab. Die Felsbilder Fezzans*. Leipzig: Harrassowitz.

Frobenius, Leo. 1937b: *Schreiben an die Deutsche Kongresszentrale vom 23.10.1937* (unpublished archive source). Frankfurt am Main: The Institute for the History of Frankfurt, magistrate file 8087. 120–121.

Frobenius, Leo. 1932: *Schicksalskunde im Sinne des Kulturwerdens*. Leipzig: Voigtländer.

Frobenius, Leo. 1930: Die Expedition von 1928–1930. In: *Mitteilungen des Forschungsinstituts für Kulturmorphologie* 5–9. 87.

Frobenius, Leo. 1929: *Monumenta Africana. Der Geist eines Erdteils (Erlebte Erdteile Bd. 7)*. Frankfurt am Main: Frankfurter Societäts-Druckerei.

Frobenius, Leo. 1925: *Vom Schreibtisch zum Äquator. Planmäßige Durchwanderung Afrikas (Erlebte Erdteile Bd. 3)*. Frankfurt am Main: Frankfurter Societäts-Druckerei.

Frobenius, Leo. 1923: *Das sterbende Afrika*. München: O. C. Recht.

Geisenhainer, Katja. 2005: [...] zwischen ‚Paideuma‘ und der ‚Rassenseele‘. Adolf Ellegard Jensen und die Auseinandersetzung um die Frobenius-Nachfolge. In: Katja Geisenhainer and Katharina Lange (eds): *Bewegliche Horizonte*. Leipzig: Universitätsverlag. 377–402.

Gingrich, André. 2005: German Anthropology During the Nazi Period: Complex Scenarios of Collaboration, Persecution, and Competition. In: Frederic Barth et al. (eds): *One discipline, four ways: British, German, French, and American Anthropology*. Chicago: University of Chicago Press. 111–136.

Kleist, Gerta. 1938. *Schreiben an Douglas Fox vom 18.5.1935* (unpublished archive source). Frankfurt am Main: Archive of the Frobenius Institute, GK 018. 5.

Kolig, Erich. 2017: Doing Research in the Kimberley and Carrying Ideological Baggage. A Personal Journey. In: Nicolas Peterson and Anna Kenny (eds): *German Ethnography in Australia*. Acton: Australian National University Press. 383–411.

Kuba, Richard and Martin Porr. 2022: Leo Frobenius' Contribution to Global Rock Art Research. In: Jamie Hampson, Sam Challis and Joakim Goldhahn (eds): *Powerful Pictures: Rock Art Research Histories around the World*. Oxford: Archaeopress. 76–88.

Kuba, Richard. 2024: Between Opportunity and Oppression. Leo Frobenius and His Institute During the Third Reich. In: Erik Tonning (ed.): *The Correspondence of Ezra Pound and the Frobenius Institute, 1930–1959*. London: Bloomsbury. 231–241.

Lommel, Andreas. 1969: *Fortschritt ins Nichts. Die Modernisierung der Primitiven Australiens. Beschreibung und Definition eines psychischen Verfalls*. Zürich: Atlantis.

Lommel, Andreas. 1952: *Die Unambal, ein Stamm in Nordwest-Australien*. Hamburg: Museum für Völkerkunde.

Love, J.R.B. 1938: *Schreiben an Helmut Petri* (unpublished archive source). Perth: State Records Western Australia, WA S2030-cons993 1937–39_0208.

Marchand, Suzanne. 1997: Leo Frobenius and the Revolt Against the West. In: *Journal of Contemporary History* 32 (2): 153–170.

Pentony, Partick. 1938: *The Dream in Australian Culture* (unpublished BA Thesis). Perth: University of Western Australia.

Petri, Helmut. 1970: Rezension von Andreas Lommel, „Fortschritt ins Nichts". In: *Tribus (N.F.)* 19. 234–236.

Petri, Helmut. 1954: *Sterbende Welt in Nord-west-Australien*. Braunschweig: Albert Limbach.

Petri, Helmut. 1952–53: Der australische Medizin-mann. In: *Annali Lateranensi* 16: 159–317 and 17: 157–225.

Petri, Helmut. 1938a: *4. Expeditionsbericht, Broome – Munja-Native Station, 1.5. – 17.5.1938* (unpub-lished archive source). Frankfurt am Main: Archive of the Frobenius Institute, HP 009.

Petri, Helmut. 1938b: *7. Expeditionsbericht, 14.7. – 21.8.1938* (unpublished archive source). Frankfurt am Main: Archive of the Frobenius Institute, HP 012.

Petri, Helmut. 1938c: *8. Expeditionsbericht, Munyastation-Drysdaleriver-Mission, 21.8. – 12.9.1938* (unpublished archive source). Frankfurt am Main: Archive of the Frobenius Institute, HP 013.

Petri, Helmut. 1938d: *Schreiben an Gerta Kleist vom 29.10.1938* (unpublished archive source). Frankfurt am Main: Archive of the Frobenius Institute, GK 0010–01.

Premier's Department Western Australia. 1937: *Schreiben an Helmut Petri vom 1.3.1937* (unpub-lished archive source). Frankfurt am Main: The Institute for the History of Frankfurt, magistrate file 8087. 115.

Schmidt-Leonhard. 1936: *Schreiben vom 12.6.1936 an Reichsminister für Wissenschaft, Erziehung und Volksbildung* (unpublished archive source). Berlin: Bundesarchiv R55-356-16A.

Schulz, Agnes. 1955: *Tagebuch, 2.2.1954 – 15.12.1955* (unpublished archive source). Frankfurt am Main: Archive of the Frobenius Institute, HvD 210.

Schulz, Agnes. 1939: *Australien-Expedition. Tage-buch 2, Mitte Juli 1938 – Mitte Januar 1939* (unpub-lished archive source). Frankfurt am Main: Archive of the Frobenius Institute, HvD 213.

Schulz, Agnes. 1938: *Schreiben an Helmut Petri und Douglas Fox vom 28.8.1938* (unpublished archive source). Frankfurt am Main: Archive of the Frobenius Institute, GK 010–08.

Stappert, Gisela. 2019: Die starken Frauen des Fro-benius-Instituts. In: Museum Giersch and Frobenius Institute (eds): *Frobenius – Die Kunst des For-schens*. Petersberg: Imhoff Verlag. 63–71.

Streck, Bernhard. 2014: *Leo Frobenius. Afrikafor-scher, Ethnologe, Abenteurer*. Frankfurt: Socie-täts-Verlag.

Streck, Bernhard. 2000: *Ethnologie und National-sozialismus*. Gehren: Escher.

Strehlow, Carl. 1907–1920: *Die Aranda- und Loritja-Stämme in Zentral-Australien*. Veröffentlichungen aus dem Städtischen Völker-Museum I, in 5 Bänden. Frankfurt am Main: Baer.

Western Australian. 1938: Kimberley Natives. Study of Their Art. In: *Western Australian*, 1 February 1938. 14.

An Eighty Year Relationship

The Country Owns Us

We Follow the Rules of *Wanjina* and *Wunggurr*

Prepared by Kim Doohan with
Rona Gungnunda Charles,
Matthew Martin, Lloyd Nulgit,
Pete O'Connor and Leah Umbagai

Located in the Kimberley region of Northwest Australia, the traditional homeland of the *Wanjina Wunggurr* people contains some of the most spectacular rock art sites in the world.[1] Although numbers are unknown, there are certainly thousands of them in the shallow caves and rock shelters that mark *Wanjina Wunggurr* Country.[2]

Wanjina Wunggurr society is a distinctive community with its members, Traditional Owners, sharing a system of beliefs and practices about their creator ancestors *Wanjina/Wandjina*, *Woongudd/Wunggurr*, and *Geeyorn/Gwion*[3]. These beliefs are foundational for belonging to *Wanjina Wunggurr* Country, being a member of the wider *Wanjina Wunggurr* community and distinguishing *Wanjina Wunggurr* society from others in Australia or the world.

The presence of *Wanjina* (as paintings) in rock shelters is a defining feature of the *Wanjina Wunggurr* community and their homeland. This attribute played a critical role in the *Wanjina Wunggurr* peoples' native title claims.[4] Any *Wanjina*-like images (as paintings) located outside this homeland were considered lost and to have accidently wandered into another Aboriginal group's Country, where they do not belong.

The senior Woddordda woman, Eewaambood, (Janet Oobagooma), explained:

> *"People who do not understand say somebody painted it but they didn't. Wanjina put themselves in the cave and they said, 'This is an important person and you have to go by the rules'"*
> (in Mangolamara et al. 2018: 9).

There are times when Traditional Owners describe themselves as belonging to named 'tribes': Woddordda, Ngarinyin, Wunambal, or Wunambal and Gaambera. These distinctions indicate localised connections to Country and associated linguistic expressions, particular narrative elements and the presence of certain *Wanjina* and/or *Wunggurr*. For instance, Wojin the big *Wanjina* of Wanalirri is primarily associated with Ngarinyin language, the shelter Wanalirri and the creation narrative of 'the big flood' (Mowaljarlai and Malnic 2001; Woolagoodja 2020: 67–69; Crawford 1968: 38–43).

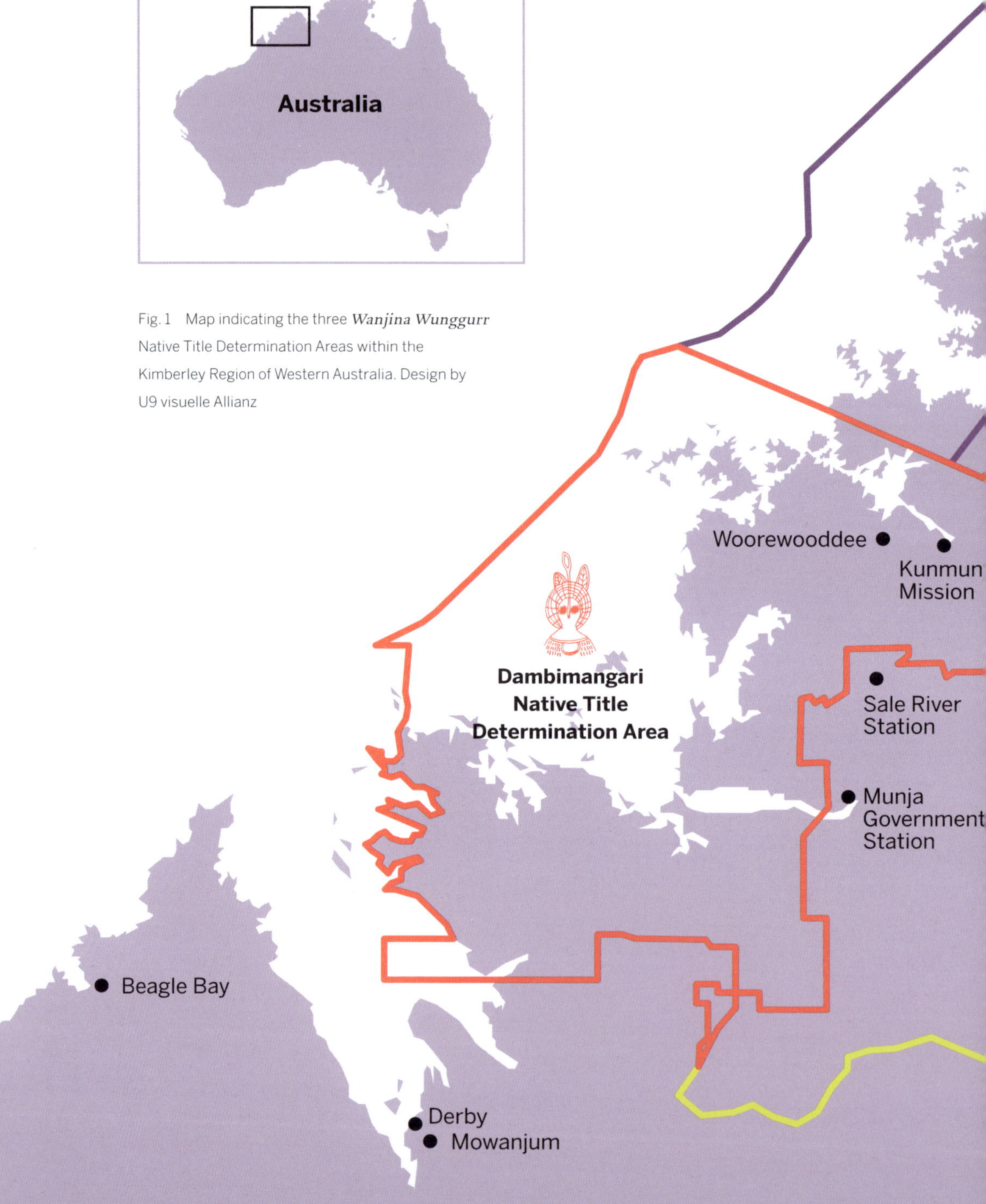

Fig. 1   Map indicating the three *Wanjina Wunggurr* Native Title Determination Areas within the Kimberley Region of Western Australia. Design by U9 visuelle Allianz

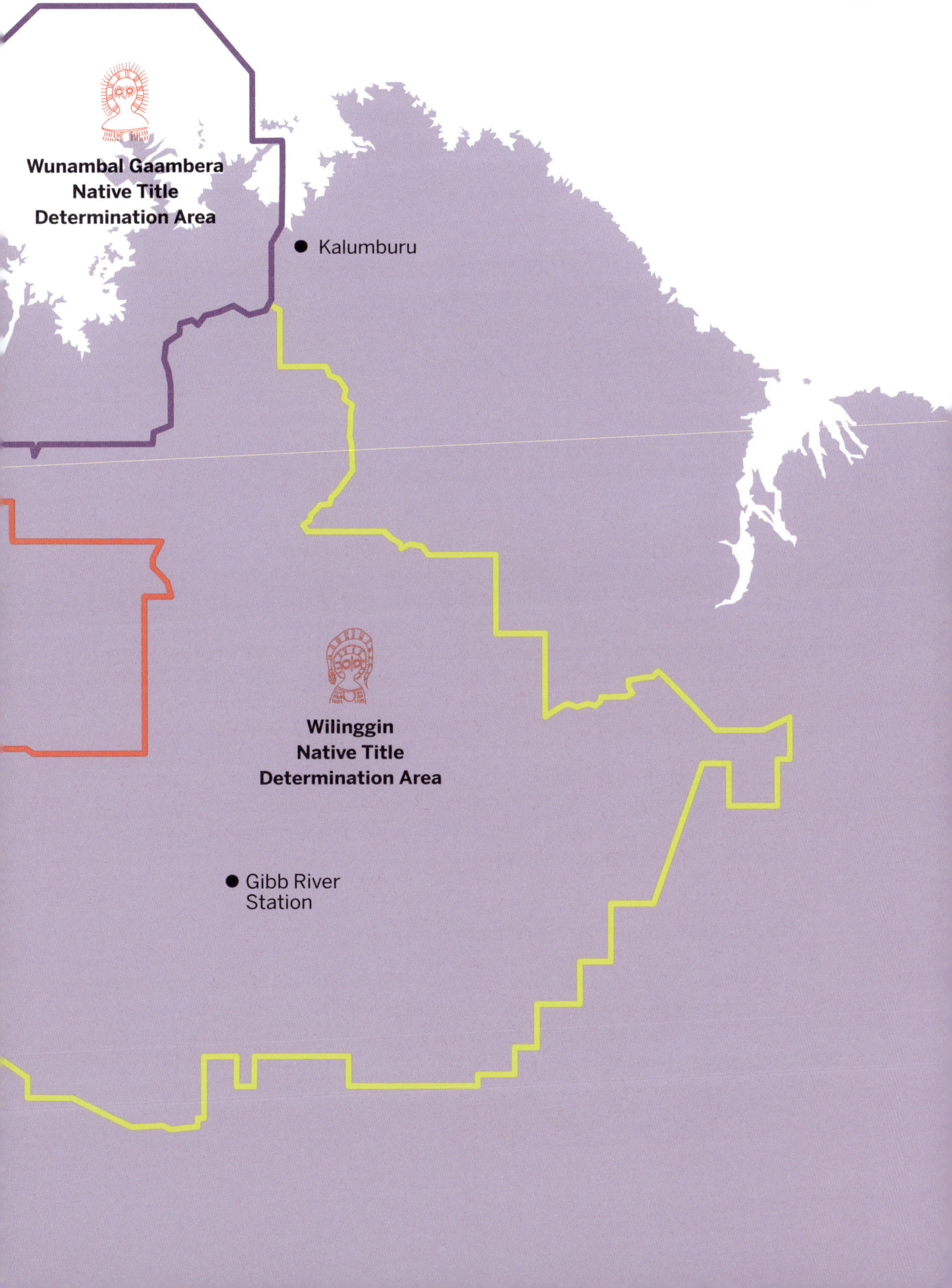

Wunambal Gaambera
Native Title
Determination Area
Kalumburu
Wilinggin
Native Title
Determination Area
Gibb River
Station

The *Wanjina Wunggurr* homeland extends in a wide arc along the Kimberley coast and inland to the range, riverine and savannah lands north of Derby to the very tip of Western Australia, just west of Kalumburu Community (formerly the Drysdale River Mission), where it meets the Balanggarra Determination Area. The southern and eastern extent takes in much of the west Kimberley pastoral lands, the Prince Regent Nature Reserve and adjoins several different native title groups along the eastern boundary (see fig. 1).

The members of the 1938 Frobenius Expedition travelled to places within *Wanjina Wunggurr* Traditional Owners' Country.[5] Andreas and Katharina Lommel undertook rock art research in and around Gibb River Station within the Wilinggin Determination Area in 1955.[6] They lived and worked with Traditional Owners, they recorded information provided to them, collected bush crafts, wrote observations of the society and landscape, painted portraits of Aboriginal people and scenes of daily life and copied rock art images onto paper. Some of these records and artefacts form part of the exhibition COUNTRY BIN PULL'EM and *Wanjina Wunggurr* Traditional Owners have granted permission for them to be displayed.

Requesting permission to enter a place where *Wandjina* are present, showing photographs or material items and demonstrating respect and reciprocity to Country and its sentient beings are integral components of Traditional Owners' lived lives. There can be adverse consequences for individuals, communities and environments if these cultural protocols are not performed appropriately. For example, paintings and sacred objects, words and pictures in books are considered sentient and capable of inflicting injurious effects on those who fail to act properly and/or even the wider community. As the senior Woddordda man, Yornadaiyn Woolagoodja explained:

> *"Wandjina and Woongudd together make the rain. If Wandjina and people work together they can make safe rain. If people do the wrong thing, then the Wandjina and the Woongudd will make a dangerous rain, a bad cyclone"* (in Mangolamara et al. 2018: 116).

Wanjina Wunggurr **Worldview:** *Lalai/Larlan*

> *"The words that we have written in this paper are trying to help you get an idea about our culture. I find it hard to get the right words but we have the words of our old people to help us. This is the best way we can think of explaining it to you"* (Leah Umbagai).

"Mamanggal birri manabadda – our family, our ancestors, were people of high knowledge. The old people's words inspire us to keep going. Their words are very powerful. Malbadda darlaj wulun di. These Ngarinyin words are saying: 'We will carry the words and the knowledge'. When we get older our words will be used by the next generations and the next generations forever" (Rona Charles).

The *Wanjina Wunggurr* worldview derives from what Wunambal, Gaambera and Woddordda people call *Lalai* and Ngarinyin call *Larlan*. This is the word used by Traditional Owners for what is widely – and inadequately – glossed as 'the Dreaming' (see i.e. Stanner 1968; Green 2012). *Wanjina Wunggurr* Traditional Owners also use the terms 'the Dreaming' and 'Aboriginal Law,' interchangeably when talking about aspects of *Lalai* or *Larlan* in trying to explain this immensely complex concept to non-Aboriginal listeners. Our Elders have said before us:

"Lalai is about the world and the stories are history, our science about the world and how Traditional Owners understand the nature of the world. What do aalmara [Europeans] think culture is because they have got a different idea from Aboriginal people? Culture to them is what they think; to us culture is the land and what is in it and every picture has a story" (Yornadaiyn in Mangolamara et al. 2018: 15).

Although much has been written about this multifaceted and regionally particular concept it continues to elude most observers. Nonetheless, Traditional Owners have attempted to explain and illustrate their beliefs in *Lalai/Larlan* in various ways, i.e. books, films and artworks (see i.e. Blundell and Woolagoodja 2005; Goring 2000; Mangolamara et al. 2018; Woolagoodja 2020). As senior Ngarinyin Traditional Owner Matthew Martin recently reiterated: "You can't pull *Larlan* apart; it is forever. The Country stays forever but we just look after it while we are alive."

Undeniably, *Lalai/Larlan* is a rich body of narratives, painted images and arranged stones. It exists as a continuum of past-present and future that creates, informs and sustains the social, spiritual, tangible and intangible worlds of the Traditional Owners. Rules for social behaviour and caring for Country are an essential component of it.

Larlan concerns the core of how and when land, sea, heavens and all that is within them came into existence by the momentous actions of Creator Beings; they continue to exist, reaffirming and re-enacting those events of creation. In this way *Lalai* is non-linear in relation to time and thus ever-present.

For Traditional Owners, this space-time continuum is not about conventional archaeological dating or sequences of events:

> *"It is not about dates; it started from Lalai. When there was no beginning of time, it was when the world started. Our evidence is all these images. We didn't have a pencil and paper to write it down. One old sacred man would be given a dream about what happened and they could tell future generations about how to live. They make the song and the dance to show the creation"* (Yornadaiyn in Mangolamara et al. 2018: 7).

Thus, that which is *Lalai* provides an intricate, potentially dangerous, and yet bountiful gossamer-like web of life and a blue print for living which continues to inform Traditional Owners' lives today.

One of the foremost *Wanjina Wunggurr* (re)creation narratives tells of the consequences of inappropriate behaviour on the part of human beings who mocked Dumbi, the owl – a child of *Wanjina*. In retribution for this bad behaviour *Wanjina* sent a cataclysmic flood to punish the people. A consequence of this action led to a dispute among the gathered *Wanjina* and the subsequent battle at Wanalirri (Woolagoodja 2020: 70). It was from these events that *Wanjina* spread throughout the *Wanjina Wunggurr* homeland to name the Country and the associated languages, to find their final resting places and to leave themselves as images to be remembered and respected and refreshed.[7] As they moved through Country, they distributed child spirits in waterholes and other locations to be born to humans. They were the ancestors of *Wanjina Wunggurr* Traditional Owners.

Wanjina, Wunggurr **and** *Geeyorn*

A full description of the pantheon of *Lalai* beings is beyond this paper. However, an explanation of *Wanjina, Wunggurr, Geeyorn* and other more prominent beings can be provided. It is important to recognise that *Lalai* beings were once both human and non-human. They are gendered and there are gendered roles. *Lalai* beings, like humans today, married, had children, had arguments, hunted, and gathered foods, died and were buried, finding their final resting places in their homes as images of their former selves. They are what is referred to as rock art by the wider public and researchers. However, Sam Woolagoodja explained that the *Wanjina* put themselves as paintings in the rock shelters (Blundell and Woolagoodja 2005: 29).

Of primary importance are *Wunggurr* and *Wanjina,* and these beings are associated with broad land, seascapes and skyscapes, as well as specific places, language areas, local regions and people. Distinctions between *Wanjina* and *Wunggurr* can be blurred or interchangeable due to their immense power in creating and sustaining the world, their tangible and intangible multiple transformational forms. There are times when they act in unison as a single force or being. For instance, as the senior Wunambal man Wilfred Goonack explained:

> ***"Wanjina make rain and sometimes Snake joins up together with Wanjina. When Gulingii, he is the most powerful Wunambal rainmaker Wanjina, they make it raining like a cyclone. That is when the Snake has joined up with Gulingii and they can sing people [cause trouble for individuals or groups of people]. Between Wunggurr and Gulingii, when they join up to make Gularndjii [cyclone], when they get wild together, then they destroy the whole thing, country, and people and all"*** (in Mangolamara et al. 2018:119).

Wunggurr also called *Woongudd* is often glossed as 'Snake'. It is the omnipresent sacred life force at the core of the material and intangible world. Humans are born of this life force. One can see *Woongudd* in many things, such as paintings and as arranged stones; but also in clouds, in waterholes, as tides and whirlpools and as the eye of cyclones.

John Rastus gave the following example: "One person moved a Wunggurr egg (in the form of a stone) from the river a couple of years ago and there was a big flood in the Kimberley. You can't do that."

Woongudd carved river beds, *Wunggurr* stands as mountains; Islands and reefs are its exposed 'backbone' or 'head' in the ocean. And in the form of arranged stones *Wunggurr* is holding back the sea from 'floods', 'tidal waves', and rising sea levels (see Mangolamara et al. 2018: 91–113).

Wanjina are mostly mouthless anthropomorphic figures that reside in their homes, their shelters, along with other *Lalai* beings. "*Wanjina* has no mouth because the sound of beginning cannot be heard by human ears" (Woolagoodja 2020: 52). "But you can hear them humming in the power of the storm; that's him talking in the thunder rolling" (Matthew Martin). *Wandjina* can also 'show themselves' in animal form like the Barramundi when she swam up the river Munja.[8] There are *Wandjina* from the land and others, saltwater *Wandjina*, who "came from the saltwater to the coast."

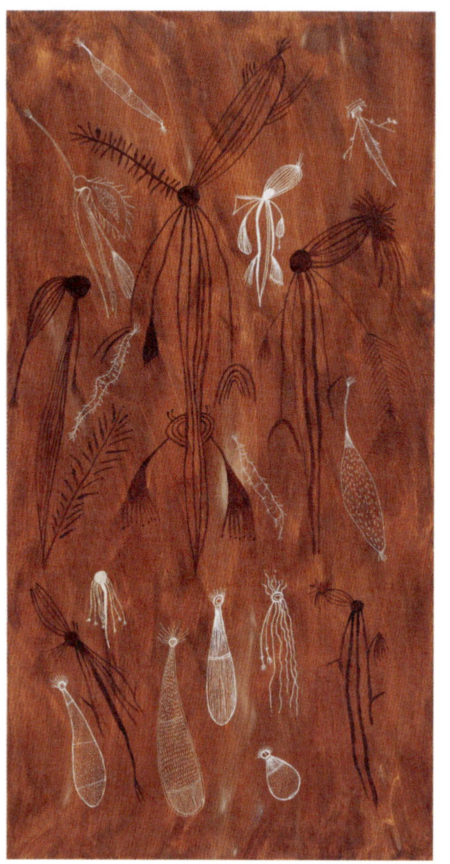

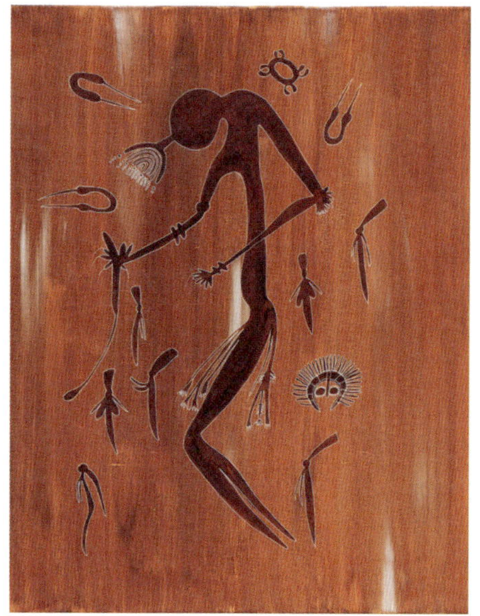

Fig. 2   Leah Umbagai, 2023: *Geeyorn Geeyorn, Maagorddeegorddee.* Acrylic paint on canvas. 60 x 120 cm. Collection: Weltkulturen Museum. Photo: Wolfgang Günzel, 2024

Fig. 3   Leah Umbagai, 2023: *Malan. Jiunya Bushwoman, Mooloomooloony*. Acrylic paint on canvas. 60 x 80 cm. Collection: Weltkulturen Museum. Photo: Wolfgang Günzel, 2024

Fig. 4   Rock art copy of the *Geeyorn*-figure at the Malan shelter by Agnes Schulz from 1938. Colour pencil on paper. 36 x 50 cm. Collection: Frobenius Institute. Photo: not stated

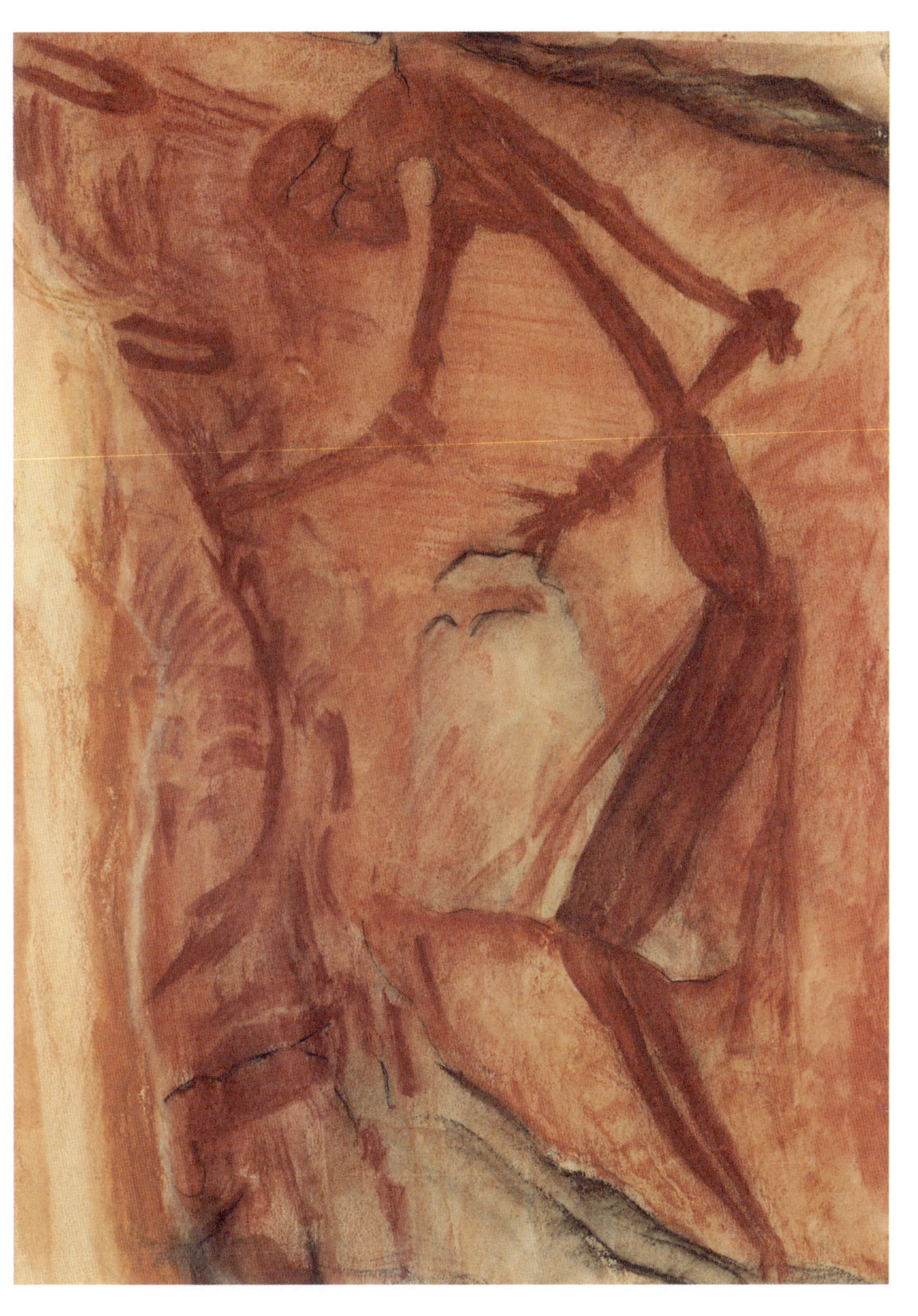

> *"Some Wanjina were always at the saltwater side; they came from the salt water and they did not go to Wanalirri. They made all the saltwater plants and animals like Jagulamarra, who created the pearl shell and left it for people to use, and Ngamalii, who pissed in the water to make it salty so that the food would taste good"* (Louis Karadada in Mangolamara et al. 2018: 80).

Geeyorn or *Gwion* are part of this relationship; they coexist and collaborate with *Wandjina*. *Gwion* are said to have been instructed by *Wandjina* to paint them on the walls of rock shelters, to paint different plants and animals in the same galleries and to care for all the different food sources found within the Traditional Owners' Country (Mangolamara et al. 2018; Doring 2000).

These beings have different forms and fulfil various roles, primarily associated with sustaining plants and animals, admonishing those who do not 'follow the rules' and presenting *Joonba* (traditional performance) to humans whilst sleeping. Furthermore, *Gwion* taught people how to make tools and how to hunt (see Mowaljarlai and Malnic 2001: 200–210).

> *"Gwion look after country and punish people if they don't. They are like a lieutenant for the Wanjina keeping things in order. Gwion got duties to do, they have to protect certain trees, plants, and Country"* (Sylvester Mangolamara in Mangolamara et al. 2018: 167).

The senior Wunambal woman, Minindil (Lily Karadada), once said "that Wanjina bin tell Gwion to put all the different tucker and look after it" (in Mangolamara et al. 2018: 151). She also noted that, as contemporary artists, "we follow the Gwion. He is a painter and we paint the Wanjina too" (in Mangolamara et al. 2018: 152). Wilfred Goonack reported: "One Wanjina married a Gwion. The Wanjina was boss for the rainforest and the Gwion is the caretaker of bush yams" (in Mangolamara et al. 2018: 184).

Another kind of *Lalai* beings are the *Agoola* or *Agula* (the 'devil devil').[9] They come in different forms and appear as images in rock shelters. They live in different environments and create various degrees of chaos and control. The *Agula* can be capricious and sometimes even dangerous. Present in the world of humans, albeit mostly unseen, they are nonetheless able to execute 'punishment' for inappropriate behaviour, and are capable of impacting on an individual's mental health (Mangolamara et al. 2018; Doring 2000; Woolagoodja 2020), or as Pete O'Connor noted: "they make you silly."

'Rock Art' in Country

The many shelters with rock paintings found throughout *Wanjina Wunggurr* homeland have long caught the imagination of the outside world. However, for Traditional Owners, there is no speculation about these images, rather they are ancestors to be visited, to be respected, to be revered and protected from physical and metaphysical damage and misrepresentation.

> *"Sometimes I hear other people talking about our country and the meaning of our images. That is not right. I want people to know that these places are our homes and what meaning they have for me. I also want to explain how it is impolite for people to go and trespass our caves with our Lalai paintings; how it is impolite to visit our country, the islands and beaches without seeking our permission. Only the Traditional Owners can really know about these places because we lived here and our old people told us and showed us our country and Lalai"* (Eewaambood in Mangolamara et al. 2018: 16).

For *Wanjina Wunggurr* Traditional Owners Country is far more than a demarcated geographic location with topography, flora and fauna. *Lalai* images, and the associated narratives, are part of Country. For them, Country is an aesthetically evocative tapestry that constitutes visible evidence of the on-going events of *Lalai*. Country is the place, or the places, that one has the obligation and right to 'speak for', to 'belong to', to 'look after', to 'care for' and to pass on to their children and grandchildren. One inherits these rights and obligations from one's parents and grandparents, who also had these rights and obligations. "We look after Country. We don't really own it but Country owns us. As Traditional Owners we have to follow the rules of what *Wanjina* and *Wunggurr* say" (Lloyd Nulgit).

Country is not considered an aspect of nature, nor is it seen as untapped wilderness. It is a culturally meaningful place articulated through the relationships that exist between people, landscapes, skyscapes and seascapes, and the all-pervasive *Lalai* beings. Adherence to *Wanjina Wunggurr* laws and customs, presence on Country and enjoying its resources, reinforce these relationships and the sustainability of Country.

Senior Traditional Owners have reported that rock shelters with images are important places; not anyone can enter them or engage with the resident *Lalai* beings. One must 'talk to the *Wandjina*', 'announce yourself' and seek permission to enter. Most importantly, these rock shelters are the homes of *Wanjina* and/or *Wunggurr* in their many manifestations; they are not caves with paintings on a wall. There are various explanations of how *Lalai* beings came to be present on these walls. For instance, Louis Karadada explained that: "When the world was soft and flat they put themselves in their country for us to see" (in Mangolamara et al. 2018: 10).

Wilfred Goonack described how "the Wanjina carried clouds as they travelled all over the country from the big battle at Wanalirri in Ngarinyin country. When they found their home, their Uunguu, they put themselves on the walls and stayed in that place" (in Mangolamara et al. 2018: 59). Louis Karadada provided further details: "The cloud went hard when they made their camp. They put themselves in their country for people to see and to know who belongs there and who was travelling to their homes. In important caves you can find more than one Wanjina. That is a sign that the Wanjina met there for a special reason, some stayed in their country and the others kept travelling to their final resting places in their own country" (Mangolamara et al. 2018: 41).

The presence of *Wanjina* images in rock shelters also adds a degree of protection to the Country. They are not passive 'paintings', but rather "where the Wandjina put themselves is bang-ganan. It means the rocks with paintings on are bang-ganan, a strong foundation and you can't take them out. They belong there. They look out over the Country; they are protecting it. They are watching to see which people are coming. They look out from their cave and listen to who is coming" (Eewaambood, in Mangolamara et al. 2018: 46).

Some of the images have been overpainted many, many times or as Traditional Owners say "refreshed". The refreshing of *Wandjina* can only be done by Traditional Owners; it can be "likened to the concept of mindfulness" (Mangolamara et al. 2018: 48). The process is of mutual obligation and physical engagement between humans and *Wandjina,* thus (re)invigorating the reciprocal relationship between humans and *Wandjina.* Scratching the body of the *Wanjina* "wakes him up", thus stimulating the process of ensuring seasonal rain and the replenishment of species (Mangolamara et al. 2018: 124–126).

> *"The older people refreshed Wandjina all the time because they were in the Country all the time. They were refreshing the images to keep the Wandjina spirit strong and alive. They were respecting their Wandjina. They did it to bring them back to life again after months of rain or just before the rains. By touching up the Wandjina, refreshing him, then he knows people still care for him. It is showing respect to the Wandjina"* (Woolagoodja 2020: 169).

"When I go to the Wandjina in the cave, what I am trying to do is not like doing it on a canvas. The Wandjina, he draws you towards him, pulls you into him and that image acknowledges what you are going to do to him. He gives you encouragement to do that thing. The feeling is like when my leeyaan (a feeling, like gut reaction) feels good because my leeyaan knows that when he looks at you, that image, he looks at you and he tells you, 'You are the right person to paint me.' There are no words, it is a feeling that I have. His leeyaan makes him know that he has the right person to paint him. The Wandjina is happy" (Woolagoodja 2020: 192).

Fig. 5   The cloud hardened to create the Malan

shelter. Photo: Joh Bornman, 2014

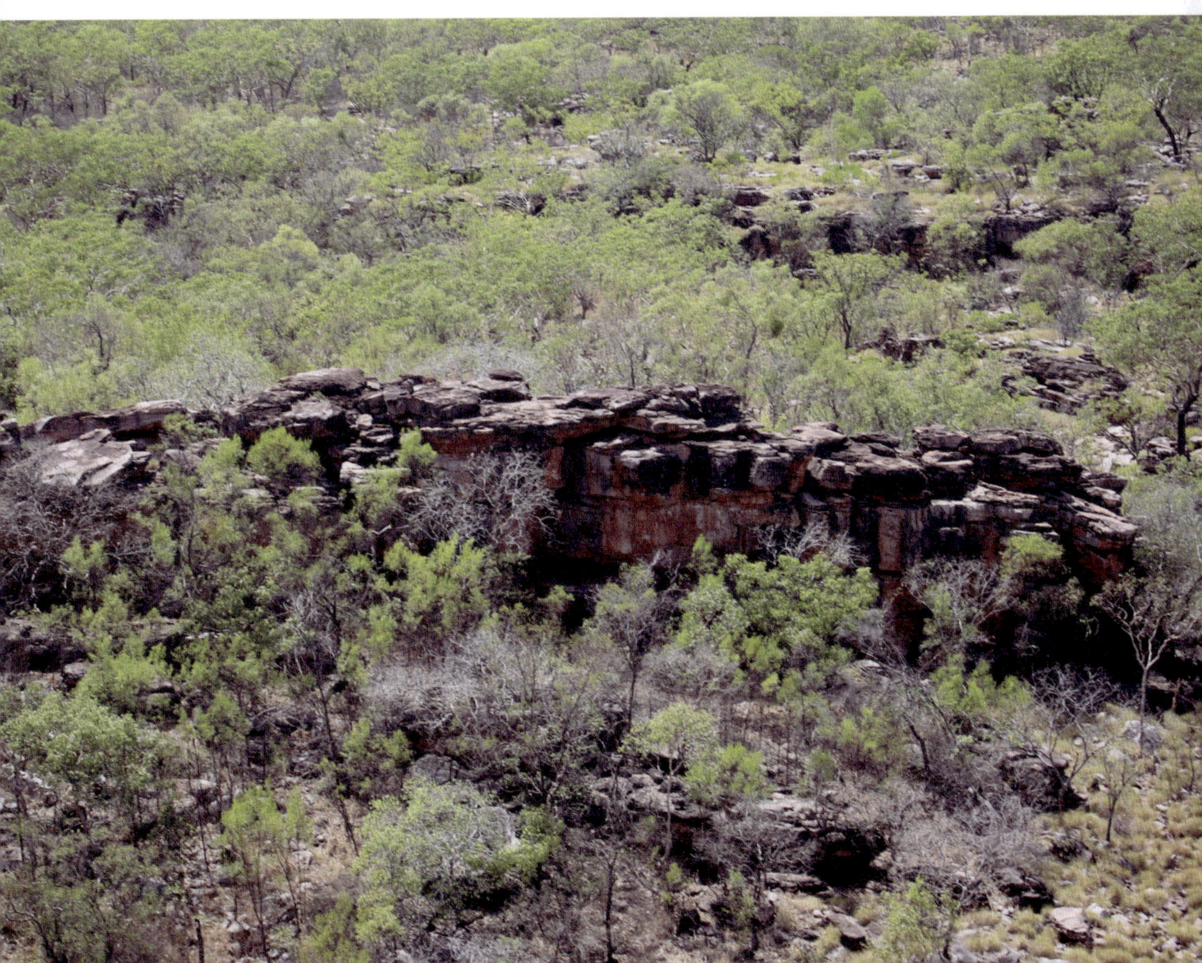

Contemporary *Wanjina Wunggurr* people regularly interact with *Lalai* beings. As their ancestors have done for countless generations, they 'visit' these paintings so that the *Wanjina* won't get 'lonely' and they restore the paintings in order to keep them 'fresh.' In return they ensure the arrival of the annual rains, replenishing food resources and sustaining land and seascapes as well as instructing their human descendants in their dreams.

Within the rock shelters there are also human skeletal remains which have been covered in red ochre and wrapped in paper bark before being lodged in the shelves and crevices of these shelters; the spirit is returned to their home. Human hand-prints stencilled onto rock faces are common, and footprints are less common. There are other forms that are said to be certain kinds of tools, domestic and ritual objects, celestial bodies and images of child spirits waiting to be born.

The rock shelters are also domestic spaces with debris in the form of stone tools, animal bones and shell deposits, remnants of ochre and other indications of occu-pation. The recently deceased senior Woddordda woman, Eewaambood, provided extensive details of her experience of living in such a shelter on one of the remote islands in the northern portion of the Dambimangari Determination Area (Ooba-gooma et al. 2016).

Leah Umbagai also explains how important the images in the shelters are to her, as a young Traditional Owner:

> *"Rock art shelters and caves are like our library; they show us younger people what has happened, what is in the country. It gives us hope for our future generations. These are the images that were put by our old people and our country. We always leave something, food, behind whenever we go camping out or hunting. It's a sign of appreciation and respect. We are taught that"* (Leah Umbagai in Mangolamara et al. 2018: 21).

Wanjina Wunggurr Traditional Owners have contributed their own creative re-sponses to the records and materials of the Frobenius Expedition collections; these art works demonstrate and re-affirm their on-going connections and rela-tionships with *Lalai* and their Country in the context of the COUNTRY BIN PULL'EM exhibition, including the message stick to Frankfurt demonstrating "we are here, our stories are still alive".

Endnotes:

1 The *Wanjina Wunggurr* homeland and associated cultural manifestations and practices have been included in the West Kimberley National Heritage Listing, 2011. For instance, *Wanjina Wunggurr* traditions including the images of *Wanjina* and *Gwion* in shelters "provides testimony of a complex association of socio-religious beliefs that continues to be central to the laws and customs of the *Wanjina Wunggurr* people" (Commonwealth of Australia Gazette No. S1232, 31 August 2011: 19).

2 The *Wanjina Wunggurr* community, Country, society, homeland and culture arose as a form of identity because Aboriginal people were trying to illustrate and reveal their shared worldview, their shared laws and customs, and their distinctiveness in contrast to other Aboriginal peoples of the Kimberley and Australia. *Wanjina Wunggurr* people are a single society in all aspects of their laws and customs, regardless of other identities articulated in terms of language, 'tribe' or 'clan'.

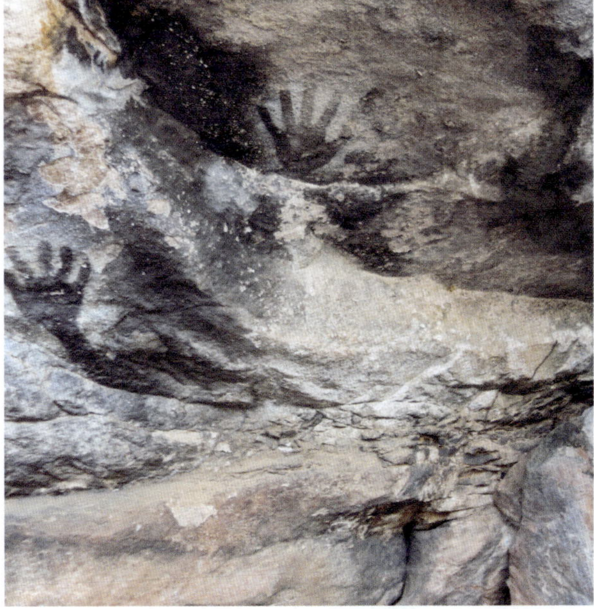

Fig. 6 Hand stencils in the rock shelter at Malan. Photo: Kim Doohan, 2014

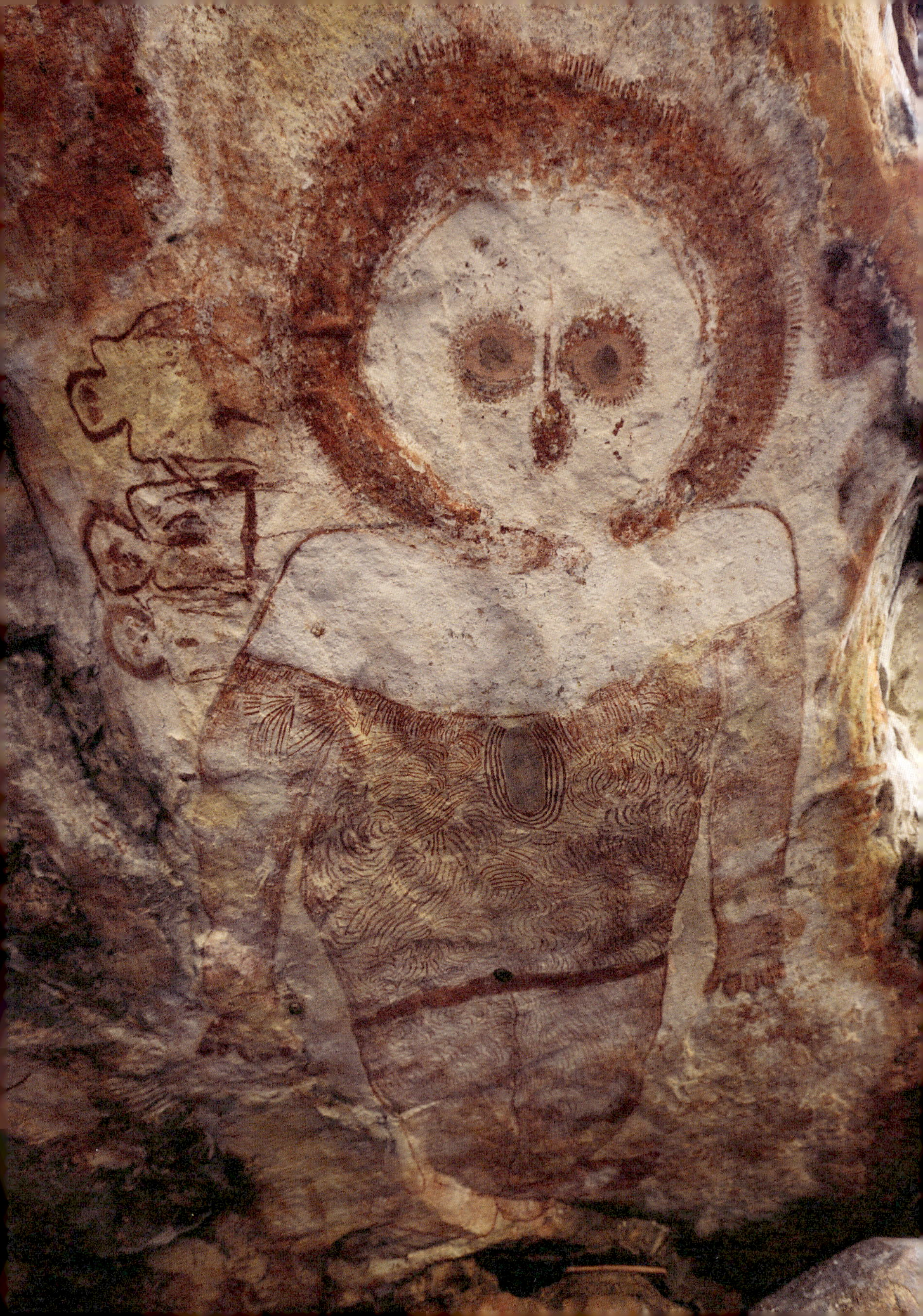

Fig. 7   Three child spirit *Wanjinas* resting on the shoulder of the big *Wanjina* at Malan waiting to be born. Photo: Joh Bornman, 2024

3   Within the **Wanjina Wunggurr** community there are several languages, dialects and accents which give rise to different spellings of words. There are two orthographies used when spelling Indigenous words. For this text, the spelling of words will alternate and be applied to the relevant language context. For example *Lalai* is used for Woddordda, Wunambal and Gaambera speakers and *Larlan* for Ngarinyin speakers. **Gwion** is used for Wunambal, Gaambera and Ngarinyin speakers, **Geeyorn** for Woddordda speakers.

4   Due to several administrative reasons, there were three applications brought on behalf of the **Wanjina Wunggurr** community. The Wilinggin claim was litigated in court, with a decision handed down in August 2004 (Neowarra v. State of Western Australia (2004) FCA 1092) recognising the native title rights in this part of the **Wanjina Wunggurr** homeland. The Wanjina Wunggurr Uunguu claim achieved a positive determination on 23 May 2011 and the Wanjina Wunggurr Dambimangari claim was recognised three days later, 26 May 2011.

5   See Richard Kuba, **An Eighty Year Relationship** in this volume.

6   See Michaela Appel, **Andreas and Katharina Lommel** in this volume.

7   See fig. 5 in Michaela Appel, **Andreas and Katharina Lommel** in this volume.

8   See Kim Doohan et al., **A Message (Stick) to Frankfurt** in this volume.

9   See fig. 5 in Eva Ch. Raabe, **Turning Points** in this volume.

References:

Blundell, Valda; Donny Woolagoodja and Members of the Mowanjum Aboriginal Community. 2005: *Keeping the Wanjinas Fresh. Sam Woolagoodja and the Enduring Power of Lalai.* Fremantle: Fremantle Press.

Blundell, Valda et al. (eds). 2017: *Barddabardda Wodjenangorddee. We're Telling All of You. The Creation, History and People of Dambimangaddee Country. Based on the Cultural Knowledge and Recollections of Janet Oobagooma, Donny Woolagoodja and Other Senior Dambeemangaddee People.* Fremantle: Fremantle Press and Dambimangari Aboriginal Corporation.

Commonwealth of Australia (ed.): 2011: *Commonwealth of Australia Gazette* No. S1232, 31 August: 19.

Crawford, Ian M. 1968: *The Art of the Wandjina: Aboriginal Cave Paintings in Kimberley, Western Australia.* Melbourne: Oxford University Press.

Doring, Jeff (ed.). 2000: *Gwion, Gwion: Ngarjno, Ungudman, Banggal, Nyawarra ; [Secret and Sacred Pathways of the Ngarinyin Aboriginal People of Australia] = Geheime und Heilige Pfade Der Ngarinyin, Aborigines in Australien.* Cologne: Könemann.

Green, Jennifer. 2012: The Altyerre Story – Suffering Badly by Translation. In: *TAJA* 23 (2): 158–178.

Mangolamara, Sylvester et al. 2018: *We Are Coming To See You: Nyara Pari Kala Niragu* (Gaambera), *Gadawara Ngyaran-Gada* (Wunambal), *Inganinja Gubadjoongana* (Woddordda). Derby: Western Australia: Dambimangari Aboriginal Corporation and Wunambal Gaambera Aboriginal Corporation.

Mowaljarlai, David and Jutta Malnic. 2001: *Yorro Yorro – Everything Standing Up Alive. Spirit of the Kimberley.* Broome: Magabala Books Aboriginal Corporation.

Oobagooma, Janet et al. 2016: Yooddooddoom: A Narrative Exploration of the Camp and the Sacred Place, Daily Life, Images, Arranged Stones and Lalai Beings. In: *Hunter Gatherer Research* 2 (3): 345–374.

Stanner, W.E.H. 1968: *After the Dreaming.* Sydney, Australian Broadcasting Commission.

Woolagoodja, Yorna. 2020: *Yornadaiyn Woolagoodja.* Derby: Western Australia: Magabala Books.

The Country Owns Us

The Archaeological Perspective

Rock Art in the Kimberley, Northwest Australia

Martin Porr

There is no doubt that the Kimberley region in Northwest Australia contains one of the most complex and diverse records of rock art anywhere in the world (David 2017). It is important to recognise and acknowledge the fact that the region is home to living Indigenous cultural traditions which integrate aspects of the rock art into their ongoing cultural practices and philosophies. The most well known of these relate to the Northwest and Central Kimberley and form the so-called *Wanjina Wunggurr* cultural bloc (fig. 1). The exhibition COUNTRY BIN PULL'EM at the Weltkulturen Museum and the related research project[1] feature and engage art and bushcraft from this tradition. But it also needs to be noted that rock art is part of the culture of many more Aboriginal groups in other parts of the Kimberley as well as throughout Australia (Donaldson and Kenneally 2007).

European engagements in the 19th and early 20th centuries

George Grey is credited with having produced the first published account of Aboriginal rock art in the Kimberley. He encountered the images in March 1838 during an overland expedition to map the region and assess the potential for settlement and pastoral use. His interactions with local Aboriginal people were hostile. He killed one Aboriginal man and was speared himself. In his report published in 1841,

Fig. 1 Craig Rustus is sitting in front of the complex rock images at Koralyi (Wilinggin Country). Most of the images are from the contemporary *Wanjina* stylistic period and show *Wanjina* and *Wunggurr* spiritual beings as well as different animal species. Photo: Richard Kuba, 2023

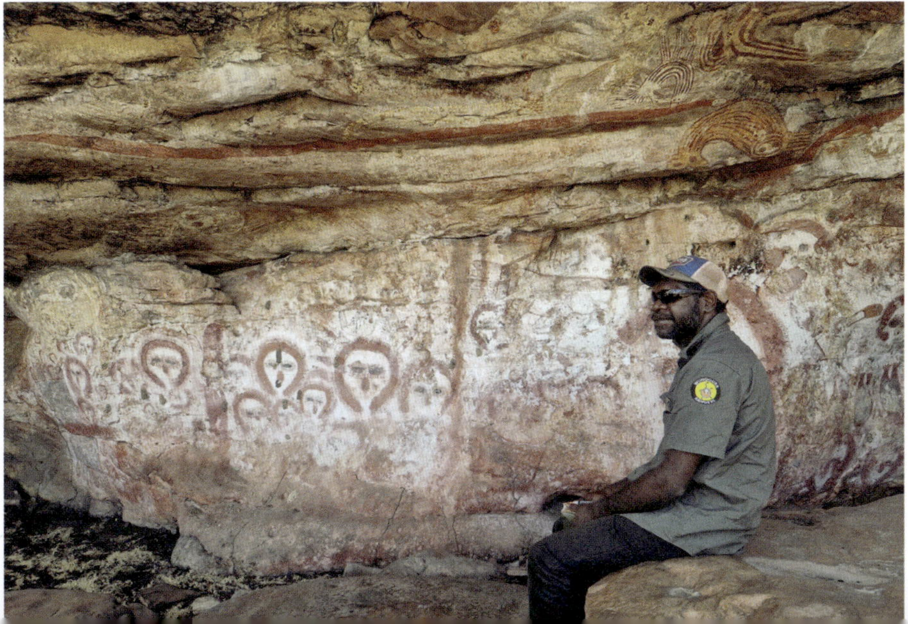

The Archaeological Perspective

he said it was unlikely that the local Aboriginal population was responsible for the art (Grey 1841: 263). Joseph Bradshaw (1892) provided another account, which related to different images within the Kimberley rock art record. In this case, Bradshaw suggested that these shared some similarities with depictions on Egyptian temples. Bradshaw also suggested that these depictions could not have been made by Indigenous Australians because he thought that the paintings were too refined and elaborate. Grey's and Bradshaw's engagement with Aboriginal people in the Kimberley and their subsequent writings reflect the colonial, intellectual, political and economic circumstances of their time.

During the nineteenth century, Aboriginal people in the Kimberley experienced an exceptional degree of violence. Aboriginal people were killed in a multitude of different situations as they resisted the incursions into their Country or were blamed for the loss of livestock (Owen 2016). Frontier violence and massacres continued into the period between the formation of the modern state of Australia in 1901[2] and the end of World War II (Jebb 2002). In terms of research into Aboriginal culture, the first systematic records were produced during this period as well. This included work by several missionaries, most prominently J.R.B. Love, who directed the Presbyterian Mission at Kunmunya in Woddordda Country (first established in 1912) between 1927 and 1940 (Choo 2012). He published the first accounts of the cosmological meanings of *Wanjina* paintings and the complex cultural practices. He thus confirmed Aboriginal authorship of local rock art in the literature (see Goldhahn et al. 2022).

The first half of the twentieth century was a period when anthropology and archaeology developed as systematic academic disciplines. In Australia, early anthropological work was strongly guided by an ethos of salvage anthropology and a functionalist orientation (Gray 2007). The Kimberley was the first research location (1927/28) of the only university-based anthropologist in Australia, A.P. Elkin, who became a professor at the University of Sydney in 1933. Elkin published several research papers on *Wanjina Wunggurr* rock art and their Indigenous mythological meanings. Goldhahn et al. correctly stress the importance of this work, which included direct interactions with Traditional Owners and informants as well as visits to significant places on Country (2022: 182–84). Even though he questioned the Aboriginal authorship of some of the images, Elkin also confirmed the integration of the art within the complex local Indigenous belief systems and worldviews (Elkin 1930).

A new phase of research in the 20th century: intensifications and confrontations

In 1938, *Wanjina Wunggurr* rock art became the subject of the Helmut Petri-led targeted expedition from the Forschungsinstitut für Kulturmorphologie (the Research Institute for Cultural Morphology, which later became the Frobenius Institute) that is at the heart of this exhibition catalogue. Archaeology in the narrow sense of the term developed in Australia only after World War II. In the case of the Kimberley, a period of integrated research emerged during the 1960s and 1970s that combined anthropological, archaeological and rock art research approaches. In contrast to earlier studies, several long-term partnerships between researchers and Aboriginal collaborators were forged. This shift changed the character of the research as well as the resulting publications. The research during this time acquired a much more personal dimension and the long-term collaborations resulted in several significant monographs (e.g. Crawford 1968, 2001). This phase of research focused primarily on contemporary meanings and issues, a type of anthropological work in which the pivotal role played by rock art and relations with Country has continued to the present day (Utemara and Vinnicombe 1992; Blundell et al. 2017; Mangolamara et al. 2019; Woolagoodja 2020).

From the 1980s onwards, discussions about Aboriginal heritage in the Kimberley were mostly dominated by the work and claims of Grahame Walsh. Walsh was an independent rock art enthusiast who became particularly interested in the Indigenous rock art of the Kimberley. Between the 1980s and his death in 2007, he created an extensive photographic and documentary archive and developed a complex chronological sequence of the art (Goldhahn et al. 2022: 189). He cultivated an independent and anti-establishment image of himself, and this made him an equally controversial and fascinating figure who received a lot of public attention (Leech 1998). While he fostered personal relationships with some Traditional Owners in the Kimberley, his work increasingly antagonised Aboriginal people and their supporters during a time in which Indigenous people were demanding more and more self-determination. Walsh's most controversial position was the idea that *Gwion* images in the sequence of Kimberley rock art were not related to today's Aboriginal groups. He argued that it was rather a product of a foreign population that possibly arrived sometime during the Pleistocene when sea levels were low and later disappeared before the ancestors of today's Aboriginal people arrived in the region (Walsh 1994, 2000; Porr and Bell 2012) (fig. 2).

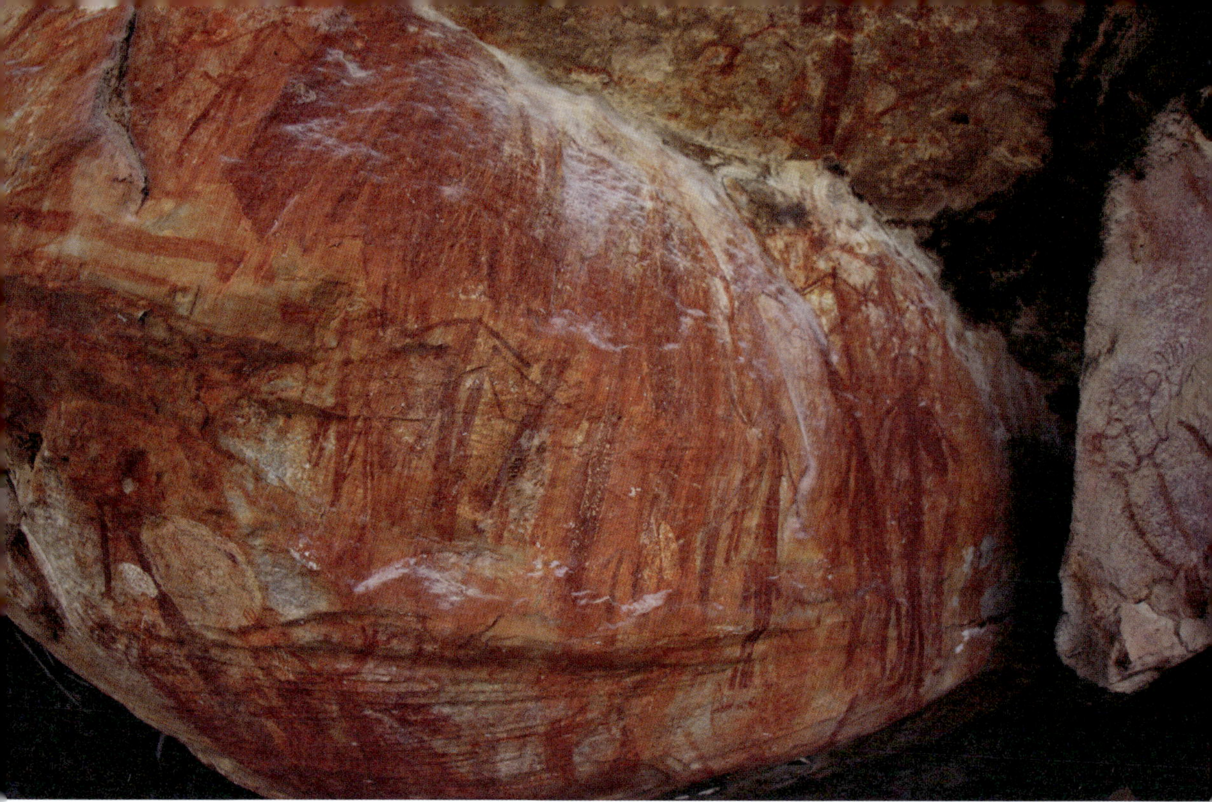

Archaeological research in the Kimberley today: collaboratively understanding the deep past

The late 1990s and early 2000s were consequently an important juncture during which archaeological and rock art research in the Kimberley took place in a highly polarised and adversarial climate. Some of these tensions that involved the restriction of access to sacred sites were resolved by the Wilinggin Native Title decision regarding the Ngarinyin claim in 2004 and the Dambimangari and Wunambal Gaambera Native Title determinations in 2011, which necessitated a realignment of permission and consent processes for research projects. Grahame Walsh died in 2007, an event that also reconfigured the landscape for archaeological and rock art research in the Kimberley. In the early 2010s, Michael Morwood and June Ross started an Australian Research Council-funded research project at Mitchell Plateau (within today's Wunambal Gaambera Native Title determination area) to conduct excavations and rock art documentation and analysis (see e.g. Travers and Ross 2016). This project established a pattern of archaeological research in the Kimberley that has continued to the present day.

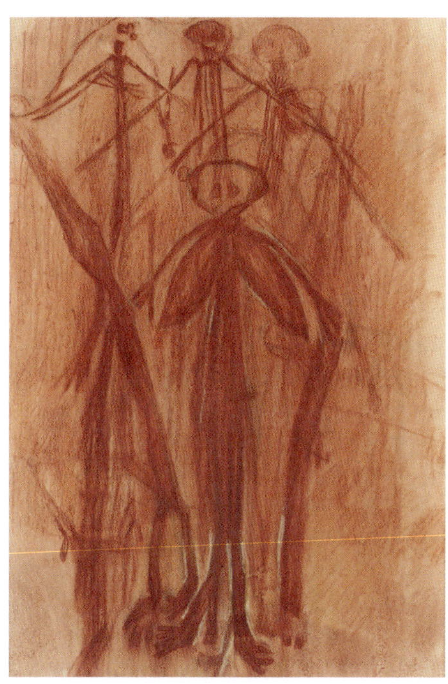

Fig. 2   One of the complex rock art panels at Malan (Dambimangari Country) shows various rock art styles from the Kimberley sequence, including *Gwion* and Static Polychrome motifs. The image also shows the challenges that archaeologists face in disentangling the repeated use of rock surfaces over time and of one artistic style being superimposed over another. Photo: Joh Bornman, 2014

Fig. 3   *Gwion* figures at the Malan rock art site. Kimberley, Northwest Australia. Rock art copy by Agnes Schulz, October 1938. Coloured pencil drawing on paper. 36 x 50 cm. Collection: Frobenius Institute. Photo: not stated

This initial project was followed by a series of other multi-year and multi-disciplinary projects that have vastly expanded our knowledge about the deep human past of the Kimberley, the development of environmental conditions from the earliest human settlement to the present day and the dating and complexity of the rock art sequence (Harper, Veth and Ouzman 2019; Veth et al. 2018). These projects were and continue to be university-based and -directed. In each case, they have been set up with the permission of the relevant Aboriginal Native Title representative body. Recent research has unequivocally demonstrated that many earlier interpretations were unfounded. Multiple strands of evidence demonstrate that the Kimberley has been continuously inhabited and several analyses have established that the development of rock art in the region was spatially and temporally much more complex than originally argued (Goldhahn et al. 2022: 189).

The Archaeological Perspective

While some important work has been conducted in different parts of the Kimberley, archaeological and rock art research work is still in a pioneering phase, especially given the Kimberley's enormous geographical size, which is broadly equivalent to that of Germany. From the latest research, a picture emerges of the Kimberley as a continuously occupied landscape with a human history that extends back at least 50,000 years. These insights are supported by detailed analyses of archaeological excavation records and genetic studies. It is likely that the region acted as a large-scale refugium throughout its human occupation and through numerous and dramatic climatic and ecological changes (Wood et al. 2016; Veth et al. 2019; Malaspinas et al. 2016). As the region is geographically vast, it contains a diversity of ecological contexts, including riverine and coastal settings, desert conditions, woodland and (sub)tropical vegetation. Archaeological studies in different regions of the Kimberley have uncovered a similarly diverse range of human adaptations from the edge of the Great Sandy Desert (Balme et al. 2019), along the Devonian reef and sandstone plateau (O'Connor and Fankhauser 2001; O'Connor, Aplin and Collins 2008) and the western and northern maritime zones and subcoastal riverine catchments (O'Connor 1999). The human settlement of the Kimberley has also been dynamic through time and is characterised by the emergence of innovative technologies such as edge-ground axes and polished bone points c. 46,000 years ago, the use of pigments c. 40,000 years ago, the long-distance transport of shells for personal ornaments c. 30,000 years ago, and the introduction of bifacial and backed stone points c. 5,000 years ago (Hiscock et al. 2016; Langley, Balme and O'Connor 2021; O'Connor and Fankhauser 2001).

The scientific dating of rock art is one of the most challenging issues in archaeological research. Archaeologically, it is generally assumed that the earliest expressions of art in the Kimberley are abstract cupule motifs (semi-spherical hollows that have been ground into vertical and horizontal rock surfaces and rock shelters) and other rock markings (abraded grooves, incisions, and similar) as well as handprints and hand stencils. These rock markings, however, appear to have been produced until recently and therefore overlap with later figurative rock art, which was dominated by the depiction of various animal species. The whole rock art sequence of the Kimberley is most often divided into six broad stylistic phases, which are sometimes divided into further sub-phases:

1. Pecked Cupules
2. Irregular Infill Animals
3. *Gwion*
4. Static Polychrome
5. Painted Hand
6. *Wanjina*

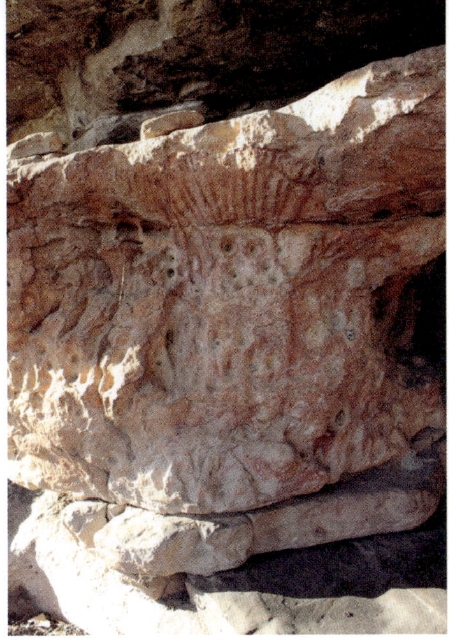

Fig. 4   At Koralyi (Wilinggin Country), so-called cupules that are visible in one section of the rock shelter have subsequently been incorporated into an anthropomorphic representation. Photo: Martin Porr, 2023

While it is tempting to provide exact start and end dates for each of these phases, the available research results currently only allow some very broad assessments. Given the evidence from outside Australia, it can be assumed that abstract markings were part of the behavioural repertoire of the first human colonisers more than 60,000 years ago. However, absolute dates within this timeframe are not yet available (fig. 4).

The earliest in situ art expressions have been dated to c. 17,000 years ago and the respective motif falls into the so-called Irregular Infill Animals period (Finch et al. 2021). From the following *Gwion* phase (fig. 5), a date of 12,000 years ago is available (Finch et al. 2020) and *Wanjina* art has been dated to as early as 5,800 years ago (Veth et al. 2021).

However, more investigations need to be undertaken on how these stylistic periods have developed over time and their possible overlaps and continuities. Within these phases, shifts in form and content can sometimes be observed, even though the exact meanings of these changes remain elusive. Within the *Gwion* art phase, for example, earlier depictions are often quite codified, and they seem to depict ceremonial scenes with richly decorated human figures. In contrast, later depictions shift towards more dynamic figures arranged in scenes that seem to depict everyday activities such as hunting or camping. Some of the human figures are now clearly gendered and depicted together with various animal species such as

The Archaeological Perspective

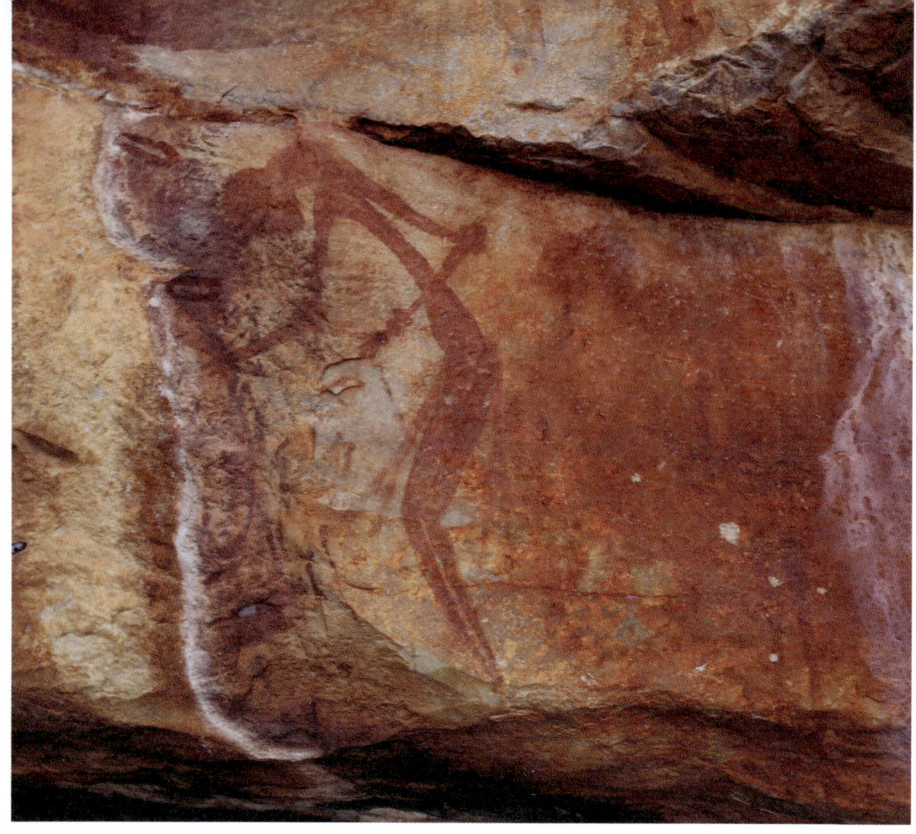

Fig. 5   This large *Gwion* figure at the site of Malan (Dambimangari Country) immensely intrigued Agnes Schulz because it seemingly did not fit into established expectations about Australian Aboriginal art expressions. Similar images from the *Gwion* period have now been dated at other sites to around 12,000 years ago. To the left and right of the large human figure are several other motifs which are barely visible; they have not been well preserved and are often impossible to identify. Photo: Joh Bornman, 2014

macropods. The placement of this art within rock shelters also changes from highly visible displays to less accessible and even hidden contexts, for example, in shelters with a very low ceiling (Veth et al. 2021). One aspect that is specific to Kimberley rock art is the regular occurrence of plant motifs. In some sites, they can constitute up to 25 percent of all depictions (Veth et al. 2018). Although there is a great deal of variation, they are represented across all stylistic phases as outlined above. In some cases, plant motifs were fused with human attributes, seemingly reflecting the close connection between the human and natural realms (Grey and Balanggarra Aboriginal Corporation 2023) (fig. 6).

While the rock art of the Kimberley is often viewed as unique and special, there is, in fact, a range of similarities that connect this region with other parts of Northern Australia, e.g. Arnhem Land. In both cases, early figurative art styles are dominated by large naturalistic animals with very few anthropomorphic motifs. The earliest emergence of these images can be dated in both cases to at least 17,000 years ago (Jones et al. 2020). Around 12,000 years ago, significant changes in the art repertoire can be observed with a shift in both regions towards anthropomorphic depictions and dynamic figures. While the exact causes behind these developments need to be examined further, the latter coincide with significant territorial losses because of rising sea levels. It can be assumed that these processes available related social responses and as these changes can be observed in both regions, this pattern very likely reflects long-distance cultural connections (Norman et al. 2024). Within the Kimberley itself, the emergence of the contemporary *Wanjina* style follows the stabilisation of sea levels and the establishment of the current seasonal monsoonal weather pattern.

This paper discusses some of the results that academic and other researchers have produced while applying archaeological and geological methods to understand the deep human past of the Kimberley. As mentioned above, these insights are not always in agreement with local Aboriginal knowledge systems. Traditional Owners of the Kimberley have no need for an official scientific validation of the deep histories and complexities of their lifeways and their connections to Country. If done in the right way, however, archaeological research can add to these understandings and show glimpses of a deep past characterised by dramatic environmental changes and the adaptability, resilience and sustainability of Aboriginal lifeways over more than 50,000 years.

Endnotes:

1 The project, called 'The German Ethnographic Expeditions to the Kimberley, Northwest Australia: A Collaborative Assessment of Research History, the Interpretation of Australian Aboriginal Heritage, and Digital Repatriation', ran from March 2020 to March 2024.

2 In 1901, the modern state of Australia was federated, which unified the different independent states and territories into a single country called the Commonwealth of Australia. Before that, the individual states had been subject to the direct control of the British colonial authority.

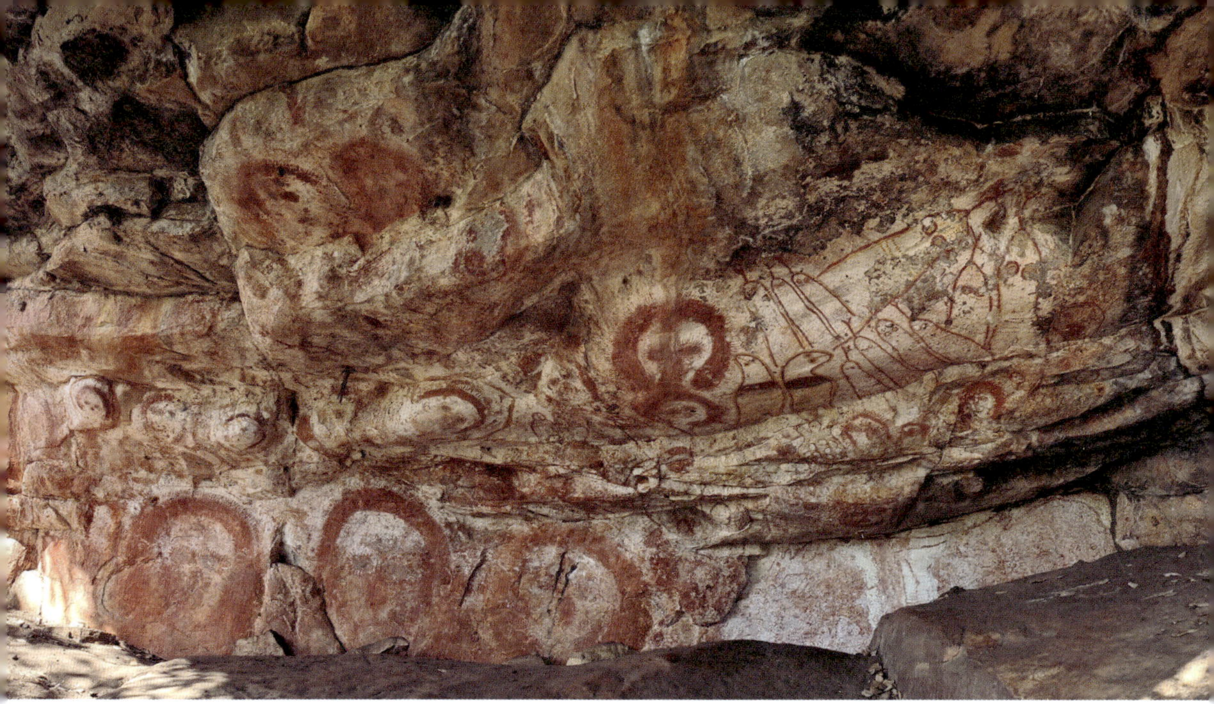

Fig. 6   The back wall of the rock shelter at Maliba I demonstrates the complexity of **Wanjina Wunggurr** rock art with different repainting episodes and a multitude of different motifs that include spiritual beings and animal species. The shelter wall also shows how the artists have used the rock wall itself to position the different images and enhance their presentation. Photo: Martin Porr, 2023

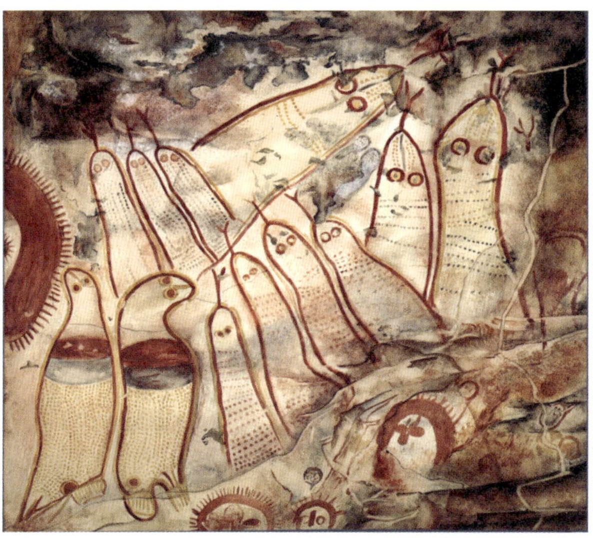

Fig. 7   The nightjar birds Wodoy and Jungurn with **Wunggurr** Snakes. Rock art site Maliba I. Kimberley, Northwest Australia. Rock art copy by Gerta Kleist, 1938. Watercolours on Paper. 108 x 98 cm. Collection: Frobenius Institute. Foto: Not stated

References:

Balme, Jane et al. 2019: Long-Term Occupation on the Edge of the Desert: Riwi Cave in the Southern Kimberley, Western Australia. In: *Archaeology in Oceania* 54 (1): 35–52. https://doi.org/10.1002/arco.5166

Blundell, Valda et al. (eds). 2017: *Barddabardda Wodjenangorddee: We're Telling All of You. The Creation, History and People of Dambiman-gaddee Country.* Based on the Cultural Knowledge and Recollections of Janet Oobagooma, Donny Woolagoodja and Other Senior Dambeemangaddee People. Fremantle: Fremantle Press and Dambimangari Aboriginal Corporation.

Bradshaw, Joseph. 1892: Notes on a Recent Trip to Prince Regent's River. In: *Proceedings of the Royal Geographical Society of Australasia, Victorian Branch* 9 (2): 90–102.

Choo, Christine. 2012: Mixed Blessings. Establishment of Christian Missions in the Kimberley. In: Cathie Clement, Jeffrey Gresham and Hamish McGlashan (eds): *Kimberley History: People, Exploration and Development.* Perth: Kimberley Society. 195–214.

Crawford, Ian M. 2001: *We Won the Victory: Aborigines and Outsiders on the North-West Coast of the Kimberley.* Fremantle, WA: Fremantle Arts Centre Press.

Crawford, Ian. 1968: *The Art of the Wandjina.* London: Oxford University Press.

David, Bruno. 2017: *Cave Art.* London: Thames & Hudson.

Donaldson, Mike and Kevin Kenneally (eds). 2007: *Rock Art of the Kimberley: Proceedings of the Kimberley Society Rock Art Seminar.* Perth: Kimberley Society.

Elkin, A.P. 1930: Rock-Paintings of North-West Australia. In: *Oceania* 1 (3): 257–279.

Finch, Damien et al. 2021: Ages for Australia's Oldest Rock Paintings. In: *Nature Human Behaviour* 5 (3): 310–318. https://doi.org/10.1038/s41562-020-01041-0

Finch, Damien et al. 2020: 12,000-Year-Old Aboriginal Rock Art from the Kimberley Region, Western Australia. In: *Science Advances* 6 (6), eaay3922: 1–9. https://doi.org/10.22459/TA55.2022.08

Goldhahn, Joakim et al. 2022: Histories of Rock Art Research in Western Australia's Kimberley, 1838–2000. In: Paul S. C. Taçon et al. (eds): *Histories of Australian Rock Art Research.* Canberra: ANU Press. 173–204.

Gray, Geoffrey. 2007: *A Cautious Silence. The Politics of Australian Anthropology.* Canberra: Aboriginal Studies Press.

Grey, Emily and Balanggarra Aboriginal Corporation. 2023: Many Ways to See Yams: An Ecological Analysis of Yam Figures in the Aboriginal Rock Art of Balanggarra Country, Northeast Kimberley, Western Australia. In: Martin Porr and Niels Weidtmann (eds): *One World Anthropology and Beyond: A Multidisciplinary Engagement with the Work of Tim Ingold.* London: Routledge. 227–243.

Grey, George. 1841: *Journals of Two Expeditions of Discovery in North-West and Western Australia, During the Years 1837, 38 and 39 […] With Observations on the Moral and Physical Condition of the Aboriginal Inhabitants*. 2 vols. London: Boone.

Harper, Sam; Peter Veth and Sven Ouzman. 2019: Kimberley Rock Art. In: Claire Smith (ed.): *Encyclopedia of Global Archaeology*. Cham: Springer International Publishing. https://doi.org/10.1007/978-3-319-51726-1_3449-1

Hiscock, Peter et al. 2016: World's Earliest Ground-Edge Axe Production Coincides with Human Colonisation of Australia. In: *Australian Archaeology* 82 (1): 2–11. https://doi.org/10.1080/03122417.2016.1164379

Jebb, Mary Anne. 2002: *Blood, Sweat and Welfare: A History of White Bosses and Aboriginal Pastoral Workers*. Crawley: University of Western Australia Press.

Jones, Tristen et al. 2020: Rethinking the Age and Unity of Large Naturalistic Animal Forms in Early Western Arnhem Land Rock Art. In: *Australian Archaeology* 86 (3): 238–252. https://doi.org/10.1080/03122417. 2020.1826080

Langley, Michelle C.; Jane Balme and Sue O'Connor. 2021: Bone Artifacts from Riwi Cave, South-Central Kimberley. Reappraisal of the Timing and Role of Osseous Artifacts in Northern Australia. In: *International Journal of Osteoarchaeology* 31 (5): 673–682. https://doi.org/10.1002/oa.2981

Leech, Graeme. 1998: Boats in the Outback. The Mystery of the Bradshaw. In: *The Australian*, 18 July 1998, 001.

Malaspinas, Anna-Sapfo et al. 2016: A Genomic History of Aboriginal Australia. In: *Nature* 538: 207–214. https://doi.org/10.1038/nature18299

Mangolamara, Sylvester et al. 2019: *We Are Coming to See You*. Derby: Dambimangari Aboriginal Corporation and Wunambal Gaambera Aboriginal Corporation.

Norman, Kasih et al. 2024: Sea Level Rise Drowned a Vast Habitable Area of North-Western Australia Driving Long-Term Cultural Change. In: *Quaternary Science Reviews* 324, 108418. https://doi.org/ 10.1016/j.quascirev.2023.108418

O'Connor, Sue. 1999: *30,000 Years of Aboriginal Occupation. Kimberley, Northwest Australia, Terra Australis*. Canberra: The Australian National University.

O'Connor, Sue; Ken Aplin and S. Collins. 2008: A Small Salvage Excavation in Windjana Gorge, Kimberley, Western Australia. In: *Archaeology in Oceania* 43 (2): 75–81. https://doi.org/10.1002/j.1834-4453.2008. tb00032.x

O'Connor, Sue and B. Fankhauser. 2001: Art at 40,000BP? One Step Closer: An Ochre Covered Rock from Carpenter's Gap Shelter 1, Kimberley Region, Western Australia. In: Atholl Anderson, Ian Lilley and Sue O'Connor (eds): *Histories of Old Ages: Essays in Honour of Rhys Jones*. Canberra: The Australian National University. 287–300.

Owen, Chris. 2016: *Every Mother's Son is Guilty: Policing the Kimberley Frontier of Western Australia, 1882–1905*. Crawley: University of Western Australia Press Scholarly.

Porr, Martin and Hannah Rachel Bell. 2012: 'Rock-art', 'Animism' and Two-Way Thinking: Towards a Complementary Epistemology in the Understanding of Material Culture and 'Rock-Art' of Hunting and Gathering People. In: *Journal of Archaeological Method and Theory* 19: 161–205. https://doi.org/ 10.1007/s10816-011-9105-4

Travers, Meg and June Ross. 2016: Continuity and Change in the Anthropomorphic Figures of Australia's Northwest Kimberley. In: *Australian Archaeology* 82 (2): 148–167. https://doi.org/10.1080/03122417. 2016.1210757

Utemorrah, Daisy and Patricia Vinnicombe. 1992: North-Western Kimberley Belief Systems. In: Mike J. Morwood and D.R. Hobbs (eds): *Rock Art and Ethnography*. Melbourne: Australian Rock Art Research Association. 24–26.

Veth, Peter et al. 2022: The Case for Continuity of Human Occupation and Rock Art Production in the Kimberley, Australia. In: Ann McGrath and Lynette Russell (eds): *The Routledge Companion to Global Indigenous History*. Abingdon: Routledge. 194–220.

Veth, Peter et al. 2019: Minjiwarra. Archaeological Evidence of Human Occupation of Australia's Northern Kimberley by 50,000 BP. In: *Australian Archaeology* 85 (2): 115–125. https://doi.org/ 10.1080/03122417.2019.1650479

Veth, Peter et al. 2018: Plants Before Farming. The Deep History of Plant-Use and Representation in the Rock Art of Australia's Kimberley Region. In: *Quaternary International* 489: 26–45. https:// doi.org/10.1016/j.quaint.2016.08.036

Walsh, Grahame L. 2000: *Bradshaw Art of the Kimberley*. Toowong, QLD: Takarakka Nowan Kas Publications.

Walsh, Grahame L. 1994: *Bradshaws. Ancient Rock Paintings of Northwest Australia*. Geneva: Edition Limitée.

Wood, Rachel et al. 2016: Towards an Accurate and Precise Chronology for the Colonization of Australia: The Example of Riwi, Kimberley, Western Australia. In: *PLOS ONE* 11 (9), e0160123. https://doi.org/ 10.1371/journal.pone.0160123

Woolagoodja, Yornadaiyn. 2020: *Yornadaiyn Woolagoodja*. Broome: Magabala Books.

The Archaeological Perspective

When the Dreaming Becomes a Night-mare

The Long, Dark Shadows of Colonial Invasion in the Northern Kimberley

Anthony Redmond

While living in Berlin in 2016, an acquaintance, on learning that I was an anthropologist, recommended visiting a nearby ethnographic exhibition[1]. Days later, not expecting a great deal, I walked into said gallery, and was immediately dazzled by a painted vision from the northern Kimberley, a *Wanjina* (rain spirit) which I was very familiar with indeed. It was as if I had unexpectedly met an old friend a very long way from home. This painting (Daylight *Wanjina*), was an image from the cave painting site Brad Wodenngarri, located on the central Kimberley plateau, which I had visited with senior Ngarinyin people in 1995. My Ngarinyin hosts had last visited this rock painting more than fifty years previously while guiding the Frobenius Expedition leader, Helmut Petri and an American companion, Douglas Fox, around their Country. Now here I was in a Berlin gallery staring with utter astonishment at Douglas Fox's life-size watercolour reproduction of that very same *Wanjina* (figs 1–3).

Fig. 1   Brad Wodenngarri rock art site. Kimberley, Northwest Australia. Rock art copy by Douglas C. Fox, September 1938. Watercolour on paper. 108 x 73 cm. Collection: Frobenius Institute. Photo: Not stated

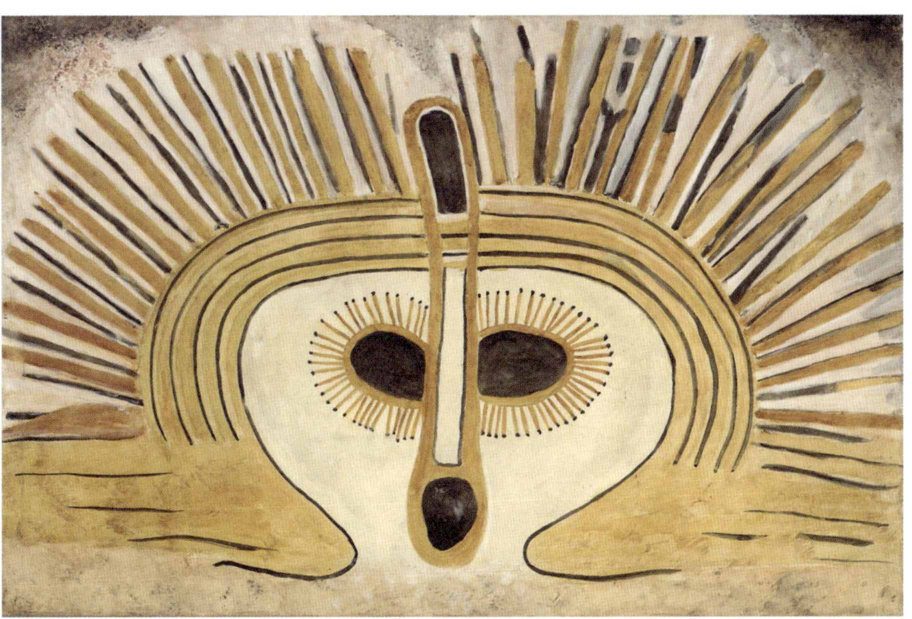

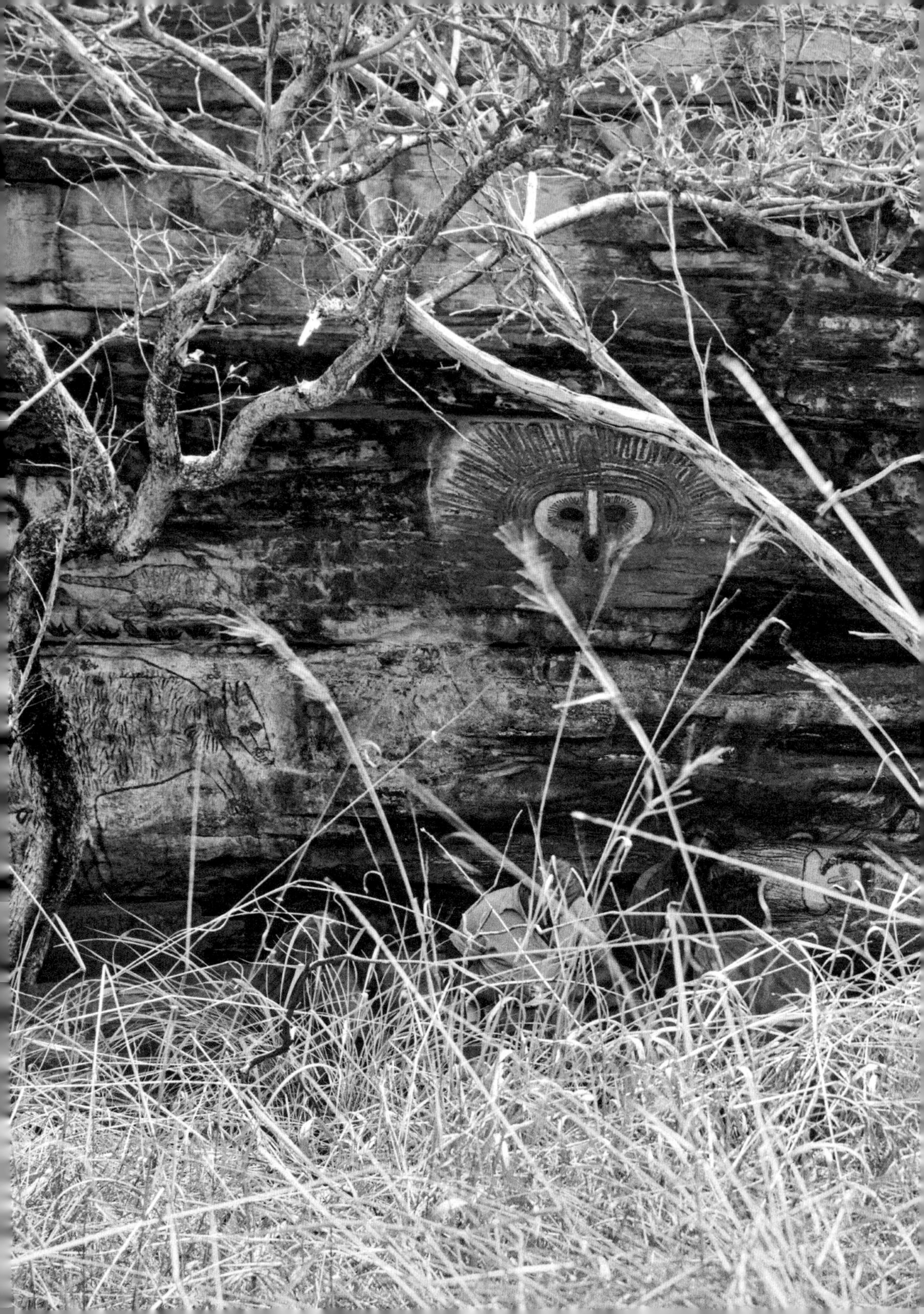

*"A head surrounded by rays, known
as Brad, the rising sun."*

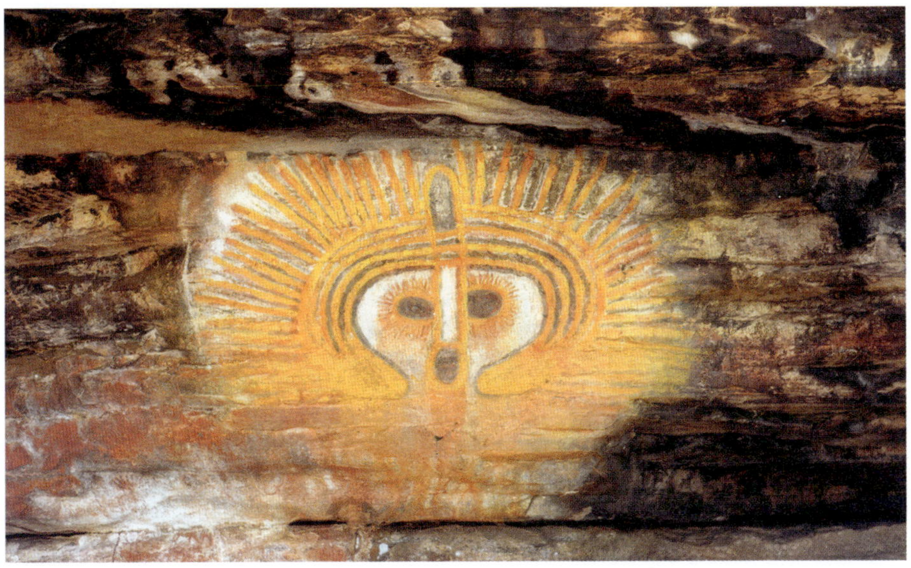

Fig. 2   View of the Brad Wodenngarri rock art site,
September 1938. Collection: Frobenius Institute.
Photo: Not stated

Fig. 3   Brad Wodenngarri – the Daylight *Wanjina*.
Photo: Anthony Redmond, 1995

When I shared this experience with another German friend, Birgit Konn, I mentioned that my Ngarinyin friends who met Lommel and Petri in 1938 had told me that the German ethnologists had brought with them a "tape recorder" of some kind but "not that square one like you got, no he had a long round one". Birgit was a keen follower of obscure clues and within a week she had tracked Lommel's "long tubes" (actually Edison wax cylinders recorded on a phonograph) to the Ethnologisches Museum Berlin. A German ethnomusicologist working in the archive kindly located and digitised the reel-to-reel recordings which had been made in 1961 from Lommel's 1938 wax cylinders and then stored away for the next half a century. My mind 'reeled' at the thread of coincidences which had led to Birgit and I sitting at a table in the museum, listening through headphones to the youthful voices of some of my older Ngarinyin, Wunambal and Worrorra mentors and some older family members singing on these very early recordings. A year or so later those same recordings became crucial source materials in a *Junba* performance (traditional dreamt songs and dances) and recording project led by a younger cohort of Ngarinyin people, working in conjunction with the ethnomusicologist Sally Treloyn.[2]

Reflecting back on his 1938 encounters with the Frobenius Expedition, my oldest Ngarinyin teacher, Laurie Gowanulli, told me how as guides they had taken good care of those visitors, despite feeling somewhat uneasy about their motives for collecting sacred ceremonial boards and making hand-drawn copies of *Wanjina* cave paintings, which were subsequently shipped back to Europe.

> *"They [his countrymen] take 'em out, stockman boy took 'em up there in that cave place and deliver 'em there, one boy look after 'em, right, they all getting all that cave drawing and mark 'em all that exactly like that thing that was in the cave too, in that paper they bin put it. They all took 'em right back there but we never got answer from all that time. We don't know what they took 'em for. That Germany is a long way from Australia."*

In those days, he said, his people typically responded to requests from apparently well-intentioned Europeans, much as they would to a request from an Aboriginal stranger in need of assistance and support in an unfamiliar social world.

> *"My time, when I bin grow, we only used do work, friend coming from there, long way we give what he ask for, he welcome, we give 'em anything, he can learn, something, well like the Germany mob they come there, we be good to them, give us everything what we needed like lolly and thing, and we give them thing and gone back home."*

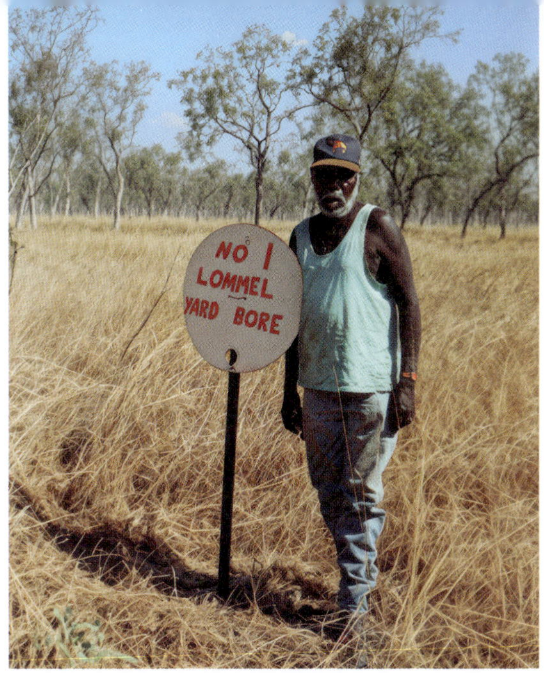

Fig. 4   David Mowaljarlai at 'Lommel Yard'. Photo: Anthony Redmond, 1996

The German anthropologists' deep interest in the *Wanjina* imagery was remarkable enough to local Kimberley people that, when Andreas Lommel returned with his wife Katharina in 1955 to conduct re-tracings of *Wanjina* images at the major sites of Wanalirri, Anggurrman and Ngalanggunda, Ngarinyin people living at nearby Gibb River Station named the base camp "Lommel Yard" (fig. 4).

Frontier violence and colonial expansion

The German anthropologists' arrival in the northern Kimberley in 1938 was just a decade or so after the worst phase of frontier violence had begun to abate. During the first violent phase of colonial expansion into the northern Kimberley (c. 1884–1910), killings and mass removal of Indigenous people from their Country had a devastating effect, forcing many older people and children into ration camps such as Munja government station (where the Frobenius Expedition members encountered them in 1938), on emerging cattle stations and around police outposts. When (and if) those arrested returned from custody, they were inducted into the unpaid workforce on the newly emerging cattle stations, while small groups of older people kept to their bush camps and avoided the stations whenever possible. The level of settler colonial violence in its initial phase was so intense that visiting German medical doctor and physical anthropologist, Hermann Klaatsch, noted during his 1904–1907 Kimberley visit that Indigenous people's relationships with whites were marked "with the dread that the natives attached to police

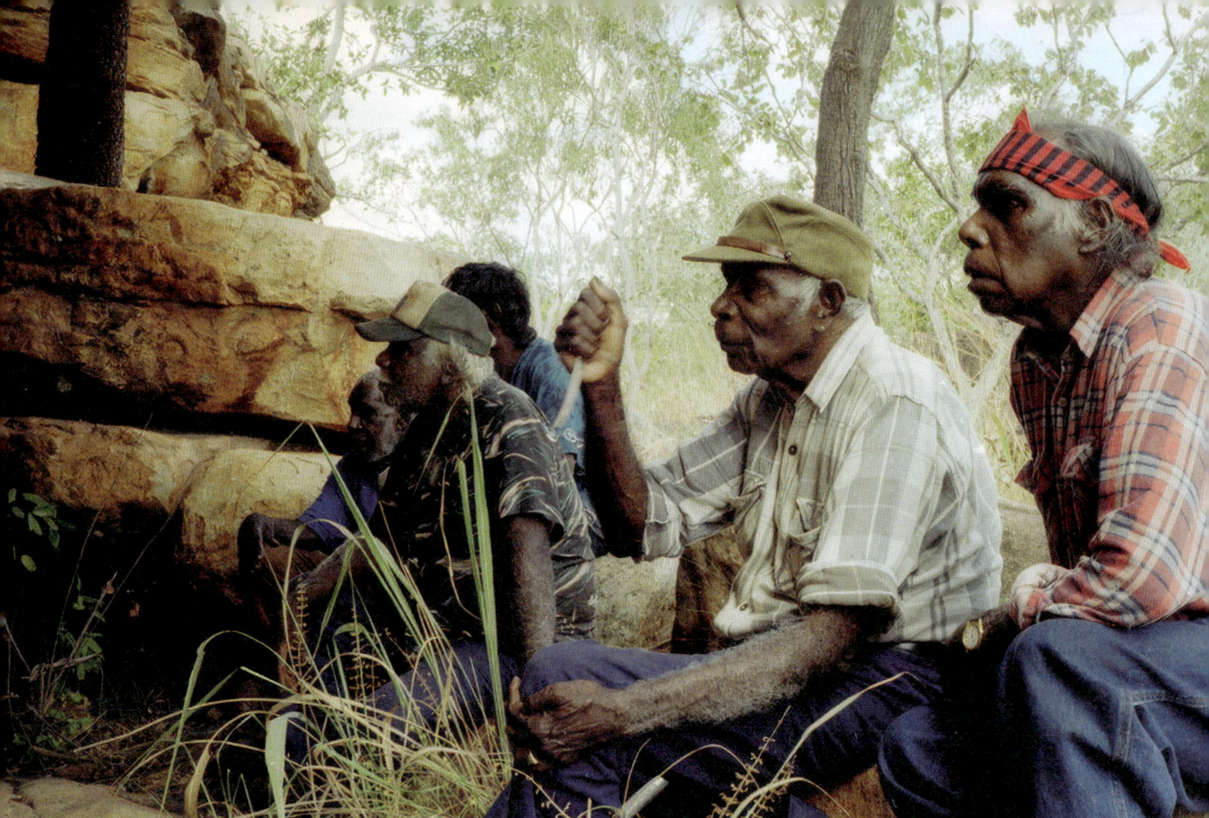

Fig. 5   Mowaljarlai, Gowanulli, Neowarra, Wama at Negamorro (from left to right). Photo: Anthony Redmond, 1996

officers, who in their mind, were likened to dangerous animals" (Klaatsch cited in Owen 2016: 418).

In 1912 the Western Australian state government, eager to be seen to be taking measures to encourage European occupation of the remote northwest, issued the Presbyterian Church with a lease to establish a mission at Port George IV (moved some kilometres further south in 1916 to Camden Harbour and renamed Kunmunya). This was the first sustained contact between Worrorra, Wunambal and Ngarinyin people and Europeans. Prior to this, Indigenous Kimberley people had had sustained contact with Macassan fishermen from Sulawesi, Indonesia (extending back to about 1720). Since the mid-nineteenth century there had been brief encounters with government appointed survey teams, pearlers and an unsuccessful group attempting a pastoral-based settlement at Camden Harbour in 1864–1866, destined to fail within a year of its commencement.

Kunmunya mission became a focus for medical interventions in the northern Kimberley, with regular inspections beginning in 1935 for leprosy, granuloma and STDs. The local population was induced to settle semi-permanently, while continuing to utilise the Country's natural and ritual resources. Over the ensuing decade, Ngarinyin and Wunambal groups visiting the area were also introduced to the notion of this permanent encampment in Worrorra Country, with its imposed regime of small-scale horticulture, rations as a supplement to the bush diet, dormitory accommodation for single girls and subjection to western work and education regimes. Nevertheless, in the context of the violent frontier conflicts which were occurring in the pastoral areas of the Kimberley, Kunmunya came to be regarded by many local people as something of a sanctuary, interspersed with outbreaks of violence and social disruption.

It was during this transitional period for Aboriginal people that the Frankfurt Frobenius Expedition was in the Kimberley, observing this incisive process of the acculturation of the Indigenous population. This probably contributed to expedition leader Helmut Petri's conclusion that the traditional way of life of the *Wanjina Wunggurr* was coming to an end, and he was indeed observing a "dying world in Northwest Australia" (as the title of his monography on the expedition suggested). Patrick Pentony, a psychology postgraduate at the University of WA, who accompanied the German researchers on the Frobenius Expedition, collected a body of dreams and their interpretations from a dozen or so Indigenous residents. In that collection of eighty three dreams, twenty two involved *Almara* (Whites), aggression or fear associated with *Almara* things, including bullocks, donkeys, houses, boats and planes. Notably, none involved direct Indigenous aggression against Whites. In one, the dreamer dreamt of Helmut Petri himself, identified as a policeman, chasing the dreamer because he had killed three Aboriginal men in a street fight in Broome.

By 1940, hundreds of the Aboriginal residents of the northwest Kimberley were concentrated in a few major encampments: mostly Worrorra and some Wunambal and Ngarinyin people at Kunmunya Presbyterian Mission; mostly Ngarinyin with some Worrorra and Wunambal people at a Government station at Munja on Walcott Inlet, 200 km north east of Derby; and mostly Wunambal/Gambre people at Pago (the Benedictines' Drysdale River Mission, today located at Kalumburu) and Kingana, an informal settlement established by White beachcombers on the far north coast.

Between 1942 and 1945, the Kimberley region of Western Australia became an intensively militarised zone. Airbases had been established near Liveringa in the Fitzroy Valley and just outside of the town of Derby. Australian and American military personnel were stationed throughout the region, including those involved in the construction of a US naval radar base at Champagny Island on the northwest coast, not far from the Presbyterian mission at Kunmunya. The town of Broome was shelled and strafed by Japanese fighter planes in 1942, killing scores of Dutch refugees who had just landed in Broome harbour aboard seaplanes that had evacuated them from Java. The Benedictine mission at Kalumburu, on the far north coast, was bombed in 1943, killing five of the Aboriginal residents as well as the mission director. A widespread fear of being shot by invading Japanese, something which had featured strongly in local rumour mills, compelled many bush-dwelling Aboriginals into settlements, in line with the prevailing government policy.

For the majority of Ngarinyin people the "Japani War" gave them their first lived experience of the real extent of modern military power and began the integration of the most remote regions of northern Australia into the centralising colonial bureaucracy of a war machine. While many Ngarinyin people had once worked for World War I veterans who had taken up beachcombing or droving after being de-mobilised from the Light Horse Brigades, and had certainly encountered murderous police patrols, formed from the same pool of hardened war veterans, this new wave of militarisation of the Top End – the upper region of the Northern Territory – was of an entirely different order.

By the end of World War II, the Kunmunya settlement was in steady decline. Scores of Ngarinyin, Worrorra and Wunambal people had been incarcerated in the Derby Leprosarium. In the early 1950s, a new community, Wotjulum, was opened near Yampi Sound where remaining residents of Munja and Kunmunya were resettled. Once Government support for remote settlements had evaporated, a decision was taken in 1956 to move the entire community to a site just outside of the township of Derby – Mowanjum Aboriginal Community. Two different sites were tried over the ensuing two decades and the present community has been located there since 1978. While *Mowanjum* is a Worrorra word meaning "settled at last", Ngarinyin Elder David Mowaljarlai was fond of saying that the settlement should have been known as *Rulug-ba-nungga* – "forever shifting".

Life in contemporary Kimberley communities

Mowanjum, and the other settlements on the Gibb River Road, are sites of dramatic economic and social change. In this era of forced reliance on government transfers, the fracturing of the cohesive bonds between ritual and economic life has shown its potential to undermine local authority structures. Some elder men and women, recognising their increasingly marginal positions in a welfare-based economy, have managed to maintain their leading positions in local bodies-politic by securing various positions: as heads of a community employment scheme, as head stockman on a cattle station, or as a well-known artist or community land rights activist with access to some material and moral resources. The occasional cash supplements, earned on mining exploration surveys or through art production, often go to repaying debts accumulated to fend off hunger amongst an extended family group.

The role played by charismatic senior people is a double-edged sword as many of them then need to commit much time and energy to negotiating with non-Aboriginal administrators. Bound by their own set of work rules, these administrators can withhold payments from those members of the group who are not seen to be satisfactorily attending to their mandatory but undervalued work, thus reducing a household's income. Senior people thus cultivate non-Aboriginal or non-local acquaintances, if he/she has them, in order to seek funding for projects which bring cash or goods into the local Aboriginal economy. In these inter-cultural transactions, the senior's local knowledge and endorsement of one or another of a set of competing projects may become a valuable resource in itself.

Amidst this complex set of intergenerational tensions, young people remain highly valued as the life-blood of the community and their senior relatives go to great effort to make life as enjoyable and meaningful for them as possible. This entails allowing ample time for young people to meet some local norms framed in terms of: "look em round country, plenty tucker, big mob to make camp lively, not too much work, don't growl 'em young ones".

Personal freedom and lively engagement with Country and kin are the most positive life values promoted by older Ngarinyin people. Young people will happily leave a town camp at the slightest notice, jumping aboard a vehicle, heading off for two or three weeks without so much as a shirt, let alone a swag (bedroll) and other basic supplies. The confidence of younger people heading 600 kilometres from town, with nothing except their basketball shorts and faith in their relatives' indulgence, is a source of mixed pleasure and chagrin for older people, who nevertheless love to see large groups of youngsters in their bush camps and are very indulgent of them.

Those older men and women often complain that during their own youth they did much forced labour for white settlers – "too much work lang *Almara*" – and because of these coercive work commitments had missed out on the infusion of some of that physical vitality which comes from experiencing the Country, as well as instruction from their Elders about various ritual sites. Thus they are keen that their children should not experience the world in the same way. When travelling, a fishing line, a gun, a swag and a tobacco supply are regarded by many older people as quite enough to get by on for a few weeks. The women of the camp tend

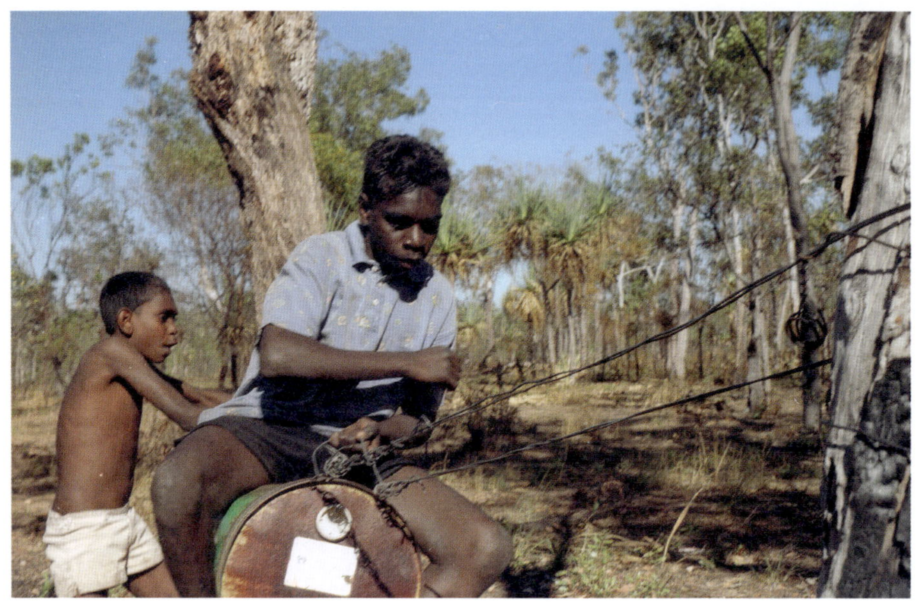

Fig. 6   Makeshift rodeo machine Maranbabidingarri.
Photo: Anthony Redmond, 1996

to carry tea and flour so that some bare essentials are usually available in unexpectedly tight situations. Older men tend to regard everything beyond these basics as an indulgence, if not a burden, and have pointed out to me the absurdity of the *Almara* obsession with horticulture when there was such an abundance of food in the bush. It was explained to me that "we don't have to carry water to get a feed". Thus, the oldest men, often glad to have put cattle work behind them, shared many common attitudes with their young relatives in regard to the value of personal freedom. Personal autonomy, offset by inevitable kin-based interdependencies, is seen as a central component of a satisfying and rewarding life. These older people were often full of good humour and can often be seen dancing in stunningly bright Western-style shirts in the town discos surrounded by their teenaged relatives. Older people also keep teenagers company on the back of trucks during bush expeditions, making jokes while calling out the traditional names of places along the road.

To a degree, once out bush, teenagers constitute their own society. Daytime hours are spent in or along the waterholes, fishing and resting. Improvised toys are constructed from basic station materials such as empty fuel drums. These include a rough and ready "rodeo machine". Fencing wire is stretched between two trees and threaded laterally through the ends of a rusting fuel drum which has had its "belly" flattened. This becomes the body of a metal "horse", which, when rocked by the wires stretched out between the anchoring trees, bucks and rolls wildly (fig. 6).

Years of impoverishment has led to Mowanjum, and the other more isolated Aboriginal settlements in the Kimberley, becoming sites of severe and chronic health crises, endemic alcohol and tobacco-related illness and deep-seated alienation from the mainstream Euro-Australian socio-economic world.

Interpersonal and family violence takes a massive toll – particularly on women. Young and middle-aged adults also suffer an extremely high rate of suicide. Diabetes is endemic – considerably increasing the probability of premature death. The incidence of children born with somatic damage from mothers consuming alcohol and tobacco during pregnancy remains disproportionately high. "Cold sick" (common cold), influenza and chronic respiratory diseases afflict a high proportion of children in the settlements, leading to the common malady of early hearing loss from ear infections and consequent learning difficulties. The Western educational levels of Kimberley children are, on average, far behind that of the metropolitan centres of Western Australia.

Although some larger and more robust houses have been constructed in Ngarinyin settlements over the last decade or so, there is a severe accommodation crisis in these communities, the townships of Derby and Wyndham and all of their satellite settlements. It is not unusual for fifteen people to be living in and around a single dwelling with three bedrooms. As a consequence of the need to share what are often well-worn foam mattresses and bedding, skin sores and head lice are re-transmitted in a ruthless cycle. Because people take their swags with them when they travel, these social afflictions also travel.

Most of the expensively built but poorly constructed dwellings at Mowanjum and other settlements have not been able to withstand the pressures put upon them by this high level of usage so that they constantly sustain structural damage. Dwellings with a single bathroom and poor drainage mean that floors are constantly covered with pools of water. Kitchens are rudimentary, and although much cooking is still done outdoors on open fires, the build-up of animal fat and flour from damper bread on bench tops and stoves means that cockroaches infest most homes in numbers that only the tropics can sustain. Infestations of mosquitoes, propagating in the tidal creeks and the thousands of hectares of long grass surrounding the communities, occur after the first rains of the wet season. This has dramatically increased the risk of infection with Ross River virus and Australian Encephalitis. Mowanjum in particular, being off-country, and the central exchange point which all remote community-based people utilise, has all the hallmarks of the "refugee camp" which many of its residents consider to be its real nature.

The neoliberal era in Australia (c. 1980 to the present day) has been marked by the dehumanisation of Indigenous welfare recipients by an increasingly coercive state apparatus. Dehumanisation of subject populations has always been part of colonial military and police training, setting the scene for a recent spate of police killings of Indigenous people in their own homes. This has facilitated racialised state violence and an ongoing displacement from Country in which Indigenous men are now imprisoned at eleven times, Indigenous women at fifteen times and Indigenous youth at twenty five times the rate of their non-Indigenous counterparts.

Imprinsonment has played a continuously destructive role in Kimberley Aboriginal communities since the early years of colonisation. The rates of Indigenous imprisonment are now much higher than reported by the 1991 Royal Commission into Aboriginal Deaths in Custody, so that, "for some cohorts of Indigenous men – such as those without formal educational qualifications living in Western Australia and the Northern Territory – the lifetime incarceration risk exceeds 50 percent" (Leigh 2020: 13).

Paint for land

Amidst these ongoing economic and social crises enveloping Kimberley communities, the Indigenous people of the region have sought and found some remarkable means for day to day survival and cultural resistance to the settler-colonial

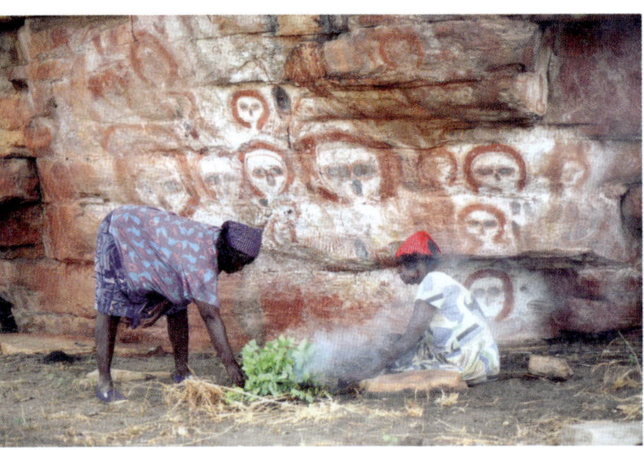

Fig. 7   Nukgit and Jordba doing a smoking ceremony at the rock art site Brad Wodenngarri. Photo: Anthony Redmond, 1995

regime. For example, in 1997, after some years in which collective artistic endeavours had been largely dormant, a move to recreate *Wanjina* imagery on canvasses emerged at Mowanjum and in the neighbouring station settlements in response to a particular set of historic conditions. Many older people had initially expressed misgivings about producing portable *Wanjina* imagery on paper or canvas because *Wanjina* are quintessentially spirits of place. The late David Mowaljarlai, in the last few months of his life (as it turned out), encouraged his countrymen and women to look seriously at the possibility of funding their own legal struggles for land rights through selling these artworks. Drawing upon a widely expressed desire for local autonomy from regional funding bodies, Mowaljarlai suggested that painting *Wanjina* on canvas might be one way in which the Ngarinyin people could fund their own Native Title claim process, without having to broker a deal with the regional state-funded land council, with which relations were in a very conflicted state.

Ngarinyin people across a wide age-span and in many remote settlements began to participate in this paint-for-land project. Special care was taken to ensure that only the people with recognised attachments to specific images and Countries painted and narrated those stories. Ochres were collected from Ngarinyin Country via traditional trade routes which have long supplied particular colours. Older Ngarinyin people took this opportunity to teach the younger generation the stories of the *Wanjina* in their own particular Countries and how to gather and prepare ochres. The project's objective was to teach the younger generation how to maintain the imagery of their local *Wanjina* cave painting galleries while raising funds for their land claim. Committing stories and images to canvas and paper, and exhibiting them in national and international galleries, became one more wave in the decades-long struggle to convince non-Aboriginal Australia to recognise and value the importance of a distinctive Indigenous lifeworld.

By 2004, in the train of these very grassroots initiatives, and following a protracted and bitterly fought legal battle, Ngarinyin people and their neighbours finally achieved Federal Court recognition of their unceded title to about 120,000 km² of their traditional Country. In addition, they have also acquired six of the major pastoral leases in the region which they run as small-scale cattle operations. In the present era, these Indigenous-owned cattle properties have the potential to significantly reshape the direction of political change by bridging Aboriginal and European interests within an expanded livestock (and possibly tourist) economy. The Indigenous people with legal rights in these tracts of land are taking their place at the centre of that process to create possibilities for the kind of economic and political future which they value and desire.

Endnotes:

1 "Kunst der Vorzeit. Felsbilder aus der Sammlung Frobenius", exhibition at the Martin Gropius-Bau, Berlin, 21 January – 16 May 2016.

2 See Sally Treloyn, *The Recordings of the "Frankfurter Expedition W-Australien"* in this volume.

References:

Leigh, Andrew. 2020: The Second Convict Age. Explaining the Return of Mass Imprisonment in Australia. In: *Economic Record* 96 (313): 187–208.

Owen, Chris. 2016: *Every Mother's Son Is Guilty: Policing the Kimberley Frontier of Western Australia 1882–1905*. Crawley, Western Australia: UWA Publishing.

When the Dreaming Becomes a Nightmare

Turning Points

Australia in the History of the Weltkulturen Museum

Eva Ch. Raabe

The collections of the Weltkulturen Museum include several holdings of Australian Aboriginal artefacts from different historical periods. Apart from the inherent meaning of the objects for their societies of origin, a number of these holdings also reflect specific epochs in the history of European ideas and the changing perception of Indigenous cultures. This account of their path to the museum's collection, their documentation and deployment in the work of the museum, is designed to provide both an impression of the European history of the Australian Aboriginal holdings in Frankfurt as well as a window onto the museum's historical development (fig. 1).

Evolutionism and cultural history

As early as 1877 the Senckenbergische Naturforschende Gesellschaft (Senckenberg Society for Nature Research) bequeathed its entire ethnographic collection to the city of Frankfurt. On its founding in 1904 the Städtische Völkermuseum[1] took over this collection of ethnographic artefacts – which also included objects which bore witness to violent encounters between Indigenous Australians and European settlers. An entry in the inventory register cataloguing a shield and a boomerang provides the following description: "in the year 1862 these two objects were taken, in an act of vengeance, from natives who had killed the Englishman Wills, along with his companions"[2]. A bestowal from 1855, consisting of objects from the Pacific Islands and Eastern Australia, originated from a Mr W. Kirchner[3] who, as a corresponding member and Consul in Sydney, is named in the register of the Senckenberg Society (1885: 29). His bestowal also originally included human remains, which however remained in the Senckenberg Museum as so-called naturalia. Consequently, they are not listed in the inventory register later compiled for the ethnological collection, but they are included in an "Inventory of the Ethnographic Section of the Collections of the Senckenberg Society for Nature Research" (Krieg and Finger 1878) handed over together with the ethnographic objects. This inventory lists a number of male skulls belonging to the Kirchner collection from the region of the Clarence River in New South Wales. The entry for two of the skulls states that the men were "killed in combat"[4] and includes details of their names and body sizes. Under the inscription "Twenty-second cabinet. Body forms," these skulls are listed together with other recent human remains and the casts of Neanderthal bones. The inventory is based on the sequence of artefacts in the historical exhibition at the Senckenberg Museum – all the bones and casts were presented in the same cabinet for the purpose of comparison. Such inventory entries express an attitude widespread in the nineteenth century: the Indigenous Australians and their cultures where assigned to the lowest developmental stage in human history. Violent conflicts were seen as a sign of their inability to adapt to 'civilised' ways of life and thus their extinction was seen

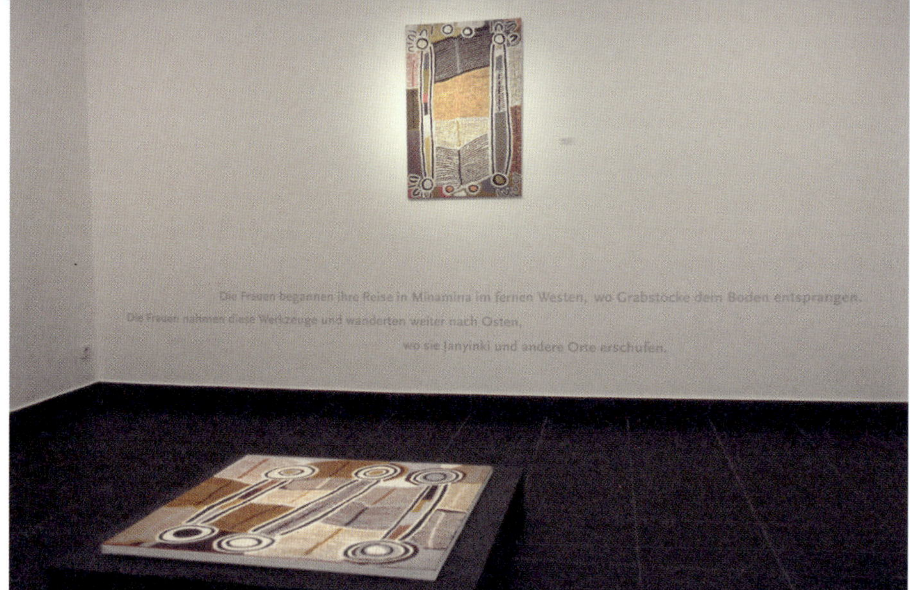

Fig. 1   View of the Australian room in the exhibition "Sinnwelten" in Gallery 37 with the paintings known as dot paintings by the artist Maggie Napangardi Watson, among others. Photo: Michael Wiener, 1997

as inevitable. This perspective was also adopted by many of the political representatives of the Australian colonies and the Australian Federation founded in 1901, a perspective that proved opportune for the European settlers who were appropriating more and more land for agriculture, cattle breeding or the extraction of mineral resources. The Indigenous population was killed, violently displaced or resettled to reservations (cf. Day 1997: 87–105; Leitner 2010: 23f.).

As Germany did not acquire colonies until the last quarter of the nineteenth century, German ethnology initially remained unaffected by the political ambition to prove the 'racial' superiority of the colonial power. Its roots go back to a philosophy that declared the study of cultural differences to be the most important instrument for understanding the different human societies. An early representative of this position was Johann Gottfried von Herder (1744–1803), who declared language, literature and oral traditions respectively to be the most characteristic forms of expression of a human group. During its early phase German ethnology developed into an empirically-based science whose representatives built up entire networks of collectors, travellers and missionaries in order to acquire as much information as possible about the different cultures (Bunzl and Penny 2003: 11f.; Kenny 2005: 15).

Missionaries in particular proved to be useful sources of information. They learnt Hebrew, Greek and Latin, and thus acquired linguistic abilities. Furthermore, they studied philosophy and religions and attempted to gain a broad understanding of the geography and culture of the regions where they were sent. In close daily contact with the Indigenous groups, many of the German missionaries in the remote Australian outback developed a deep understanding of the local language, culture and way of life. The Städtische Völkermuseum stood in close contact with Carl Strehlow, who from 1893 was the director of the Hermannsburg Lutheran mission station on the Finke River. During his lengthy period of missionary work amongst the Aranda of Central Australia Strehlow collected numerous objects which he offered for sale to German museums (fig. 2). Through the mediation of Baron Moritz von Leonhardi the Städtische Völkermuseum purchased the majority of this collection of Aranda artefacts between 1907 and 1913.[5] Von Leonhardi, who was extremely interested in ethnological matters, was unable to travel for health reasons. In order to clarify questions for his own writings on the beliefs of the Indigenous peoples he followed the reports of the German missionaries stationed in Australia in the ecclesiastical memorandums and specialist journals and corresponded with them.[6] At the same time he read the writings of Australian ethnologists, e.g. the book *The Native Tribes of Central Australia* by Walter Baldwin Spencer and Francis James Gillen, published in 1899. However, von Leonhardi had his reservations about this book, doubting the validity of the generalisations it contained which were applied to the whole of Central Australia. He saw the different local myths and customs collected through empirical research in the field as merely the basis for an elaboration of universal, common features to be conducted at a later date on the theoretical plane (Kenny 2013: 114f.). In his critical assessment of the Australian studies and their sources von Leonhardi repeatedly drew on Strehlow's information for verification, i.e. the correction of ethnological details (cf. Leonhardi 1907 and 1908). A scientific exchange extending over many years developed between the two and von Leonhardi ultimately secured the publication of five volumes of Strehlow's writings on the Aranda and Loritja by the Städtische Völkermuseum (1907–1920). To this end he personally edited Strehlow's manuscripts and prepared them for publication.

Strehlow had studied the language of the Aranda, compiled a dictionary and was so familiar with linguistic methodology that he could transcribe myths and songs, translated into phonetics, in the original language. His books contain numerous texts in the language of the Aranda, accompanied by direct, literal translations. However, his interpretation of these religious songs, in which he saw evidence for the existence of a highest being in the belief of the Aranda, was subject to serious criticism. It did not fit with the idea advocated at the time, above all by the British ethnologists James George Frazer and Edward Burnett Tylor, that every religion has its origin in magical beliefs. The representatives of British evolutionism placed

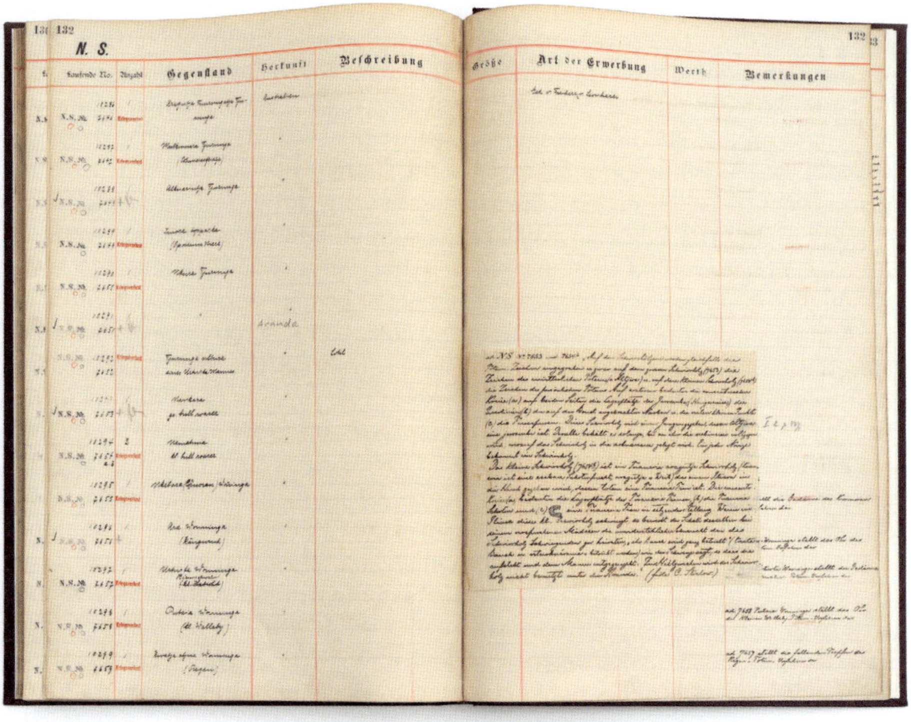

Fig. 2 A look at the inventory book of the Weltkulturen Museum: the detailed entries on the symbolism and ritual use of the sacred objects demonstrate the effort to understand the spirituality of the Aranda in depth. Photo: Wolfgang Günzel, 2024

the Aranda in a pre-religious stage of humanity (Kenny 2013: 105). For his transcriptions Strehlow had the religious songs recited – as a missionary he refused to personally participate in the rituals. For this reason Frazer and Spencer accused him, despite his superior knowledge of the language and his intensive discussions with the Aranda Elders, of flawed scientific methods. A response to these attacks not only came from Strehlow's publisher, Baron von Leonhardi (1908: 285 and 1910), but above all from an important representative of the cultural-historical school of ethnology, namely the founder of the so-called Vienna School, Father Wilhelm Schmidt (1908: 622f. and 1911: 430f.). For Schmidt, Strehlow's data on the religion of the Aranda appeared to provide clear proof of his own theory of a primordial monotheism at the root of all later forms of religion. Strehlow's work triggered a scientific discussion which profoundly reflected the controversy between British cultural evolutionism and the German Kulturkreis theory which was based on the historical dissemination of cultural elements as opposed to stages of human development. The Aranda objects housed in the Weltkulturen Museum, together with their inventory entries, must be considered as part of this history of European science. At the beginning of the twentieth century the majority of the collection documentation consisted of hand written inventory books. In many cases the incoming artefacts were merely listed with inventory numbers and details of their origin. In contrast, the entries for Strehlow's collection were, in many cases, more detailed. At the time, the scientific exchange between Carl Strehlow and the museum could only proceed in written form. Letters were conveyed through the outback via camel trek, then via rail to Port Adelaide, via ship to Hamburg or Bremerhaven and finally via mail coach to Frankfurt (cf. Kenny 2013: 104). Postal dispatches took a long time, were subject to delays or could be lost – which made it all the more important to preserve Strehlow's valuable information. Thus the collector's explanations were frequently committed to the inventory register. Although the respective entries do not reveal the theoretical dispute which was heatedly conducted at the time, they do point to a scientific approach based on the inherent meaning of an object, as opposed to any evolutionist classifications. In particular, the detailed entries on symbolism and the ritualistic use of the sacred objects provide evidence of the efforts made to gain an in-depth understanding of the Aranda's spirituality.

Breaks in the museum's history

The Australia Hall in the Städtische Völkermuseum in the Palais Thurn und Taxis, in which the Aranda objects purchased from Strehlow dominated, was once one of Frankfurt's major sights (cf. Petri 1937). Amongst ethnological experts the museum made its name, above all, with the publication of Carl Strehlow's books. As late as 1937, when the Frobenius Expedition to Northwest Australia of 1938–39 was being prepared, the Australian ethnologist Charles Chewings, who had translated Strehlow's writings into English and who the museum had asked for a letter of recommendation, referred to this important scientific heritage.[7] In 1934 the city of Frankfurt appointed the Africa explorer Leo Frobenius as director of the Städtische Völkermuseum and declared its willingness to assume responsibility for his own research facility. Initially run under the name Institut für Kulturmorphologie (Institute for Cultural Morphology), it was renamed Frobenius-Institut in 1946 in honour of the founder who had died in 1938. Frobenius stood in the tradition of cultural-historical ethnology, however he had formulated his own cultural theory, namely cultural morphology. Here he compared the development of a culture, from its birth to its decline, with the human life cycle – in prehistoric rock paintings he saw important testimonies to an early stage of human development (cf. Schuster 2006: 121f.). Frobenius established the documentation and exploration of rock painting sites as one of the institute's main areas of scientific work, and it was he who instigated the expedition to Northwest Australia, a region with important rock paintings (Petri 1954: 350). Participants in the expedition included the research assistants Andreas Lommel and Helmut Petri. While Lommel (1952) conducted research amongst the Wunambal, Petri's goal was to conduct a comprehensive study of the material and spiritual culture of the Ngarinyin (Petri 1954: 14). As in the case of Carl Strehlow, he recorded myths in the Indigenous language, adding interlinear literal translations. A few months after the end of the research expedition World War II broke out and Petri was conscripted into the army. His notes, along with the majority of his extensive collection of ethnographic objects, were destroyed during the bombing of the Rhine-Main region in 1944. Petri repeatedly compared the living conditions of the Ngarinyin at the time of his pre-war stay with their way of life in the post-war period. Disillusioned, he stated that the "old tribal culture" had disappeared and that open questions could no longer be clarified (Petri 1954: 350, cf. Petri and Schulz n.d.). He gave the monograph of his field research the title *Sterbende Welt in Nordwest Australien* (Dying World in Northwest Australia) (Petri 1954). It almost appears as if Petri's doubts concerning the survival of the Ngarinyin culture was an attempt to come to terms with the trauma of his lost field notes. In 1953 he returned to Northern Australia for further research, together with his later wife Gisela Odermann. The graphic artist Agnes Schulz, who had already accompanied Petri on the first expedition, conducted her own independent rock art research in Arnhemland. The bark paintings and objects that she collected also became part of the museum collection (Schulz 1971).

Over many decades the museum and the Frobenius Institute were run as an institutional unit under one director, during which time the museum profited from the collection activities conducted on the different Frobenius Expeditions. However, as the reports on the research expeditions were published by the institute, the priority for many of the expedition participants was their own publications. The processing of their collections for the museum often had to wait, which occasionally resulted in gaps in the documentation of the objects. As Petri was not available for the immediate documentation of his collection due to his military service, a scientific appraisal of his collection only took place after the war. Although, Petri was personally involved in the documentation of the objects, the only reliable source remaining to the museum is his publication from 1954. Eventually, at the end of the 1960s, the museum, now known as the Museum für Völkerkunde, and the Frobenius Institute were separated again as the financing of an additional research facility had become too expensive for the city of Frankfurt. A contractual agreement was signed which left the copies of rock paintings and photographs in the possession of the Frobenius Institute, while the collections, many of which had been purchased with municipal finances, remained the property of the museum. This resulted in the breakup of connected sources – due to the institutional split it was no longer possible to readily establish the important correspondence between the bark paintings in the museum depot and the copies of the rock paintings in the Frobenius archive. The bark paintings originating from the expeditions of 1938–39 and 1953–54 were hardly ever included in exhibition projects, and the Frobenius Institute's research into Australian rock paintings remained just a brief episode in the museum's history (fig. 3 and 4).

Fig. 3 and 4   Exhibition views "Ferne Völker – Frühe Zeiten". View of the section on Northwest Australia. Exhibition of the Museum für Völkerkunde and the Frobenius Institute at the Messe Frankfurt am Main. 5.5. – 30.6.1957. Collection: Weltkulturen Museum. Photo: Gisela Simrock, 1957

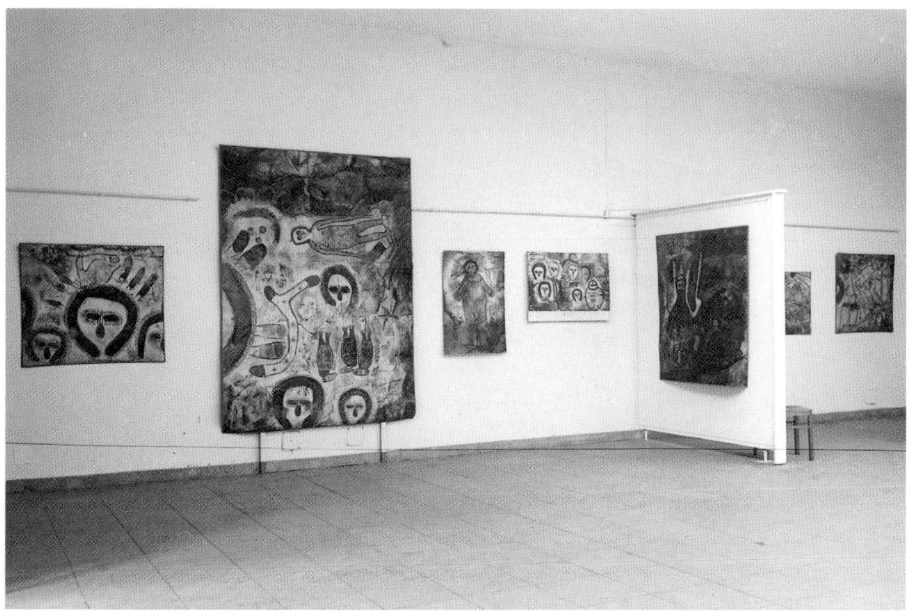

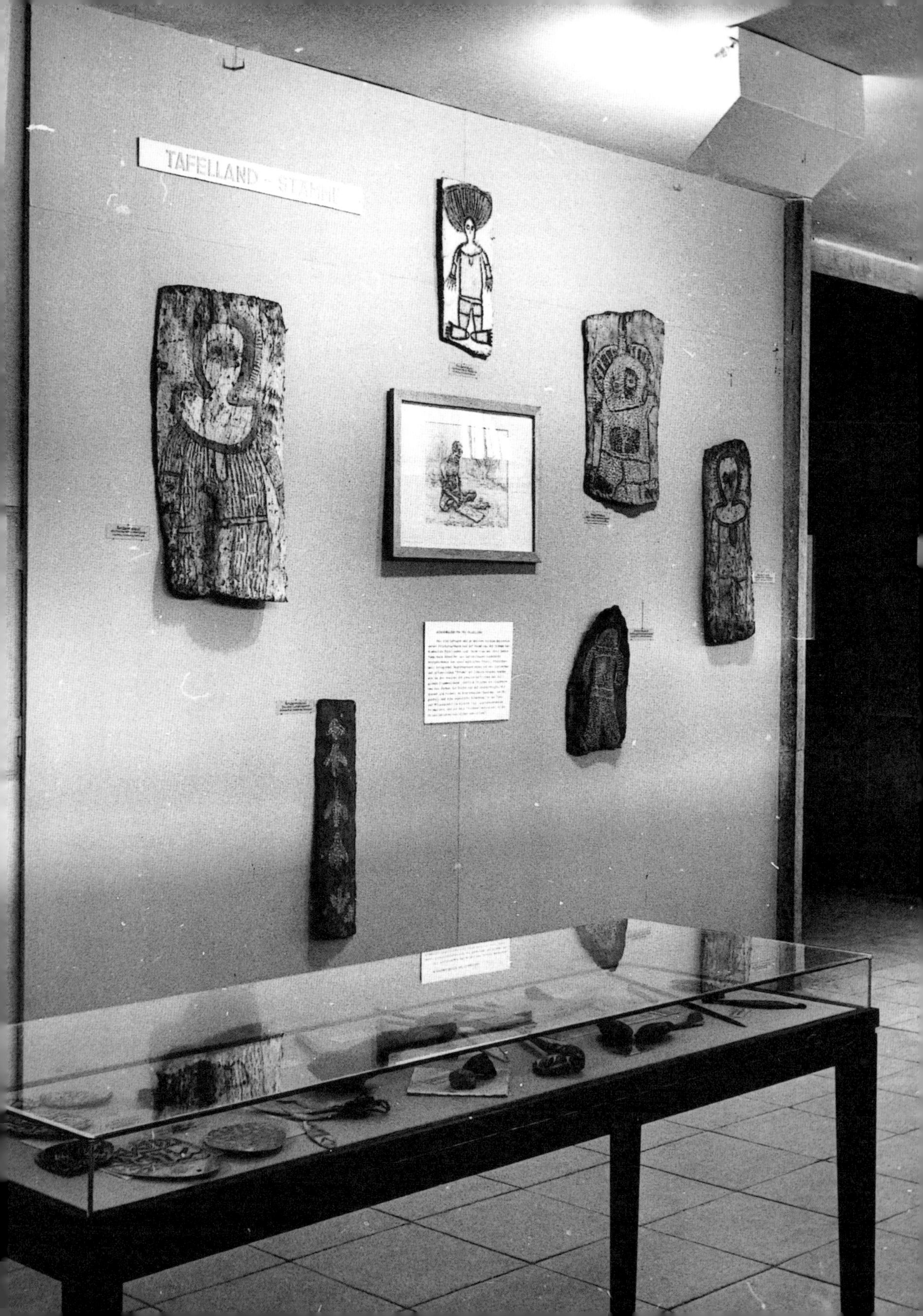
TAFELLAND - STAMM

Contemporary art

Overall, in the following decades, the Australian collection featured less and less in the museum's projects. A reason for this was the growing sensitivity and associated uncertainty in dealing with collections consisting in large part of sacred objects.[8] In 1967 the Australian government granted the Indigenous Australians civil rights and in 1976 passed the Aboriginal Land Rights Act (Leitner 2010: 74ff. and 2016: 235). The land rights movement also led to many of the Indigenous communities demanding respect for their beliefs from the majority of Australian society and insisting on the secrecy required by rituals and cult objects. This resulted in a re-think by many Australian museums. The affected objects were no longer shown publicly, were stored separately in the depots according to their groups of origin and access for outsiders strictly controlled (Fenner 1990: 34; Raabe 2018: 140). While Australian politics was concerned with reparations and taking responsibility for injustices committed against the Indigenous minority at home, in Germany it was primarily the anti-nuclear movement that awakened a broad interest in the Indigenous Australians and the threat to their living space as a result of the expansion of uranium mining. In 1979 Janine Robert's documentation of the struggle of the Indigenous communities against land grabbing and uranium mining was published in German translation in the series pogrom, published by the Gesellschaft für bedrohte Völker (Society for Threatened Peoples). This issue was accompanied by a foreword from the Bundesverband Bürgerinitiativen Umweltschutz e. V. (Federal Association of Environmental Action Groups – BBU). In this document the association, which was in contact with Indigenous activist groups, stated that the "industrialised nations' addiction to atomic energy" had led to the "destruction of cultures and genocide", and cited the ancient Aboriginal knowledge of the dangers of uranium mining as preserved in myths (Vorstand BBU 1979: 9). Although the German environmental movement used the Indigenous Australians' spiritual connection to their land for their own aims, they failed to engage with the complex secret/sacred knowledge in any greater depth. For a large group of young, politically alternative Germans the Indigenous Australians, analogous to the First Nations in the USA or Canada, were ideal examples of a life in harmony with nature. Thus in Germany the mythologies and ritual systems of the Indigenous Australians commonly provided a foundation for scientific theories and environmental appeals. Awareness and consideration of a purely Indigenous perspective, namely the opposition to the public display of sacred objects, only gradually gained ground in German cultural institutions during the course of the 1980s. The major, pioneering exhibition *Dreamings* at the Asia Society Galleries in New York in 1988 and the major exhibition *Aratjara*, held at the Kunsthalle Düsseldorf in 1993, generated international interest for the contemporary art of various Indigenous communities (Sutton 1989; Lüthi 1993). As the content of Indigenous artworks almost always referred to mythology, the wanderings of mythical ancestors or sacred sites, the religious philosophy, and with it the principle of secrecy, soon generated public interest beyond the circles of ethnological experts. This occasioned many ethnological museums to consciously engage with their Australian collections and their exhibition contexts. Secret objects were no longer displayed in the travelling exhibition *Der Flug des Bumerangs* (The Flight of the Boomerang), shown in Bremen, Hamburg and Cologne. The decision not to exhibit them was also thematised for museum visitors. From the beginning of the 1990s at the latest there was hardly a German ethnological museum that publically displayed ritual objects clearly identified as sacred and secret (cf. Fenner 1990; Raabe 2018: 141f.). –

For the Weltkulturen Museum Aboriginal art played an important role in the development of its own concepts. Even as the Museum für Völkerkunde it declared contemporary art from non-European, non-Western societies in general as an important focus of its collection activities and prepared the opening of Galerie 37, which was designed to provide a platform for Indigenous artists. For many of them it was still difficult to gain a foothold and receive recognition as a creator of modern art in the Western-oriented art scene of the 1980s and 1990s.[9] In order to lay a foundation stone for this concept in the Oceania department, in 1991 the museum commissioned the author of this article, at the time the curator of the Oceania collection, to journey to Australia and Papua New Guinea in order to purchase works from different Indigenous art movements. From a European perspective modern art meant a break with tradition – in contrast, Indigenous art was exclusively seen in a 'traditional' context and overlaid with phrases such as primitivism and authenticity. Western cultural institutions displayed a special ambivalence in their handling of contemporary central Australian acrylic painting, the so-called dot paintings. Although they were especially sought after on the art market, this did not prevent, for example, the Melbourne-based gallery owner Gabriella Pizzi from being refused a stand at the Art Cologne art fair on the grounds that the works of the artists she represented were not modern art but the traditional art of an ethnic collective (Raabe 1995: 102). The goal of the Museum für Völkerkunde at the time was to show the vital, creative autonomy of the Indigenous painters beyond all aesthetic categorisations. For this reason, the focus of the acquisitions in Australia in the 1990s was on paintings from the well-known art communities of the Western and Central Desert, namely Papunya, Yuendumu, Lajamanu, Balgo Hills and Utopia. Their presentation within the context of the Sinnwelten exhibition, which opened the Galerie 37 in 1997, was the start of a new working method for the museum, not just in the Oceania department. Nevertheless, the exhibiting of the art works and their explanation was still only an indirect representation of Indigenous positions (Raabe 1997b) (fig. 5).

Today ethnological collections are seen as a shared heritage, as a common cultural legacy whose documentation and research can only be conducted collectively by museums and the communities of origin. The current reappraisal of the long neglected collection of the Frobenius Expedition of 1938–39 is one such cooperation. The project was launched in 2015 with an initial visit to the museum for a viewing of the bark paintings by representatives of the Wanjina Wunggurr cultural bloc, and now culminates in a new exhibition jointly curated with the communities of origin. With the title COUNTRY BIN PULL'EM, they aim to express their conviction that it was the spiritual power of their country that drew the Frobenius Expedition to the Kimberley at the time, a power which over recent years has also

Fig. 5   The bark painting painted on both sides with earth pigments shows a *Wanjina* and an *Agula* (or "Devildevil") – the bringer of order and chaos. In 2009 it featured as part of the Masterpieces exhibition at the Weltkulturen Museum. Wunambal. Woorewooddee, Kimberley. Acquired by Andreas Lommel during the Frobenius Expedition to Northwest Australia, 1938. Collection: Weltkulturen Museum. Photo: Wolfgang Günzel, 2023

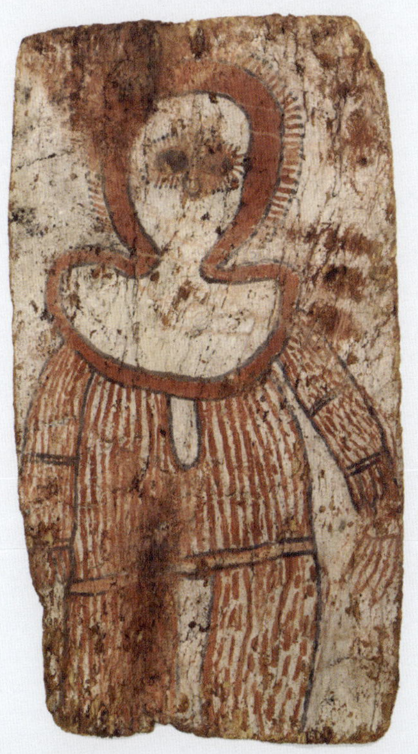

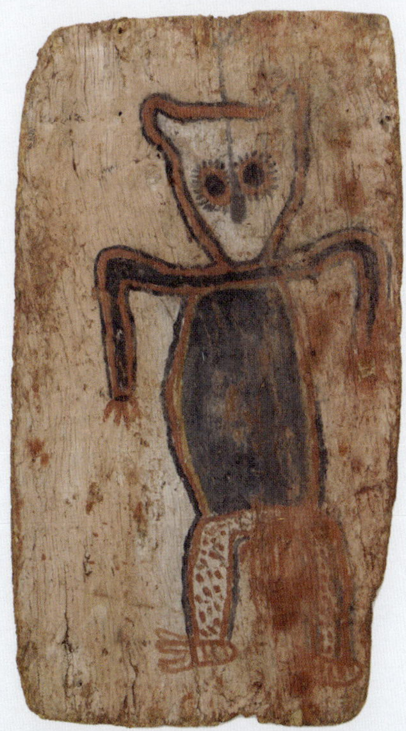

facilitated the return of the archive materials in digital form. And this title also applies to the history of the museum – for it is surely the unbroken bond between the Ngarinyin, Wunambal and Woddordda and their Country, together with the associated interest in their rock and bark paintings, that have reunited within this exhibition the collections stored separately in the Weltkulturen Museum and the Frobenius Institute.

Endnotes:

1 After World War II the Städtische Völkermuseum was renamed the Museum für Völkerkunde der Stadt Frankfurt am Main. It was subsequently renamed the Museum der Weltkulturen in 2001. Since 2010 it has used the title Weltkulturen Museum.

2 Shield (E742) and boomerang (E743, losses due to war), Mr Ehren 1864; entry in Old German Script and old spelling.

3 In all likelihood Karl Ludwig Wilhelm Kirchner who emigrated in 1839, was active in Frankfurt as recruiter of emigrants for New South Wales from 1848 until c. 1850, served as Consul for Hamburg and Prussia in Sydney and from 1851 established himself as a businessman in New South Wales (Clarence River Historical Society and German Australia).

4 The skulls have since been repatriated by the Senckenberg Museum (Schrenk et al. 2018: 51).

5 For today's approach to secret/sacred objects from the Strehlow collection and the theme of repatriation see Raabe 2018.

6 Amongst others with the Lutheran missionary Otto Siebert (see Leonhardi 1909: 1068). The Anthropologische Gesellschaft placed his collection of objects from the Diyari on permanent loan to the Städtische Völkermuseum in 1904 and bequeathed the collection to the museum in 1910.

7 I thank Christina Henneke for directing my attention to the letter to the Department of the Prime Minister in Canberra (document Ex-AU-WA S2030-cons933 1937-0223 in the Archive of the Frobenius Institute).

8 The description of this atmosphere provided by the author Eva Raabe, curator of the Oceania department from 1985 to 2018, is drawn from her own experience.

9 Galerie 37 operated from 1997 to 2010. For the concept and aims see Raabe 1997a.

References:

Bunzl, Matti and H. Glenn Penny. 2003: Introduction. Rethinking German Anthropology, Colonialism, and Race. In: H. Glenn Penny and Matti Bunzl (eds): *Worldly Provincialism. German Anthropology in the Age of Empire.* Ann Arbor: University of Michigan Press. 1–30.

Clarence River Historical Society (ed.). Undated: *German Settlers on the Clarence.* https://www.clarencehistory.org.au/html/germans.html (22.03.2024).

Day, David. 1997: *Claiming a Continent. A New History of Australia.* Sydney: Angus & Robertson.

Fenner, Burkhard. 1990: Nur für Eingeweihte. Zur Ausstellung geheimer Sakralgegenstände aus Australien. In: *Kölner Museums Bulletin* 1: 29–40.

German Australia (ed.). Undated: *Neu-Süd-Wallis. Wilhelm Kirchner.* https://www.germanaustralia.com/d/d-kirchner.html (20.03.2024).

Kenny, Anna. 2013: *The Aranda's Pepa. An Introduction to Carl Strehlow's Masterpiece Die Aranda- und Loritja-Stämme in Zentral-Australien (1907–1920).* Canberra: The Australian National University.

Kenny, Anna. 2005: A Sketch Portrait. Carl Strehlow's German Editor Baron Moritz von Leonhardi. In: Anna Kenny and Scott Mitchell (eds): *Collaboration and Language.* Alice Springs: Northern Territory Government. 54–70.

Krieg, G. L. and F. A. Finger. 1878: *Verzeichnis der ethnographischen Section der Sammlungen der Senckenbergischen naturforschenden Gesellschaft* (unpublished archival source). Frankfurt am Main: Archive Weltkulturen Museum.

Leitner, Gerhard. 2016: *Geschichte Australiens.* Stuttgart: Philipp Reclam jun.

Leitner, Gerhard. 2010: *Die Aborigines Australiens.* München: Verlag C.H. Beck.

Leonhardi, Moritz von. 1910: Vorrede. In: Carl Strehlow: *Die Aranda- und Loritja-Stämme in Zentral-Australien. part 3. Die Totemistischen Kulte der Aranda- und Loritja-Stämme. Section 1. Allgemeine Einleitung und die totemistischen Kulte des Aranda-Stammes.* Veröffentlichungen aus dem Städtischen Völker-Museum I. Frankfurt am Main. III–VXIII.

Leonhardi, Moritz von. 1909: Der Mura und die Mura-Mura der Dieri. In: *Anthropos* 4: 1063-1068.

Leonhardi, Moritz von. 1908: Über einige religiöse und totemistische Vorstellungen der Aranda und Loritja in Zentralaustralien. In: *Globus. Illustrierte Zeitschrift für Länder- und Völkerkunde* 91: 285–290.

Leonhardi, Moritz von. 1907: Vorwort. In: Carl Strehlow: *Die Aranda- und Loritja-Stämme in Zentral-Australien. Part 1. Mythen, Sagen und Märchen des Aranda-Stammes in Zentral-Australien.* Veröffentlichungen aus dem Städtischen Völker-Museum I. Frankfurt am Main.

Lommel, Andreas. 1952: *Die Unambal. Ein Stamm in Nordwest-Australien.* Monographien zur Völkerkunde 2. Hamburg: Museum für Völkerkunde.

Lüthi, Bernhard (ed.). 1993: *Aratjara. Kunst der ersten Australier. Traditionelle und zeitgenössische Werke der Aborigines und Torres Strait Islanders.* Düsseldorf: Kunstsammlung Nordrhein-Westfalen.

Petri, Helmut. 1954: *Sterbende Welt in Nordwest-Australien.* Braunschweig: Albert Limbach Verlag.

Petri, Helmut. 1937: *Der Australiensaal im Völkermuseum.* Schriftenreihe Frankfurter Sehenswürdigkeiten. Issue 9. Frankfurt am Main: Stadt Frankfurt am Main.

Petri, Helmut and Agnes Susanne Schulz. Undated: *Bericht von der Frobenius-Expedition 1938 nach Nordwestaustralien.* Düren: Schoellershammer.

Raabe, Eva Ch. 2018: Secret/Sacred. Die tjurunga aus Australien im Weltkulturen Museum Frankfurt am Main. In: Anna-Maria Brandstetter and Vera Hierholzer (eds): *Nicht nur Raubkunst! Sensible Dinge in Museen und universitären Sammlungen.* Mainz: Mainz University Press. 135–146.

Raabe, Eva Ch. 1997a: Alte und neue Ziele. Warum eine Galerie für außereuropäische Kunst im Museum für Völkerkunde? In: Eva Ch. Raabe and Mona B. Suhrbier (eds): *Sinnwelten.* Galerie 37. Kunst im Museum für Völkerkunde. Vol. 1. Frankfurt am Main: Museum für Völkerkunde. 7–12.

Raabe, Eva Ch. 1997b: Künstlerische Freiheit – kulturelle Traditionen. In: Eva Ch. Raabe and Mona B. Suhrbier (eds): *Sinnwelten.* Galerie 37. Kunst im Museum für Völkerkunde. Vol. 1. Frankfurt am Main: Museum für Völkerkunde. 13–24.

Raabe, Eva Ch. 1995: Modernism or Folk Art? The Reception of Pacific Art in Europe. In: *Art and Asia Pacific* 2(4): 96–104.

Schmidt, Wilhelm. 1911: Is Ethnological Information Coming From Missionaries Sufficiently Reliable? In: *Anthropos* 6: 430–431.

Schmidt, Wilhelm. 1908: C. Strehlow, Die Aranda und Loritja-Stämme in Zentral-Australien. I. Teil: Mythen, Sagen und Märchen des Aranda-Stammes in Zentral-Australien, bearbeitet von Moritz Freiherrn von Leonhardi. Review. In: *Anthropos* 3: 622–625.

Schrenk, Friedemann et al. 2018: Menschen in Sammlungen. Geschichte verpflichtet. In: Anna-Maria Brandstetter and Vera Hierholzer (eds): *Nicht nur Raubkunst! Sensible Dinge in Museen und universitären Sammlungen.* Mainz: Mainz University Press. 45–61.

Schulz, Agnes Susanne. 1971: *Felsbilder in Nord-Australien. Ergebnisse der Frobenius-Expedition nach Nord-Australien 1954/55.* Ergebnisse der Frobenius-Expeditionen vol. 15. Wiesbaden: Franz Steiner Verlag.

Schuster, Meinhard. 2006: Museum und Institut. Zu Genealogie und Vernetzung zur Frankfurter Ethnologie 1904–1965. In: Karl-Heinz Kohl and Editha Platte (eds): *Gestalter und Gestalten. 100 Jahre Ethnologie in Frankfurt am Main.* Frankfurt am Main and Basel: Stroemfeld Verlag.

Spencer, Walter Baldwin and Edgar Francis Gillen. 1899: *The Native Tribes of Central Australia.* London: Macmillan and Co.

Strehlow, Carl. 1907–1920: *Die Aranda- und Loritja-Stämme in Zentral-Australien.* Veröffentlichungen aus dem Städtischen Völker-Museum I, in 5 volumes. Frankfurt am Main: Baer.

Sutton, Peter (ed.). 1989: *Dreamings. The Art of Aboriginal Australia.* Ringwood: Viking.

Senckenbergische Naturforschende Gesellschaft, Frankfurt am Main (ed.). 1885: Verzeichnis der Mitglieder. In: *Bericht über die Senckenbergische naturforschende Gesellschaft.* 21–32. https://www.

zobodat.at/pdf/Berichte-der-Senckenberg-naturf-Ges-Frankfurt_1885_0021-0032.pdf (20.03.2024)

Vorstand BBU. 1979: Vorwort des Bundesverbandes der Bürgerinitiativen Umweltschutz e. V. (BBU). In: Janine Roberts: *Nach Völkermord. Landraub und Uranabbau. Die Schwarzaustralier (Aborigines) kämpfen ums Überleben.* Series *pogrom* (1003). Göttingen: Gesellschaft für Bedrohte Völker. 9–10.

Celebrated and Lost

The Remains of a Collection from Northwest Australia

Matthias Claudius Hofmann

Anyone who spends time exploring the Frobenius Expedition to Northwest Australia and the resulting collection of material culture in the Welt-kulturen Museum will come to realise that it comprises no more than the sparse remains and fragments of a once extensive ethnographic collection. A glance at the inventory, which is the primary record in this case, underscores the extent of the devastation. We see page upon page of entries accompanied by a red stamp denoting a war loss. Of the 632 entries listed in the inventory under "Frobenius Expedition 1938/39", only ninety-six have survived today.

During World War II, the heavy aerial bombardment of Frankfurt in March 1944 led to the complete destruction of the Völkermuseum, as the Weltkulturen Museum was then called, which had been housed in Palais Thurn und Taxis since 1908. While much of the museum's collection and the entire library had already been removed and stored elsewhere, almost all the objects that remained in the exhibition spaces and in the basement were destroyed, along with the objects from the Northwest Australia expedition which had only arrived at the Völkermuseum five years previously (see Agthe 1994: 14). In addition to countless testaments to the region's material culture, all the expedition's film recordings and some of the field research notes were lost. Fortunately, the copies of rock art, paintings, and the photographic negatives had not been kept on the museum premises, which allowed them to survive the bombing undamaged.

Even though the few remaining objects that came from the Kimberley region of Northwest Australia (particularly from Ngarinyin and Wunambal areas) in the 1930s are undoubtedly significant in terms of the cultural evidence they provide, and some individual pieces are of exceptional quality, the issue of the war losses has always concerned me when working on this collection, and I have found myself unable to let it go.

What can still be discovered about these lost things, if we follow traces of them in the Weltkulturen Museum archives and in the expedition's diaries and research reports? What findings can we conclude about the original collection as a whole? What does this collection tell us about the expedition, about the acquisition histories of the objects, and about the relationship between the researchers and the Indigenous people? Below I would like to examine in greater detail the collection of material culture from the *Wanjina Wunggurr* community, who come from the Kimberley region of Northwest Australia. I believe it is meaningful to look at the surviving objects alongside the war losses in order to get an overall impression of the collection, while also examining it in connection with the history of the expedition and retracing the contexts in which the objects were acquired.

One of the world's best collections on Australia

After the participants returned from Australia in spring 1939, the press coverage testifies to the great interest taken in reports about the expedition and its research findings. Someone reading the headlines today might even occasionally discern exuberant enthusiasm: "Australia's gods and demons", "We immersed ourselves in a world of mythical and cultic processes and customs" (Kölnische Zeitung, 9 April 1939), "Exceptional findings for the Petri expedition" (Hamburger Abendblatt, 19 July 1939) and "German scholars research Australia: the secret of ancient rock art decoded" (Münsterischer Anzeiger, 12 April 1939).

On 8 April 1939, the Deutsche Gesellschaft für Kulturmorphologie (now the Frobenius Society) invited journalists to a press event in Frankfurt, at which Helmut Petri, as the expedition leader, gave all those assembled in the research institute's large conference hall "the first ever detailed depictions of the scholarly findings from the research trip, [while also] presenting a selection of rock art images and cultic objects in a small exhibition". During the press conference, Petri also spoke about the extent of the collections that had been brought to Germany. The reporter from the Kölnische Zeitung wrote that "over a hundred full-size copies of rock art were made, around two hundred myths were collected, some hundred phonographic recordings were produced of cultic songs and speech samples of the natives, and an ethnographic collection of over a thousand items was brought back. The latter", continued the article, "will be added to Frankfurt's Völkermuseum, which will now [...] house what is, after Adelaide, the world's most extensive and significant collection of Australian cultural objects within its walls" (Kölnische Zeitung, 9 April 1939).

Petri and the managements of both institute and museum seem to have thought it vital to emphasise the considerable size and importance of the acquired collections to the general public: an earlier article in the Kölnische Zeitung had already reported on the number of collections, and the fact that there had been "particular success [...] in exchanging cultural objects". The talk was of "a total of fifty boxes" of ethnographic objects on their way to Frankfurt. The reporters were informed that, in light of the sheer overwhelming amount of material, the "Forschungsinstitut für Kulturmorphologie [...] would be busy for years to come with working through the findings of this trip". The report goes on to mention the issue of duplicates: "The Frankfurt Völkermuseum will exchange any duplicated items with other museums in order to expand its own collections" (Kölnische Zeitung, 5 March 1939).

It was actually common practice until the 1960s for ethnological collections to exchange duplicates – in the sense of objects that were identical in typology or appearance – among each other in order to increase the size of their own collections. If one institution had several paintings on bark or wood, for example, it seemed sensible to swap these doubles with other museums in return for objects that had not yet been added to the collection. The individual ethnographic objects were viewed not as unique items but rather as prototypical representations within a culture's material repertoire. It was a practice that failed to acknowledge the importance of provenance and split up sets of objects in collections, which is why it was ultimately abandoned in the 1960s.

Indeed, we find an indication in one report prepared by Petri for the institute in Frankfurt that he was already mulling over this idea with an eye to the collection's planned expansion:

> *"Moreover, we completed our ethnographic collection here, which has now increased to circa 300 [catalogue] numbers. Assuming that we manage to transport [these objects] to [Frankfurt] undamaged, we really do have an exceptional collection which can be used for a wide range of exchanges"* (Petri 1938a: 4).

While Petri was still in Australia he exchanged objects from the collection with the South Australian Museum in Adelaide and with a museum in Melbourne. This is revealed in the inventory, where the fact of the exchange and the objects received in return are listed under "provenance". It seems that Petri was systematically trying to acquire older objects from the Kimberly region for comparative purposes. Petri had already developed an interest during the research itself in processes of cultural change and their impact on material culture. Indeed, he began setting up a network of museums, colleagues and specialists in the field. Very soon after his return in Frankfurt he also initiated a further exchange with the British Museum in London.

Petri seems to have been attempting to establish research into Australian ethnology as a specialisation in Frankfurt. The researchers threw themselves into the work just a few months after their return from Australia. The collections were swiftly catalogued in the museum and work began on the scientific evaluation. In addition, a temporary exhibition in the Völkermuseum was conjured up in just a few months, opening on 14 July 1939 as *Die Ergebnisse der Australien-Expedition 1938–39* (The Findings of the Australian Expedition 1938–39). It presented the extensive collection from Northwest Australia to the people of Frankfurt until the museum closed in 1940.

A series of articles accompanied the opening, appearing on 15 July in edition 29 of the Frankfurter Wochenschau, with contributions from Helmut Petri, Andreas

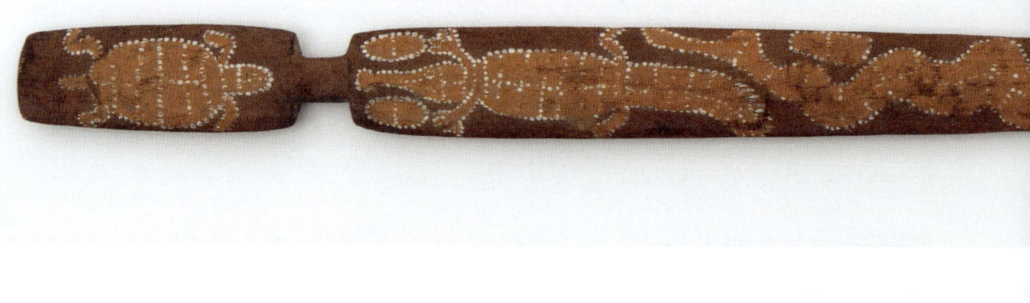

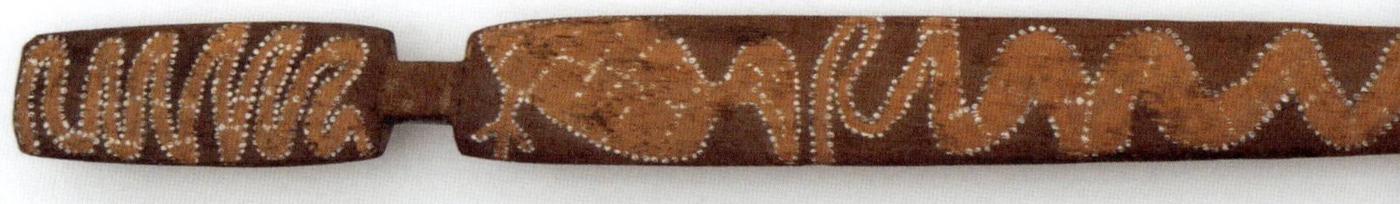

Fig. 1 Spear thrower, *Yamálba*, made from corkwood *(Hakea)* painted on both front and back. Ngarinyin. Sale River, Kimberley. Acquired by Helmut Petri during the Frobenius Expedition to Northwest Australia, 1938. Collection: Weltkulturen Museum. Photo: Wolfgang Günzel, 2023

Lommel, Douglas Fox and Agnes Schulz that would act as a "guide through the aforementioned special exhibition, giving [visitors] a brief, selective impression of the activities of the last Frobenius Expedition" (Petri et al. 1939: 345).

Sadly, we know very little about this exhibition: no pictures of the display space have survived, there are no precise descriptions or lists of exhibits detailing what was on show and how it was presented, and we cannot even tell if the exhibition was of a somewhat improvised nature on account of the short time available. All we can say with certainty is that most of the objects were shown to the general public in Frankfurt for the first and last time before they went up in smoke along with the museum building just five years later. We can gain at least some impression of the exhibition from the 15 July article in the Frankfurter Zeitung about the opening ("New Display in the Ethnological Museum: The Findings of the Australia Expedition"):

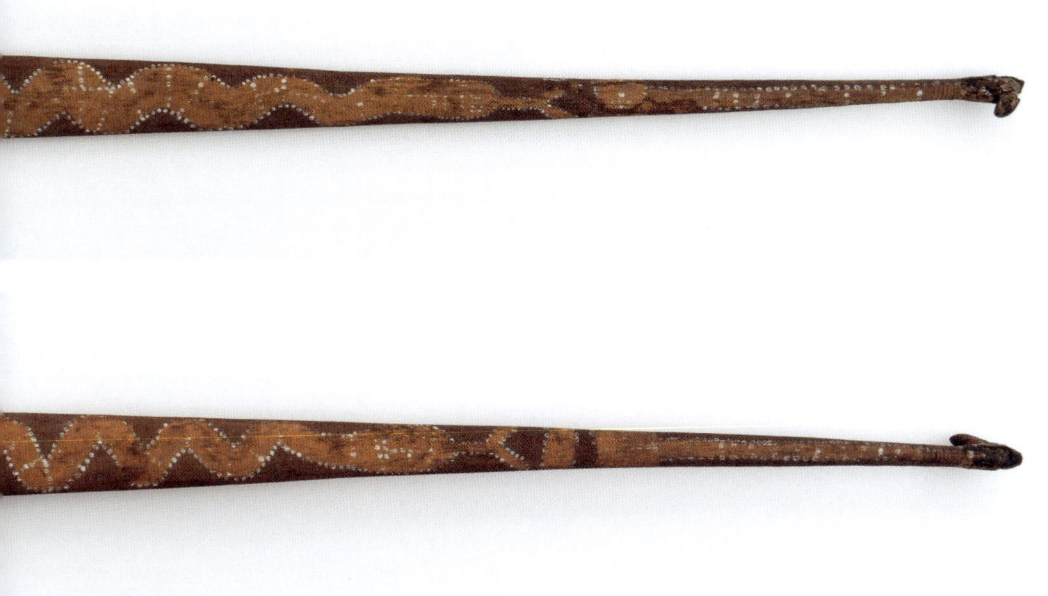

"The results of the expedition, which can now be seen in a temporary exhibition at the city's ethnology museum, significantly expand our knowledge of Australia's native cultures. Ornamentally decorated ceremonial boards give us insights not only into certain prehistoric legends but also into initiation rituals that are still held today. Devices resembling antennas convey a tangible impression of the Indigenous dream world: the world of the imagination. Stone axes, spears, arrows, belts and bags as well as the most interesting bark paintings testify to their technical skill. But the rock paintings are of particular value. As they are still looked after by the Indigenous people, the content and meaning of these visual depictions can be accurately explained."

These newspaper articles, alongside the piece written by Petri in the Sunday edition of the Kölnische Zeitung on "Sorcery and Black Magic in Northwest Australia" (1939), show not only that the participants threw themselves obsessively into their work almost as soon as they had returned, but also that they tried to do so in a manner that generated the maximum amount of positive publicity.

Fig. 2 *Wanjina* painting with earth pigments on eucalyptus bark. Wunambal. Prince Regent River, Kimberley. Acquired by Andreas Lommel during the Frobenius Expedition to Northwest Australia, 1938. Collection: Weltkulturen Museum. Photo: Wolfgang Günzel, 2023

Evaluating the findings, war losses and remains

Helmut Petri had similarly big plans for publishing his research findings. He regarded himself as the scholarly successor to the missionary Carl Strehlow, whose ethnographic collection of the Aranda in Central Australia has been part of what is now the Weltkulturen Museum since 1907. Petri knew this collection as much as he was familiar with Strehlow's multi-volume work *Die Aranda- und Loritja-Stämme in Zentral-Australien* (The Aranda and Loritja Tribes of Central Australia, 1907–1920), which had also been published by the museum and which he regarded as "among the best works on Australian ethnology" (Petri 1939: 345). Petri was undoubtedly envisaging a similarly comprehensive publication detailing the expedition and his research findings, which would stand up to any comparison with Strehlow's work. Instead, there was a certain bitterness to his tone when he finally concluded the expedition report fifteen years after returning from Australia. His book, which bore the suggestive title *Sterbende Welt in Nordwest-Australien* (A Dying World in Northwest Australia), catalogued the concessions that the chaos of war had forced him to make in publishing the findings: "In some respects," he wrote in the afterword, "this book has remained a fragment" (Petri 1954: 350).

It is true that the evaluation of the expedition's findings was abruptly suspended by the outbreak of World War II. The male members of staff were called up for military service, while the museum was closed to visitors in 1940 and two years later Karin Hissink undertook the highly difficult task of coordinating the gradual evacuation of the collections (Agthe 1994: 13). The interruption of the work is reflected, for example, in the inventory records, which remained fragmentary. At that time, individual objects would first be listed in the inventory itself and then documented in more detail on index cards. In addition to information such as dimensions, material, collector, and geographical information, there were notes – some more extensive than others – on the object's function and cultural significance. Moreover, it was still common practice to include sketches or watercolours of the work being described on the index card, to aid identification. While the index cards of surviving objects have been replaced over time by typed equivalents, the cards that Petri completed by hand in 1939 to describe objects that would later be destroyed in the war are still available. The sudden abandonment of the work is

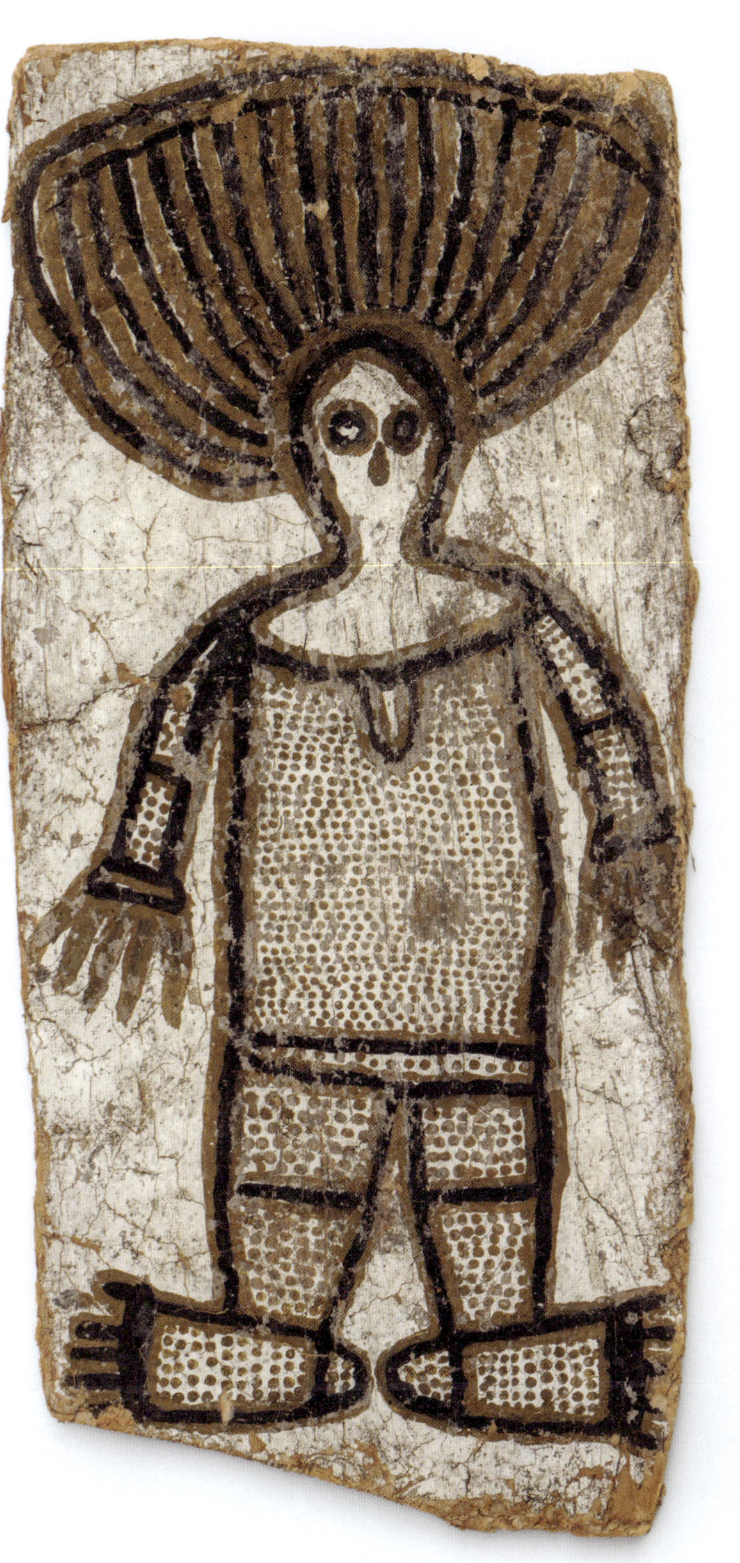

Celebrated and Lost

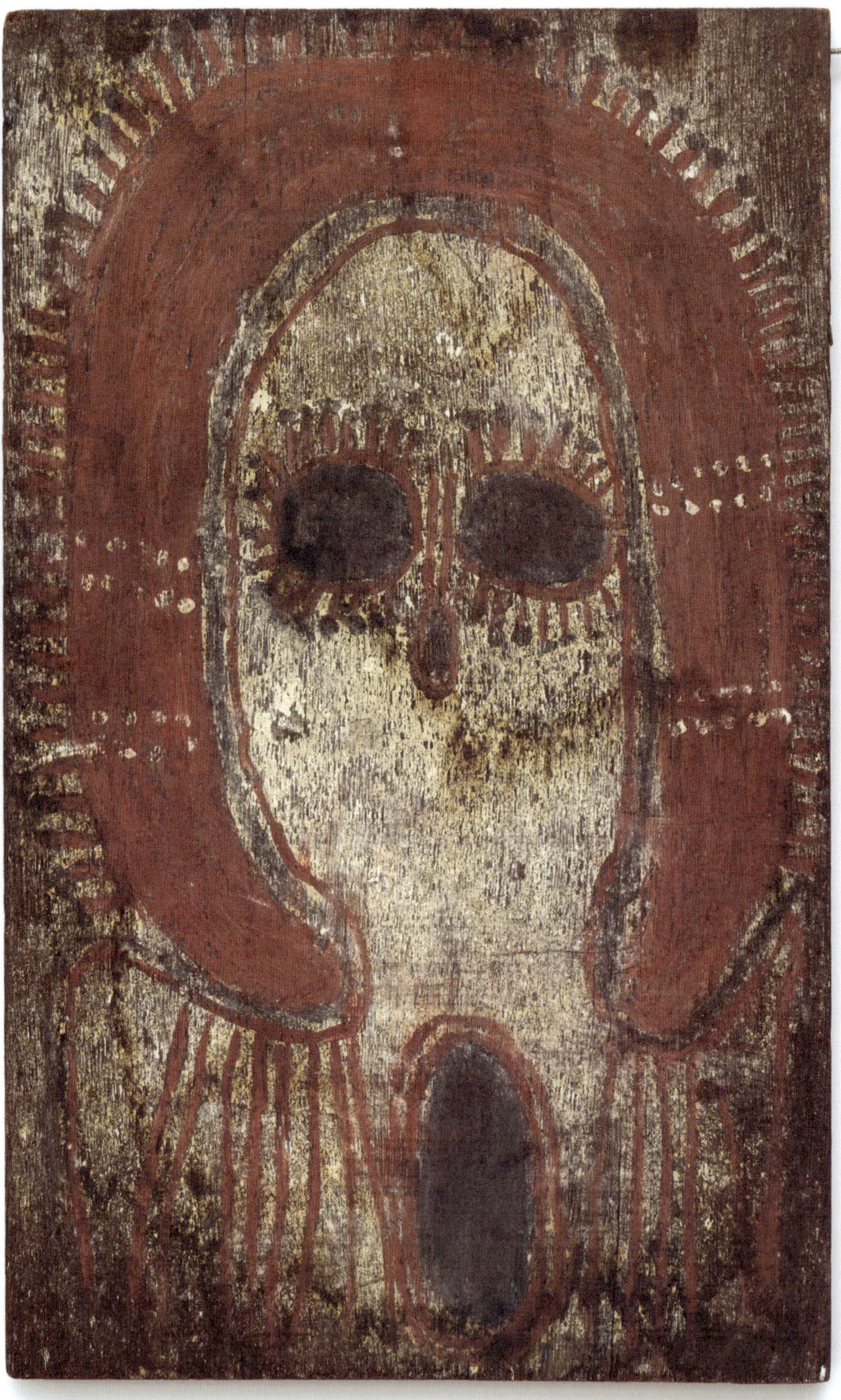

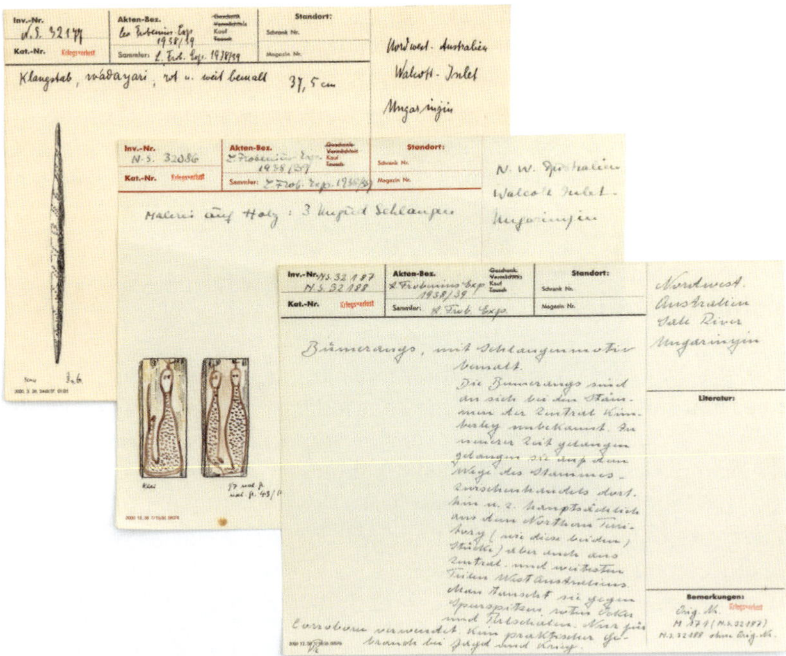

Fig. 3 *Wanjina* image on board from a wooden crate.
Ngarinyin. Walcott Inlet, Kimberley. Probably acquired
by Helmut Petri during the Frobenius Expedition
to Northwest Australia, 1938. Collection: Weltkulturen
Museum. Photo: Wolfgang Günzel, 2023

Fig. 4 Index cards of objects lost in the war: a
clapping stick and a painting on wood of a *Wunggurr*
Snake, with watercolour drawings by Agnes Schulz
and Gerta Kleist, plus index card of two boomerangs
with extensive description by Helmut Petri.
Collection: Weltkulturen Museum. Photo: Wolfgang
Günzel, 2024

easy to see. Fewer than half the objects (only 167 catalogue numbers) were recorded as described above. Only three index cards were accompanied by a drawing
done by Agnes Schulz or Gerta Kleist (fig. 4). Nonetheless, these documents are
particularly revealing with respect to the collection as it originally existed, because
Petri, with the memories of his Australian experiences still fresh in his mind, recorded meticulous details about the objects and categorised them thematically.

Celebrated and Lost

After the end of the war, Karin Hissink set about ensuring that Petri, now no longer held as a prisoner of war, should return to the museum and the institution in order to continue the evaluation of the research findings. As well as viewing his own records, the idea was that he would support the museum in returning the evacuated holdings and help recover the collections from what remained of the museum (Hissink 1945). What might Petri have been thinking as he stood in front of the ruins of the collection he had amassed and realised that all his work, plans and intentions had gone up in smoke amidst the chaos of war?

Acquisition histories

Nonetheless, by taking a look at the remaining field notes that are now in the Frobenius Institute we can glean some knowledge about the contexts in which the objects were acquired and the practices followed in collecting them. A vividly described example of acquiring an object is found in one of the expedition reports compiled by Douglas Fox (in the following cited after Fox 1938b: 18ff.). He had set up camp near the Kalingi-Odin rock art site with Agnes Schulz as well as with their Indigenous companions Munyat and Korelli and the latter pair's wives Dernowall and Aunie. It was here that Schulz recorded the rock art gallery with her striking paintings.

> *"On 1 August we saw a big cloud of smoke above the mountain to the north, and we knew that a 'mob' of blackfellows were hunting kangaroo. So, I made my way there with the two boys [Munyat and Korelli] and after a while we saw six completely naked hunters streaking through the blackened, burned and still smoking bush."*

Fox invited the group to come into camp the next morning, and was astonished when a total of twenty-five men of various ages appeared instead of the six from the day before, all requesting food. "I baked two huge loaves", wrote Fox, "and cooked a big meat dish. I was certainly not prepared for twenty-five people." After hosting the group, Fox tried to barter for a few objects, even though they "didn't have all that much with them, but in exchange for some tobacco I received half a dozen balls of baobab string and two tschanguns [hairstring belts] made of kangaroo hair, two lovely spearheads, a polished axe without a shaft, and three beautifully painted boomerangs".

After preparing a shared supper, Fox and Schulz sat down with their Ngarinyin guests and listened to their *Corroborees* [song and dance performances]:

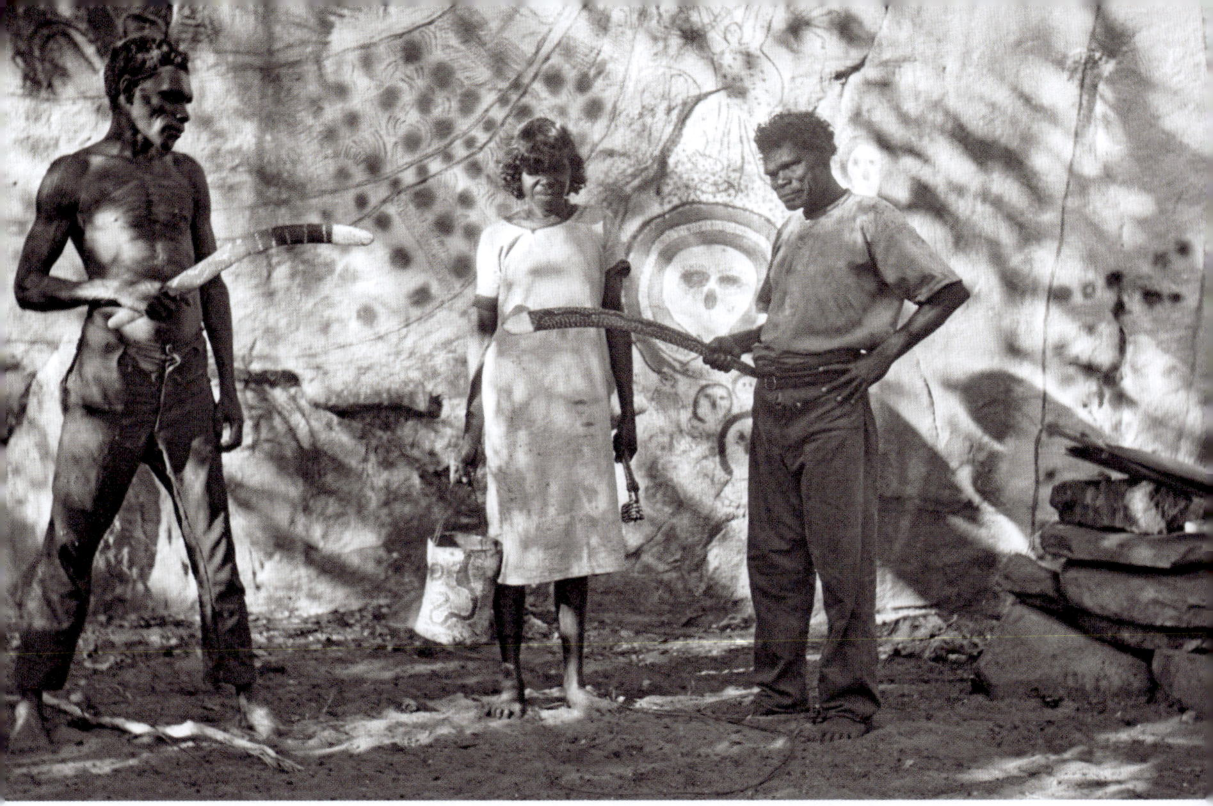

Fig. 5   Korelli, Aunie and Munyat present the objects that Douglas Fox has recently acquired in front of the main painting at the Kalingi-Odin rock art site: two boomerangs, a stone axe and a bark bucket. Collection: Frobenius Institute. Photo: Douglas Fox, 1938

Fig. 6   A bark bucket, *Karáki*, painted with a *Wunggurr* Snake. Ngarinyin. Walcott Inlet, Kimberley. Collected by Douglas Fox during the Frobenius Expedition to Northwest Australia, 1938. Collection: Weltkulturen Museum. Photo: Wolfgang Günzel, 2023

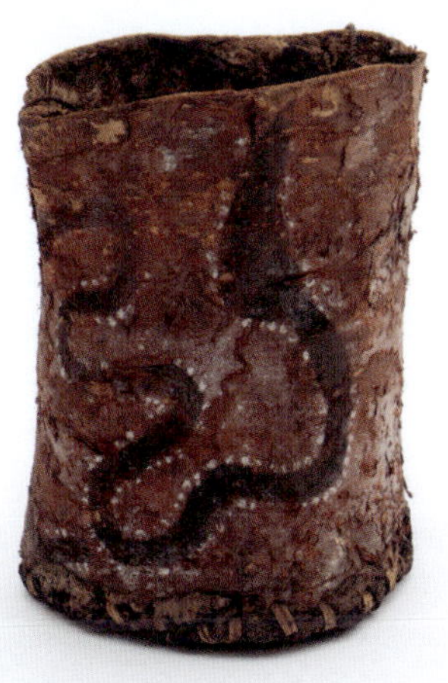

"At night the shadows of a dozen campfires flickered on the rocky walls of the gorge and the staccato sound of corroboree songs resonated."

Following breakfast the following morning, when Fox served the men a "huge quantity of wheat", as he wrote, the Ngarinyin wandered back towards their own camp. Fox accompanied them in the hope "of finding something that I could exchange for the rest of my tobacco. I also took a film camera, a Rolleiflex, sugar and tea with me".

Once they had reached the camp, where the Ngarinyin women were already waiting for their men, Fox immediately initiated the exchange process:

"I ordered tea to be made for everybody several times, with lots of sugar. They had no food. I didn't either, but intentionally so. If I had had some on me I would have had to share it with them – and then, with full stomachs, they would not have been quite so dependent on my remaining tobacco as the Völkermuseum needed them to be."

The haul was accordingly meagre, at least numerically speaking. Fox was nonetheless satisfied: "They are actually the best pieces we have." Apart from the rarely found "bush billy-cans" – small pails made of bark – there were two polished stone axes with a shaft, and a spearhead. One of the billy-cans described by Fox can be unequivocally identified in photos on account of its painted decoration, while the other objects presumably did not survive the tumult of war (fig. 6).

These accidental encounters and occasions frequently served as opportunities for bartering. The friendly and generous approach towards the Ngarinyin as well as the interest shown in their culture generated a sense of trust and aided the process of exchange based on mutual consent.

Moreover, the acquisition of ethnographic objects during the expedition was facilitated by what Helmut Petri termed a "system of intertribal trade" – the traditional *Wurnan* system of exchange. He identified a number of trading hubs or "meeting grounds" where various Aboriginal groups from surrounding parts of the country gathered to exchange *Corroborees*, for initiation ceremonies, and other rituals. At the same time these ritual events also provided an opportunity for "negotiating barters" (1950: 34). These gathering places thus served as a focal point for cultural exchange. "What is being exchanged", explains Petri, "comprises in the wider sense the entire material, and in some cases spiritual, cultural inventory of the Kimberley peoples." These include items such as stone spearheads, boomerangs, red ochre earth for ceremonial painting, bullroarers and decorated pearl shells (Petri 1950: 35).

In the era when the expedition took place, the repertoire of Indigenous gifts to be exchanged was already being supplemented by European goods. These primarily included pressed loose tobacco, tea, sugar, flour, bottle glass, iron shovels, wire, nails, tins of conserves, knives and axes. Petri notes that the European goods were viewed as being of equal value or higher (because of their rarity) and were integrated into the traditional bartering system (Petri 1950: 35).

Moreover, at the time of the Frobenius Expedition the pay for Indigenous employees on cattle farms and stations was composed exclusively of foodstuffs, clothing and tobacco rations. The relationship between farm owners and the Aboriginal workers on farms was also highly feudal in nature and characterised by exploitation (Skyring 2012: 155).

The goods with which Petri, Fox and Lommel paid for their acquisitions – as well as the ever-popular tobacco there was tea, sugar, flour, meat conserves and, in particular, strawberry jam – were regarded as appropriate by the Indigenous sellers, as the examples listed in this essay show. The Indigenous system of exchanging goods meant that pre-established values were used as the basis for negotiating gifts and what would be given in response.

Sacred wooden boards

Petri was particularly interested in changes to religious practices among the *Wanjina Wunggurr*. He identified one of the forms of "magic boards" as sacred objects from the deserts of Central Australia, and observed that they were among objects to have made the journey to the Kimberley region via traditional trading hubs. These objects facilitated the establishment of new cults, such as the gender restricted cult he described (Petri 1952). Fascinated by the complex trade network and the cultural transformation it wrought, Petri tried to purchase one of these sacred boards for the museum:

> *"We witnessed one of these trades in magic boards at the [ceremonial ground] on Sale river, and tried to acquire one for our collection. This desire triggered a huge and extremely lively palaver. Various men offered theirs, because we had promised a sack of flour and several jars of strawberry jam. This offer was regarded as not bad at all. Nonetheless, it took a fairly long time until Willy, the [ceremonial] boss, had given his consent for a Kunyu to be handed over"* (Petri 1952: 67f.).

It was the head or 'boss' of the particular ceremonial community who would negotiate the magic boards being bartered for pearl shells and foodstuffs, and he would then hand them on to the members of his cultic society in exchange for food. Without his permission it would have been impossible for Petri to even participate in the ceremony (Petri 1952: 67). In the expedition report he goes into more detail about how the acquisition proceeded:

> *"A ceremonial handover followed. The men formed a semi-circle and I had to stand in the middle. The Kunyu that was to be mine was buried in the ground at the edge of the Marallje [ceremonial square] [...] directly opposite where I was positioned. Then a man hurried out of the group, fetched the Kunyu, inserted it into the ground briefly in front of each person, and finally placed it in front of me. While this was happening the men struck their claves and sang extremely monotonously in a high-pitched voice [...] The Kunyu then belonged to me"* (Petri 1938c: 18–19).

Petri did, on the one hand, indulge in this kind of ceremonial exchange of gifts in order to find out more about the cultural contexts of the ritual, but at the same time he immediately disregarded the taboo beliefs that were associated with the sacred board he had acquired. He was never permitted to show the board to women or talk about it in their presence – this was a reference to Agnes Schulz and Gerta Kleist. Moreover, rather than being a purely secular bartering process it was actually an initiation into a cultic society. The previous owner of the board, Mengalilli, was henceforth known as Petri's "tribal brother". They were bound to each other by the exchange of gifts. In return, the former received a sack of flour from his "tribal brother" Petri, as well as some tea, sugar and tobacco. The headman of the cult site, who was in charge of the proceedings, also demanded a gift, and was satisfied with a jar of strawberry jam (Petri 1938c: 19).

Targeted acquisitions and systematic documentation

In addition to opportunistic acquisitions as described above, Petri, Fox and Lommel, in their role as collectors, also commissioned specific objects to be manufactured for the museum. A good example is the set of stone spearheads, whose production and use in situ must have made a great impression on all three researchers because they studied them extensively and reported on them in just as much detail in diaries, expedition reports and later publications (see Petri 1954 and 1952; Lommel 1952; Fox 1938b). In Petri's report dated 19 May, he lamented the fact that they had not yet been able to observe the men hunting, particularly for kangaroo, and had instead only been able to hear several detailed accounts (Petri 1938c:

21–22). But he was all the more impressed by the hunting weapons they used, particularly the spears with their stone heads shaped like laurel leaves, which were attached to a thin bamboo shaft by kangaroo sinews and spinifex or beeswax. Hunters were dependent on their spears, but the fine tips broke off easily and thus every adult Ngarinyin would know how to make stone spearheads, if for no other reason than to ensure they would have enough material for their own hunting (Petri 1938c: 22). This gave Petri and Fox the idea of documenting exhaustively how such an essential tool was made: "We filmed the individual steps, making notes and drawings along the way (fig. 7), and in addition to creating a collection of finished spearheads we also assembled a number of them at various stages of production" (Petri 1938c: 22).

Fox describes in detail how he immersed himself in the production of the spearheads over a period of three days with his Indigenous informant Umbagun. This included looking into the tools that were required and the process that was followed. He listed objects such as

> *"two bone tools made from the lower leg of a kangaroo, a wooden rod, paper bark and several stones"* (Fox 1938b: 15).

After the raw materials had been obtained, a kangaroo had been slain, dismembered and consumed, and all the tools had been made by Umbagun, the task at hand was to manufacture the stone tips:

> *"The material is worked from two edges and two sides until it becomes pointed. Then the retouching is done in the same manner with the Djumbi, the first piece of bone, and the fine serrations are carved out with the second piece, the Tingal. An experienced man would have to work hard all day long in order to produce a tip in this manner"* (Fox 1938b: 16).

The researchers enthusiastically assembled a fascinating collection: in addition to around fifty stone spearheads and other spearheads fashioned from bottle glass and window glass, the inventory lists sixteen bamboo spears with tips made of stone and glass. A number of tips with shafts were also collected, in order to illustrate how they were affixed. The collection, moreover, comprised several workpieces, stone tips at various stages of completion, and complete sets of tools for their production. These were supplemented by various surface finds of broken spearheads and flakes that were evidence of their production. Not only was the collection structured in a manner that made it possible to follow the production of raw stone through to the finished spear, it also documented the use of more recently introduced materials such as glass.

Tools for the production of spearheads – Ngarinyin

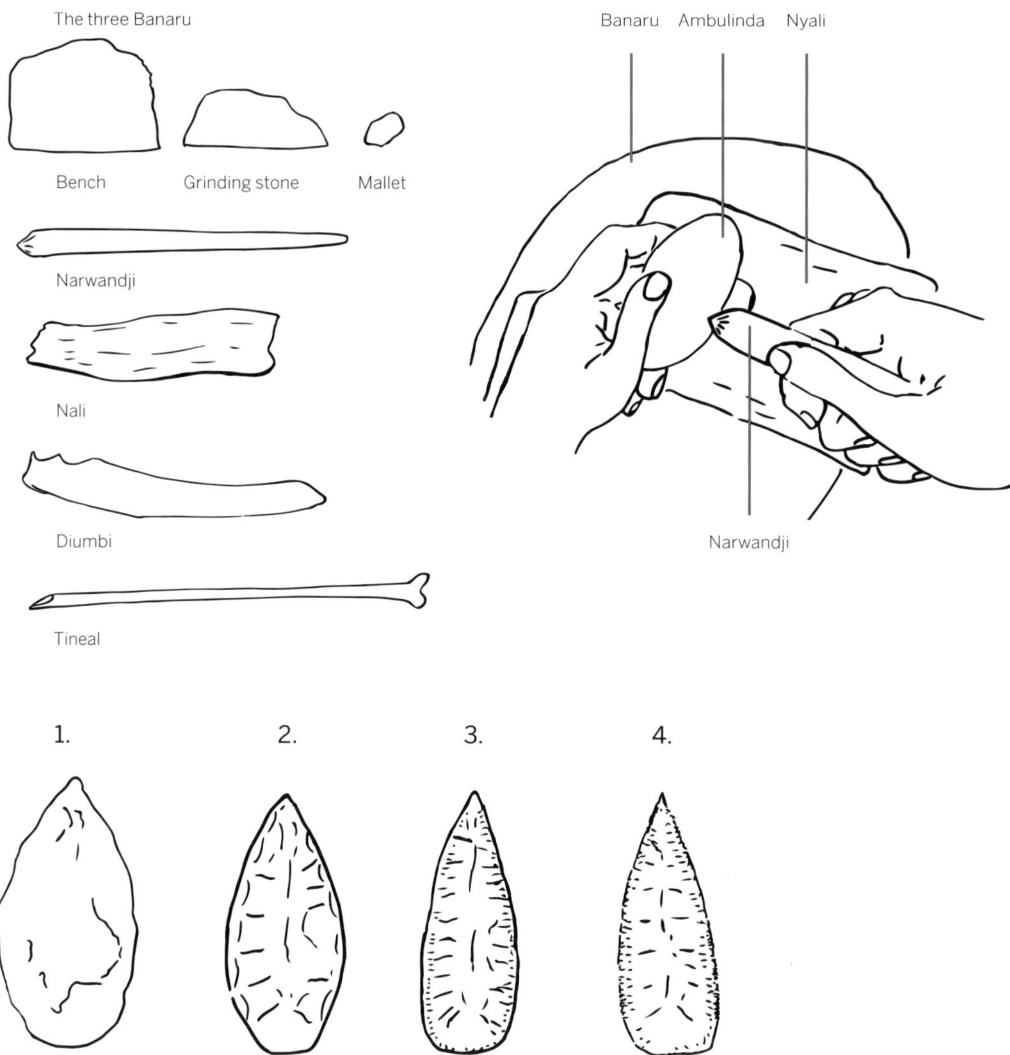

1.   after working with the Banaru
2.   after working with the Narwandji
3.   after working with the Djumbi
4.   after working with the Tinea

Fig. 7   Sketch of the tools and steps involved in manufacturing spearheads. From drawings in Douglas Fox's field notes, 1938. Collection: Frobenius Institute. Design by U9 visuelle Allianz

Only a minuscule portion of this extensive collection has survived: just thirteen stone spearheads that can be traced back to Andreas Lommel's collecting activities with the Wunambal (fig. 8), and six more spearheads of Ngarinyin origin that came from an exchange Petri agreed with the museum in Adelaide.

Bark paintings

At the heart of the *Wanjina Wunggurr* ethnographic collection is the set of bark and wood paintings, most of which were acquired as commissioned pieces during the expedition. The motifs they show overlap with those on the rock paintings to such an extent that the researchers ultimately concluded they only actually differed in terms of their material:

> *"These bark paintings are, with respect to their technique, colour, brushwork, and often their subject matter too, exactly the same as the rock paintings. The only difference is [that they are] stone rather than bark"* (Fox 1938c: 2).

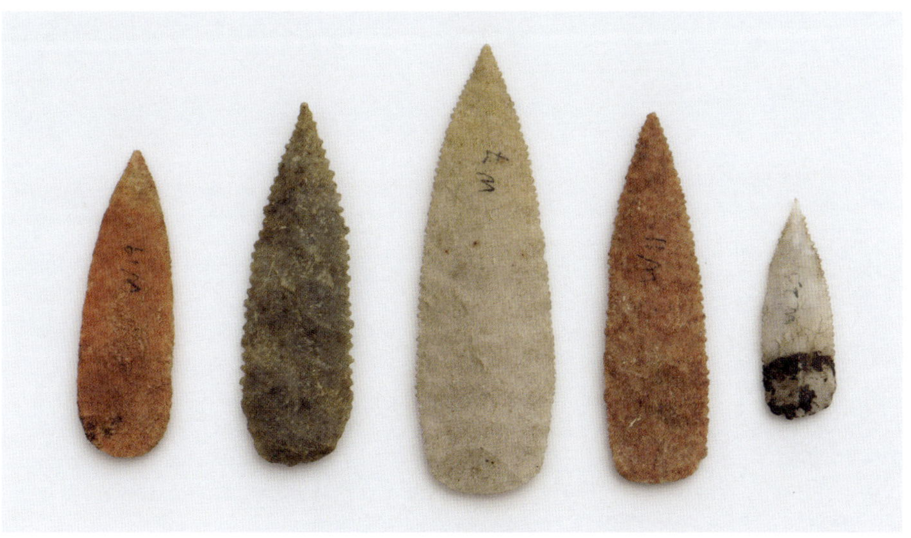

Fig. 8   Five spearheads from quartzitic sandstone. Wunambal. Woorewooddee, Kimberley. Acquired by Andreas Lommel during the Frobenius Expedition to Northwest Australia, 1938. Collection: Weltkulturen Museum. Photo: Wolfgang Günzel, 2023

Petri similarly sees the analogy to the rock paintings:

> *"Here too, it is impossible to describe them as new creations,*
> *because what is being depicted are strictly speaking copies:*
> *they paint local Wóndjina figures and Ungud snakes which have*
> *their galleries here somewhere in the Country"* (Petri 1954: 203).

The sheer number of assorted large paintings that originally existed is impressive. Petri, Fox and Lommel acquired a total of fifty paintings on bark, wood and cardboard. Only seven works on bark have remained out of this set, with four more made from the wood used for packing crates.

The researchers documented the process of manufacturing the paintings they had commissioned in Yaburunda, near Walcott Inlet (fig. 9): some white clay is chewed in the painter's mouth, then mixed with a little water and blown onto the inside of a dry piece of bark. The outlines of the head and eyes are sketched out in a red paint that is a mixture of ochre, spit and water, applied with the chewed end of a small twig. Using a somewhat thicker twig as a tool, the inside of the eye is filled in with ochre and then retraced in a mixture of water, spit and charcoal. Finally, the hair and eyelashes are added and the outlines of the shoulder are drawn in (Fox 1938a: 47).

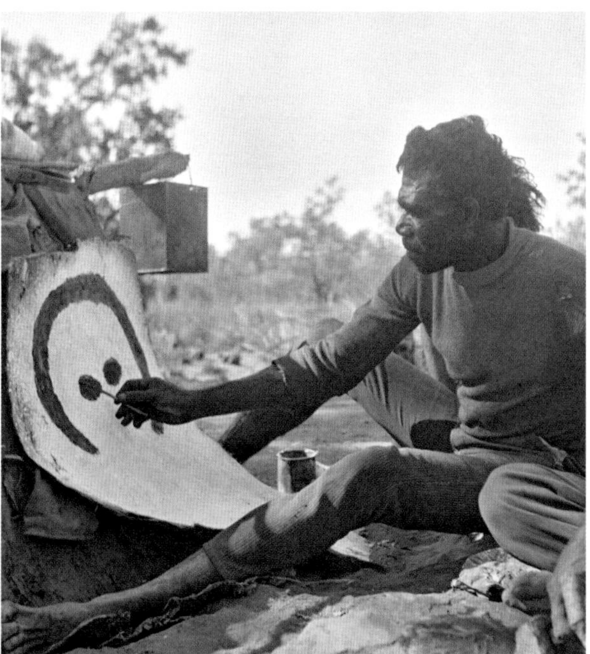

Fig. 9   Making of a bark painting as documented in Yaburunda. Commissioned for the museum collection, this bark painting was later destroyed in the war. Collection: Frobenius Institute. Photo: Douglas Fox or Helmut Petri, 1938

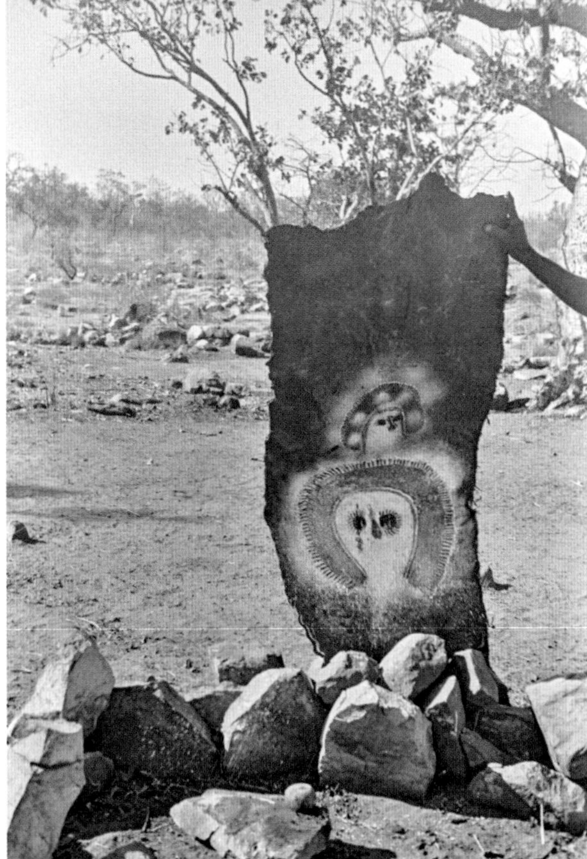

Fig. 10   The bark painting erected in the stone circle in Yaburunda. Collection: Frobenius Institute. Photo: Douglas Fox (presumed), 1938

Ritual bark painting

According to Akerman (2000: 228), representations of *Wanjina* and *Wunggurr* motifs had been painted on eucalyptus bark or packing-case wood since the 1930s, upon the instigation of missionaries and ethnologists. This means that the paintings collected in the course of the 1938 expedition are today among the oldest manifestations of this early form of commissioned art. Yet there is also evidence that the traditional motifs were once painted on bark for ritual purposes, too. A rare example of the ritual use of a bark painting was observed by Petri and Fox in Yaburunda, at a traditional gathering place in the district of Gungunda, a few miles from Walcott Inlet:

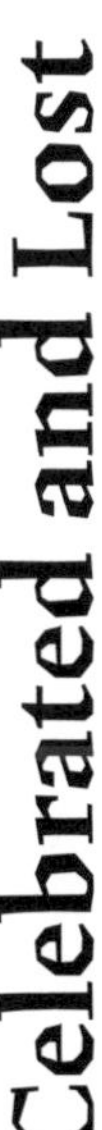

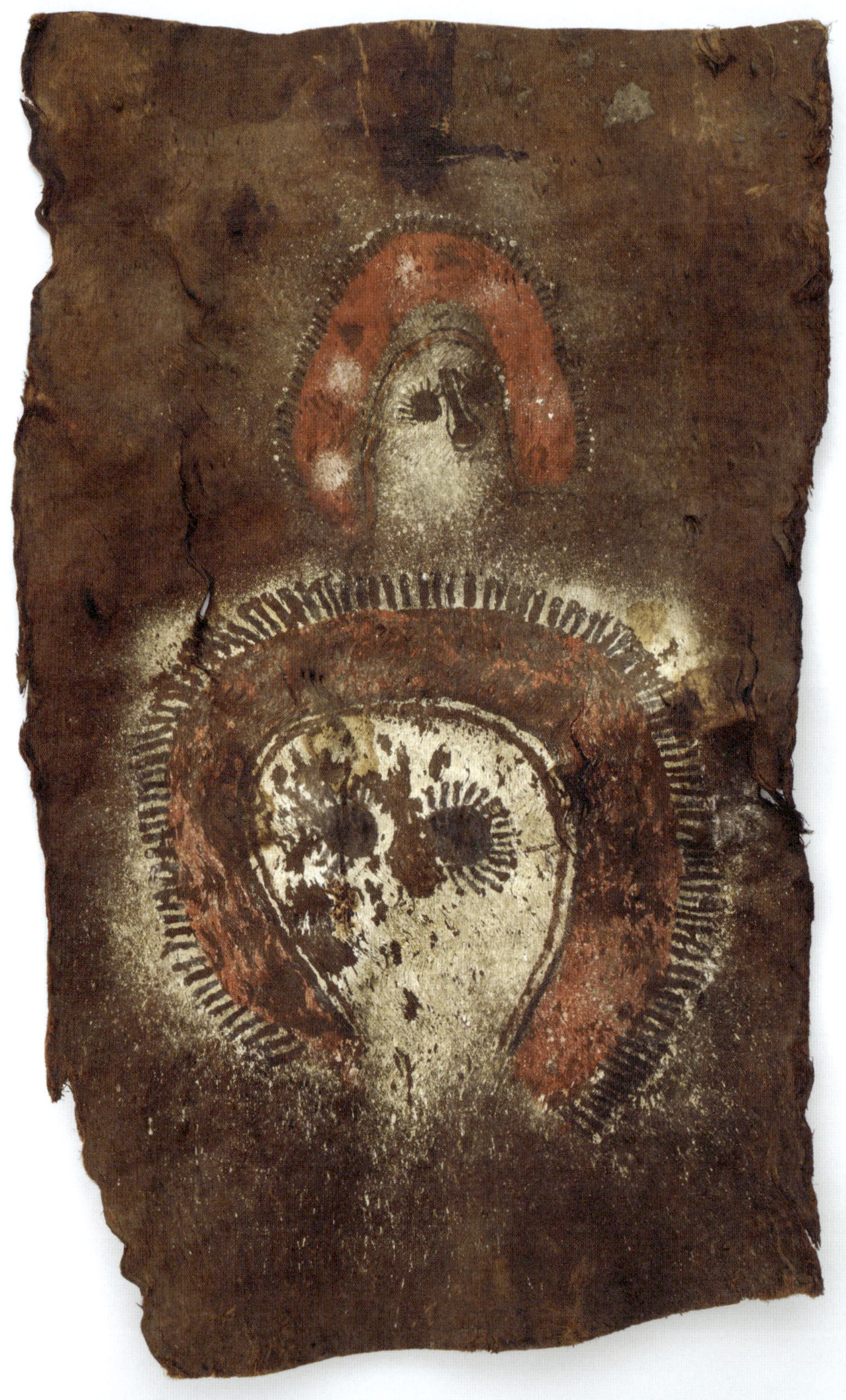

Fig. 11   The bark painting of the *Wanjina Yilmpudmara* which was erected in the stone circle at the traditional meeting place Yaburunda and later acquired by Helmut Petri and Douglas Fox. Ngarinyin. Walcott Inlet, Kimberley. Frobenius Expedition, 1938. Collection: Weltkulturen Museum. Photo: Wolfgang Günzel, 2023

"Monday, 13 June […] Moving northwards, we crossed the muddy inlet at low tide and went to Gungunda, a native camp. The two men who look after the banana grove live there, under 'breakwinds' and sunshades […] In the middle of the camp was the low stone circle, which we had photographed on 10 May, the last time we were there. […] a large curved piece of bark stood there, with two Wondjina heads painted on its inner side. […] All that could be ascertained was that it was designed with rain in mind ('cold fella come down'), perhaps because the bananas that the painter was in charge of were failing to thrive: as a consequence, he would rather have rain now in the dry season" (Fox 1938c: 2).

The stone circle at the end of which the bark painting had been erected belongs to a particular type of ritual place in Kimberley, which Petri called "stone or megalithic propagation sites" (Petri 1954: 207). In addition to refreshing the paintings in the rock art galleries, certain round stones were rubbed at these sites as annual cyclical propagation rites that would ritually assure the presence of edible plants, game and rain. Neither Petri nor Fox were able to discover much more from the camp's residents about the meaning and purpose of the stone circle. They were simply told that "the medicine man […] would go there in order to make rain" and that the stone circle was named Yilmpud and the local *Wanjina* was called Yilmpudmara (Petri 1954: 210). This was the same mythical ancestor depicted on the bark painting (fig. 10 and 11).

A few days later, Petri and Fox purchased the bark painting – after it had fulfilled its ritual purpose – for a few jars of strawberry jam and some tobacco. In addition, they asked the producer to make some more paintings for them and promised that they would pay the same price (Fox 1938c: 8). It is an immense stroke of luck that specifically this bark painting survived the chaos of war, given that it is described so extensively and the circumstances of its acquisition are documented so precisely. Unfortunately, the field notes do not tell us how many bark paintings Petri and Fox later received from the artist in Yaburunda. But by looking through the inventory we can identify at least two more paintings, which are listed as bark paintings depicting "Yaburunda Wondjina" and "Gugunda Wondjina". These two works were sadly lost during the war.

Conclusion

Although the devastation of the war years wrought gaping holes in what had once been a magnificent collection, and these losses cast a long shadow on the comparatively modest 'remains', it is difficult to resist being drawn in by them. Not only do the objects give us an intriguing glimpse into the culture of the *Wanjina Wunggurr* in the late 1930s, they are also the end result of the complex relationships between the researchers and their Indigenous partners during the expedition. Just like the photos, field notes, rock art copies and research reports, they also tell the story of the Frobenius Expedition to Northwest Australia.

Fig. 12   Andreas Lommel documented the making of the *Wanjina* image (see fig. 3) by an unnamed Wunambal artist before he acquired the painting. Collection: Frobenius Institute. Photo: Andreas Lommel, 1938

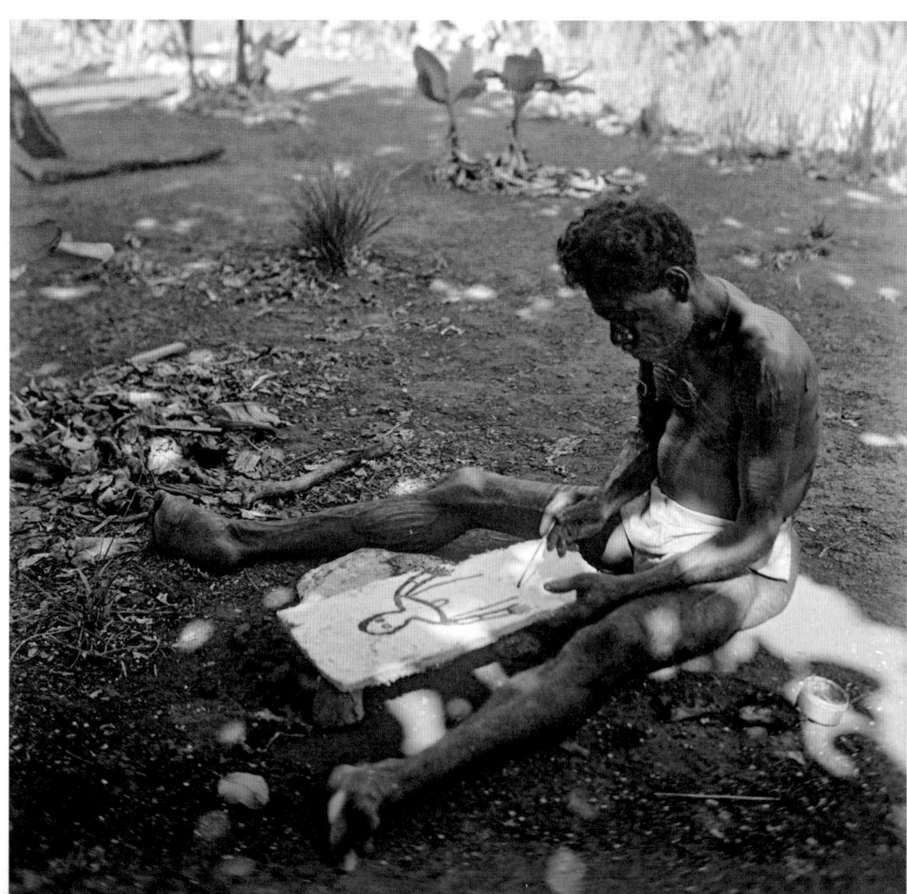

Helmut Petri was only able to utilise the surviving parts of the collection for his expedition report on the "dying world in Northwest Australia", in which he emphasised his deep respect for the artistic expressiveness of *Wanjina Wunggurr* material culture, as reflected in those examples. It was true, he wrote, that the material culture was "simple, concise and limited in form" but "at the same time, one should not on any account confuse this with cultural poverty". In fact, the overall cultural inventory was "expedient and perfectly formed". If we look at the evidence of material culture, encompassing everything from stone spearheads to painted bark billy-cans and spear throwers, and ultimately the impressive bark paintings, with the style "of such paintings revealing [...] a surprising artistic sensibility and pleasure taken in beautiful colour compositions" (Petri 1954: 44).

Anyone who spends any time with this collection will undoubtedly support his conclusion, and will moreover discover a continuum between the ethnographic objects of the past and the wonderful *Wanjina Wunggurr* art of the present day, which is no less artistic in nature.

References:

Agthe, Johanna. 1994: *Wer jetzt kein Haus hat, kriegt auch keines mehr. Zur Geschichte des Frankfurter Museums für Völkerkunde.* Frankfurt am Main: Museum für Völkerkunde.

Akerman, Kim. 2000: The Traditional Aboriginal Art of the Kimberley Region. In: Sylvia Kleinert and Margo Neale (eds): *The Oxford Companion to Aboriginal Art and Culture.* Melbourne et al.: Oxford University Press. 226–230.

Deutsche Gelehrte erforschen Australien: Das Geheimnis uralter Felsbilder enträtselt. In: *Münsterischer Anzeiger.* 12.04.1939. Unpaginated.

Fox, Douglas C. 1938a: *Tagebuch.* 19.05.1938 – 18.08.1938 (unpublished archival source). Frankfurt am Main: Archive of the Frobenius Institute, HP 030-1.

Fox, Douglas C. 1938b: *Expeditions-Bericht.* 04.08.1938 (unpublished archival source). Frankfurt am Main: Archive of the Frobenius Institute, HP 028.

Fox, Douglas C. 1938c: *Expeditions-Bericht.* 19.07.1938 (unpublished archival source). Frankfurt am Main: Archive of the Frobenius Institute, HP 027.

Götter und Dämonen Australiens. In: *Kölnische Zeitung.* 09.04.1939. No. 180: 6.

Hervorragende Ergebnisse der Petri-Expedition. In: *Hamburger Abendblatt.* 19.07.1939: 2.

Hissink, Karin. 1945: *Antrag auf Weiterbeschäftigung des aus der Gefangenschaft zurückgekehrten Dr. Petri.* Archive of the Frobenius Institute. Verwaltungsarchiv, VA 2820-07.

Lommel, Andreas. 1952: *Die Unambal: Ein Stamm in Nordwest-Australien.* Monographien zur Völkerkunde 2. Hamburg: Museum für Völkerkunde.

Neuaufstellung im Völkermuseum: Die Forschungsergebnisse der Australien-Expedition. In: *Frankfurter Zeitung.* 15.07.1939. Unpaginated.

Petri, Helmut. 1954: *Sterbende Welt in Nordwest-Australien.* Braunschweig: Albert Limbach Verlag.

Petri, Helmut. 1950: Wandlungen in der geistigen Kultur nordwestaustralischer Stämme. In: *Special Edition of the Veröffentlichungen aus dem Museum für Natur-, Völker- und Handelskunde in Bremen.* Series B. No. 1: 33–121.

Petri, Helmut. 1939: Zauber und schwarze Magie in Nordwestaustralien. In: *Kölnische Zeitung.* 05.11.1939. Sonntagsblatt No. 561: 7.

Petri, Helmut. 1938a: *Expeditions-Bericht.* 14.07.1938 (unpublished archival source). Frankfurt am Main: Archive of the Frobenius Institute, HP 012.

Petri, Helmut. 1938b: *Expeditions-Bericht.* 09.06.1938 (unpublished archival source). Frankfurt am Main: Archive of the Frobenius Institute, HP 011.

Petri, Helmut. 1938c: *Expeditions-Bericht.* 19.05.1938 (unpublished archival source). Frankfurt am Main: Archive of the Frobenius Institute, HP 010.

Petri, Helmut. 1938d: *Expeditions-Bericht.* 16.05.1938 (unpublished archival source). Frankfurt am Main: Archive of the Frobenius Institute, HP 009.

Skyring, Fiona. 2012: Low Wages, Low Rents, and Pension Cheques: The Introduction of Equal Wages in the Kimberley, 1968–1969. In: Natasha Fijn et al. (eds): *Indigenous Participation in Australian Economies II.* https://doi.org/10.22459/IPAE.07.2012.08

Strehlow, Carl. 1907–1920: *Die Aranda- und Loritja-Stämme in Zentral-Australien.* Veröffentlichungen aus dem Städtischen Völker-Museum I, in 5 vols. Frankfurt am Main: Baer.

Vorgeschichtliche Kulturen in Australien: Der Abschluß der 2. Frobenius-Expedition in Australien. In: *Kölnische Zeitung.* 05.03.1939: 3.

Andreas and Katharina Lommel

as Researchers in the Kimberley

Michaela Appel

ndreas Lommel (1912–2005) was Head of the South Seas Department at the Museum Fünf Kontinente in Munich[1] from 1948 to 1956 and director of the same institution from 1957 to 1977. He had originally studied Chinese and Japanese language, art and culture in Munich and then moved to what is now known as the Frobenius Institute in Frankfurt am Main in 1935. Leo Frobenius (1873–1938), who founded the Forschungsinstitut für Kulturmorphologie (Research Institute for Cultural Morphology) in 1923, was particularly interested in rock paintings as the earliest documents of human culture. He tried to decode them, to compare them and to set up an archive of copies of rock paintings from all over the world.

To build up this 'world rock art archive', Frobenius organised expeditions to Africa, Spain, Norway, the Middle East, to the Moluccas and to Northwest New Guinea and finally Australia. However, unlike the places they had travelled to so far, in Australia the Frobenius researchers had the opportunity to meet people who had painted or repainted these rock paintings themselves and were able to explain their meaning.

In the late 1930s, when Lommel was asked by Frobenius whether he would like to take part in an expedition to Australia, he saw his chance, said "yes" – unlike two other students – and began preparations for this expedition (Lommel 1997a: V-VI).

Katharina Lommel, née Marr (1911–2004), was also closely associated with the Frobenius Institute even before her marriage in 1949. As a trained graphic artist and advertising designer, she had already worked at the institute as a scientific draughtswoman for fifteen years and taken part in five expeditions to Jordan and Libya, France, Spain and Italy (Stappert 2019). The fact that Andreas and Katharina Lommel would once again go on a research trip together to Australia in 1954–55, in particular to the Kimberley region, was a logical continuation of their work for the two 'Frobenius students'.

Andreas Lommel and the Frankfurt Frobenius Expedition 1938–39

The aim of the 1938–39 Frobenius Expedition was to explore the culture of the Ngarinyin, Woddordda and Wunambal, on whose lands the rock paintings known to Europeans since 1838 can be found, and who are known today as the *Wanjina Wunggurr* cultural community. The leader of the expedition, Helmut Petri, was an anthropologist, an assistant at the Frobenius Institute and had worked for a time at the Städtisches Völkermuseum in Frankfurt. Other participants were Agnes Susanne Schulz and Gerta Kleist, both artists with experience in copying rock paintings, and Douglas C. Fox, an American journalist with an interest in rock paintings.[2] In Australia, the linguist Arthur Capell and the psychology student Patrick Pentony also joined the expedition for a period.

The starting point of the expedition in the Kimberley region was initially the Munja government station at Walcott Inlet and the Kunmunya Mission. Agnes Schulz and Gerta Kleist were guided to different rock painting sites in the vicinity of the station by Aboriginal guides from Munja. Fox and Lommel accompanied them in turns, whereas Petri tried to find knowledgeable persons amongst the Indigenous population to work with. Lommel accompanied Schulz and Kleist to Modum, Maliba and Koralyi and joined them again in Marie Springs, the small peanut farm belonging to Bob Thompson on the headwaters of the Glenelg River. Here he worked with the Aboriginal guides, tended horses and camels, hunted with these men and listened to their stories – only making notes afterwards in order not to spoil the atmosphere (Lommel 1997a: VII).

Later, when Helmut Petri made an overland trip from Sale River to Kalumburu, Lommel stayed with Agnes Schulz and Gerta Kleist in Marie Springs. While they copied rock paintings from the surrounding sites, Lommel was introduced to the poet Allan Balbunga and later to ritual performances. It was during this visit that Lommel first met the Aboriginal boy David Mowaljarlai (fig. 1), who was then about ten or twelve years old (Mowaljarlai and Malnic [1993] 2001: X) and who later became a well-known author, artist and activist.

During the expedition Lommel focused on the Wunambal. From his publications it seems that his interests – apart from rock paintings – were initiation ceremonies, the role of the healer *(Banman)* and ritual performances. He took impressive photographs of some of these events, which are now held by the Frobenius Institute in Frankfurt am Main.

Although Lommel met members of all three groups of the *Wanjina Wunggurr* community, the artefacts he collected in 1938 are mostly from the Wunambal and include: painted bark containers, spear throwers, spear points made from stone, ceramic and glass as well as bark paintings which are now in the Museum Fünf Kontinente in Munich (Lommel 1997b: 4).

With respect to the rock paintings, Agnes Schulz and Gerta Kleist primarily copied depictions of the *Wanjina*, the ancestral creators of the Ngarinyin, Woddordda and Wunambal. *Wanjina* are among the most powerful supernatural beings portrayed in Kimberley rock art. Painted using natural earth pigments that were generally applied over a white background made of the mineral huntite, *Wanjina* typically have a horseshoe-shaped ring encircling their heads. They appear as solitary paintings or in groups, and most figures are frontal images that depict the

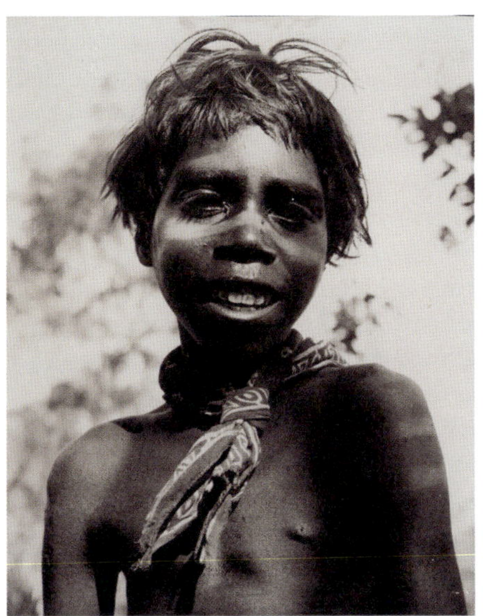 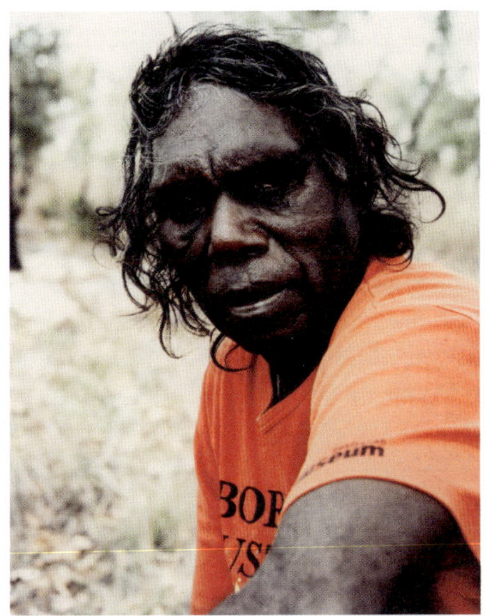

Fig. 1   David Banggal Mowaljarlai (1925–1997) at the age of about 12 during the Frobenius Expedition and at the age of about 60. Collection: Frobenius Institute. Photo: Andreas Lommel, 1938 and Collection: Museum Fünf Kontinente. Photo: Jutta Malnic, 1988

entire body or just the head and shoulders. There are both male and female *Wanjina*. A range of other paintings are associated with these figures, including depictions of plants and animals, some of which are said to be *Wanjina* in their animal or plant form. Paintings of snakes are common. They are among the many manifestations of an ancestral creator Snake called *Wunggurr* who, along with the *Wanjina*, is especially prominent in the cosmology of the *Wanjina Wunggurr* people. However, Schulz and Fox also found paintings known today as *Gwion Gwion*, slender little human-like figures depicted in highly animated dancing and hunting poses (Blundell and Woolagoodja 2012). Agnes Schulz was the first who referred to them as "Bradshaw paintings" (Schulz 1956: 45ff.) after Joseph Bradshaw, who discovered them in Kimberley rock art sites in 1891 while assessing the area's potential for cattle breeding (Bradshaw 1892).

The expedition returned to Germany shortly before the outbreak of World War II. However, only a small publication accompanying the exhibition on the results of the expedition could be printed in 1939 (Petri et al. 1939). Andreas Lommel's further publications on the results of the expedition were – like those of his colleagues – delayed by World War II. He was first offered the opportunity to publish some of his results in the journal *Oceania* (1949; 1950) – years before he could publish his study of the Wunambal (1952) in German.

Andreas Lommel was drafted into the army and was initially stationed in France and Russia until he was transferred to Rommel's Africa Corps as an interpreter, where he became a British prisoner of war in Egypt. Lommel returned to Munich in 1946 and initially worked for the Bayerischer Rundfunk before being employed at the Staatliches Museum für Völkerkunde in Munich in 1948. Initially he was primarily responsible for the repatriation of the evacuated objects and the reconstruction of the partially destroyed museum. In 1952–54 he was appointed deputy director and curator for the South Pacific and Australia due to the departure of the director, Heinrich Ubbelohde-Doering, on a research trip to Peru. With the support of Katharina Lommel as a volunteer and in collaboration with the American diplomat and art patron Stefan P. Munsing, the director of the Central Collecting Point[3] in Munich, Lommel was able to present two exhibitions outside the museum in 1949 and 1952, before the Staatliches Museum für Völkerkunde reopened in 1954 with the exhibition *Asiatische Kunst* (Asian Art) (Stappert 2021).

The Munich Australia Expedition 1954–55

In December 1954, Andreas and Katharina Lommel set off from Munich on their joint expedition to Australia and the Kimberley region, which was financed by the German Research Foundation. Their main aim was to find and copy further rock paintings, but also to gain more insights into art, mythology and ritual performance.

On 2 January 1955, Andreas and Katharina Lommel arrived in Perth on a Lloyd Triestino steamer. They initially worked in the museums of Perth, Sydney, Melbourne and Adelaide before continuing their research in the Kimberley region. In these museums Katharina Lommel was able to make numerous copies of bark paintings and other objects together with rubbings of ornamented ritual artefacts, which are no longer accessible to the public (Lommel 1955).[4] Today, it seems rather unusual to make such artistic copies of museum artefacts. However, Andreas and Katharina Lommel believed that the copies could be used in exhibitions to provide an overview of the art of Australia as a whole, of stylistic groupings and perhaps even developments. Copies would enable scientific research and comparisons, while the originals would remain in situ and not be damaged (Lommel 1997b: 7).

In 1954, Andreas and Katharina Lommel had written to a number of stations in the Northwest of Australia where they knew there must be rock painting sites. The owners either failed to answer or flatly refused their request for assistance. The only helpful reply came from Gibb River station and the Russ family. As it turned out later, the farmer's wife, Laura Booty – an Aboriginal woman – and his head stockman[5], Joe White, had met Andreas Lommel during his previous visit to the Kimberley in 1938, and still remembered him.[6]

Andreas and Katharina Lommel travelled from Adelaide by train to Alice Springs and from there to Darwin, Wyndham and Gibb River by plane. They stayed at the station from May to September 1955 – during the dry season – and Fred Russ provided them with Aboriginal guides who knew the sites where rock paintings could be found. Their main guide, whose name was Nipper, was "a tall, powerful, man, who was also very knowledgeable" (Lommel and Lommel 1989: 15). He was accompanied by his second wife, Jabel, and his four-year-old son, Jerry, from his first marriage. They rode to the sites on horseback, with mules to carry their camping equipment and drawing utensils, where they stayed and worked for several days or even weeks while the Aboriginal people tended to the animals (fig. 2).

The sites where Katharina Lommel copied a total of thirty five rock paintings are all in the area around Gibb River station and on Ngarinyin Country. Their names are Molcott, Awulen, Nallanganda, Wanalirri and Sundron[7]. All these sites feature *Wanjina* or Snakes and the smaller *Gwion Gwion* paintings.

Fig. 2   Andreas Lommel with Nipper and Jabel at the rock art site Wanalirri. Collection: Museum Fünf Kontinente. Photo: Katharina Lommel, 1955

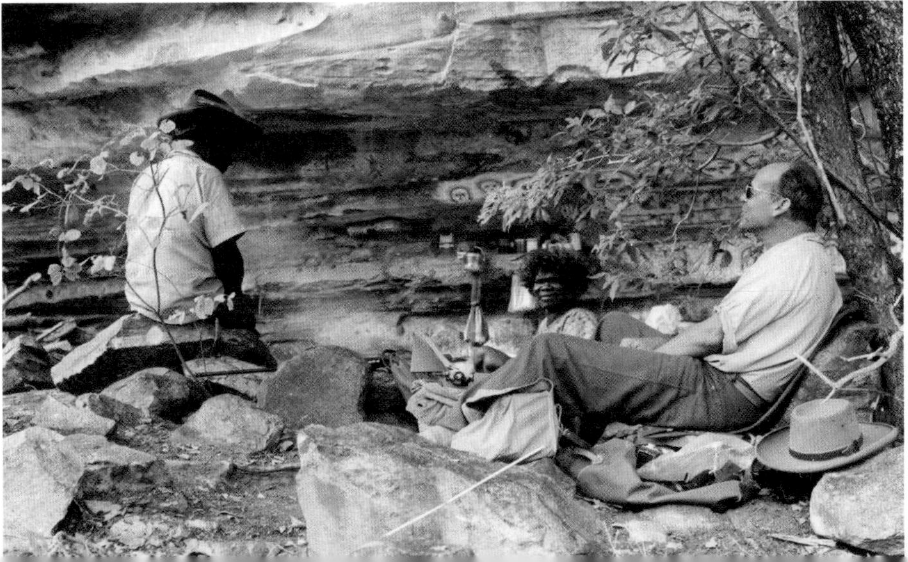

Andreas and Katharina Lommel

During the copying process the rock paintings had to be touched, although the Lommels had been advised by their Aboriginal guides not to do so. They and their ancestors had not painted the pictures, and they themselves only touched them when repainting to promote rain and fertility and to ensure the survival of the animals depicted. The touch of a stranger – one never knew – could bring disaster! On a number of occasions rain did indeed fall in the middle of the dry season. While Fred Russ merely commented that their work was evidently good for the grass, it was viewed critically by the Aboriginal people (Lommel and Lommel 1989: 15–16). Indeed, they still talk about the fact that the Lommels touched the rock paintings to this day.

At Molcott, the first rock art site the Lommels visited in May 1955 (fig. 3 and 4), the main image of four snakes had obviously undergone recent repainting. On the ground beneath the painting[8] they found several bark palettes, together with lumps of paint and chewed sticks which had been used to apply the colour (Lommel and Lommel 1989: 28–29).

The main painting at Wanaliri shows Wojin, the dangerous, powerful *Wanjina* who features in a story shared by the Ngarinyin, Woddordda and Wunambal people, the story of Dumbi, the owl:

> *"[Wojin] raged when he heard how two boys had teased and hurt Dumbi, plucked his feathers, flicked the naked little bird with speargrass and had then thrown him into the air: 'Now see how you can fly!' When Dumbi told the Wandjina his misfortune, Wojin brought on an enormous flood that killed all people in the area – except the two mischievous boys. They hid in the pouch of a kangaroo and started the whole tribe afresh"* (Mowaljarlai and Malnic [1993] 2001: 15).

Wojin is holding *Guloi*, a native plumtree with sweet green fruit (fig. 5). As the tree of life the *Guloi* tree *(Terminalia carpentariae)* is a symbol of birth and regeneration, revered in numerous rock paintings as a visual metaphor for the step-by-step acquisition of knowledge and its transmission (Doring 2000: 323).

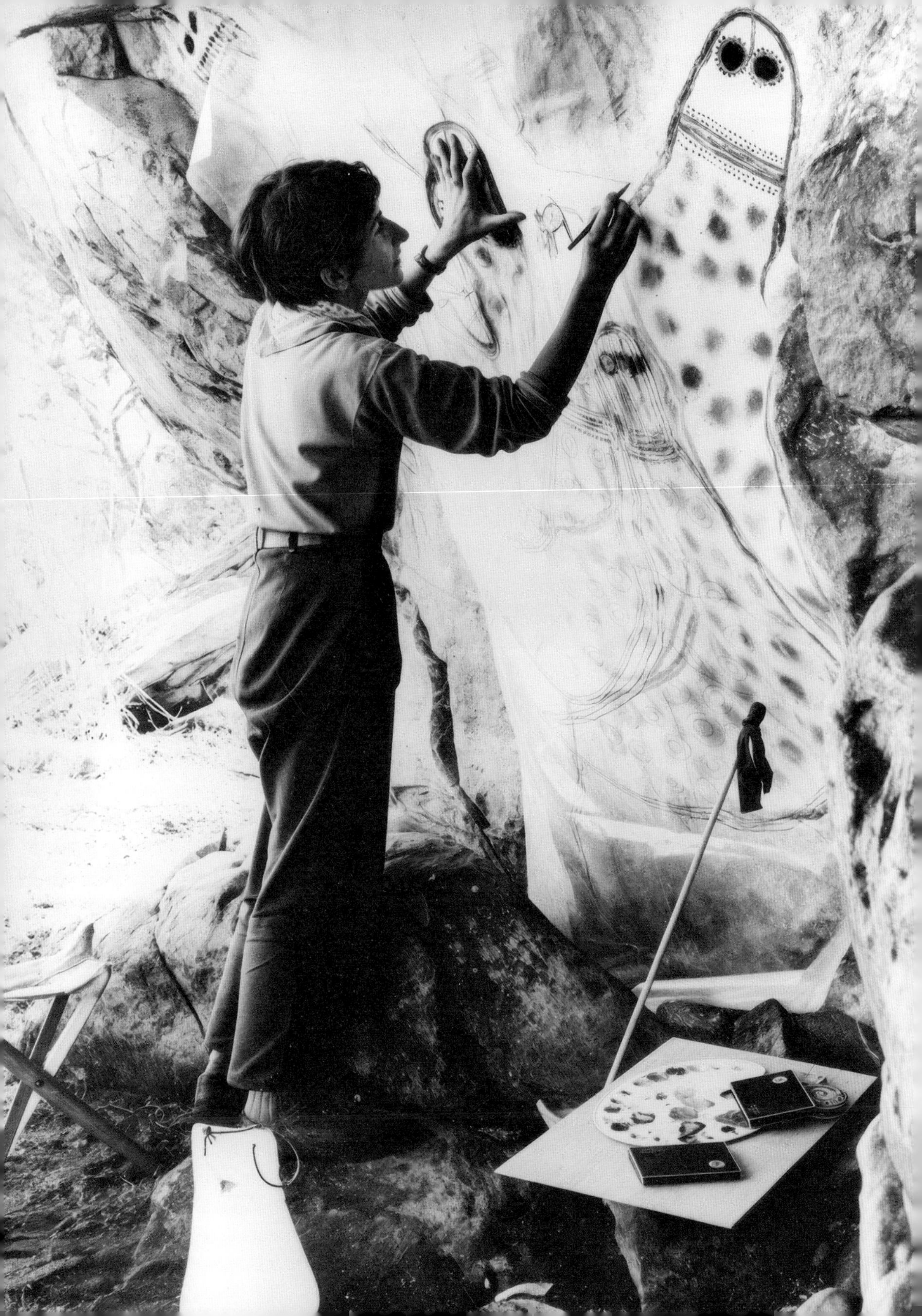

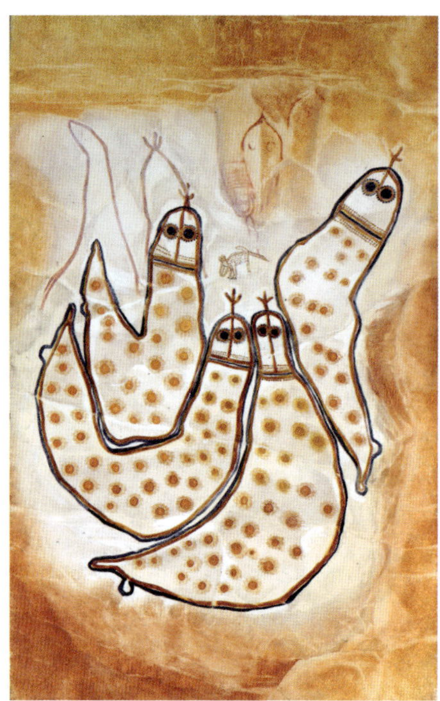

Fig. 4   Four Snakes, Molcott rock art site. Kimberley, Northwest Australia. Watercolours on canvas. 152 x 247 cm. Rock art copy by Katharina Lommel, 1955. Collection: Museum Fünf Kontinente. Photo: Marianne Franke, 2023

Fig. 5   *Wanjina* with plumtree, Wanalirri rock art site. Kimberley, Northwest Australia. Watercolours on canvas. 573 x 153 cm. Rock art copy by Katharina Lommel, 1955. Collection: Museum Fünf Kontinente. Photo: Nicolai Kästner, 2024

In Lommel's publications this painting has the title "*Wanjina* with Plumtree", but, unfortunately, the story of Wojin and Dumbi the owl is missing in his commentary.

After their return to Germany, Andreas and Katharina Lommel conceived the exhibition *Die Kunst des fünften Erdteils* (The Art of the Fifth Continent) presenting the results of their research expedition, which opened on 8 June 1959 and was subsequently also shown in Amsterdam (van Baal 1960). From the exhibition catalogue (1959) and Andreas Lommel's further publications it is clear that he was less interested in documenting the religious beliefs of the people and the associated mythical content and meanings of the rock paintings in a particular region such as the Kimberley, than in broader theoretical questions such as style regions, the spread of certain motifs or the relationship between cultures, which identify him as a student of Frobenius (see e.g. Lommel 1961, 1970). The notion of the "degeneration" of art and of the "psychological decay" of the people comes up repeatedly.

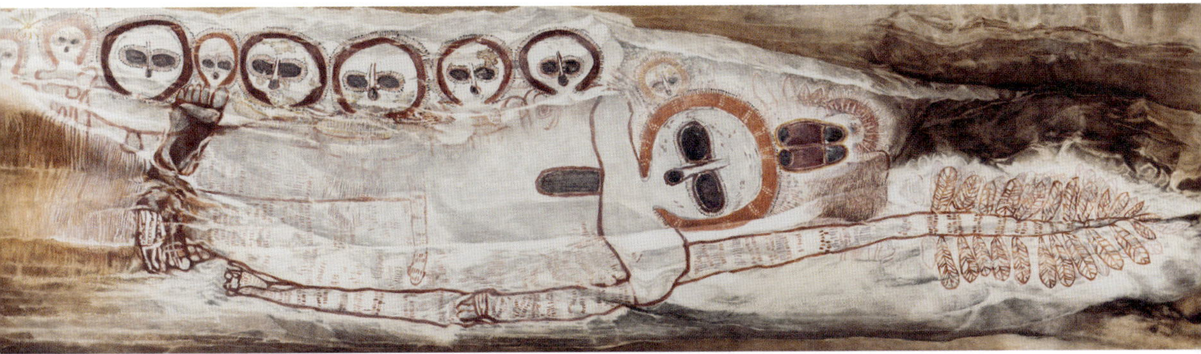

Lommel's theories on rock painting styles (1970) led to harsh criticism by the Australian archaeologist Lesley Maynard (1979: 89, 109, note 1). His book *Fortschritt ins Nichts* (Progress into Nothingness) (1969) also provoked very different reactions. While Theodor Strehlow (1973) judges it very positively, Helmut Petri (1970) vehemently contradicts – among other things – the concept of a general cultural degeneration of Aboriginal people by an author "who draws exclusively from within himself" because his views in this book are not substantiated in any way (see also Beinssen-Hesse 1991).

The same pessimism is still expressed in the publication *Die Kunst des alten Australien* (The Art of Ancient Australia) (1989) which accompanied the last exhibition Andreas and Katharina Lommel had the honour of conceiving for the Museum Fünf Kontinente on the occasion of the Australian bicentenary year 1988. It is here that Lommel talks about the founding of the Australian Institute of Aboriginal Studies in 1964 and its great commitment to creating a permanent place for the culture of the Aboriginal people in general consciousness. He then continues:

> *"Unfortunately, many of these efforts have come too late, as there are no longer any Indigenous people who could still embody the special spiritual culture, the unique psychological structure unscathed. Apart from political, social and biological damage, psychological degeneration has now affected everyone"* (1989: 154).

This stance is all the more surprising as Andreas and Katharina Lommel had received a visit from the Australian photographer Jutta Malnic before the publication of *Die Kunst des alten Australien* – and thus indirectly resumed contact with David Mowaljarlai (fig. 1), whom Lommel had met in 1938 and who was now working with Jutta Malnic.

Andreas and Katharina Lommel

In the meantime Mowaljarlai had become a respected Ngarinyin Elder and lived in Mowanjum near Derby. He had been raised in the Kumunya Mission in both Ngarinyin and Christian religious traditions and his life was marked by an ability to move in two worlds. Mowarljarlai not only had extensive knowledge of Ngarinyin culture, but was also committed to passing on this knowledge to the younger generation and sharing elements of his understanding of Kimberley cosmology with others. He worked with a series of scholars, recording languages, ceremonies and rock art sites. He sought and received support from government agencies for his work, among them the Australian Institute of Aboriginal Studies (Ward 1997).

The contact with Jutta Malnic and Mowaljarlai seems to have brought about a change of mind on the part of Andreas Lommel, as he subsequently provided them with photos and wrote an extremely positive foreword to their joint publication *Yorro Yorro – Everything Standing Up Alive. Spirit of the Kimberley* which was published in 1993 (Mowaljarlai and Malnic [1993] 2001: IX-X). This book stimulated another indirect cooperation between Andreas Lommel and David Mowaljalai: an article with the title "Shamanism in Northwest Australia" that was published in the journal Oceania in 1994.

In 1994, the independent rock art researcher Grahame L. Walsh (1944–2007) published his book *Bradshaws. Ancient Rock Paintings of Northwest Australia.* Walsh was of the opinion that the *Gwion Gwion* paintings originated from a different, extinct culture that had nothing to do with the contemporary Kimberley culture, and thus triggered a heated political debate in Australia which, among other things, had an impact on the land claims of the Ngarinyin (McNiven 2011).

Andreas and Katharina Lommel were also enthusiastic about the anthropomorphic *Gwion Gwion* depictions that appear alongside the *Wanjina* paintings, and which they described as "rock paintings of the small-figure Bradshaw style" (Lommel and Lommel 1989: 24). The figures are almost always depicted in motion, carrying boomerangs, spears and spear throwers; they are richly decorated with exaggerated hairstyles and painted in dark red tones directly on the rock surface (fig. 6). The name *Gwion Gwion* imitates the call of the mysterious "cave bird"[9] who wiped its bloody beak on a cave wall and thus created the first rock painting (Doring 2000: 120).

Andreas Lommel was of the opinion that the *Gwion Gwion* depictions were older than the *Wanjina* paintings and that both must be due to contact with cultures outside Australia, as they are only found in the northwest of the continent. He described them as the "climax of Australian art" (Lommel 1970: 234), an art that the people no longer knew anything about, while the *Wanjina* depictions were a degenerated form of this elegant style (Lommel and Lommel 1989: 24–25). The

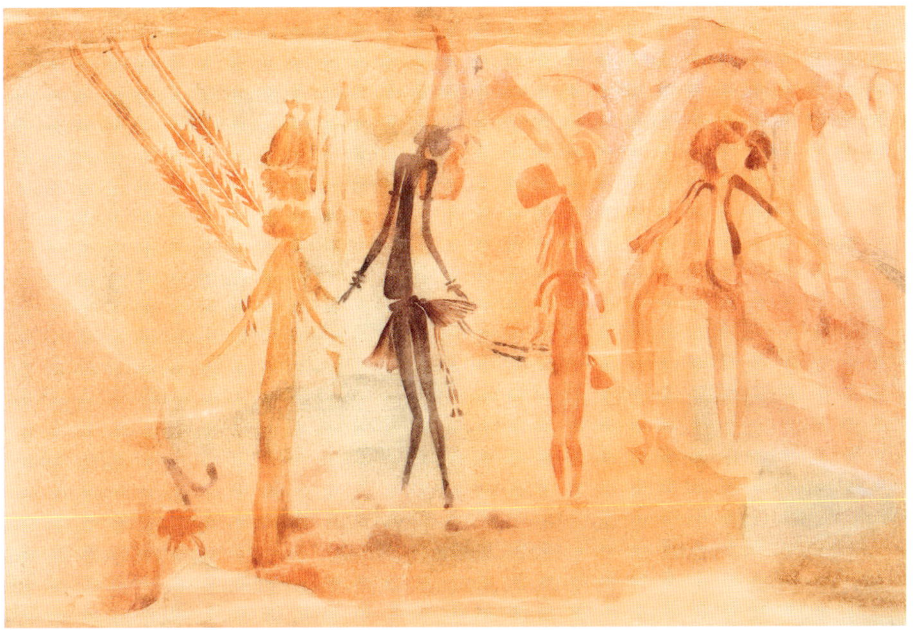

Fig. 6   *Gwion Gwion* dancers, Awulen rock art site. Kimberley, Northwest Australia. Watercolours on canvas. 72.5 x 56 cm. Rock art copy by Katharina Lommel, 1955. Collection: Museum Fünf Kontinente. Photo: Marietta Weidner, 2020

dating of the Bradshaw paintings in 1997 at 17,000 years old (Roberts et al. 1997) was also interpreted by Lommel as evidence of a succession of different Aboriginal cultures (Lommel 1998). It would appear that Walsh and Lommel became friends, as in 1997 Walsh published *The Unambal. A Tribe in Northwest Australia*, the English translation of Lommel's 1952 book, in his own publishing house Takarakka Nowan Kas Publications (Lommel 1997a: V).

David Mowaljarlai passed away in September 1997, however in June 1997 he managed to visit Paris to present the so-called Pathway Project to UNESCO. This project was initiated in collaboration with biologist and filmmaker Jeff Doring when in 1992 Mowaljarlai and three other senior Elders, *Munnumburra*, decided to reveal their ancestral connection to *Gwion* rock art and some of the previously secret pathways *(Dulwan Mamaa)* to the roots of their history in order to secure the Ngarinyin's legal claim to land under Australian law. As part of this project these men demonstrated that the *Gwion Gwion* were the first ancestors to be credited with the discovery of the practical use of fire and the invention of many hunting techniques, in particular the making of stone blades. The *Gwion* also created the *Wunan* Law, which governs the kinship system of two intermarrying groups as well as a system of sharing. Furthermore, the *Gwion* also gave the people the initiation ceremonies with the associated songs and dances (Doring 2000).

David Mowaljarlai did not live to see the completion of the Pathway Project with the publication of the book *Gwion Gwion. Secret and Sacred Pathways of the Ngarinyin Aboriginal People of Australia* (2000) and the presentation of the film *GWION* (2001) at the Australian Centre for the Moving Image (ACMI) in Melbourne. Ultimately, the book served as evidence for the Ngarinyin's land rights claim, which in 2004 resulted in the plaintiffs being awarded ownership of all *Wanjina* and *Gwion* rock art "against the world" (Doring with Paddy Nyawarra 2014: 4–5).

To mark Andreas Lommel's 90th birthday in 2002, the Munich museum organized an exhibition of Katharina Lommel's rock art copies, which was also visited by Damon de Laszlo and John Robinson, representatives of the Bradshaw Foundation, an association for the study of rock art worldwide. They also met with Andreas and Katharina Lommel, who provided photos and extracts from *Die Unambal* and *Die Kunst des alten Australien* in English translation for the Bradshaw Foundation's homepage. Until recently, the images, some of which also show ceremonies classified as secret/sacred, could be viewed there by the general public.

In 2023, within the framework of the DFG project "The German Ethnographic Expeditions to the Kimberley, Northwest Australia. A Collaborative Assessment of Research History, the Interpretation of Australian Aboriginal Heritage and Digital Repatriation", and at the request of the Wunambal Gaambera Aboriginal Corporation, it was decided to delete these pictures. Thus, after more than eighty years, the Traditional Owners were able to regain a degree of control over the visual documentation of their culture.

Endnotes:

1 The name of the institution was Staatliches Museum für Völkerkunde (State Museum of Ethnology) at the time.

2 In 1937 Douglas C. Fox, together with Leo Frobenius, published a catalogue for the exhibition *Prehistoric Rock Pictures in Europe and Africa* in the Museum of Modern Art, New York, as well as the book *African Genesis* with drawings from Katharina Marr.

3 The Central Collecting Point in Arcisstraße in Munich was the collection point for museum objects that were evacuated during the war or looted by the National Socialists in Germany and abroad (Smyth 2022).

4 Ritual objects and photos that show ritual acts and are therefore categorised as secret/sacred by the Aboriginal people are no longer shown in public.

5 "Stockman" is an Australian term for labourers on a cattle farm. Aboriginal people were often employed as stockmen and played an important role in the successful management of many farms. As a rule, the Indigenous stockmen only received food and clothing as wages. It was not until the 1950s and 1960s that they were also paid a small salary, although this was usually far lower than that of their white colleagues (see Skyring 2012).

6 The photo exhibition *Stockyards and Saddles. A Story of Gibb River Station* curated in 2018 by Vanessa Russ, the granddaughter of Fred Russ, included photos taken by Andreas and Katharina Lommel in 1955 which they had given to the Russ family (Russ 2018).

7 The Sundron rock art site was lost after the death of Charlie Numbulmoore (1907–1971), the Lommels' Aboriginal guide there, and was only rediscovered in 2021 by Butch Maher, Joh Bornman and Kim Doohan as part of the DFG project "The German Ethnographic Expeditions to the Kimberley, Northwest Australia. A Collaborative Assessment of Research History, the Interpretation of Australian Aboriginal Heritage and Digital Repatriation".

8 The copy of this rock painting, following its digital repatriation as part of the DFG project mentioned in endnote 7 in June 2022, inspired Donny Woolagoodja to create his own painting. See Matthias Claudius Hofmann and Richard Kuba, *Introduction* in this volume.

9 Schulz (1956: 47) and Lommel (1952: 12) mentioned the bird Kujon.

References:

Baal, Jan van. 1960: *Palet van het stenen tijdperk in Australie.* December 1960 – April 1961. Amsterdam: Tropenmuseum.

Beinssen-Hesse, Silke. 1991: The Study of Australian Aboriginal Culture by German Anthropologists of the Frobenius Institute. In: David Walker and Jürgen Tampke (eds): *From Berlin to the Burdekin. The German Contribution to the Development of Australian Science, Exploration and the Arts.* Kensington, NSW: New South Wales University Press. 135–150.

Blundell, Valda and Donny Woolagoodja. 2012: Rock Art, Aboriginal Culture, and Identity: The Wanjina Paintings of Northwest Australia. In: Peter Veth and Jo McDonald (eds): *A Companion to Rock Art.* Chichester: Wiley-Blackwell Publishing Ltd. 472–487.

Bradshaw, Joseph. 1892: Notes on a Recent Trip to Prince Regent's River. In: *Transactions of the Royal Geographical Society of Australasia, Victorian Branch Proceedings* 9 (2): 90–103.

Doring, Jeff with Paddy Nyawarra. 2014: Gwion Artists and Wunan Law. The Origin of Society in Australia. In: *Rock Art Research* 33 (1): 3–13.

Doring, Jeff (ed.). 2000: *Gwion Gwion. Secret and Sacred Pathways of the Ngarinyin Aboriginal People of Australia.* Köln: Könemann Verlag.

Lommel, Andreas. 1998: Aboriginal-Kunst in deutschen Museen. In: *Museum Aktuell* 32: 1094–1997.

Lommel, Andreas. 1997a: *The Unambal. A Tribe in Northwest Australia.* Primary English translation by Ian Campbell. Carnarvon Gorge, Qld: Takarakka Nowan Kas Publications.

Lommel, Andreas. 1997b: Die Australiensammlung Lommel im Staatlichen Museum für Völkerkunde in München. In: *Nah und Fern. Zeitschrift für Volks- und Völkerkunde* 1: 4–12.

Lommel, Andreas. 1970: Changes in Australian Art. In: Arnold R. Pilling and Richard A. Waterman (eds): *Diprotodon to Detribalization. Studies of Change among Australian Aborigines.* East Lansing, Mich.: Michigan State University Press. 217–236.

Lommel, Andreas. 1969: *Fortschritt ins Nichts. Die Modernisierung der Primitiven Australiens. Beschreibung und Definition eines psychischen Verfalls.* Zurich: Atlantis Verlag.

Lommel, Andreas. 1961: The Rock Art of Australia. In: Hans-Georg Bandi et al.: *The Art of the Stone Age. Forty Thousand Years of Rock Art.* Art of the World. New York: Crown Publishers Inc. 205–231.

Lommel, Andreas. 1952: *Die Unambal. Ein Stamm in Nordwest-Australien.* Monographien zur Völkerkunde 2. Hamburg: Hamburgisches Museum für Völkerkunde.

Lommel, Andreas. 1950: Modern Culture Influences on the Aborigines. In: *Oceania* 21 (1): 14–24.

Lommel, Andreas. 1949: Notes on Sexual Behaviour and Initiation, Wunambal Tribe, North-Western Australia. In: *Oceania* 20 (2): 158–164.

Lommel, Andreas and Katharina Lommel. 1989: *Die Kunst des alten Australien.* Munich: Prestel Verlag.

Lommel, Andreas and Katharina Lommel. 1959: *Die Kunst des fünften Erdteils. Australien.* Munich: Staatliches Museum für Völkerkunde.

Lommel, Andreas and David Mowaljarlai. 1994: Shamanism in Northwest Australia. In: *Oceania* 64 (4): 277–287.

Lommel, Katharina. 1955: *Tagebuch.* 02.01. – 07.11.1955 (unpublished archival source) Munich: Museum Fünf Kontinente, Slg. Manuskripte und Schriften, SG-739-1-0.

Maynard, Lesley. 1979: The Archaeology of Australian Aboriginal Art. In: Sidney M. Mead (ed.): *Exploring the Visual Art of Oceania, Australia, Melanesia, Micronesia, and Polynesia.* Honolulu: University Press of Hawaii. 83–110.

McNiven, Ian J. 2011: The Bradshaw Debate. Lessons Learned from Critiquing Colonialist Interpretations of Gwion Gwion Rock Paintings of the Kimberley,

Western Australia. In: *Australian Archaeology* 72: 35–44.

Mowaljarlai, David and Jutta Malnic. [1993] 2001: *Yorro Yorro – Everything Standing Up Alive. Spirit of the Kimberley.* New edition. Broome: Magabala Books.

Petri, Helmut. 1970: Buchbesprechung: Andreas Lommel. Fortschritt ins Nichts. In: *Tribus* 19: 234–236.

Petri, Helmut et al. 1939: Die Frobenius-Expedition nach Nordwest-Australien 1938–39. In: *Frankfurter Wochenschau* 29: 345–355.

Roberts, Richard et al. 1997: Luminescence Dating of Rock Art and Past Environments Using Mud-Wasp Nests in Northern Australia. In: *Nature* 387 (6634), 12 June 1997: 696–699.

Russ, Vanessa (ed.). 2018: *Stock Yards and Saddles. A Story of Gibb River Station.* Crawley, WA: Berndt Museum at the University of Western Australia.

Schulz, Agnes S. 1956: North-West Australian Rock Paintings. In: *Memoirs of the National Museum of Victoria (Melbourne)* 20: 7–57.

Skyring, Fiona. 2012: Low Wages, Low Rents, and Pension Cheques: The Introduction of Equal Wages in the Kimberley, 1968–1969. In: Natasha Fijn et al. (eds): *Indigenous Participation in Australian Economies II. Historical Engagements and Current Enterprises.* Canberra: ANU E Press. http://doi.org/10.22459/IPAE.07.2012.08

Smyth, Craig Hugh. 2022: *The Central Collecting Point in Munich.* Veröffentlichungen des Zentral-instituts für Kunstgeschichte München 63. Passau: Dietmar Klinger Verlag.

Stappert, Gisela. 2021: De «Frobénide» à directeur du Musée d'ethnologie de Munich: vie et œuvre d'Andreas Lommel. In: *Bérose – Encyclopédie internationale des histoires de l'anthropologie.* Paris. https://www.berose.fr/article2261.html

Stappert, Gisela. 2019: Katharina Marr (Hamburg 1911 – 2004 München). In: Birgit Sander et al. (eds): *Frobenius. Die Kunst des Forschens.* Petersberg: Michael Imhof Verlag. 211–215.

Strehlow, Theodor G. H. 1973: Book Review: Fortschritt ins Nichts by Andreas Lommel. In: *Current Anthropology* 14 (4): 459–460.

Walsh, Grahame L. 1994: *Bradshaws. Ancient Rock Paintings of North-West Australia.* Geneva: Edition Limitée.

Ward, Graeme K. (ed.). 1997: Obituaries: D. Mowaljarlai, OAM 1925–1997. In: *Australian Aboriginal Studies* 1997 (2): 78–85.

Andreas and Katharina Lommel

The Recordings

...of the "Frankfurter Expedition W-Australien"

Sally Treloyn

Multiple audio recordings were collected by the Forschungsinstitut für Kulturmorphologie in the course of the Frobenius Expedition to Northwest Australia in 1938–39, and these are referred to as the "Frankfurter Expedition W-Australien" recordings.[1] A detailed examination of the content of these recordings that draws upon knowledge of performance traditions in the region has never been undertaken before. This essay presents the results of a preliminary analysis of the content of the recordings, which serves the dual role of contributing to the catalogue for the exhibition COUNTRY BIN PULL'EM and providing information that will help the *Wanjina Wunggurr* community assess and, through local creative practice, realise the recordings' significance and value. Moreover, in giving details of the content and organisation of the recordings, the essay will facilitate not only community use and management but also appropriate management by the archive. The analysis draws upon several different strands: a previous comparative analysis of *Wanjina Wunggurr* musical styles by the author; a documentation of the *Junba* referenced in "Corroboree of Kurangali and Banad" provided by an expert advisor to Lommel (1997: 84–87); and information about *Junba* repertories dated to the time of the expedition by *Wanjina Wunggurr* Elders in 2002.

Such an examination is challenging, as there is limited documentation to accompany the recordings, the singing is obscured by mechanical and medium (wax cylinder) noise, and there is distortion of the performed tempo and pitch. Each of these factors is intertwined with the need to take great care in managing and using underdocumented recordings. In order to support access, the *Wanjina Wunggurr* community have to ascertain if the content only includes the public genre *Junba* performed by *Wanjina Wunggurr* peoples, and potentially other genres that are also performed in public contexts. But in light of the fact that the expedition also encountered a genre that has particular sensitivities (and was documented elsewhere), they also need to determine if the recordings include material that is restricted and has to be handled accordingly.

The essay is structured in five parts. The first introductory section gives a brief overview of the dance-song traditions (i.e. cultural performance practices that feature dance and song) of *Wanjina Wunggurr* peoples and, with a particular focus on *Junba* as a genre, of the place of the "Frankfurter Expedition W-Australien" recordings in the larger history of recording in the region. The second part of the essay briefly describes how the recordings are organised, involving a description of the digital files and information provided in the labels that accompany the source reel-to-reel tapes. The third part of the essay gives an overview of the distribution of distinct genres in the recordings. It identifies the items within the recordings that are clearly *Junba*, in the *Jadmi/Jodmolo/Ngodben Junba*-style, and those for which – based upon available information – the genre is unclear, although it is possibly *Gulowada Junba* and *Wangga/Lirrga* or *Nyindinyindi*. Advice is provided about further steps for managing these as long as the genre remains undetermined. The fourth part of the essay examines the *Jadmi/Jodmolo/ Ngodben Junba*-style items in the recordings in more detail. Not only the number of distinct songs is identified but also the likely composers of those songs, drawing upon the co-occurrence of three songs in a repertory documented by Ngarinyin Elders Mr Paddy Neowarra, Mr Jimmy Maline and Mr Paddy Wama in 2002, and in the documentation provided by an expert advisor to Lommel related to the "Corroboree of Kurangali and Banad" (1997: 84–87). The essay concludes with some reflections on the significance and value of the "Frankfurter Expedition W-Australien" recordings in light of the preliminary analysis as described above, and informed by contemporary uses of archival recordings and other materials in community initiatives for revitalising *Junba*.

Wanjina Wunggurr dance-song: *Junba*

Wanjina Wunggurr peoples have a rich and diverse heritage of creative practices and traditions that involve dance and song among other artistic forms.[2] The genre known as *Junba* is perhaps most distinctive to the region, and the dance-songs reflect *Wanjina Wunggurr* peoples' places, languages and histories. It is a living tradition that originates with *Wanjina*, in which repertories are devised by living composers and by spirits of deceased family members who visit or are visited by composers in dreams. There are two primary styles of *Junba*: one (referred to as *Jadmi*, *Jodmolo* or *Ngodben*, depending on the language group) that is characterised by the use of paperbark headdresses and leaf adornments representing the distinctive brolga bird; and one (referred to as *Jerregorl*, *Galinda* or *Balga*, depending on the language group) that is characterised by large dance totems depicting ancestors and places. A third style known as *Gulowada* is less common but is distinct from the other two styles both musically and in relation to dance. What distinguishes *Junba* from other genres that are used only in ceremonial and similar sensitive or restricted contexts is that it is practiced in schools, community gatherings, festivals and other public and private venues.

Significantly, *Junba* has remained prolific in the Kimberley throughout the twentieth and into the twenty-first centuries. Composers and performers have used these repertories to manage massive environmental and regime shifts from deep history to the present, exemplifying a tradition of artistic and musical resilience that co-sustains people, places and creative traditions. The song lyrics accompanying the dance choreography, in addition to other *Junba* design elements, record ancestral stories and Law as well as more recent historical and contemporary events. Moreover, as documented by Ngarinyin Elder Mr Paddy Neowarra and other

Wanjina Wunggurr Elders in 2002, *Junba* is used to build and negotiate relationships with neighbours and strangers. In each performance of *Junba* there is an area for visiting strangers to sit and *dawul* (listen to and learn from) the performance. This is the case when repertories are shared or sold in relation to *Wurnan* Law and its associated conventions of transmission. It is also the case when performance (at present-day festivals, for example) is used to teach non-Indigenous audiences about the importance of *Wanjina Wunggurr* cultural beliefs, society and practices.

It is therefore not surprising that the members of the Frobenius Expedition to the Kimberley witnessed *Junba* when attending community gatherings in *Wanjina Wunggurr* territories in 1938–39. The attendance of Andreas Lommel and other members and what they witnessed was reported by Mr Neowarra, Mr Maline and Mr Wama, who were children at the time, along with other members of the *Wanjina Wunggurr* community[3] in areas such as Munja and Pantijan. The *Junba* witnessed by Lommel is also described and represented in the monograph *Die Unambal* (Lommel 1997) and elsewhere (Lommel and Mowaljarlai 1994; Redmond 2017).

That recordings were created during the Frobenius Expedition to the Kimberley in 1938–39 has long been known within the *Wanjina Wunggurr* community. Mr Laurie Gowanulli, for example, told anthropologist Anthony Redmond that he had seen Lommel record onto wax cylinders (2017: 417). However, the location of any extant recordings had remained unclear until the recent emergence of the "Frankfurter Expedition W-Australien" tapes. These recordings on five tapes – copied from the wax cylinder originals in the 1960s – add to the history of *Junba* composers and performers who have adopted new audio technologies, both in order to create an enduring recording of their traditions and practices and to communicate with audiences who are separated by time and place.

Matthew Dembalali Martin, a contemporary Ngarinyin and Wunambal singer and dance master, has explained that he sees the recordings as a gift of singers from the past to future generations. As such, Dembalali continues, they contribute to *Wurnan:* a law and ethos of sharing for the collective good (Treloyn, Martin and Charles 2016: 98–99).

Recordings of *Wanjina Wunggurr* dance-song

After the "Frankfurter Expedition W-Australien" recordings, the next known recordings of *Junba* were those recorded by *Wanjina Wunggurr* Elders, including Worrorra composer and singer Watty Ngerdu with Peter Lucich in Mowanjum in

1963 and with Alice Moyle in 1968. More recently, Elders including Demabalali Martin's father, Ngarinyin and Wunambal composer and singer Scotty Martin, worked with various researchers to record *Junba* performances and document *Junba* histories, knowledge and practices. These researchers included ethnomusicologists Linda Barwick and Allan Marett with the Ngarinyin Aboriginal Corporation (NAC), anthropologist Anthony Redmond with the Kamali Land Council, and me with the NAC and Elders. Significant group-performed *Junba* events have been recorded, including but not limited to those by Alice Moyle in Mowanjum, Gibb River and elsewhere in 1986, Lesley Reilly in Kalumburu in 1974, Ray Keogh in Kalumburu in 1985, and later by Barwick, Marett and Redmond in various sites throughout the northern Kimberley. The collective record of *Junba* indicates that from the early 1900s there have been at least thirty-five composers of *Junba* from the *Wanjina Wunggurr* groups, responsible for more than fifty repertories (Treloyn 2006).

In recent years the body of work left by Elders in audio collections has been taken up by contemporary practitioners in *Wanjina Wunggurr* communities. In particular, archival recordings are used to support the recovery of dance-songs that had fallen out of usage, to support the learning of singing style and conventions, and to inform dance choreography (Treloyn, Martin and Charles 2019; Treloyn, Charles and O'Connor 2021). Dembalali has explained that, like the act of recording, the work of return – involving repatriation and the use of recordings to renourish contemporary practice – maintains *Wurnan*. The Old people are resident in the recordings, Dembalali says, and recordings must come back to renourish Country and its people, and for the sake of future generations (Dembalali Martin in Treloyn, Martin and Charles 2019: 599). The value of these audio collections is thus far-reaching: they could possibly contribute to increasing musical and linguistic diversity in *Wanjina Wunggurr* communities. They also hold the prospect of supporting the wider goals of community, social and global wellbeing and sustainability. The "Frankfurter Expedition W-Australien" recordings therefore contain a great deal of potential, significance and value. Information about the song material located within them is, however, critical to their usefulness. Other factors are equally decisive: the accessibility of the format, the organisation of the recordings, the nature of the content and the quality of the sound. The intent of this essay is to provide a preliminary assessment of these elements and provide some insights that may aid any future management and use of the recordings.

The recordings: tapes, numbered tracks, items and digital files

The "Frankfurter Expedition W-Australien" recordings are located on five tapes labelled WU 216, WU 217, WU 218, WU 219 and WU 220 (see figs 1 and 2). The audio content was sourced from galvanos (copper negative moulds) of the wax cylinder recordings collected in the course of the Frobenius Expedition to Northwest Australia in 1938–39. These were, in turn, transferred directly to tape in the 1960s.

The labels on the reels of tape identify fifty-nine numbered pieces in total. These will be referred to in this essay as 'tracks', whereas the term 'item' is used in line with ethnomusicological conventions to describe periods of singing within recordings. The first track is labelled No. 1 and the final one is No. 66, although several numbers are omitted from the sequence of track labels (Nos 5, 25, 27, 35, 38, 40, 41, 59 and 62). Some audio content occurs in multiple tracks (e.g. the content of 22_1 also occurs in 22_2). One digital audio file is provided for each of the labelled tracks. The exceptions to this include No. 37, for which no corresponding digital file is provided, and No. 58, the content of which is included in the digital audio file that is labelled 57. Each labelled track and corresponding digital file contain between one and three sung items. These items are labelled a, b and c on the tape labels. In total, 130 sung items are included in the available recordings.

Fig. 1 Tape label for WU 220, showing track numbers and item labels. Collection: Berliner Phonogramm-Archiv. Photo: Albrecht Wiedmann, 2024

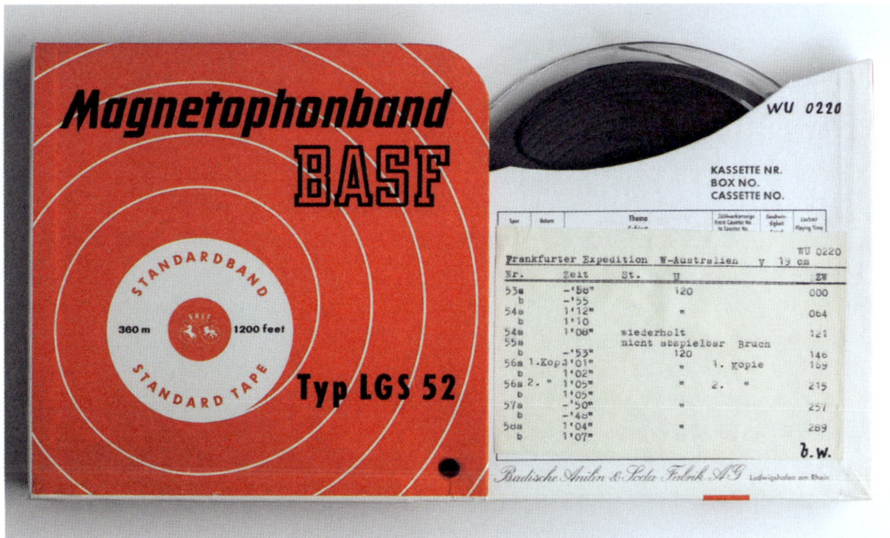

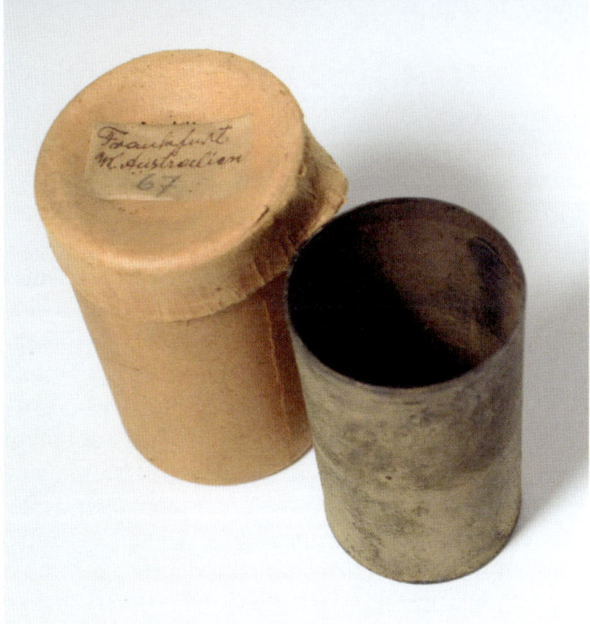

Fig. 2 Original phonograph cylinder made of hard wax, No. 67 in the "Frankfurter Expedition W-Australien" audio recordings. Collection: Berliner Phonogramm-Archiv. Photo: Albrecht Wiedmann, 2024

Identifying genre in the "Frankfurter Expedition W-Australien" recordings

Performances of at least two *Junba* repertories were witnessed by the expedition group. One of these was the *Galinda*-style *Junba* that was composed by the Worrorra composer Alan Balbungu. Under the heading "The Poet Allan's Great Corroboree", Lommel provides transcriptions of the lyrics of thirty-eight of these songs, with an abbreviated gloss, and descriptions of the accompanying dances for many (Lommel 1997: 77–84). As noted above, Ngarinyin Elder Laurie Gowanulli recalled seeing Balbungu record these songs with Andreas Lommel (Redmond 2017: 417). Additionally, twenty-one song lyrics of another repertory that was performed during the expedition are represented under the heading "Corroboree of Kurangali and Banad" (Lommel 1997: 84–87), referring to the skin heroes (the totem animals associated with moieties) Brolga and Bush Turkey, who often feature in the *Jadmi/Jodmolo/Ngodben*-style of *Junba*. Four of the songs in this set are similar or identical to four that were attributed by Neowarra, Maline and Wama in 2002 (fig. 3) to the shared *Jadmi/Jodmolo/Ngodben*-style *Junba* repertory of Wunambal-Gambere composers Mick Bungguni and Wabi 'Bobby' Wundhalmanja. Neowarra, Maline and Wama also recalled a further eight dance-songs from this set and described dances based on their childhood experiences of dancing the *Junbas*, which included performing in the presence of the Germans.

One might therefore expect that the "Frankfurter Expedition W-Australien" recordings would include *Junba*, and most likely that of Balbungu, given Gowanulli's account provided by Redmond (2017). As explained above, however, many genres have been practiced in the region and there are various impediments to identifying the content on the recordings. These obstacles include such factors as organisation and sound quality. This part of the essay provides the results of a preliminary analysis of the recordings, identifying the items that are clearly *Junba*, and specifying where other genres are located.

Aspects of musical style, incorporating voicing, melody, rhythm, lyrics and instrumentation, may enable the genre of sung items to be determined from audio recordings. The recordings do present challenges due to the level of sound distortion. However, a significant portion of the sung items in the recordings can be identified by turning to previous comparative analysis of *Wanjina Wunggurr* musical styles (Treloyn 2006, 2014) as well as information about *Junba* repertories (namely Bungguni and Wundhalmanja) that were dated to the time of the expedition by Neowarra, Wama and Maline in 2002. Table 1 shows that eighty-three of the 130 sung items can be identified as *Junba*, and specifically *Jadmi/Jodmolo/Ngodben*-style *Junba*. Eighty of these are recordings of unique performances, with at least three (22_IIa, 22_IIb, 22_IIc) being a duplication in the recording of the previous three items.

Fig. 3 Paddy Neowarra, Paddy Wama and Jimmy Maline during a **Junba** documentation session with the author in Derby. Collection: The Kerry Stokes Collection. Photo: Kevin Shaw, 2002

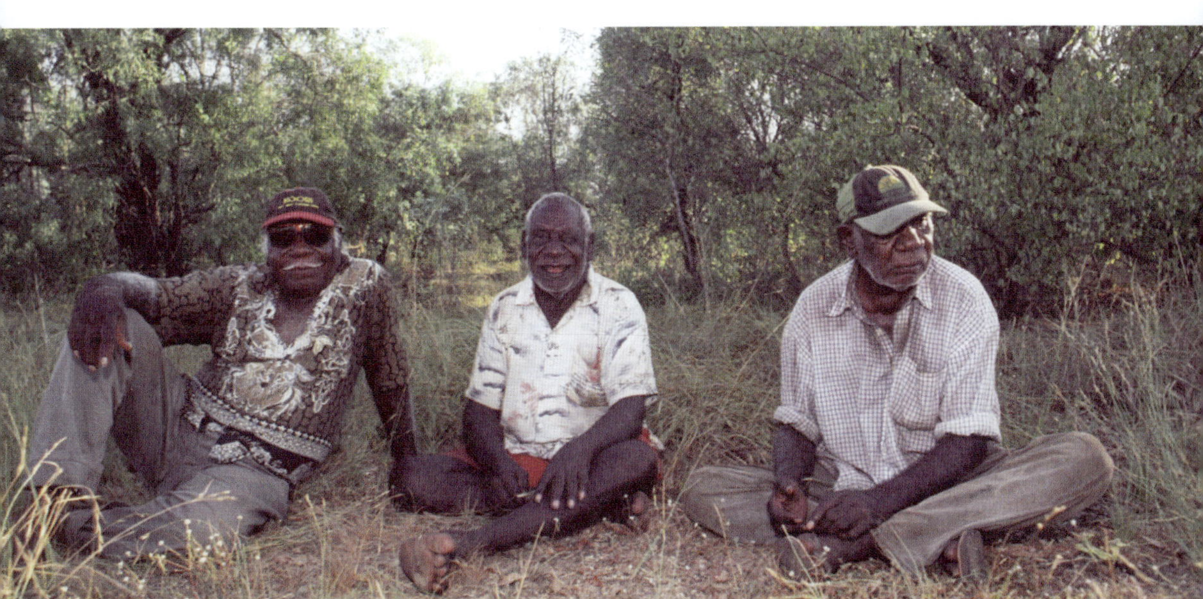

At least two other genres are exhibited in the remaining forty-seven sung items. Twenty-nine of these exhibit characteristics that also feature primarily or exclusively in the *Gulowada*-style *Junba* (namely a melodic suffix "aa"), however these should be reviewed privately within the community, bearing in mind that the expedition elsewhere documented material of a sensitive nature. Thirteen exhibit some characteristics shared with *Wangga/Lirrga*, which is performed in both public and private contexts, and possibly *Nyindinyindi* (a genre accompanied by didjeridu that preceded the arrival of *Wangga* and *Lirrga*). These should also be reviewed privately within the community. The musical characteristics of the remaining five items are obscured by mechanical noise or the recording is absent, thereby making it impossible to determine the genre at this stage.

Identifying a *Junba* repertory and songs in the "Frankfurter Expedition W-Australien" recordings

As is the case when identifying genre, issues with clarity of the recorded sound impedes any identification of *Junba* repertories and songs. Notably, recordings of Balbungu's *Junba*, the creation of which were witnessed by Gowanulli as reported by Redmond, are clearly not present in tapes WU 216, WU 217, WU 218, WU 219 and WU 220. The key to which repertory does lie in the body of eighty-three *Jadmi/Jodmolo/Ngodben*-style *Junba* items on the tapes, however, lies in the work done by Neowarra, Maline and Wama in 2002, more specifically in their work to document the shared repertory of Bungguni and Wundhalmanja, which as noted they had danced as children and attributed to the period of the Frobenius Expedition.

Close listening to the *Jadmi/Jodmolo/Ngodben*-style *Junba* set indicates that in the eighty distinct sung items, at least twenty-eight distinct songs are performed. That is, there are twenty-eight distinct sets of lyrics, each corresponding to one distinct song. As these all have the same melodic features and appear to demonstrate a symmetrical range and distribution of rhythmic mode, it can be concluded with some certainty that these belong to a single repertory. Table 2 provides an identifier for each *Jadmi/Jodmolo/Ngodben*-style *Junba* song, and the sung items performed for each, using track numbers and item labels provided by the collection.

Track and item	No. of items	Genre
1a, 1b, 2b, 2c, 3a, 3b, 3c, 6a, 6b, 6c, 7a, 7b, 8a, 8b, 9a, 9b, 10a, 10b, 10c, 11a, 16a, 16b, 21a, 21b, 22_Ia, 22_Ib, 22_Ic, 22_IIa, 22_IIb, 22_IIc, 23a, 23b, 24a, 24b, 29a, 42a, 42b, 43a, 43b, 44a, 44b, 45a, 45b, 46a, 46b, 47a, 47b, 48a, 48b, 49a, 49b, 50a, 50b, 51a, 51b, 52a, 52b, 53a, 53b, 54a, 54b, 55b, 56_Ia, 56_Ib, 56_IIa, 56_IIb, 57a, 57b, 58a, 58b, 60a, 60b, 61a, 61b, 63a, 63b, 64a, 64b, 65a, 65b, 66a, 66b, 66c	83 (80 distinct items)	*Jadmi/Jodmolo/ Ngodben*-style *Junba*
4a, 12a, 12b, 13a, 13b, 13c, 14a, 14b, 15a*, 15b, 18a**, 18b, 20a, 20b, 30a, 30b, 31a, 31b, 32a, 32b, 32c, 33a, 33b, 33c, 34a, 34b, 34c, 36a, 36b	29	Unknown genre – possibly *Gulowada Junba*
17a, 17b, 17c, 19a, 19b, 19c, 26a, 26b, 28a, 28b, 39a, 39b, 39c***	13	Unknown genre – possibly *Wangga/Lirrga* or *Nyindinyindi*
2a, 23c, 55a	3	Indistinguishable
37a, 37b	2	Missing audio file
Total	130	

*   Labelled "15 I"

**   Labelled "18 I"

***   Not labelled

Table 1   Distribution of genres in the "Frankfurter Expedition W-Australien" recordings

Song identifier	Track and item	No. of sung items for each song
S01	1a, 1b, 55b, 65b	4
S02	2b	1
S03	2c, 58a, 58b	3
S04	3a, 3b, 47a, 47b	4
S05	3c, 10a, 56_IIa, 56_IIb	4
S06*	6a, 6b, 46a, 46b	4
S07*	6c, 45a, 45b	3
S08	7a, 7b	2
S09	8a, 64a, 64b	3
S10	8b	1
S11*	9a	1
S12	9b	1
S13	10b, 48a, 48b	3
S14	10c, 53a, 53b	3
S15	11a, 56_Ia, 56_Ib	3
S16	16a, 16b	2
S17	21a, 21b	2
S18	42a, 42b	2
S19	43a, 43b	2

S20	44a, 44b	2
S21	49a, 49b, 63a, 63b	4
S22	50a, 50b	2
S23	51a, 51b, 57a, 57b	4
S24	52a, 52b	2
S25	54a, 54b, 60a, 60b	4
S26	61a, 61b	2
S27	65a	1
S28	66c	1
Lyrics indistinguishable	2a, 23c, 29a, 55a, 66a, 66b	6

Table 2   Summary of songs and the sung items performed for each song

Three of the songs attributed by Neowarra, Maline and Wama to Bungguni and Wundhalmanja share lyrical content with three songs (performed across eight of the eighty sung items) in the expedition recordings (these are marked with an asterix in table 2). Two of these (the ones that feature lyrics with the closest similarity between the expedition recording and Neowarra, Maline and Wama's version), are provided in table 3. In the table the songs have been named according to glosses and descriptions provided by Neowarra, Maline and Wama: "Stranger in an open place" and "Crocodile dance". Beyond some phonemic variation, in each case the main difference between the versions in the recordings and Neowarra, Maline and Wama's versions is the order of phrases, which are reversed. For example, in the first song in the expedition recording, "Stranger in an open place" (item nos 1a, 1b, 55b), the phrases "mayarn barrana" and "badada bana" are performed in succession and repeated. In Neowarra, Maline and Wama's version the phrase "badada bana" is followed by "mayarn barrana" before repeating. This manner of reversing lines is common in the *Junba* genre in cases where songs are transmitted across time and place (Treloyn 2014) and in cyclical, isorhythmic genres throughout Central Australia and into the Kimberley.

Source	Song lyrics as transcribed with gloss
Song: "Stranger in an open place"	
Frankfurter Expedition W-Australien, 9a	"mayarn barrana, badada bana" (repeated)[4]
Neowarra, Maline, Wama 2002	badada bana, mayarn barrana" (repeated) Gloss: In that open place there they are telling stories. I am a stranger in that country.
Song: "Crocodile dance"	
Frankfurter Expedition W-Australien, 6a, 6b, 46a, 46b	"jali mawana, ngarrngarr embewe" (repeated)[5]
Neowarra, Maline, Wama 2002	"ngerrngerr embewe, jali mawana" (repeated) Gloss: Going to the flat country. Dancers move as crocodiles.

Table 3   Two *Jadmi/Jodmolo/Ngodben*-style *Junba* songs attributed to the shared repertory of Mick Bungguni and Wabi 'Bobby' Wundhalmanja: versions in the "Frankfurter Expedition W-Australien recordings" and by Neowarra, Maline and Wama

Sounding the archive

This essay has provided a preliminary description and analysis of the organisation and distribution of genres in the "Frankfurter Expedition W-Australien" recordings. It may be used to prepare the recordings for safe management by the archive and for community use. Three genres have been identified: *Jadmi/Jodmolo/Ngodben Junba*; an unknown genre, possible *Gulowada*; and another unknown genre, possibly *Wannga/Lirrga* or *Nyindinyindi*. The essay has also drawn upon comparative analysis of *Junba* repertories and recordings, along with documentation provided by *Wanjina Wunggurr* Elders in 2002 to identify the repertory and composers of eighty-three of the 130 sung items in the collection. Three songs which are found in the recordings, in documentation from these Elders and in Lommel's monograph have also been identified.

In recent years, members of the *Wanjina Wunggurr* community have used recordings and archived documents to recover, re-choreograph and return numerous dance-songs to performance programmes in the Kimberley. These had for the most part last been performed in the 1990s, and in some cases as long ago as the 1960s. Since 2018, however, attention has also turned to dance-songs with earlier dates, including the period that corresponded with the German Frobenius Expedition in 1938–39.

The songs and dances recovered include one from Alan Balbungu's Garlgudada *Junba* dance-songs, using documentation by Neowarra and others, and one from Wundhalmanja and Bungguni's shared *Jadmi/Jodmolo/Ngodben* repertory. The latter example was prompted by a photograph of a dance originating from the expedition (fig. 4).[6]

Undertaking this work of returning cultural heritage contributes to increasing musical and linguistic diversity in performed repertoire today, while also providing opportunities for knowledge transmission and for participation (Treloyn, Charles and Nulgit 2013). As proponents of the practice today have noted elsewhere, this helps establish a sense of pride, plays a role in increasing youth participation, and contributes to the renourishment of people and place (Parke 2021; May 2022). Continuing the research to link photographs and other documentation from the Frobenius Expedition with the identified recordings, based on the documentation done by Elders in the early 2000s, has immense potential to further these efforts. This 'linking' work increases the significance of the recordings exponentially. As noted above, it means that audio collections – and the work undertaken in making them accessible – has a far-reaching value, contributing to ongoing community goals for wellbeing and sustainability.

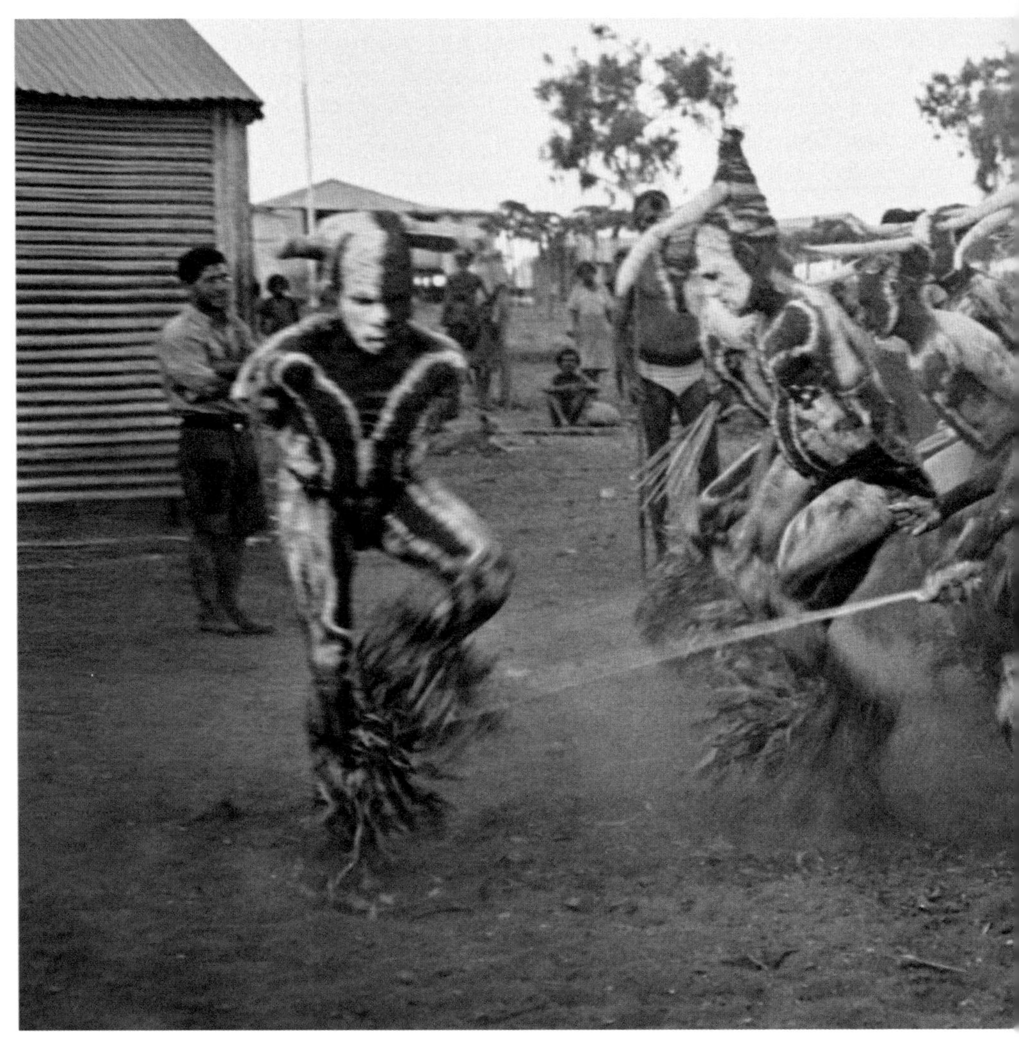

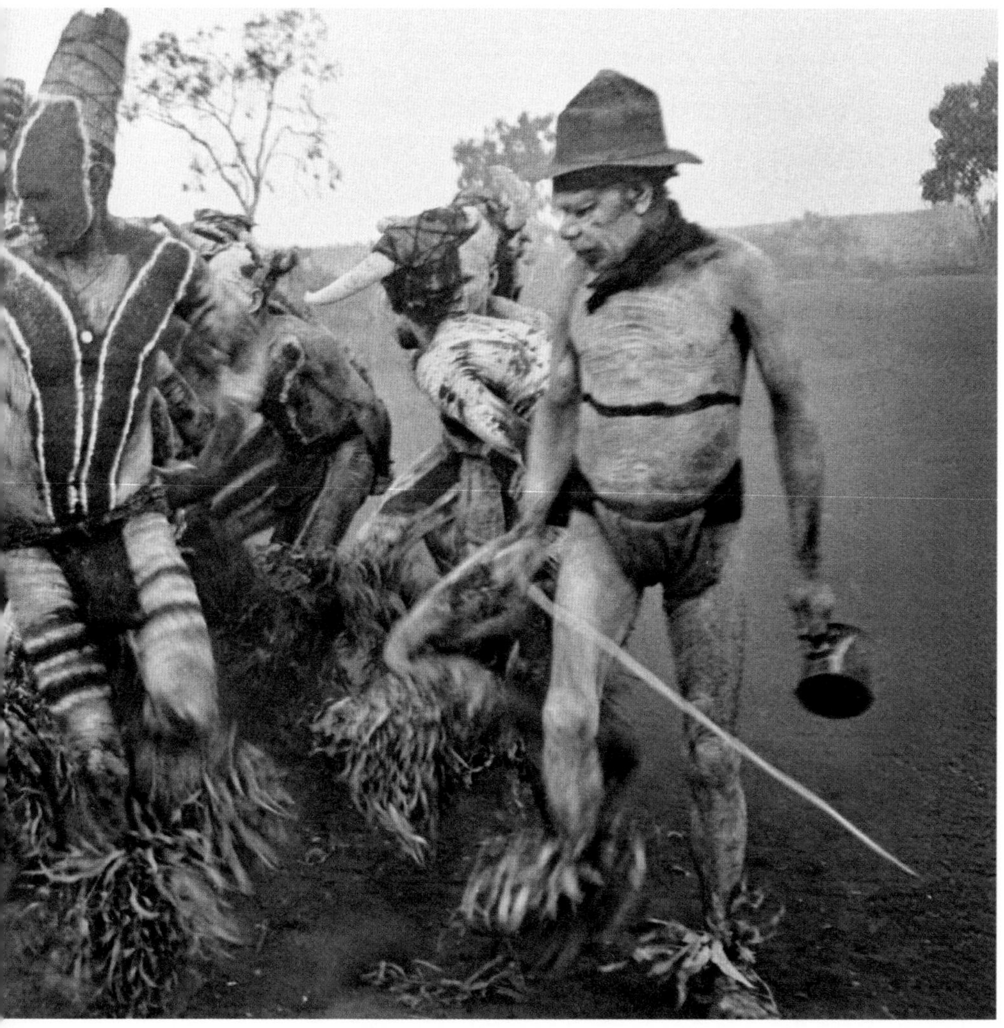

Fig. 4   Photograph of a performance of the *Bulamana Junba* in Kalumburu during the Frobenius Expedition in 1938 which inspired the revival of this *Junba* in 2019. Collection: Frobenius Institute. Photo: Not stated

The Recordings

Endnotes:

1   As soon as the Frobenius Expedition had returned, the wax cylinders containing the recordings were sent to the Berliner Phonogramm-Archiv, which is what enabled them to survive the aerial bombing in World War II. The recordings are listed in the archive's inventory as catalogue no. 94 "Frobenius-Expedition NW-Australien" (Ziegler 2006: 134–135).

2   The research presented in this essay was made possible by many members of the *Wanjina Wunggurr* community from 2000 through to the present day. Writing the essay was supported by the Special Studies programme at the University of Melbourne Faculty of Fine Arts and Music and the German Ethnographic Expeditions to the Kimberley, Northwest Australia project. Particular thanks is noted to Matthew Dembalali Martin, Jeremy Lami Kowan, Rona Googninda Charles, Lloyd Nulgit, Jason Lee, Mariangela Lanza, Wilinggin Aboriginal Corporation and Wunambal Gaambera Aboriginal Corporation for reviewing and offering comment on this essay as it developed.

3   See the account of Laure Gowanulli reported by anthropologist Anthony Redmond (2017: 417).

4   This matches the song transcribed as "bada banga maian buruna" with the gloss "The spirits say to him: 'Look round on the whole plain'" in Lommel (1997: 85).

5   This matches the song transcribed as "ngernger rembeuwe dschali mauane" with the gloss "At the mountain Ngernger Kurangali canot advance, snakes are coming towards him" (Lommel 1997: 86).

6   See Rona Gungnunda Charles et al., *Bringing It Back to Life* in this volume.

References:

Lommel, Andreas. 1997: *The Unambal: A Tribe in Northwest Australia.* Primary English translation by Ian Campbell. Carnarvon Gorge, Qld: Takarakka Nowan Kas Publications.

Lommel, Andreas and David Mowaljarlai. 1994: Shamanism in Northwest Australia. In: *Oceania* 64 (4): 277–287.

May, Catriona. 2022: Sustaining Song and Spirit. In: *Pursuit*, 2022. https://pursuit.unimelb.edu.au/articles/sustaining-song-and-spirit

Parke, Erin. 2021: Rare Captain Cook Dance among Hundreds Revived in the Kimberley. *ABC News*, 12 July 2021. https://www.abc.net.au/news/2021-07-12/captain-cook-yagan-dance/100284908

Redmond, Anthony. 2017: Tracks and Shadows. Some Social Effects of the 1938 Frobenius Expedition to the North West Kimberley. In: Nicolas Peterson and Anna Kenny (eds): *German Ethnography in Australia.* Canberra: ANU Press. 413–434.

Treloyn, Sally. 2014: Cross and Square. Variegation in the Transmission of Songs and Musical Styles between the Kimberley and Daly Regions of Northern Australia. In: Amanda Harris (ed.): *Circulating Cultures: Exchanges of Australian Indigenous Music, Dance and Media.* Canberra: ANU Press. 203–238.

Treloyn, Sally. 2006: *Songs That Pull: Jadmi Junba from the Kimberley Region of Northwest Australia.* PhD dissertation. The University of Sydney.

Treloyn, Sally; Rona Goonginda Charles and Pete Myadooma O'Connor. 2021: Dancing with the Devil (Spirit). How Audiovisual Collections Reveal and Enact Social and Political Agency in Dance and Song (A Case from the Kimberley). In: *Preservation, Digital Technology & Culture* 50 (3–4). 117–129.

Treloyn, Sally; Matthew Dembal Martin and Rona Goonginda Charles. 2019: Moving Songs: Repatriating Audiovisual Recordings of Aboriginal Australian Dance and Song (Kimberley Region, Northwestern Australia). In: Frank Gunderson, Robert C. Lancefield and Bret Woods (eds): *The Oxford Handbook of Musical Repatriation.* New York: Oxford University Press. 591–606.

Treloyn, Sally; Matthew Dembal Martin and Rona Googninda Charles. 2016: Cultural Precedents for the Repatriation of Legacy Song Records to Communities of Origin. In: *Australian Aboriginal Studies* 2. 94–103.

Treloyn, Sally; Rona Googninda Charles and Sherika Nulgit. 2013: Repatriation of Song Materials to Support Intergenerational Transmission of Knowledge about Language in the Kimberley Region of Northwest Australia. In: Mary Anne Norris et al. (eds): *Endangered Languages Beyond Boundaries: Community Connections, Collaborative Approaches and Cross-Disciplinary Research Proceedings of the 17th FEL Conference.* Ottawa, Canada: Foundation for Endangered Languages. 18–24.

Ziegler, Susanne. 2006: *Die Wachszylinder des Berliner Phonogramm-Archivs.* Berlin: Ethnologisches Museum, Staatliche Museen zu Berlin.

"Rubbish" Painting

Impressions of Site-Focused Archival Research with Ngarinyin Traditional Owners on their Country

Christina Henneke in collaboration with
Rona Gungnunda Charles and John Rastus

The rattle of the helicopter blades is ear-deafening; communication is only possible via the headset.[1] On the pilot's small display screen we can see ourselves approaching the coordinates of our destination. As we start descending, numerous small patches in shades of brown and green deep below us are gradually transformed into clearly distinguishable trees, bushes and boulders that characterise the landscape in this area. Craggy, jagged rocks of golden-brown sandstone jut out from the tall, withered grass, and the plains are covered with bright green, spiky spinifex tufts. There is scattered low tree growth in between them. We search for a suitable landing spot. Suddenly, two rings of light-coloured stones stand out below us, one around the other. Ngarinyin Traditional Owner Rona Charles, sitting next to me in the back seat, points her finger in that direction. From the front seat, John Rastus, another Traditional Owner of the Ngarinyin, nods at her. We are in the right place.

A good hundred metres away, the pilot finds a rocky plateau to land on. The helicopter's landing skids touch the stony ground and now everything happens really quickly. We undo our seatbelts and remove our headsets, jump out of our seats and run, our heads bowed beneath the rotating blades of the helicopter. A few seconds later, the pilot is back in the air to pick up the next passengers, and the droning noise and oppressive rotor wind fade away. It gets quieter and quieter. Now we are alone. There are no other people for many kilometres, no telephone reception and of course no road. I am overcome by feelings of dependence on my two companions, but also of gratitude that I am able to share this moment with them. I realise that I am their guest here, and that this role should guide my behaviour.

The rock painting site Maliba II

We had memorised where we saw the stone formations from the air and walk cross-country in that direction. John Rastus leads the way. After a few minutes we reach the spot. Tall yellow grass surrounds a small green area with vegetation covering the ground, which makes it very easy to see the two stone circles in its centre. Rona Charles and John Rastus explain that these two circles refer to a public dance during initiation that is called *Walangarri* (Blundell et al. 2017: 383–384; Mangolamara et al. 2018: 257; Petri 1954: 221). The inner circle is for women and the outer one for men. "*Wanjina* sits in the middle and starts singing," says John Rastus. Both of them examine the stone circles closely. From here, they spot another sight they saw the night before in the online database of the research project: the protected inner side of a rocky outcrop leaning over at a steep angle holds the rock painting that was recorded in the Frobenius archive as Maliba II (fig. 1). Some *Wanjina* heads are already visible from here. Rona Charles and John Rastus walk over a good twenty metres and gesture for me to wait. They approach

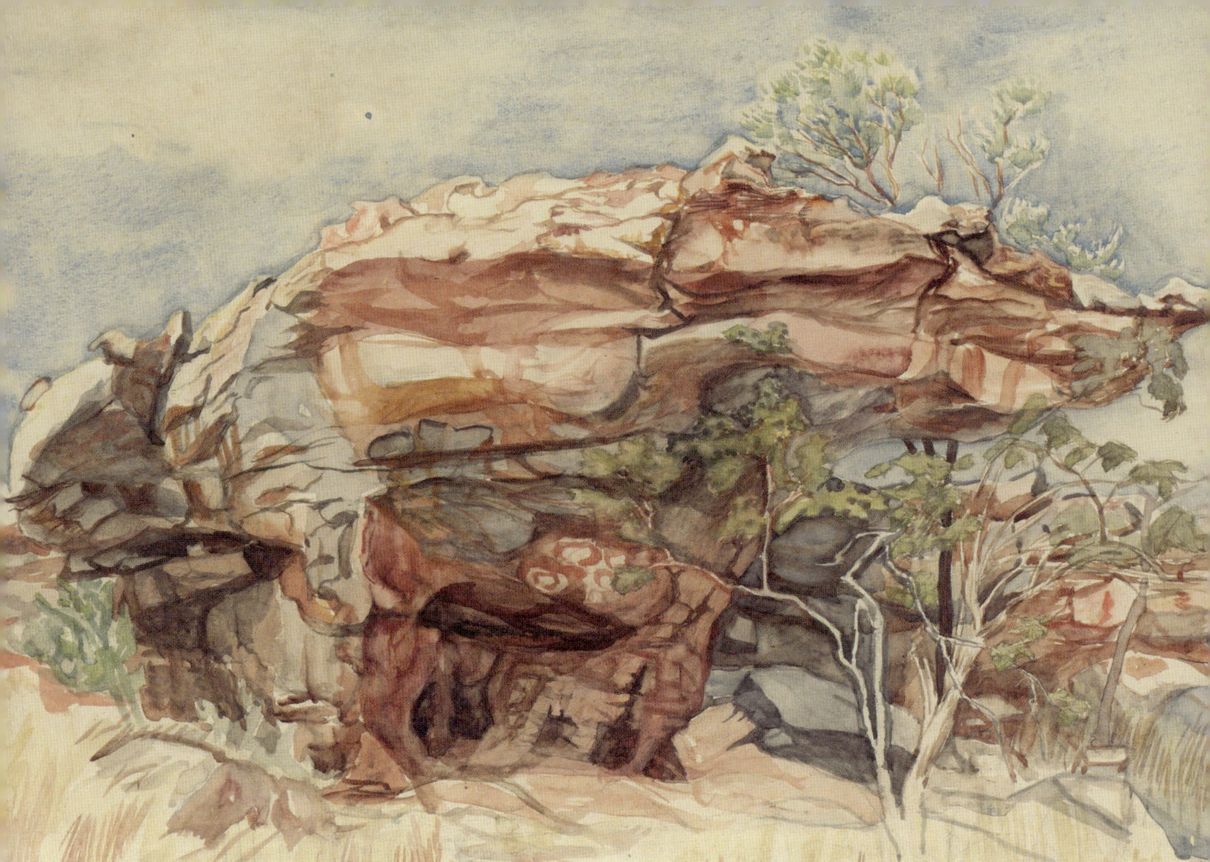

Fig. 1   Watercolour painting of the Maliba II rock shelter by Agnes Schulz, 1938. Collection: Frobenius Institute. Photo: Not stated

in stages and announce their coming to the *Wanjina* by singing in Ngarinyin. "They are looking at us," Rona Charles explains later. In calling out, the Traditional Owners are informing the *Wanjina* that they are approaching them and that they are bringing visitors. It is a way of showing respect to Country that is important for it to open up so that the spirit of Country will listen to the visitors and provide them with what they need (Woolagoodja 2020: 56–57).

I watch from a distance as John Rastus walks closer to the rock painting, examines it and looks into the deeper niches and corners of the shelter. He checks for ancestral remains, as *Banja Odin* (rock painting sites) are often burial sites, and also looks for possible damage from wildlife, cattle, insect nests or weathering. Rona Charles keeps a little further away. From her position, she examines the ochre paintings on the ceiling and the back of the ledge. After a while, I ask if I can come closer and they both agree. John Rastus' first question to me is about who guided the German expedition to this site in 1938. Rona Charles recalls the readings in the archive material from last night, and replies on my behalf that they came here with the Indigenous man Lorri (fig. 4) as their guide. But that would not have been his Country, John Rastus promptly replies. And with this, he sets out a central theme for our visit.

Next, the Ngarinyin man wants to see the historical photos and paintings from the Frobenius archive. So he flips through the booklet with all the information about the site and keeps looking up at the original in front of him. The main painting of Maliba II consists of five *Wanjina* heads without bodies on a white background (fig. 2). They stand together like a family portrait, emerging from beneath the overhanging roof of the shelter. We are all amazed at how intensely the red and white colour has been preserved. There is a striking similarity to the copy painted eighty-five years ago, which I know from the archive and which has been shown in several exhibitions (fig. 3). At first, nothing seems to have changed. But then John Rastus notices that one of the round stones, which are placed on a ledge before the painting, is missing in the historical photos. John Rastus suspects that Jonny Umbagun – another Aboriginal man who was working with the Frobenius Expedition – returned here after the expedition to "keep the Country fresh".

John Rastus turns around. He is the first to hear the buzzing of the returning helicopter; the second half of our group is approaching. Our concentrated, almost contemplative mood is interrupted for the time being. The smoking ceremony known as *Bijagun* needs to be prepared! The Traditional Owners search for leaves of the *Unggarrun*, or ironwood tree. John Rastus roams around and returns just in time with a large branch as the helicopter lands in the distance. The leaves are pulled off and piled into a small heap in front of the rock shelter. John Rastus lights the fire. With the help of water from Rona Charles' drinking bottle, which he drips over the leaves, smoke starts to rise. My colleagues Martin Porr and Richard Kuba make their way through the tall grass. Having been through a smoking on previous days, everyone knows what to do. "Smoke yourself," John Rastus comments on the routine procedure. One by one we stand in the smoke, bend over the small fireplace and wave the smoke at ourselves from the front and back. Immersion in the smoke is a cleansing mechanism that pushes away the negative energy before visiting the *Banja Odin* (Woolagoodja 2020: 61). After we are all cleansed by the smoking, our actual engagement with the painting site can start.

Together we examine the surroundings of Maliba II, take photographs and look at the archival materials in an attempt to determine where the photographers would have stood in 1938. The stone circles in the foreground and the rock shelter of Maliba II in the background appear in my camera's viewfinder. It is as if someone had added colour to the old black-and-white photographs. Other than that, the

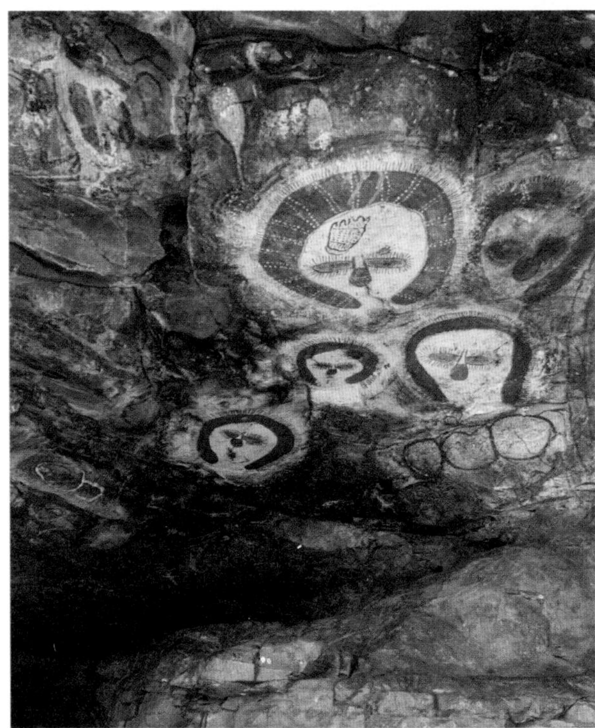

Fig. 2   View of the Maliba II rock art site, 1938. Kimberley, Northwest Australia. Collection: Frobenius Institute. Photo: Not stated

Fig. 3   *Wondjina Heads,* Maliba II rock art site. Kimberley, Northwest Australia. Watercolour on canvas. 77 x 106.5 cm. Rock art copy by Gerta Kleist, 1938. Collection: Frobenius Institute. Photo: Not stated

historical images are barely distinguishable from what I see before me in real life. We also study the written material in the presence of the original rock painting. Sitting in the shade of the shelter, Rona Charles and John Rastus are distilling the information from their ancestors contained in Agnes Schulz's writings. The following is a key passage about Maliba II that the German artist wrote in her diary in June 1938:

> *"On a foray into the area, Lommel found another grotto with Wonjina heads [Maliba II], about 20 metres away from which were two stone circles, a smaller one and a larger one in front of it about 2.50 metres and 6 metres in diameter respectively. One stone positioned similarly in each of the inner and outer circles actually stands upright, two thin slabs of the modest height of 34 and 39 centimetres. The remaining pieces of stone are quite irregular, and spaced about 1 metre apart [...]. Referring to the stone circles, Lorri told me that the main Wondjina [sic] of this tambun [clan estate] had sat there and ordered his subordinate Wondjinas to do the*

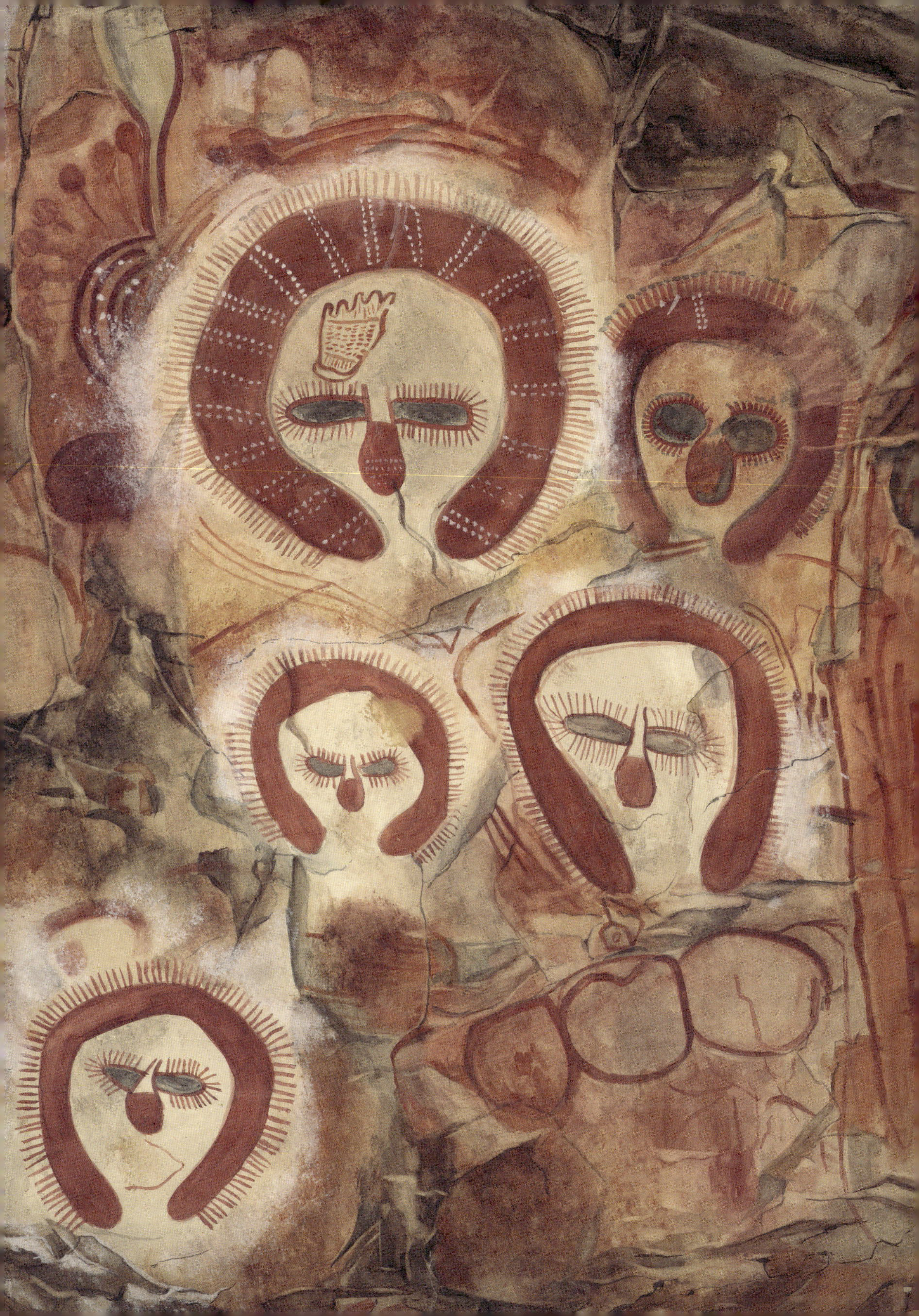

> *paintings in the grotto – this is called Maliba. Of the second group that Lommel found [Maliba II], he explained that it was rubbish, and that it was made not by Wondjina"* (Schulz 1938a: 33; translation by C.H.).

The Traditional Owners have already spent the previous evening studying the compiled archival sources, but now at the original site they seem to be literally diving into it again. Why did Lorri call the rock painting "rubbish"? What did it mean? Last night they already identified Lorri as John Rastus' grandfather (i.e. his mother's father) and deconstructed the name "Maliba" that the Frobenius archive used to describe this place. "Maliba" was puzzling the two as it makes no sense in Ngarinyin language. John Rastus and Rona Charles picked the word apart, dissecting, varying and swapping out each syllable. "We are pushing that word out," Rona Charles explains. *"Barlimba"*, which stands for "Let's go over there. Follow me", emerged as a potential alternative.

Another aspect, the two stone circles that we first saw from the air still remain largely free of overgrowth, as described by Schulz in 1938. Rona Charles and John Rastus discuss what Schulz wrote about the main *Wanjina* sitting in the middle of the stone circle and giving orders to his subordinate *Wanjina*. This essentially tallies with John Rastus' assertion that the *Wanjina* sat here in the centre during the *Walangarri* dance. However, the topic of initiation which is linked to these stone circles was not mentioned in the archival sources on Maliba. The Traditional Owners regard the two stone circles as one of the most important aspects of Maliba, because they represent young men entering adulthood and the law of *Wanjina*. What similarly remained unaddressed in the archival source was the painting of an *Agula* (a type of spirit) on a side wall to the right of Maliba II's main painting. A small sketch in Schulz's field notes proves that she must have seen this spot during her fourteen-day stay here, but it was not identified or interpreted in her writings (Schulz 1938b: 78).

The rock painting site Maliba I

Before commenting further on the historical records, Rona Charles and John Rastus would like to take a look at the second painting on this site, Maliba I. According to the archival sources, it is only 150 metres south of Maliba II, so we head south, all equipped with radio and GPS devices. John Rastus and Rona Charles go on ahead, with my colleague and I some distance behind. After only a few metres of walking through the shoulder-high grass, I realise that I have already lost my bearings and can no longer tell which of the many rocky outcrops behind us house the Maliba II painting. On my own, I would be lost here. Although we are all familiar with the images from the archival material, Maliba I is difficult to spot as it is located in a very low-lying grotto that can only be seen when standing a few metres in front of it. We fight our way through scrub and fallen trees that block the entrance until we finally come face to face with two *Wanjina* heads of Maliba I positioned a little higher. Suddenly they are there, and it is impossible to overlook them. "They are looking out who is coming and letting them [the other *Wanjina*] know who is coming. They are looking out on Country to see. No changes, no disturbances," is how Rona Charles explains the role of the two 'scouts'.

Maliba I was where the Indigenous guide Lorri had escorted the Frobenius Expedition on horseback from Munja.[2] Andreas Lommel, Agnes Schulz, Gerta Kleist and Lorri had camped in the shelter of this rocky outcrop from 15 to 28 June 1938. It was here that they worked, cooked, slept and even celebrated Kleist's twenty-first birthday (fig. 5). The female artists copied the rock paintings and sketched the landscape while Andreas Lommel was gathering information from Lorri about the site and explored the area.

Just like my German colleagues and I, Rona Charles and John Rastus are also here today for the first time in their lives. They start to examine the paintings and the general condition of the *Banja Odin*, as they have done at Maliba II. Since the grotto is so low in height, we lie down on our backs beneath it to view the painting as a whole. Besides the *Wanjina* figures, John Rastus and Rona Charles identify a *Yaali* [kangaroo], a *Belngerr* [cockatoo], a *Wulumbara* [turtle] and numerous *Gambin* [eggs]. Our rocky base is smooth and level, having been flattened over the millennia by kangaroo urine, as the archaeologist in our team explains. The sandy areas directly in front of the rocks are intermixed with black particles, reflecting a presumably long use as a fireplace. Moved by the sight of the fairly well preserved paintings, John Rastus and Rona Charles look towards the future. In the years to come, they want to bring their children and grandchildren to show them these rock paintings, to teach them and tell them the stories. They are also talking about refreshing the paintings (traditional repainting)[3] and re-arranging the partially scattered bones from the burial site we saw yesterday. But for that to happen, they both agree, they would need the guidance of a more senior man: Matthew Martin, who is John Rastus' uncle. This would take some time, but it is an important matter: "We are looking towards that future plan," says Rona Charles.

The other members of our group trickle in one by one. The loud shouting of one teammate to another who could not find the site breaks the concentrated yet dignified atmosphere. John Rastus points out that loud shouting is inappropriate here and becomes even more upset when it occurs a further time. Behaviour at the painting site is subject to specific protocols. Shouting is viewed as impolite. A woman I talked to a few weeks later compared this to the code of conduct in a

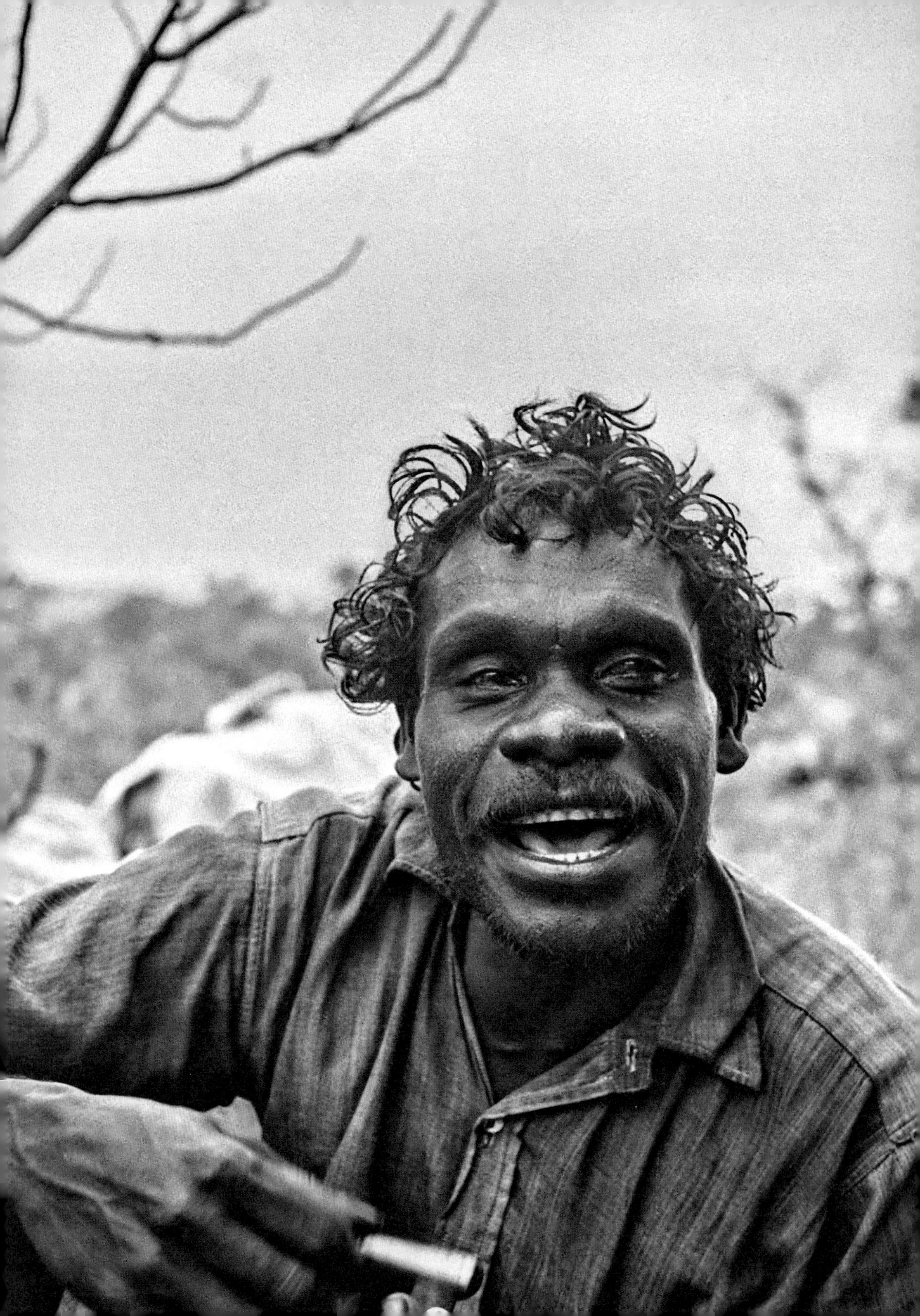

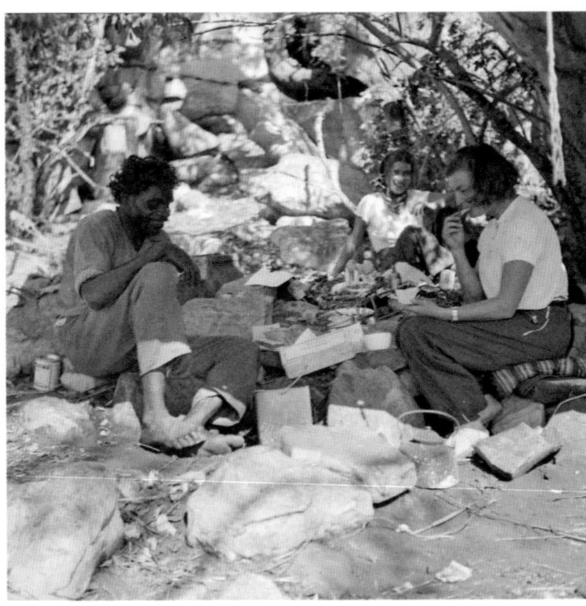

Fig. 4 Lorri singing at the Maliba rock art grotto, June 1938. Collection: Frobenius Institute. Photo: Not stated

Fig. 5 Lorri, Gerta Kleist and Agnes Schulz celebrating Kleist's birthday at Maliba I in 1938. Collection: Frobenius Institute. Photo: Not stated

library or church. The Traditional Owners feel a responsibility towards the *Wanjina* and the Country for the behaviour of their guests that they have brought here. But the mood quickly lightens again given the fascinating rock paintings around us.

A protective claim

We set up a tripod with a camera for a planned film documenting this site visit (fig. 6), which would later become part of the exhibition at the Weltkulturen Museum. In front of the camera, Rona Charles reflects on their experiences today and the significance of the returned archival materials (fig. 7):

> *"We are able to look at the painting a hundred or eighty years ago. And we can see the difference. What was the painting like then and now? We can see if any damage has been done, or if anything has happened around the site. We might see that cattle have ruined some of the paintings. And also the stories – some families probably have not learned the story. But the stories were written down [almost] a hundred years ago so that young people can read that now. And we [John Rastus and Rona Charles] are able to say, yes, this is right because we know most of these stories. That knowledge is on paper,*

> *but it didn't come from them [the expedition]. They didn't have the knowledge, but the people who gave them that information, that's our knowledge, for the future too. And we are able to still carry on that knowledge of the stories. And the knowledge of the people for the Dambun [clan estate], people who belong here, the people who took them out on the expeditions."*

In making this statement, Rona Charles and John Rastus are unmistakably claiming ownership of the cultural knowledge that is embedded in the archival records. In front of the camera, the new impressions blend with those from the endless campfire discussions over recent days. Rona Charles and John Rastus use Agnes Schulz's notes as the basis for interpreting Lorri's reaction. We are all a little puzzled by Lorri's alleged description of Maliba II as "rubbish", which Schulz has recorded. I am immediately reminded of other occasions well known from literature when this term has led to fatal misinterpretations of Aboriginal interlocutors (Redmond 2002: 58; Walsh 1994: 13; Crawford 1968: 86). In our case, too, the term "rubbish", which initially seems so clear cut, conceals a deeper misunderstanding in the intercultural genesis of the archival records. Based on her notes, Agnes Schulz had summarised the respective scene later again in a publication and added her own interpretation of the event:

> *"We were greatly surprised when the attending Ungarinyin [sic] qualified this painting as 'rubbish'. It was done by blackfellows; it was not done by Wond'ina [sic]. We could not get anything more out of him. Possibly his remark sprang from disappointment, since the place had been found by Lommel without his assistance. He was a vivacious young man who seemed to be attached to the spirit world of the traditions by imagination rather than esoteric knowledge"*
> (1956: 29f).

From the start, Rona Charles and John Rastus find the interpretation – that Lorri called the rock painting "rubbish" out of disappointment and that he lacked "esoteric knowledge" – unconvincing. Since they had already identified Lorri and situated him within their kin relations, they knew that this was not his Country and that he accordingly did not possess the full rights to speak for it. But they presume that he had received permission from a *Munnumburra* [fully initiated] man at Munja to escort the group here. Otherwise, it would have been unimaginable. Lorri must have had cultural knowledge about this place from being a classificatory in-law of the Country through his wife – John Rastus' maternal grandmother.

Rona Charles explains this to the camera as she sits on a rock in front of the low roof painting:

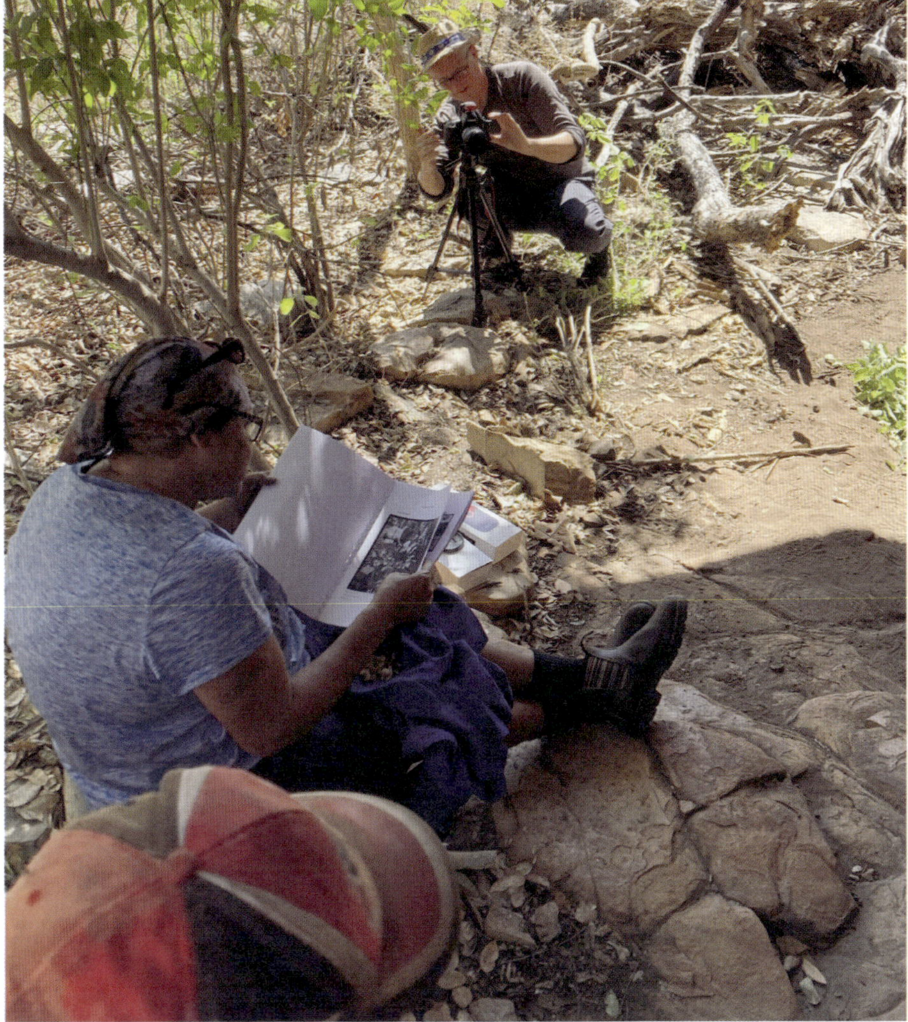

Fig. 6   Rona Charles studying the archival records.
Photo: Christina Henneke, 2023

"His grandmother, his Gaja [John Rastus' mother's mother], was the youngest wife of Lorri. He [Lorri] had five wives and she was the youngest. And she had a daughter to Lorri, which is John's mother. But the mythological narrative of this area relates more to his father's mothers [John Rastus' father's mothers]. So this is the other line."

While Rona Charles is describing his relationship to the site, John Rastus points to the three *Wanjina* figures behind him that refer to the women from his paternal

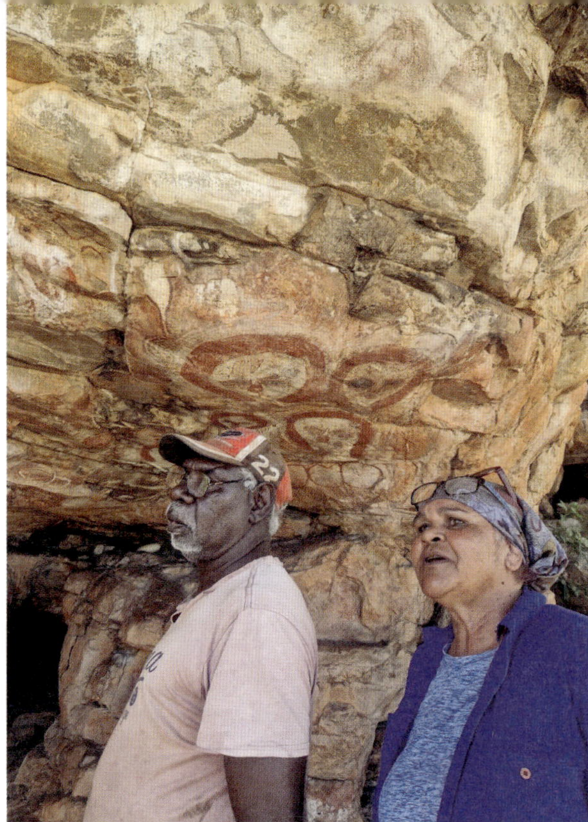

Fig. 7 Rona Charles and
John Rastus in front of Maliba II.
Photo: Richard Kuba, 2023

ancestry. "This is all his *Maga* [father's mother and her sisters], the three females, three *Maga*," Rona Charles explains. Painted using ochre on rock, the *Wanjina* figures of Maliba I are more than a symbolic representation of John Rastus' ancestors; they embody his paternal grandmother and her sisters – the family of the Traditional Owners of this Country. As their descendant, John Rastus is allowed to speak about and for this place today and at the same time bears the personal responsibility to preserve this legacy. Rona Charles and John Rastus agree that Lorri neither lacked knowledge about Maliba II nor did he call the painting "rubbish" because of a hurt ego. In actual fact, he had only been able to talk about a few things because he was not the Traditional Owner of the site and, as an in-law, was not allowed to say much more. Rona Charles imagines herself in Lorri's position:

> *"He wasn't comfortable with Lommel going there by himself, obviously because in any circumstances when you are going on Country and visiting the cave sites, there has to be a older person or a couple of people being in front: the Custodians or the Traditional Owners of that Country. And when I look at it, I was thinking that he felt so uncomfortable that he could not say anything."*

They suspect that he did not want to show Maliba II to the Germans because he was not the Traditional Owner of this area and also because of the *Agula* painting, which surely would have scared him. "It will make you mad, your mind twists," is how John Rastus explains the potential risk posed by the *Agula* on the side of the rock face. When Lommel then discovered the site himself, Lorri felt bad as he was responsible for the wellbeing of the group. He had wanted to protect them by not revealing Maliba II. But Lommel had violated cultural protocols by making his own inquiries to find the site, and this must have frightened Lorri. Schulz reported in her diary that Lorri would not go out of the camp at night for fear of *Agula* and kept asking when other Indigenous companions from Munja station would be sent to join him. One day he disappeared altogether, despite being well aware that this could lead to punishment from the station manager (Schulz 1938a: 34; Fox 1938: 11).

After their visit to the site, Rona Charles and John Rastus are now even more certain than they were the night before when they first looked at the archival sources: the statement that the Maliba II images were "rubbish" was a protective claim that was intended to avert potential danger and harm for the group of visitors as well as for himself.

The more Rona Charles and John Rastus put themselves in Lorri's shoes while we are filming in Maliba, the more I learn to see the place as Lorri saw it. After a lot of talking about the archive and the intense impressions this place has left on all of us, everybody is exhausted. John Rastus and Rona Charles want to pursue another passion: fishing. The Calder River, just fifteen kilometres away, provides the best opportunity for this. Our pilot gives them an airlift. After the fishing trips of the last few days have only been moderately successful, today they return with numerous bags of black bream.

Endnotes:

1 The field visit took place in July 2023 and was jointly organised by the Wilinggin Aboriginal Corporation and the DFG research project "The German Ethnographic Expeditions to the Kimberley, Northwest Australia: A Collaborative Assessment of Research History, the Interpretation of Australian Aboriginal Heritage, and Digital Repatriation". The text is written from Christina Henneke's perspective with cultural knowledge provided by Traditional Owners Rona Charles and John Rastus.

2 Munja was a government-run Aboriginal station on Walcott Inlet in Ngarinyin Country, where the Frobenius Expedition had set up their research base for a few months in 1938.

3 See Kim Doohan et al., *The Country Owns Us* in this volume.

References:

Blundell, Valda et al. (eds). 2017: *Barddabardda Wodjenangorddee. We're Telling All of You. The Creation, History and People of Dambimangaddee Country.* Based on the Cultural Knowledge and Recollections of Janet Oobagooma, Donny Woolagoodja and Other Senior Dambeemangaddee People. Fremantle: Fremantle Press and Dambimangari Aboriginal Corporation.

Crawford, Ian. 1968: *The Art of the Wandjina.* Oxford: OUP in association with the Western Australian Museum.

Fox, Douglas C. 1938: *1. Bericht Fox, 19.7.1938* (unpublished archival source). Frankfurt am Main: Archive of the Frobenius Institute, HP 027.

Mangolamara, Sylvester et al. 2018: *Nyara Pari Kala Niragu (Gaambera), Gadawara Ngyaran-Gada (Wunambal), Inganinja Gubadjoongana (Woddordda): We Are Coming to See You.* Derby, WA: Dambimangari Aboriginal Corporation and Wunambal Gaambera Aboriginal Corporation.

Petri, Helmut. 1954: *Sterbende Welt in Nordwest-Australien.* Braunschweig: Albert Limbach.

Redmond, Anthony. 2002: 'Alien Abductions', Kimberley Aboriginal Rock-Paintings, and the Speculation about Human Origins: On Some Investments in Cultural Tourism in the Northern Kimberley. In: *Australian Aboriginal Studies* (2): 54–64.

Schulz, Agnes Susanne. 1956: *North-West Australian Rock Paintings.* Memoirs of the National Museum of Victoria, Melbourne (20): 7–57.

Schulz, Agnes Susanne. 1938a: *Australien – Expedition, Tagebuch I, Frau Schulz, 9.2. – 27.6.1938* (unpublished archival source). Frankfurt am Main: Archive of the Frobenius Institute, HVD 207.

Schulz, Agnes Susanne. 1938b: *Fieldnotes* (unpublished archival source). Frankfurt am Main: Archive of the Frobenius Institute, LF 1681.

Walsh, Grahame L. 1994: *Bradshaws: Ancient Rock Paintings of Northwest Australia.* Geneva: Edition Limitée.

Woolagoodja, Yornadaiyn. 2020: *Yornadaiyn Woolagoodja.* Broome: Magabala Books.

Bringing It Back to Life

The Re-Creation of the *Bulamana Junba*

Group discussion with Rona Gungnunda Charles,
Lloyd Nulgit, Pete O'Connor and Leah Umbagai,
edited by Christina Henneke and Isabel Kreuder

During a three-week residency at the Weltkulturen Museum in Frankfurt in November 2023 four *Wanjina Wunggurr* Traditional Owners discussed a collection of twenty-five historical photographs that were taken during the Frobenius Expedition in 1938. While the Traditional Owners were familiar with some of these photos before coming to Germany, most were new to them. As part of the residency, they wanted to give exhibition visitors an explanation of the important role played by these archival materials in re-remembering and reviving the historical *Junba*[1] (song and dance tradition) being depicted there. The following text is an edited transcript of a group discussion in which the Traditional Owners sat in front of these historic images and held some of them in their hands, while also talking about this *Junba* called *Bulamana* (fig. 1).

Pete: That is our dance, our Joonba. That was recorded back in 1938. Here we are looking at the archival material that was created back then. It tells the story about the Brahman cattle[2] and the first time Brahman cattle would walk through our Country. These images were taken back in 1938. For a long time we didn't even know they were taken. And then there was this project called the 'Joonba project' which goes into a lot of archives and materials, and these images were sourced out.

Rona: These pictures themselves not only tell us about the dance, they tell us a lot of story [...]. They talk about and show us how our old people performed and how we [the people in 1938] were painted and how the materials on the actual performers looked like. They gathered the

Fig. 1 The four Traditional Owners Leah Umbagai, Pete O'Connor, Rona Charles and Lloyd Nulgit (from left to right) together with filmmaker Florian Kluck during recordings in the studio of the Weltkulturen Museum. Photo: Kim Doohan, 2023

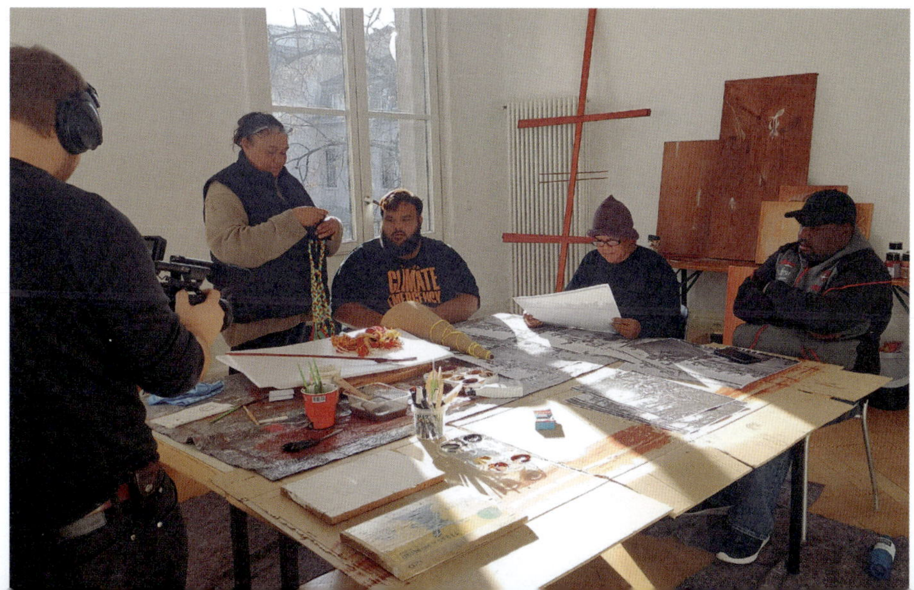

Bringing It Back to Life

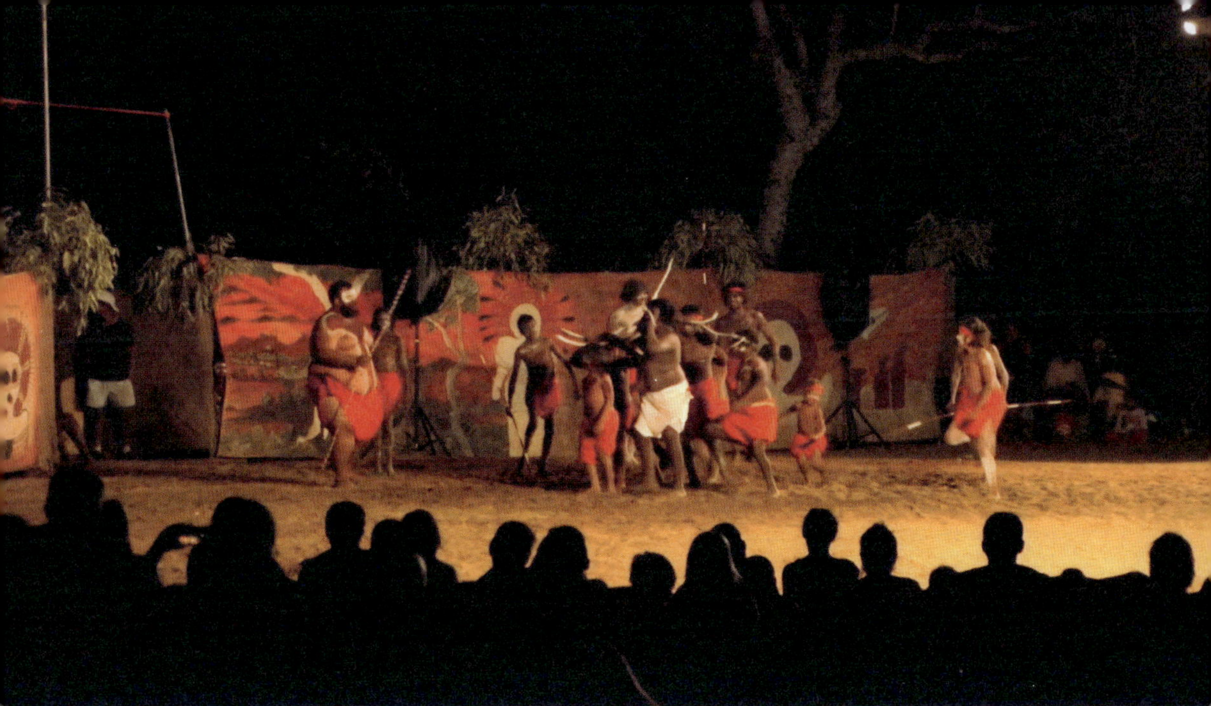

Fig. 2   Film still showing the contemporary *Bulamana*
Junba performed for the first time during the 2019
Mowanjum Festival. Photo: PAKAM, 2019

natural resources such as red and white ochre in order to perform this
dance. And as we look at these pictures, the body paintings tell us about
the two different skin groups [moiety groups]. These are part of the
three Wanjina Wunggurr groups and how we perform our identity –
you can be Jungoon or Wodoy [names of the two moieties].

Before the Junba project we had no idea about this particular song, this
Bulamana. We all wanted to know the lyrics of the song. We didn't
have any recordings. But one of our senior Ngarinyin leaders, Mr Paddy
Neowarra – he saw these performances when he was a young child.
I'm thinking of him sitting in Country with the singers and watching
maybe his father and uncles, grandfathers, great-grandfathers performing,
dancing. He was sitting in the crowd in the back with the mothers and
grandmothers watching these men performing the Junba. So he wanted to
bring that back. Prior to looking at the photographs, he remembered
the dance and he also remembered the lyrics to this song. And he also spoke

about how important it is to paint the style of the body paint when you're performing this Junba. So he actually started drawing how the dancers would have looked like. When doing that he also remembered to sing the lyrics and we started recording him. It took us a couple of years – two or three years – to work on this particular performance. When we finally performed it, unfortunately that year the old fella [Paddy Neowarra] passed away. He was so passionate to see that he brought this Junba back for the young ones to learn it. Even the lyrics, the young men were singing. So, we performed it that night at Mowanjum Festival [in 2019] and he didn't get to see it. As those dancers were performing that night at the Mowanjum Festival, I started to think of him. I was thinking of some of the little ones that evening sitting in the back with the singers and watching this dance.

These photographs gave us that opportunity of also looking at the characters of the dancers and how they come out of the Wurawun. A Wurawun is like a screen on the dance ground that is made by gathering the natural resources of the leaves and the wood. First the dancers are behind the Wurawun and then they come out. And looking at the photographs – well, you can see that they came out here. It tells us how the dancers on the dance ground came out towards the singers. They used the right side, then they did a curve as they came towards the singers. It is said that the composer is pulling them towards them as they are singing. When they came around, they went back behind [the Wurawun] and then they repeated [the movement in the other direction].

This material, these photographs, are also showing and teaching us the characters and how their bodies were painted. This includes the materials they use on their body, but also the way they dance and perform. There are many different dances. This one is showing you how to dance this Bulamana dance. But it is also learning material for future generations.

Rona to Pete: During that performance at the Mowanjum Festival[3], I think I recall you were performing [as] one of the managers? Were you the manager? In one of the photographs we see him with a hat.

Pete: Yeah, in this dance you got a lot of different characters, like Aunty Rona was speaking. You got the people that dress up like cattle and then also there is the old man dressed as the station manager (fig. 3). *So when we performed it at the Mowanjum Festival, I was the manager and had to paint myself with Ornmol, which is the white ochre from the Country. I had painted my whole body white.*

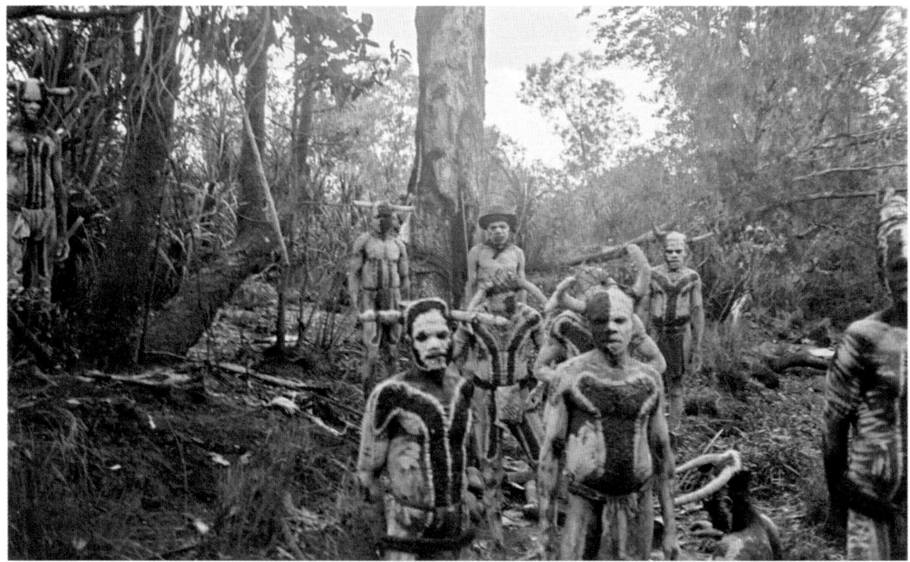

Fig. 3   Dancers preparing for the performance of *Bulamana Junba* in Kalumburu in 1938. Collection: Frobenius Institute. Photo: Not stated

At first, I tried to understand what this dance was about. It was about when cattle first roamed the Country. Cattle is not native to our land and it was the first introduced species of animals in our Country. And so my ancestors created the song. The station manager with his cowboy hat Nagala painted in white with his stick, which would have been a whip. And another performer was the Aboriginal, like a head stockman. He was the second in charge. And he would walk around with his Ngaadaddee paperbark hat and stick. He used to be the station manager's first hand. They used to keep cattle in areas where there was no fence to keep them together (fig. 5).

We did, like, a re-choreography of that Joonba. We recreated this dance just by looking at the photos and listening to the stories what Mr Neowarra told us. It was a fun project, revitalising this dance. And it was good to get all the kids involved to make their spirit happy and to make ancestors happy. You know, like when they first saw this and first created this dance. It was an awesome experience to bring something so old back to life. Often people, white men, they say the old Joonba are gone, but they are not, they are just resting. That spirit was resting and now we brought it

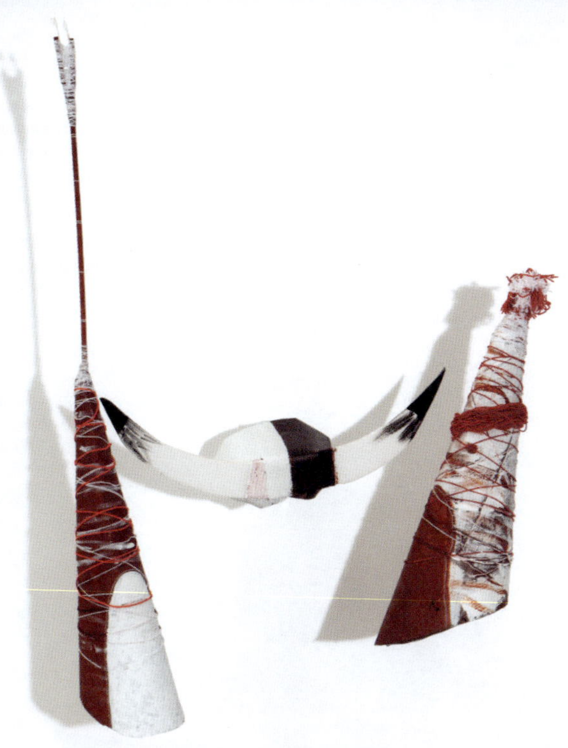

Fig. 4 Headdresses, which are worn during the *Bulamana* dance, made by Leah Umbagai and Pete O'Connor during the artist residency in November 2023. Photo: Wolfgang Günzel, 2024

back to life. And thanks to, you know, the Frobenius Expedition that has done this trip long time ago, they were able to record it and put it in their archive that is still here today for us to look at it. That is a bit of a blessing in disguise to have something like this and to bring it back to life. If it wasn't this expedition and that old man Mr Neowarra, this Joonba would have been lost. But it isn't and we have put it back to life again. So, that is the importance of some of these archival materials and stuff, because even now that it is not in Country, it is good to see that we can bring it back. We brought it back to life. And me as a dancer and per-former, I feel happy, honoured to dance this Joonba, and being one of the first people to recreate something that was not lost, but misplaced.

Rona: I was just thinking about the composer. He was a Wunambal person who had this song performed in 1938. I am thinking about him as he was singing about the cattle and kind of imagine him walking through Country. In his early years through his teenage or infancy, he saw how the cattle as an introduced species impacted his Country. It damages rock art, the vegetation, or waterholes. And there is a message that maybe he wanted to tell us: the cattle does have a lot of impact on our Country.

Bringing It Back to Life

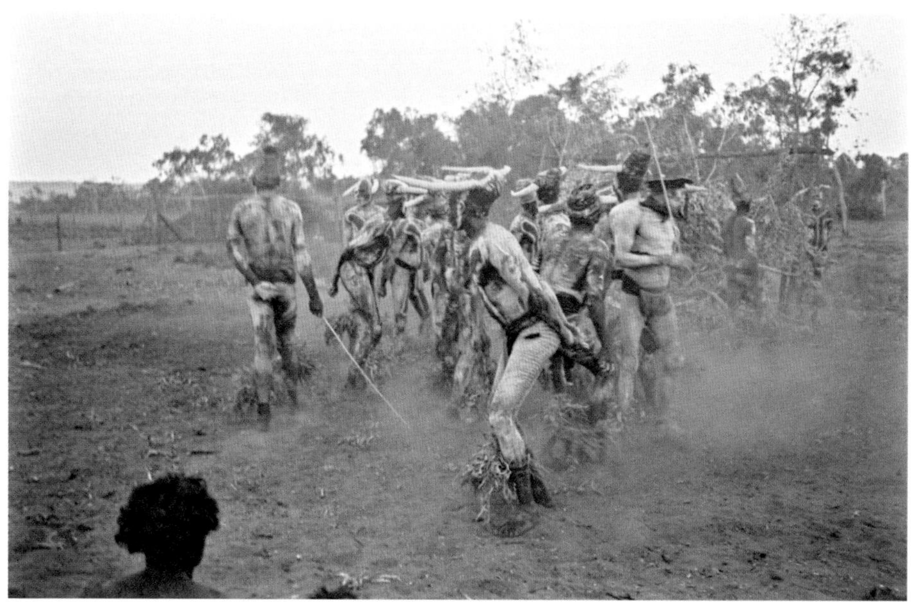

Fig. 5   Performance of the dance in Kalumburu in 1938.
Collection: Frobenius Institute. Photo: Not stated

Leah: I suppose as people of today, we practise, we gather, we take children out and we do the performance today. For us it is a privilege to continue our traditions. Our ancestors have done it then and we have old people to bring it back to life. [Nowadays] we are giving it a little bit of flavour to how young people today dance. Like Pete said, it has been a tradition then, and now we are bringing it back to life. It is part of our story of Country. It is part of how we were back then to how we are today.

I was still able to sing the song of this Joonba with the old women that have left us now. It has been a privilege to sing with them the old songs which have been performed during the Mowanjum Festival. It feels really good in here, that we brought something to life but also that our children today are still performing songs and dances. And we will continue to do that.

Rona: Yes, looking at the photography in front of me, it is bringing me back, like I am sitting with the old ladies in the back and the singers. I am thinking of Mr Neowarra, you know, sitting there. The photograph, it feels alive. I imagine myself, like him back then, sitting there and watching this performance.

Lloyd: When you are dancing and stamping the ground, you are waking up the spirits – whether you are on Country or whether you are away from Country. Especially when we are back home dancing and singing on Country, we can feel this, you can feel the spirits of our ancestors, they are there. You can feel the presence of them, like they are singing and dancing with you. That makes you stronger and gives you more confidence and makes you healthy in spirit.

And when they dance, the dancers are listening to the Borndorra. The Borndorra, that is the clapsticks that we use as an instrument to keep the beat going; you got two different ways: the Jadmi and the Jerregorl dance.[4] These are the two principal forms of Junba. The Bulamana belongs to the Jadmi repertoire. It is good that we are continuing our traditional Junba, our Law and culture today as some people may say that we have lost it, but to us, as Traditional Owners of this Country, we feel that it is not lost. We are continuing it and saving it on for the next generations and making it stronger. We sing it today in communities and festivals and on bush trips and kids enjoy it today. It makes me feel happy, my own personal feelings, you know. I've been around Law and culture since I could walk, and somewhere in between we saw the senior people dying away, because our old people were moved away from Country. But with all the materials being recorded back in 1938, we are able to bring it back to life and continue it on.

The historical records and photographs are an important source for the Traditional Owners, not only to re-choreograph the *Junba* but also to keep it alive for generations to come. Making the archives and various kinds of information accessible via an online database and digital repatriation as in this project are vital aspects of the collaboration between communities of origin and institutions holding collections of a shared heritage.

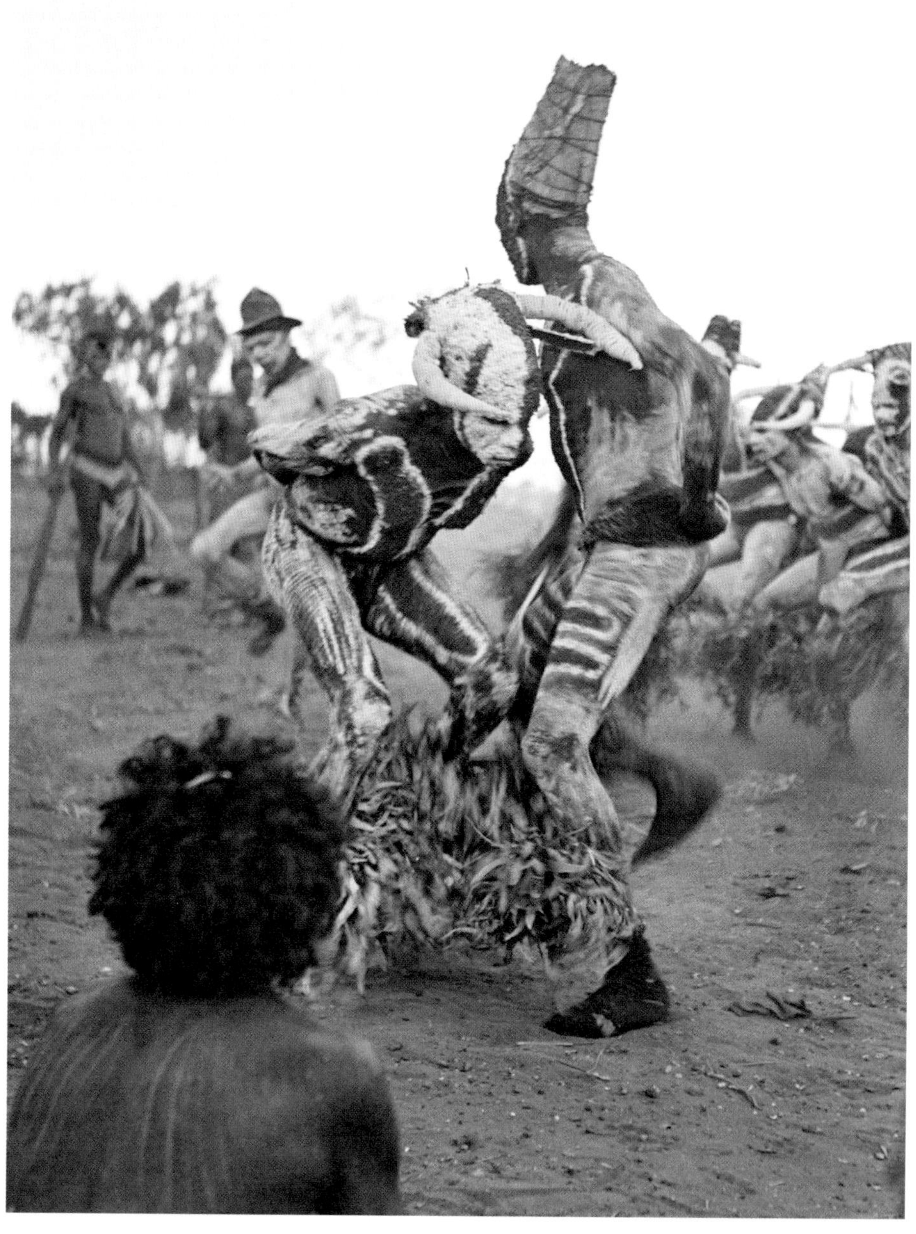

Fig. 6   Performance of the *Bulamana Junba* in Kalumburu in 1938. Collection: Frobenius Institute. Photo: Not stated

Endnotes:

1. There are different orthographies used for the different languages: Ngarinyin, Woddordda, Wunambal and Gaambera. In this text the spelling for the different languages for common cultural practices is used for the relevant speaker, i.e. the Woddordda word *Joonba* is spelt *Junba* for Ngarinyin speakers.

2. Today, Brahman cattle are the most widespread breed in Australia. Developed from the progeny of Indian Zebu, the Brahman was introduced to Australia because of its high tolerance to heat, sunlight and humidity. There have been different breeds of Brahman cattle over time; the early variety depicted in this *Junba* is recognizable by its horns. Nowadays the term Brahman is more likely to be used for a breed with no horns at all. The impact on the environment is nevertheless extensive.

3. The Mowanjum Festival is an annual dance festival held on the outdoor grounds of the Mowanjum Arts Centre near Derby. As one of Australia's oldest Indigenous cultural festivals, it brings together Aboriginal dancers from across the Kimberley region to perform their traditional dances for local people and tourists.

4. The *Wanjina Wunggurr* distinguish two main types of *Junba*. In *Jadmi*, the dancers wear *Ngardarri* (a paperbark headdress) and *Yirrminjal* (leaves) as part of their outfit. Their bodies are also painted with the typical designs of their moiety groups. The *Bulamana* is also a *Junba* in the *Jadmi*-style. In *Jerregorl*, the dancers are equipped with *Ornod Jirri* (dancing boards and string totems).

A Message (Stick) to Frankfurt

"We Are Here, Our Stories Are Still Alive!"

Kim Doohan with Rona Gungnunda Charles, Lloyd Nulgit, Pete O'Connor and Leah Umbagai

Four Traditional Owners from the *Wanjina Wunggurr* community of the North West Kimberley region of Western Australia arrived in Frankfurt on 13 November 2023 for a three-week artists' residency. Travelling from the very hot Kimberley region – where there is no need for coats, scarves, warm shoes, or gloves – required planning and preparation.

They were Leah Umbagai and Pete O'Connor, who represented the Dambimangari Aboriginal Corporation, and Rona Charles and Lloyd Nulgit, who represented the Wilinggin Aboriginal Corporation, with the Wunambal Gaambera Aboriginal Corporation representatives in constant telephone and email contact with those in situ. Kim Doohan, an anthropologist and human geographer, accompanied the Traditional Owners to provide some inter-cultural assistance to the project participants (fig. 1).

The four Traditional Owners accepted their responsibility to represent and communicate the fundamental cultural values of the wider *Wanjina Wunggurr* community and their Country whilst working with the Weltkulturen Museum and Frobenius Institute staff and researchers. They were invited to undertake four important and emotionally demanding tasks whilst in Frankfurt:

1. to visit and review the material and digital collections at the Weltkulturen Museum and at the Frobenius Institute from the 1938 Frobenius Expedition to places in *Wanjina Wunggurr* Country;
2. create new, contemporary art works both in response to the archival materials held in the Frobenius Institute's and the Weltkulturen Museum's collections and as a matter of cultural continuity;
3. to participate in informing and co-curating an exhibition of archival and contemporary materials for the planned exhibition in 2024 – namely COUNTRY BIN PULL'EM; and were expected
4. to report back to *Wanjina Wunggurr* Traditional Owners about what they saw, how they felt, what they did and what might be next in the relationships renewed through the residency and exhibition.

The residency members were accommodated in the visitor apartments at the Weltkulturen Museum courtesy of the City of Frankfurt. Traditional Owners noted that the buildings associated with the Weltkulturen Museum were situated along the banks of the river Main; Munja, the location of much of the 1938 expedition's research is located on the banks of Jilai (the Walcott River). This concurrence stimulated Traditional Owners to contemplate the implications of this apparently random coincidence.

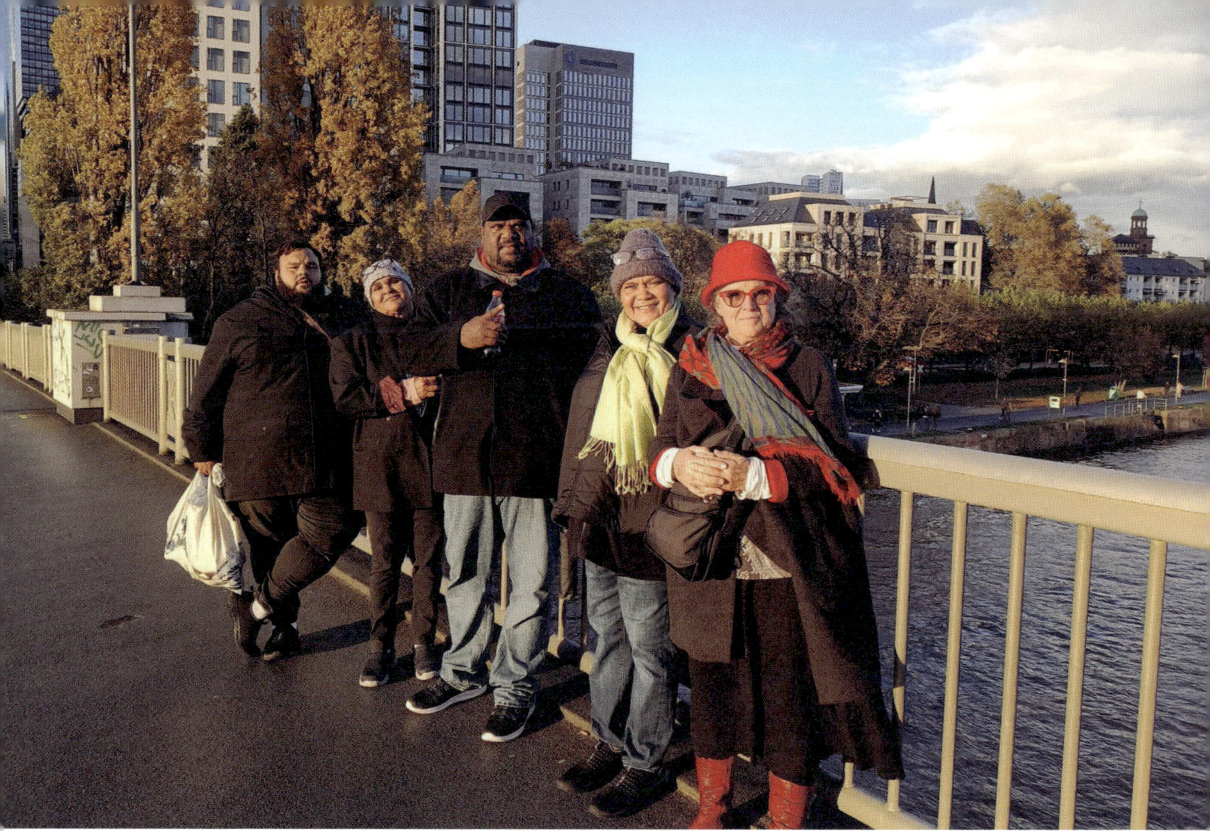

Fig. 1   Traditional Owners Pete O'Connor, Rona Charles, Llyod Nulgit, and
Leah Umbagai with Kim Doohan (from left to right) on arrival in Frankfurt.
Photo: Christina Henneke, 2023

However, on reflection and over the course of working on their artworks and reviewing the collections, it became apparent that profound influences were oper-
ating through time and space, reinforcing the deep connections between the
Traditional Owners, their old people and their German colleagues. The Traditional
Owners believe that Country is an enlivened place with interactive powers that
engage with, and influence people. The Traditional Owners believe that, far from
the German researchers being independent agents, it was the power of their
Country that called the researchers and pulled them to the Kimberley, thus establishing a relationship which lasts until today. From this deep, metaphysical posi-
tioning, and with hours of discussion, debate and collaboration between the participants, there emerged the title of the exhibition COUNTRY BIN PULL'EM. The
phrase best reflects the culturally enmeshed nature of the relationship between
the Frobenius Expedition members and *Wanjina Wunggurr* Traditional Owners.

Residency context

More than ten years ago Traditional Owners began to reinvigorate their connection with the German institutions. They wanted to locate and review archival records and materials, including items such as bush crafts, tools and art works created by their ancestors, as well as notebooks, drawings and art works created by expedition members whilst working with their ancestors. The Traditional Owners were essentially unfamiliar with these collections. They were keen to know why researchers back then took things back to Germany, what was written about them and why; they were keen to know how their society and cultural values were represented in the archival records and subsequent publications.

For the Traditional Owners, this was an active re-invigoration of a dormant relationship. A relationship with their archived cultural heritage materials, derived from their old peoples' sharing of knowledge, with the Institutions that hold these records and their staff, as well as the beginning of a new and renegotiated chapter in that relationship.

In 2020 the new chapter took shape as a formally agreed research collaboration between the three Aboriginal representative bodies; Dambimangari, Wilinggin, and Wunambal Gaambera Aboriginal Corporations and members of the Frobenius Institute, the Weltkulturen Museum, the Museum Fünf Kontinente in Munich, the University of Western Australia, as well as the Western Australian Museum and the Mowanjum Art Centre. Funding was secured through the Deutsche Forschungsgemeinschaft (DFG). Further funding for aspects of the project and the Frankfurt residency was also provided by the Weltkulturen Museum, the Frobenius Institute, the Aboriginal Corporations and private donations. The project functioned successfully over four years with the residency and exhibition as one of the affirmative outcomes.[1]

Making art and review of collections

Upon arrival, the museum and institute staff made the Traditional Owners feel welcome, they provided orientation documents and travel cards, and generally eased the transition to life in Frankfurt. The apartments provided a sense of home and the artists' studio on the floor below was spacious, light and still, thereby providing an ideal creative environment and the luxury of supported time away from the demands and distractions of daily life in the home communities. A wide range of art materials were delivered to the studio; work commenced immediately.

Visits to the Weltkulturen Museum's and the Frobenius Institute's collections were undertaken on several occasions throughout the residency. The residency also attracted the attention of the Australian Embassy in Germany. Kate Luxford (Chargé d'Affaires, Australian Embassy Germany) accompanied Traditional Owners on one of their visits to inspect materials in the Frobenius Institute.

The artists became deeply immersed in the process of responding to the collections; the collections inspired the works – the works were modified and enhanced. The staff from the Frobenius Institute and the Weltkulturen Museum visited the studio and apartments for consultations. Access to the digital archive database was made possible through a computer in the studio; there was an atmosphere of dynamic exchange and creativity.

The combination of comfortable domestic and calm studio environments enabled the Traditional Owners to create 29 new works, as well as providing time and space to quietly review database entries, connect with, and exchange knowledge and practices with numerous staff members throughout the residency. It was also a time to reflect on each day's experiences and how to convey these experiences to kin back home.

For the Traditional Owners, travelling to be in the presence of cultural items taken from their home a long time ago, presented some challenging emotions and anxious moments. The first visit was to the Weltkulturen Museum's collection, at a depot which stores materials from other countries and peoples. The presence of other peoples' cultural materials was a bit disconcerting for the Traditional Owners; how were they to know if these cultural materials were safe? Would the Traditional Owners of these other materials be happy for them to be visited? These apprehensions were also felt when Traditional Owners were visiting the Frobenius Institute and encountered the extensive collection of copies of rock art from around the world.

Despite their initial uneasiness, the Traditional Owners were relieved to see that the collections were being carefully curated in the German institutions and respectfully handled by staff. Traditional Owners were then also excited to be encountering their own cultural materials in the collections. Sometimes there was a sense of being transported back to Country, and at other times, if the records were unclear, there were concerns about which people had created these materials. Rona Charles said:

> *"As I came into the store room, it was strange. As I walked through the door I felt as if the whole room was alive and looking or questioning me. I could sense a strong powerful energy in there.*

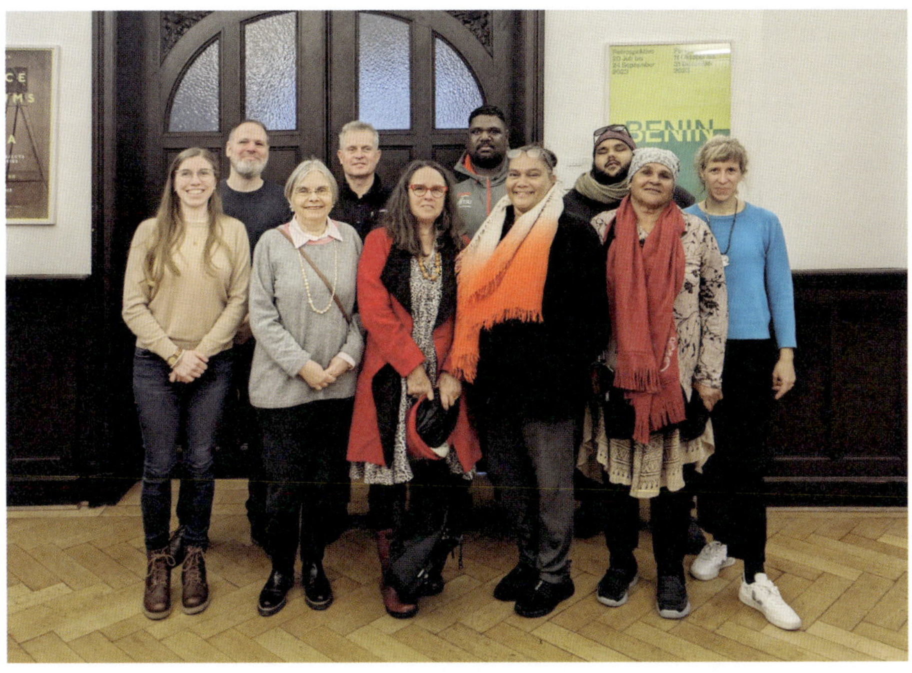

Fig. 2   First formal meeting between partners during the Frankfurt artists residency in November 2023: Matthias Claudius Hofmann, Richard Kuba, Lloyd Nulgit, Pete O'Connor, Christina Henneke, Isabel Kreuder, Eva Ch. Raabe, Kim Doohan, Leah Umbagai and Rona Charles (from left to right). Photo: Claudia Bodens, 2023

It felt like I was a stranger in a different place full of different tribes. 'Nyanggi nyinda? Who is she?' As I came closer to the bark paintings, my leeyaan (like a gut reaction or intuitive sense) felt good. It was as if the artist of the bark painting was talking to me. 'Nyinda gungunda nyi ngarri ngin mamagul biddi Ngarinyin damb. This is Rona my family.' That painting was Gungunda and my name is Gungunda Nyi Ngarri or Gungunda."

Each of the Traditional Owners had similar experiences. The two men were burdened with the extra responsibility of encountering and identifying objects of a potentially secret/sacred character, which might also be (spiritually) dangerous to non-initiated persons, especially women. They viewed the full range of material items first to safeguard the women from any potentially dangerous encounters with restricted objects. Gender restricted materials were identified and appropriately labelled and stored.[2] It was also the expressed wish of the Oceania curator Matthias Claudius Hofmann to have the collection evaluated by the Traditional Owners and to identify objects in the collection that are considered secret/sacred to ensure an appropriate and respectful handling of these cultural artefacts in the future.

Unfortunately, some of the restricted information and photographs of secret/sacred materials and ritual information has been incorporated in at least one of the publications that came out of the 1938 expedition. The original expedition report by Petri was published in 1954 in German. An English translation was only published in 2011 and made the material accessible to the Traditional Owners for the first time (Petri 2011). The men were deeply concerned. There are certain things that cannot be publicly shown, mentioned in public or revealed between genders. The apparent disregard for these important practices, and the constant push to make these secret aspects of their culture public, is a long standing, unresolved issue of genuine concern. It was regretted that Traditional Owners were not involved in the publication process.

Pete O'Connor was unsettled by his encounter with these powerful materials. He was unsure how to react, a disquiet that troubled him even after he returned home:

> *"When I was there, it was like the spirit was telling me that they wanted to get back home; they were lost for a long time. And we don't know if any of those things will come back. Especially that men's stuff. It should really come back and go back to bush where it belongs. When I got home, I talked to our senior old men about the feeling that I got in that room and what that spirit was saying to me. They understood me, those old men, but I am not sure if I will be believed by other people."*

When discussing the residency back in Derby, the senior Ngarinyin man, Matthew Martin said: "They should not have taken them, even then, in those days." Traditional Owners feel that these matters remain for future discussion now that communication channels have been re-established and knowledge exchanges have commenced.

Despite coming to terms with some of the unsettling elements of reviewing collections and being in the presence of other cultural material, the flow of the creative artistic stream persisted. The residency provided the time to reflect and create, to check the archival records, view the collections' material pieces and provide additional information and corrections where needed. There were also ongoing reflections on the social and political context of the period within which the records were created, and how this might have influenced what was written and understood by the expedition members. The Traditional Owners were distressed to hear that so many of their ancestors' materials had been lost during bombing raids in World War II.[3] As Pete O'Connor commented: "There was a loss of spirit of our old people and the Country when that happened."

These collaborative efforts and research process offered Traditional Owners the opportunity to gain a better appreciation and enhanced understanding of how archival records were created, to reflect on how their old people responded and to think differently about the process of research and curation of archival materials. It also alerted Traditional Owners to some of the ways they have been portrayed, some of the predictions that were made about their cultural survival and stimulated them to find ways to articulate responses.

Traditional Owners' cultural responses in Frankfurt

It became evident to the Traditional Owners that there was a pervasive theme of 'what once was' in the archives and some of the resultant publications. A sense of impending cultural loss, decline of connections to Country and expressions of being *Wanjina Wunggurr* people. In essence, an underlying theme of a dying culture.

The Traditional Owners felt they needed to rectify this situation and ensure that the collections, and particularly the exhibition, did not relegate them to the past. They wanted to demonstrate, by way of curation, presence, and preparation of contemporary works, that they were alive and well. They wanted to show their continuing cultural expressions of *Wanjina Wunggurr* traditions. They wanted to demonstrate that their stories travelled with them and that their Country retained power. The kind of power that had, indeed, pulled the 1938 expedition members to the West Kimberley, so that a relationship could be formed.

One of the powerful *Lalai* creator beings, the Barramundi Fish, pulling the expedition members into the community at Munja, was given contemporary manifestation in a collaborative art work with the painting created by Rona Charles and the 'final touches' provided by Leah Umbagai (fig. 3 and 5). "She [the Barramundi] came from Dambeemangaddee saltwater country. She was travelling to get to freshwater because she wanted to lay her eggs. The *Wunggurr* stopped her. This is the same way that the Frobenius people came into Munja Station. They came the same way" (Rona Charles).

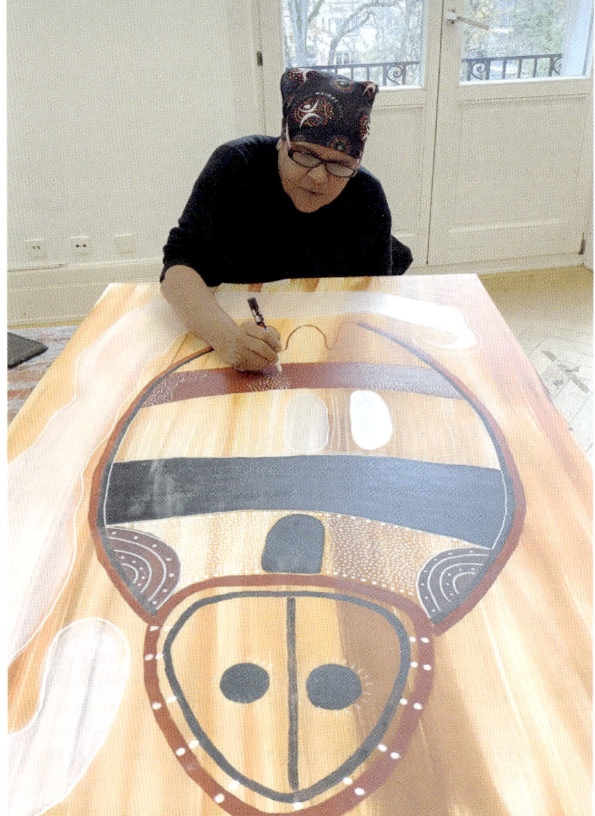

To reinforce these points, Leah Umbagai created a contemporary 'message stick' showcasing Wanalirri (Ngarinyin), Namaralay (Woddordda) and Rumidjmarra (Wunambal) and a *Woongudd* Snake as a way of emphasising continuity and on-going presence, and as an invitation to the public to visit the exhibition (fig. 4).

Other works created during the residency were directed to revealing cultural knowledge and practices embedded in *Lalai*, and to enlighten those who visit the exhibition or the collections in years to come. For instance, several of the works were created to reflect some of the meanings embedded in rock shelters where the creator *Lalai* beings, *Wanjina* in their anthropomorphic and other forms, are located as images. Images left to be seen, to be refreshed and to be respected as a reminder of appropriate social, economic, ritual and ecological behaviour.

Following the senior Wunambal man, William Bunjuck who stated: "That painting, he is holding the land – that paint" (in Mangolamara et al. 2018: 10), the Traditional Owners were attentive to the choices of colours used in the paintings and *Joonba* totem production. They were diligent in choosing colours that best reflected their

Country and the solemnity of the relationship between themselves and what they were preparing for the exhibition. These decisions and choices are understood to act as a reminder of obligations that Traditional Owners have to their Country, where they come from and where they will go after they have lived their lives.

Leah Umbagai explained the meaning of the seemingly simple and pale images of *Wandjina* and *Woongudd*, created to express the continuing importance of *Lalai* to Traditional Owners today (fig. 6). Leah Umbagai described how looking at these images, as paintings, reminds you of the much broader account of the creation of the world as Traditional Owners know it today. For instance, in this image one is reminded of the creative forces of the world which are omnipresent, powerful and largely unknowable, but nonetheless affect humans and their environment; *Wandjina* and *Woongudd*. Their all-pervasive power resides within and does not need to be made bold with colour.

Fig. 4   The two sides of the contemporary message stick created for the people of Frankfurt. Leah Umbagai, 2023. Acrylic paint on wood. 4.5 x 24.5 x 1.5 cm. Collection: Weltkulturen Museum. Photo: Wolfgang Günzel, 2024

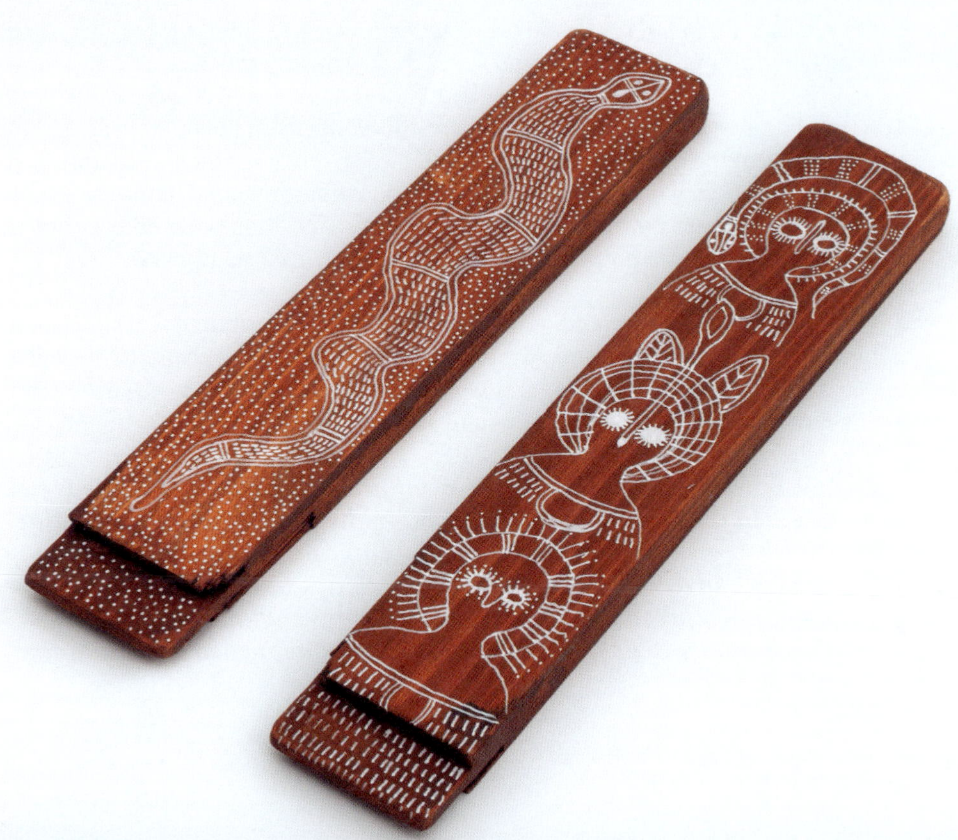

As noted, for the *Wanjina Wunggurr* Traditional Owners 'rock art' is one part of the overall cosmology *Lalai/Lalarn*. Images are alive, they are powerful and an integral aspect of each person, their Country and their worldview. So too are the paintings of *Wanjina* (in their various forms) created by humans, powerful and conveying important knowledge and reinforcing narratives of creation and connection to Country.[4]

Being away from Country, being in Frankfurt or anywhere else, but painting *Lalai* and Country keeps the connection alive. There is a relationship between the images in the art, the ochres and colours of the paint, and the power associated with those images. There are ideas about how a painting or *Joonba* (dance performance with song) will look that come to you when you are in Country, when you are dreaming and from spirits of the Country or your old people. As Leah Umbagai noted, "Sometimes *Wandjina* come to you when you are asleep and ask you: 'When are you going to paint me again?'"

Stimulated by seeing the full collection of archival photos of a performance based on the coming of cattle to their Country from 1938, Traditional Owners spoke of how they had reinvigorated this very *Joonba*. Based on discussions with an Elder, and one of the 1938 images which they had acquired from the Australian Institute of Aboriginal and Torres Strait Islander Studies, the process of recovery began. The Traditional Owners prepared several items that are in the repertoire of the contemporary *Bulamana Junba*.[5] This includes a range of different, colourful, and spectacular 'totems' that are created for each new performance.

The Traditional Owners wanted to include some words from their Elders as part of this story about the residency. They felt that it was because of their ancestors that they could be present in Frankfurt, respond to questions, respond to the collection materials and create new pieces for the exhibition and thus become part of the ongoing corpus of work prepared by *Wanjina Wunggurr* Traditional Owners.

Several senior *Wanjina Wunggurr* Traditional Owners contributed to a significant publication where they explained aspects of their 'rock art' worldview to the wider public. Sadly, these senior men and women are no longer alive, however, their words remain potent, relevant and inspire younger generations.

> *"Everybody likes to look at our Wandjina and our art. This site is there, in the home where our ancestors lived. It was their protection. Different groups had different representation in the cave, all the images had different languages and groups but everybody knew about it, it spread like a fire. Geeyorn and Wandjina started it up. This is evidence of Lalai, creation and what happened in the country.*

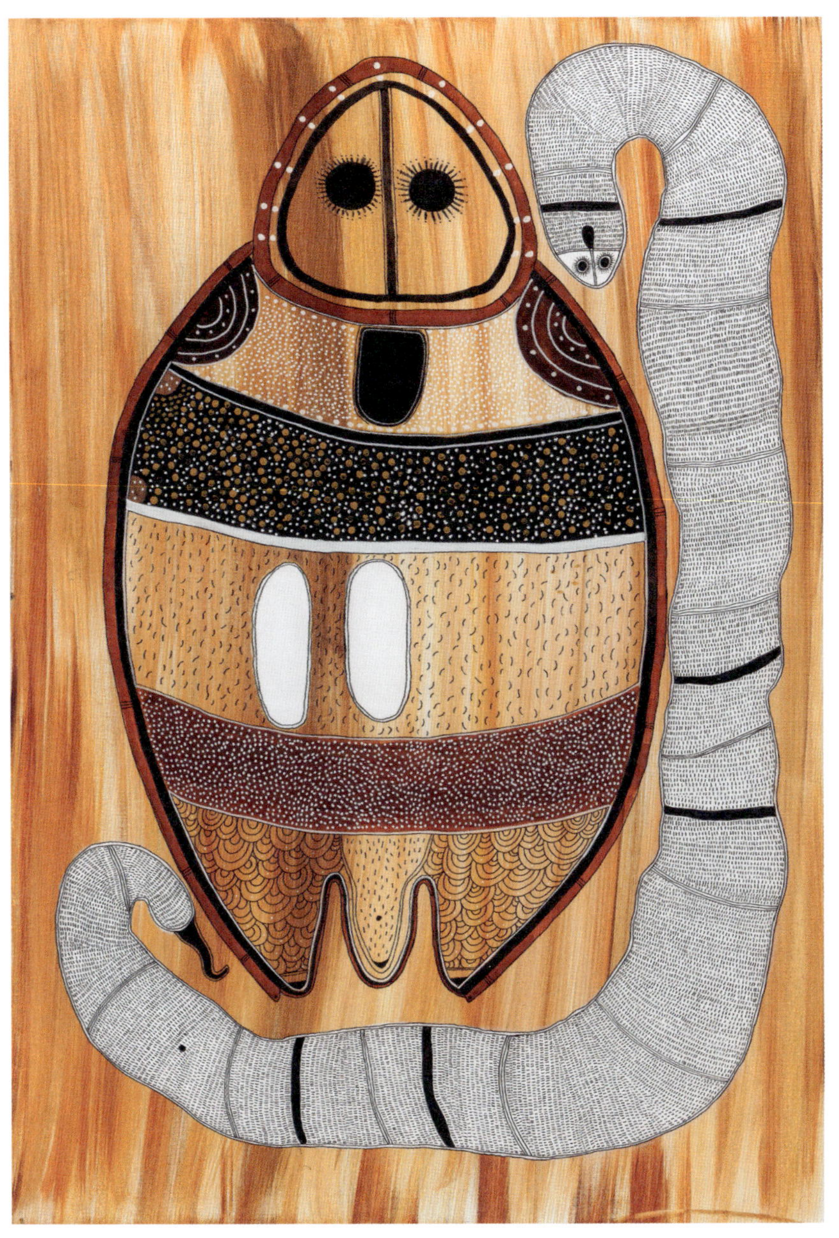

Fig. 5   Rona Gungnunda Charles, 2023: *Barramundi Dreaming.* Acryl auf Leinwand. 80 x 120 cm. Collection: Weltkulturen Museum. Photo: Wolfgang Günzel, 2024

A Message (Stick) to Frankfurt

It is not about dates; it started from Lalai. When there was no beginning of time, it was when the world started. Our evidence is all these images.

The images teach us what the land provides for us: it's our histories. The rock art represents all of these kinds of stories about the Woonan, Woongudd baby spirit, the fish, animals, honey, bush fruits and different kinds of snakes, and the country itself. It's our ancestors that put this for us and our future generations. When we are looking at country and rock art, it's not about things but the spirit of the country itself and the rock art and stone arrangements represent that" (Yornadaiyn Woolagoodja in Mangolamara et al. 2018: 7).

In summary, the creative actions of Traditional Owners during the residency, the act of 'painting' or creating *Joonba* totems, was an act of echoing *Lalai* stories and strengthening those stories, albeit in Frankfurt. Thus, Traditional Owners were enlivening and reinforcing what is already in their Country, already in *Lalai*, already in *Joonba* and in dreams given to them by the spirits of Country, including *Gwion*. The Traditional Owners felt that they were continuing their cultural practices; their ancestors had done something similar when they prepared enlivened materials for the German researchers in 1938, which are now in the Weltkulturen Museum and the Frobenius Institute collections. These materials are about honouring and respecting *Wanjina Wunggurr* culture and associated traditions; not finding individual expression but asserting continuity and connection. By way of explaining art creation and the reciprocity between Traditional Owners and *Lalai*, the well-known artist Yornadaiyn once said "Even if we just paint them on the canvas, they know that we are respecting them" (Woolagoodja 2020: 44). These are beliefs and practices held by *Wanjina Wunggurr* Traditional Owners in the past and the present, and presumably in the future. Painting images reminds Traditional Owners and others of this reality. Being away from Country can be hard, painting and thus communicating with *Lalai* retains the connection, identity and thus capacity to engage in the world.

It took all the days and nights being in Frankfurt, discussing, showing and illustrating their culture for this final recognition of engaged encounters, active agency, and long-term relationships to find its expression in the title for the exhibition: COUNTRY BIN PULL'EM. For the Traditional Owners this short title encapsulates a process whereby the spirits embedded in Country pulls people into it, embedding them in the totality of an enlivened cultural space. Furthermore, the Traditional Owners felt that in being in Germany they were proof that, "we are here, our stories are still alive!" This was expressed in the form of a contemporary articulation of the message stick – something sent to others to convey a message – an invitation to come together and share. Sharing in ceremony, reciprocal exchange, sharing plentiful resources and social interaction. Indeed, the message stick has fulfilled its purpose with the exhibition COUNTRY BIN PULL'EM in the Weltkulturen Museum in 2024.[6]

The process of exploring the cultural needs of the Traditional Owners and the needs of a German museum found a comfortable fit with an agreed exhibition outline developed to incorporate the history of the German expedition to the Northwest Kimberley in 1938 as well as the perspectives of relevant Traditional Owners of the past and present.

The discussions, explanations and regular engagements allowed for a reimagining and fresh interpretation of the archival materials and how they are important for Traditional Owners, institution workers, and German visitors. Most important was the growth of a new awareness and articulation of the Traditional Owners' world-view, their aesthetic, and their responsibilities as representatives of their community whilst visiting Germany.

In addition, wider issues surrounding collections, the display of and references to Traditional Owners' cultural heritage, and the continuation of that heritage, were also regularly discussed and explored. The complexity surrounding the concept of 'permission' was sometimes challenging for Traditional Owners to explain. However, the strength of the relationships, and the commitment to appropriate and respectful cultural protocols, provided the basis for working out an agreed and suitable process in choosing materials for display and appropriate curatorial practices.

During the residency the Traditional Owners followed a demanding and tight work schedule with many intensive meetings and discussions. Conversations revolved around the design and the structure of the exhibition as well as the selection of appropriate items to be displayed. This process continued after the residency, with other Traditional Owners being regularly involved in the final choice of items for display and the associated text.

On their return to the Kimberley the four Traditional Owners, in discussion with their senior community members, reflected on their experiences in relation to the collections, their creation of new works and the COUNTRY BIN PULL'EM exhibition. They felt it was just the beginning of a renewed relationship; one that started many years ago. They hope that other Traditional Owners will be able to experience the collections, either in Germany or preferably in Australia.

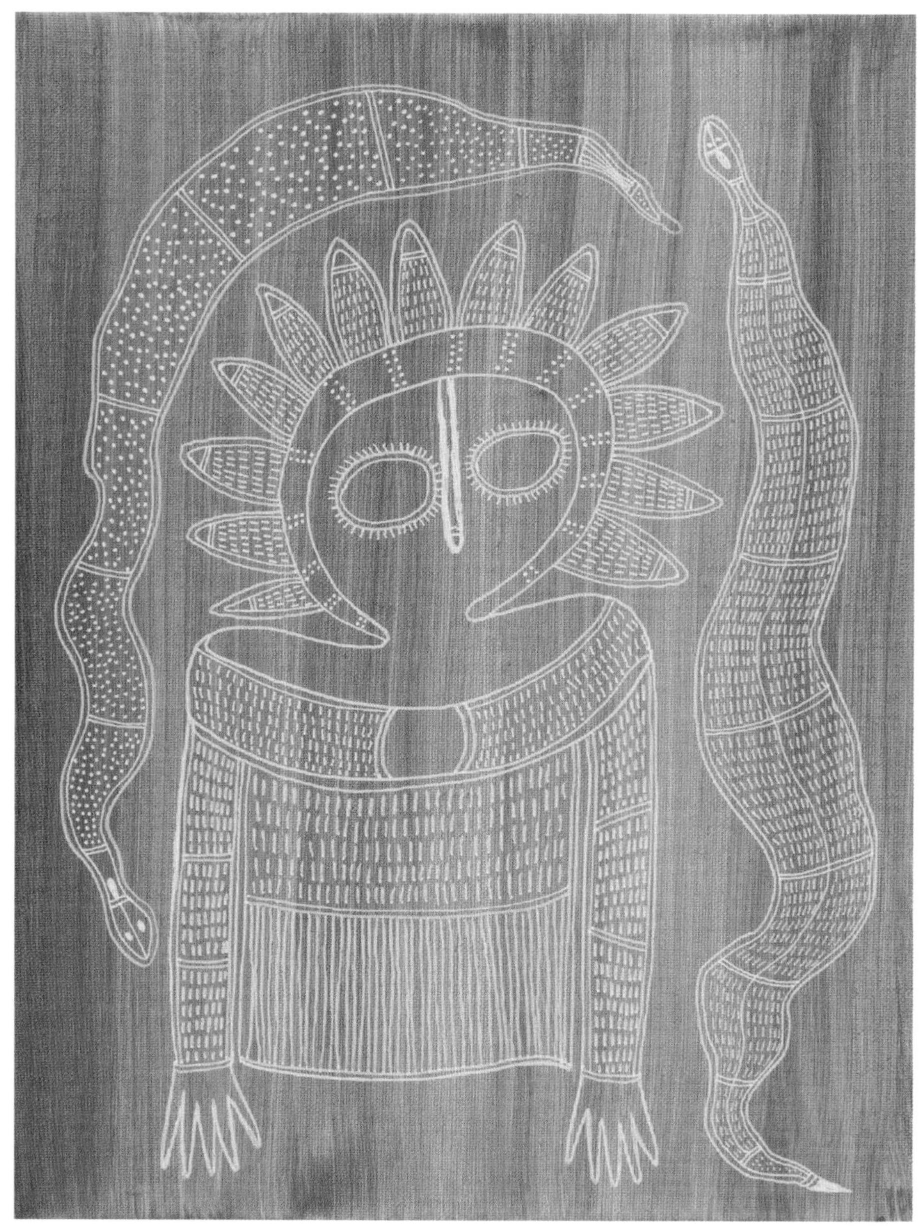

Fig. 6   Leah Umbagai, 2023: *Wandjina and Woongudd (Snakes).* Acrylic paint on canvas. 30 x 40 cm. Collection: Weltkulturen Museum. Photo: Wolfgang Günzel, 2024

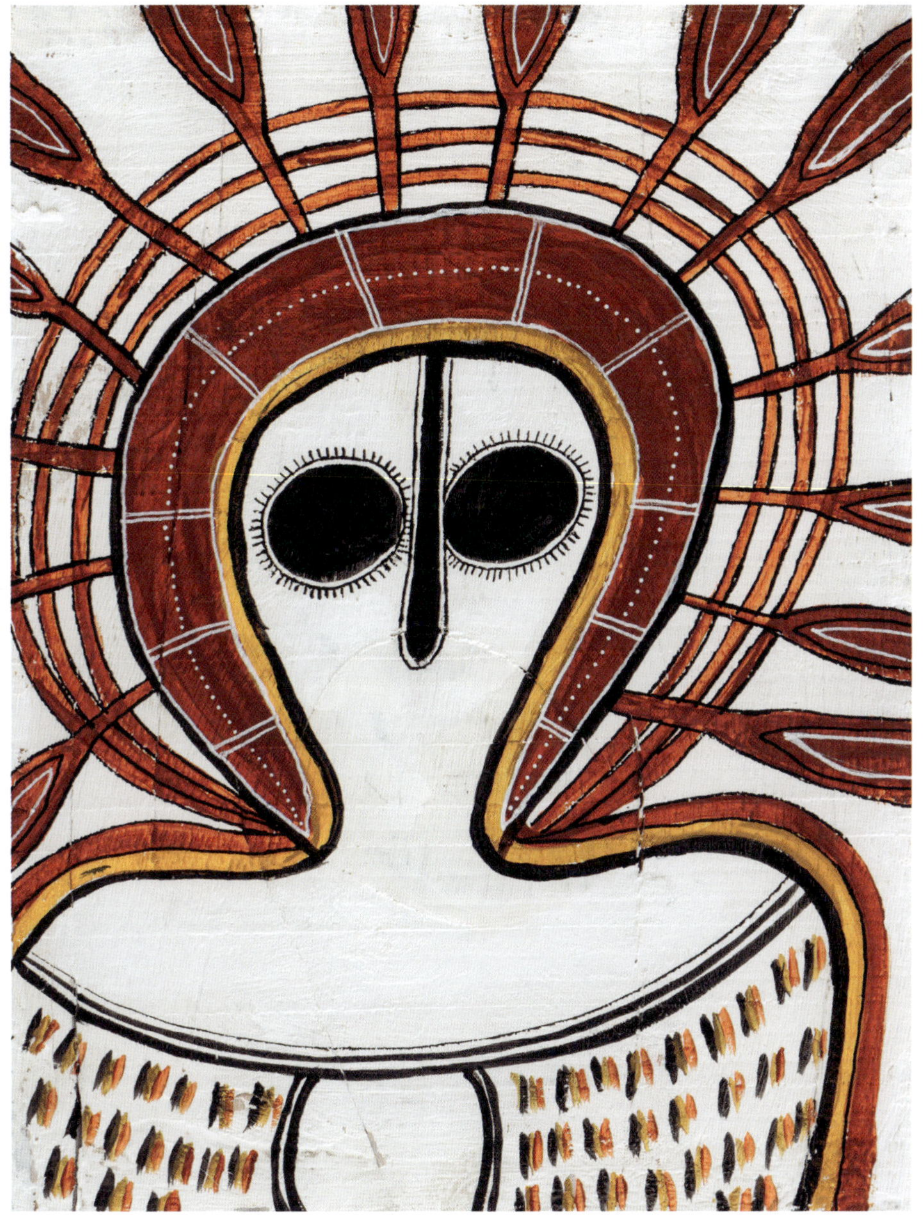

Fig. 7   Leah Umbagai, 2023: *Wandjina*. Acrylic paint on wood. 20 x 30 cm. Collection: Weltkulturen Museum. Photo: Wolfgang Günzel, 2024

Endnotes:

1   "The German Ethnographic Expeditions to the Kimberley, Northwest Australia: A Collaborative Assessment of Research History, the Interpretation of Australian Aboriginal Heritage, and Digital Repatriation" (March 2020 to March 2024).

2   Gender restrictions on some of the photographs had been determined in consultation with senior and younger men in Derby prior to the journey to Frankfurt and these decisions were integrated into relevant databases as part of the residency undertakings.

3   See Matthias Claudius Hofmann, *Celebrated and Lost* in this volume.

4   See Kim Doohan et al., *The Country Owns Us* in this volume.

5   See Rona Gungnunda Charles et al., *Bringing It Back to Life* in this volume.

6   At the time of the Frobenius Expedition to Northwest Australia, message sticks were an Aboriginal means of communication.

References:

Blundell, Valda et al. 2017: *Barddabardda Wodjenangorddee. We're Telling All of You. The Creation, History and People of Dambimangaddee Country.* Based on the Cultural Knowledge and Recollections of Janet Oobagooma, Donny Woolagoodja and Other Senior Dambeemangaddee People. Fremantle: Fremantle Press and Dambimangari Aboriginal Corporation.

Mangolamara, Sylvester et al. 2018: *We Are Coming To See You. Nyara Pari Kala Niragu (Gaambera), Gadawara Ngyaran-Gada (Wunambal), Inganinja Gubadjoongana (Woddordda).* Derby: Western Australia: Dambimangari Aboriginal Corporation and Wunambal Gaambera Aboriginal Corporation.

Petri, Helmut. 2011: *The Dying World in Northwest Australia.* Translated by Ian Campbell. Carlise: Hesperian Press.

Petri, Helmut. 1954: *Sterbende Welt in Nordwest-Australien.* Braunschweig: Albert Limbach Verlag.

Woolagoodja, Yorna. 2020: *Yornadaiyn Woolagoodja.* Derby: Western Australia: Magabala Books.

A Message (Stick) to Frankfurt

Exhibition Views

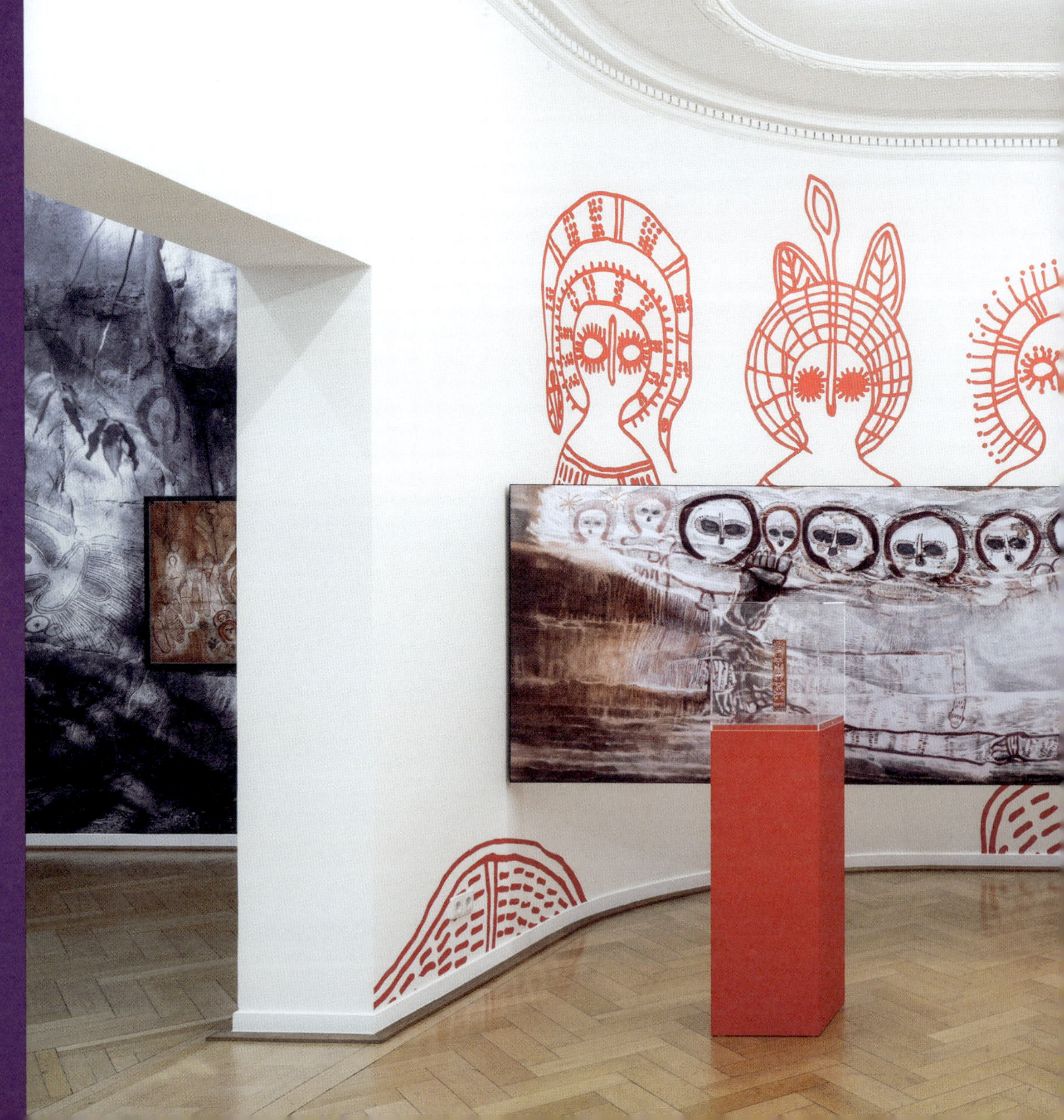

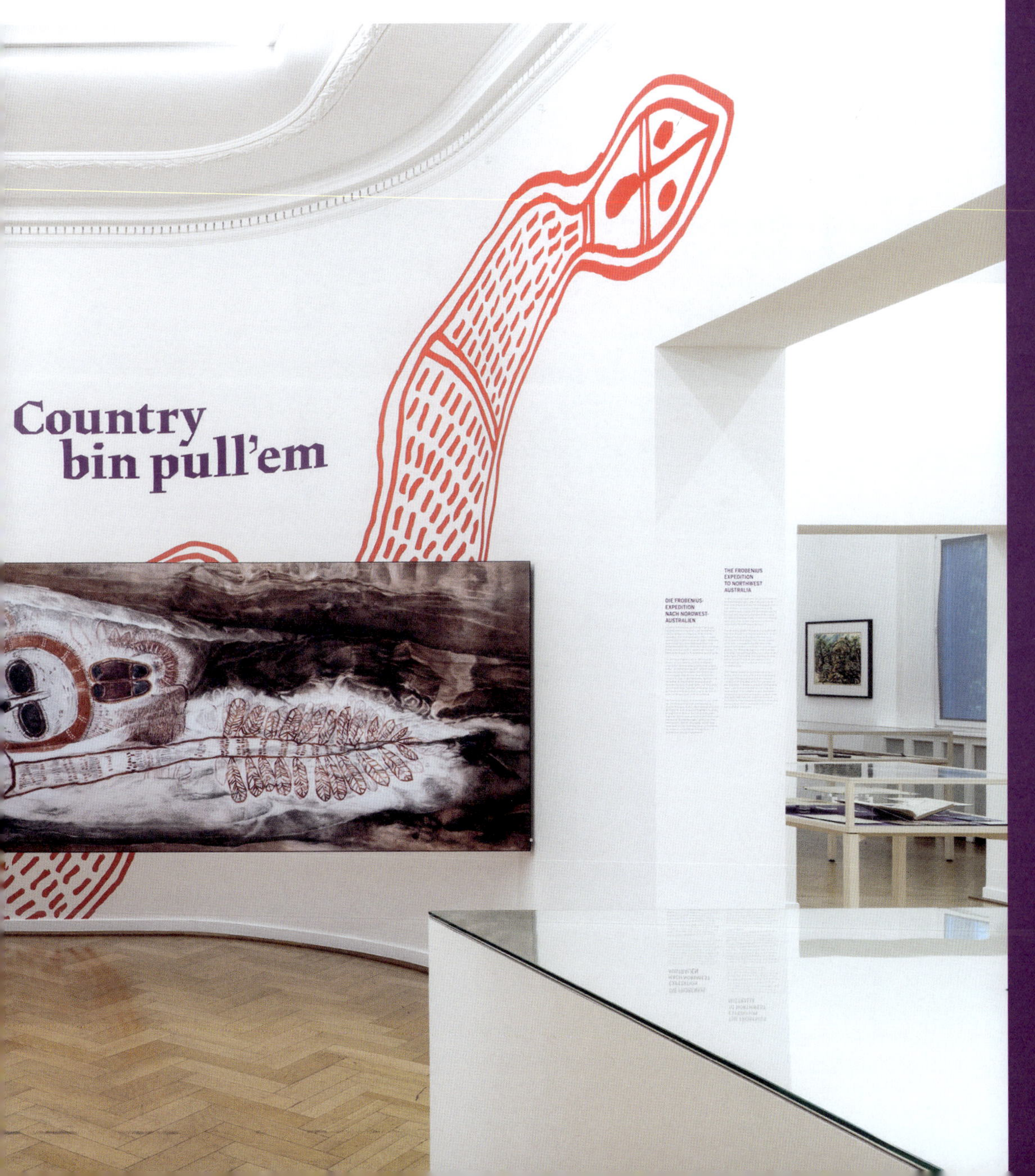

Exhibition view COUNTRY BIN PULL'EM. Entrance area with installation of the Wanalirri rock art copy. Photo: Wolfgang Günzel, 2024

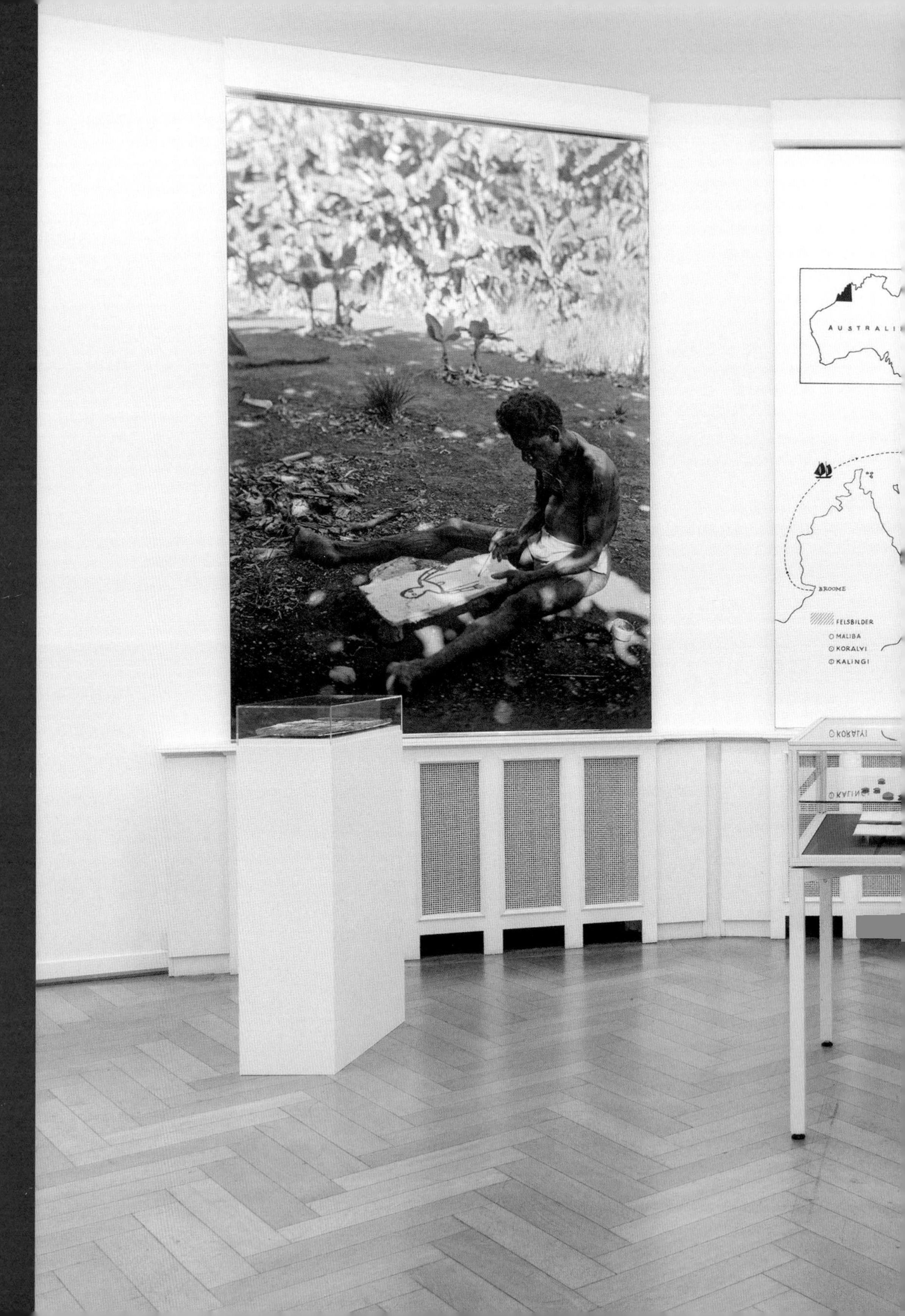
AUSTRALIEN
BROOME
FELSBILDER
MALIBA
KORALYI
KALINGI

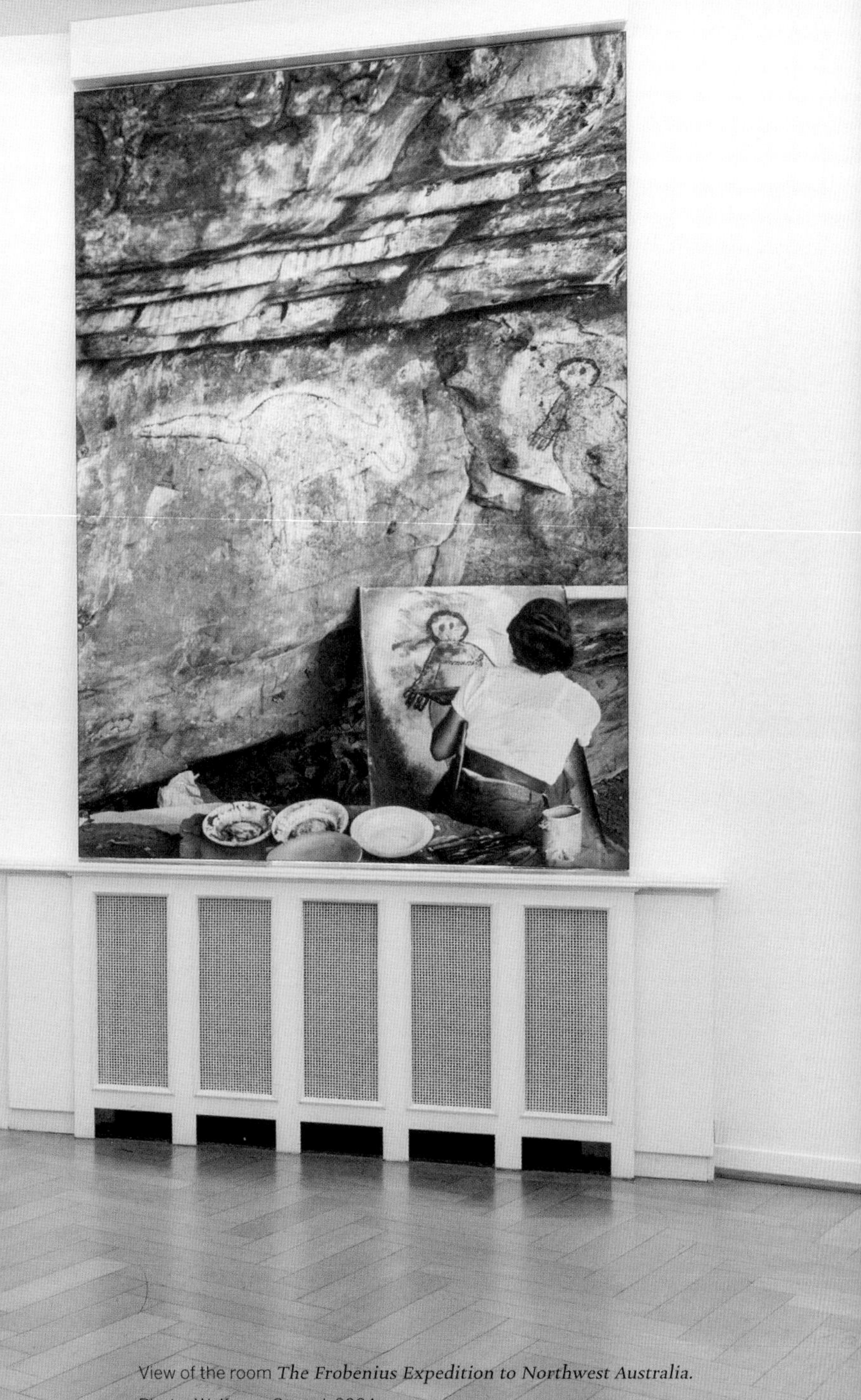

View of the room *The Frobenius Expedition to Northwest Australia.*
Photo: Wolfgang Günzel, 2024

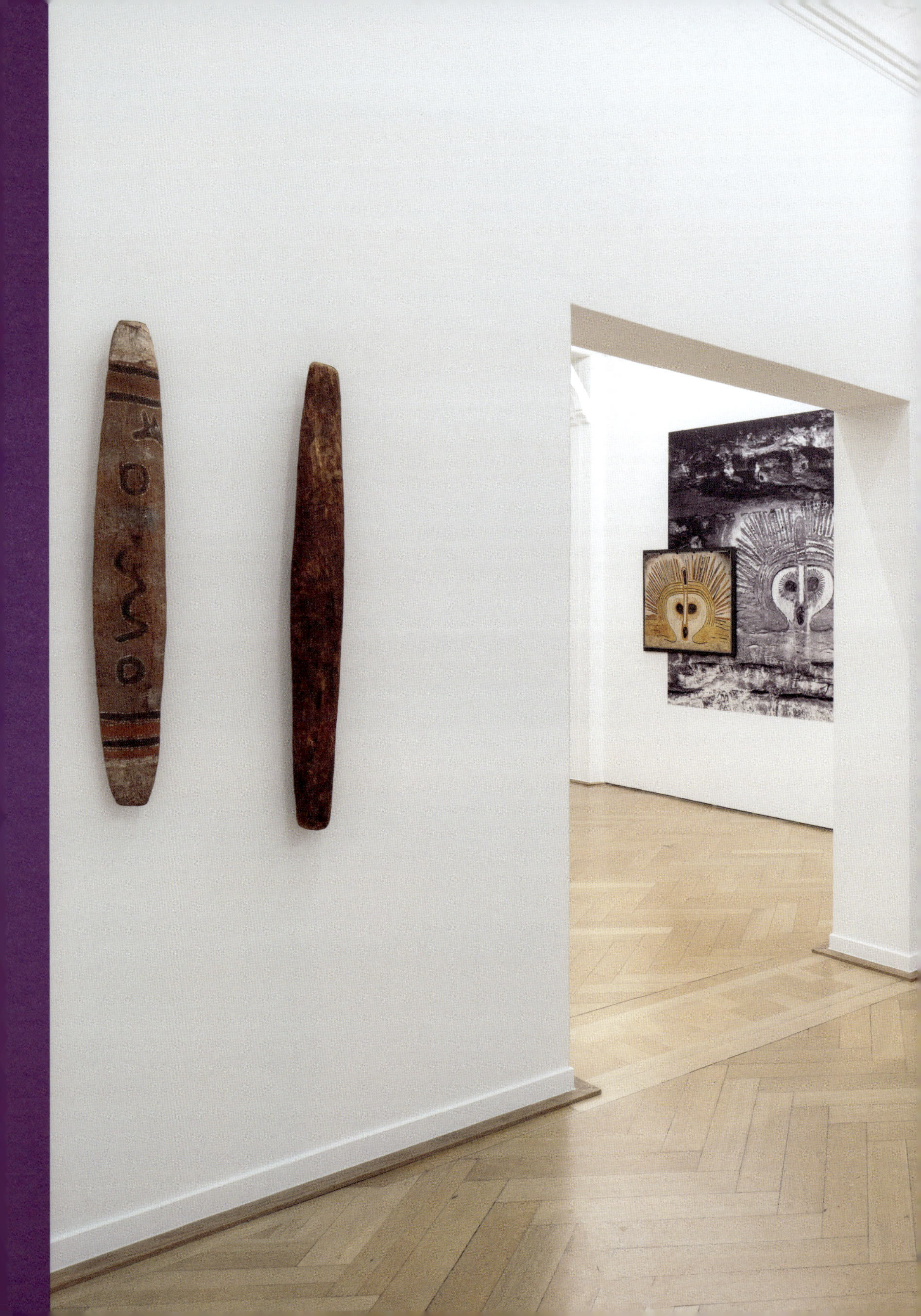

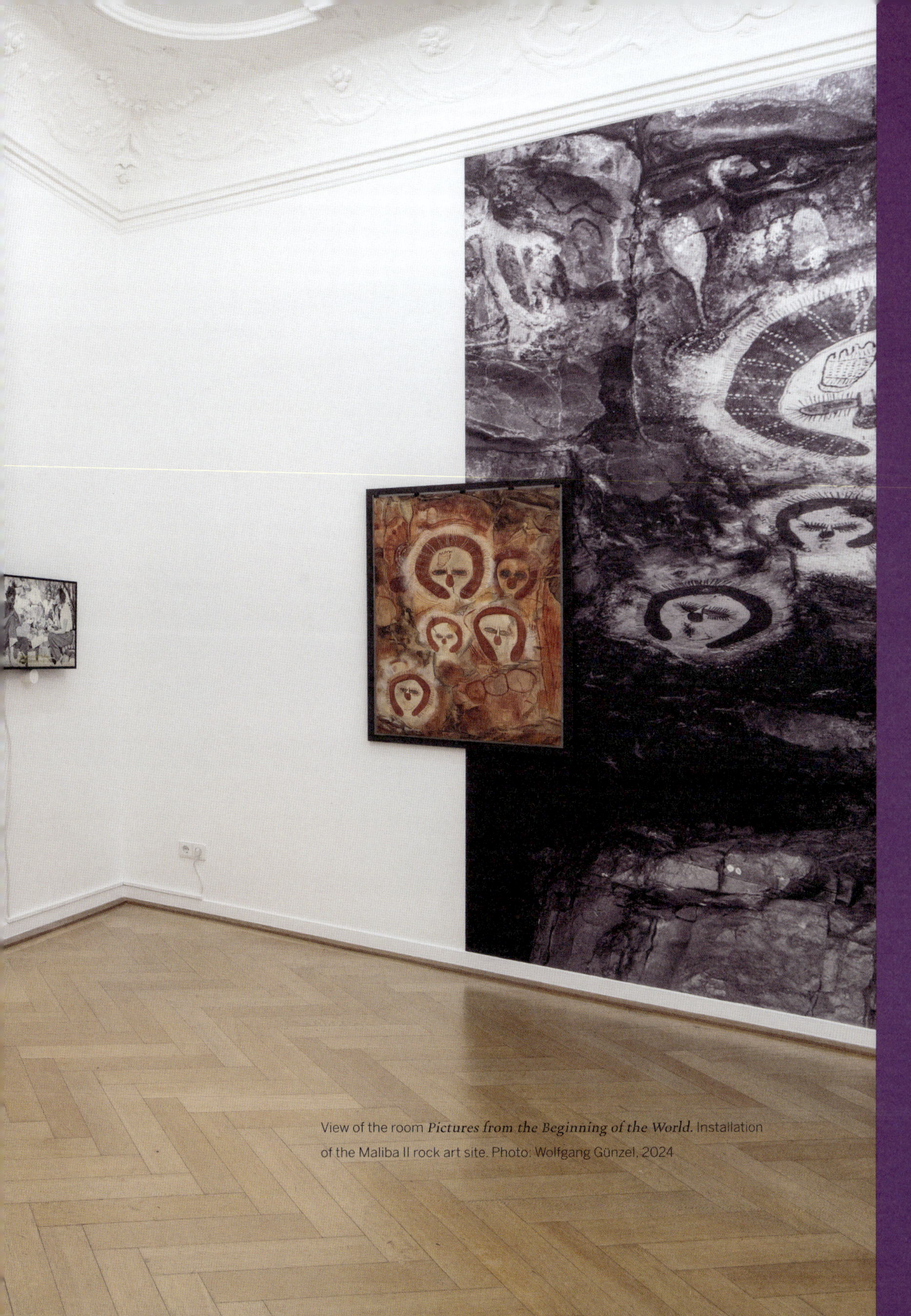

View of the room *Pictures from the Beginning of the World*. Installation of the Maliba II rock art site. Photo: Wolfgang Günzel, 2024

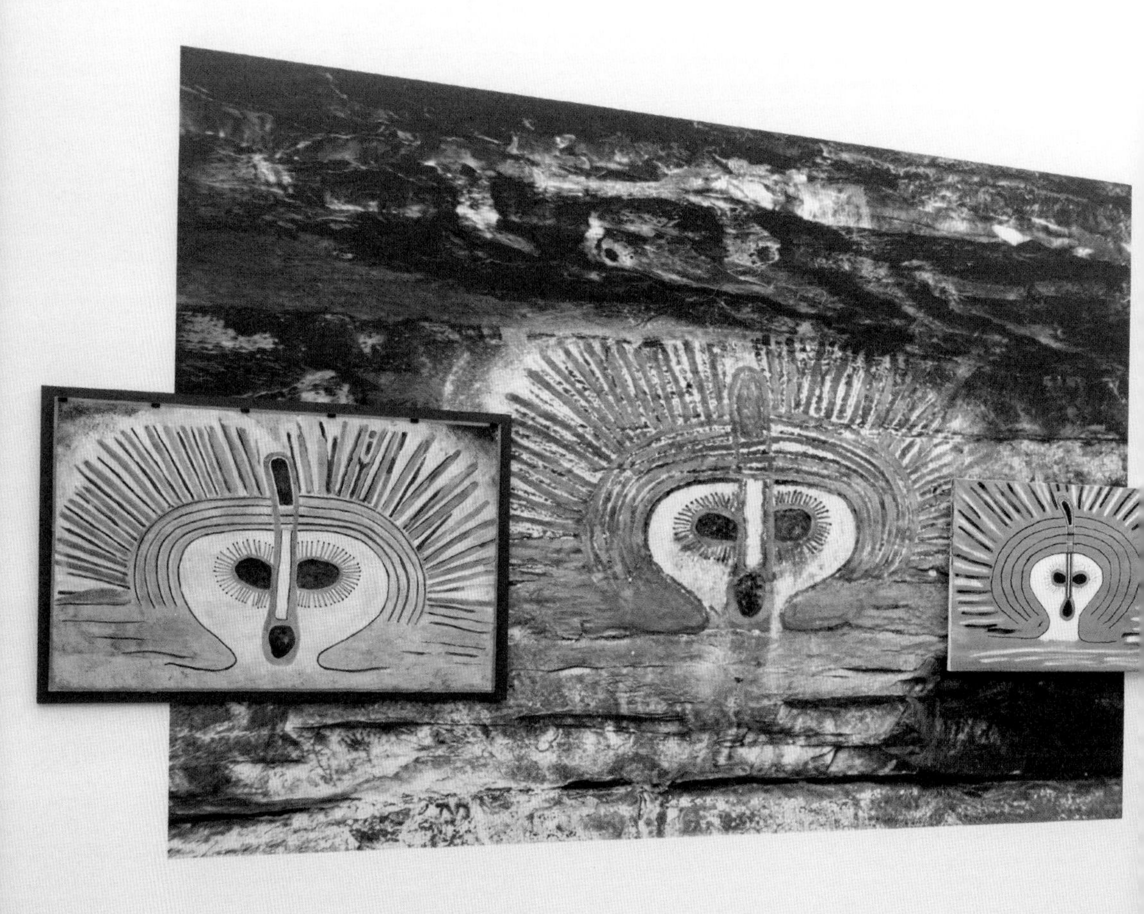

View of the room *Every Picture Tells a Story*. Installation of the
Brad Wodenngarri rock art site. Photo: Wolfgang Günzel, 2024

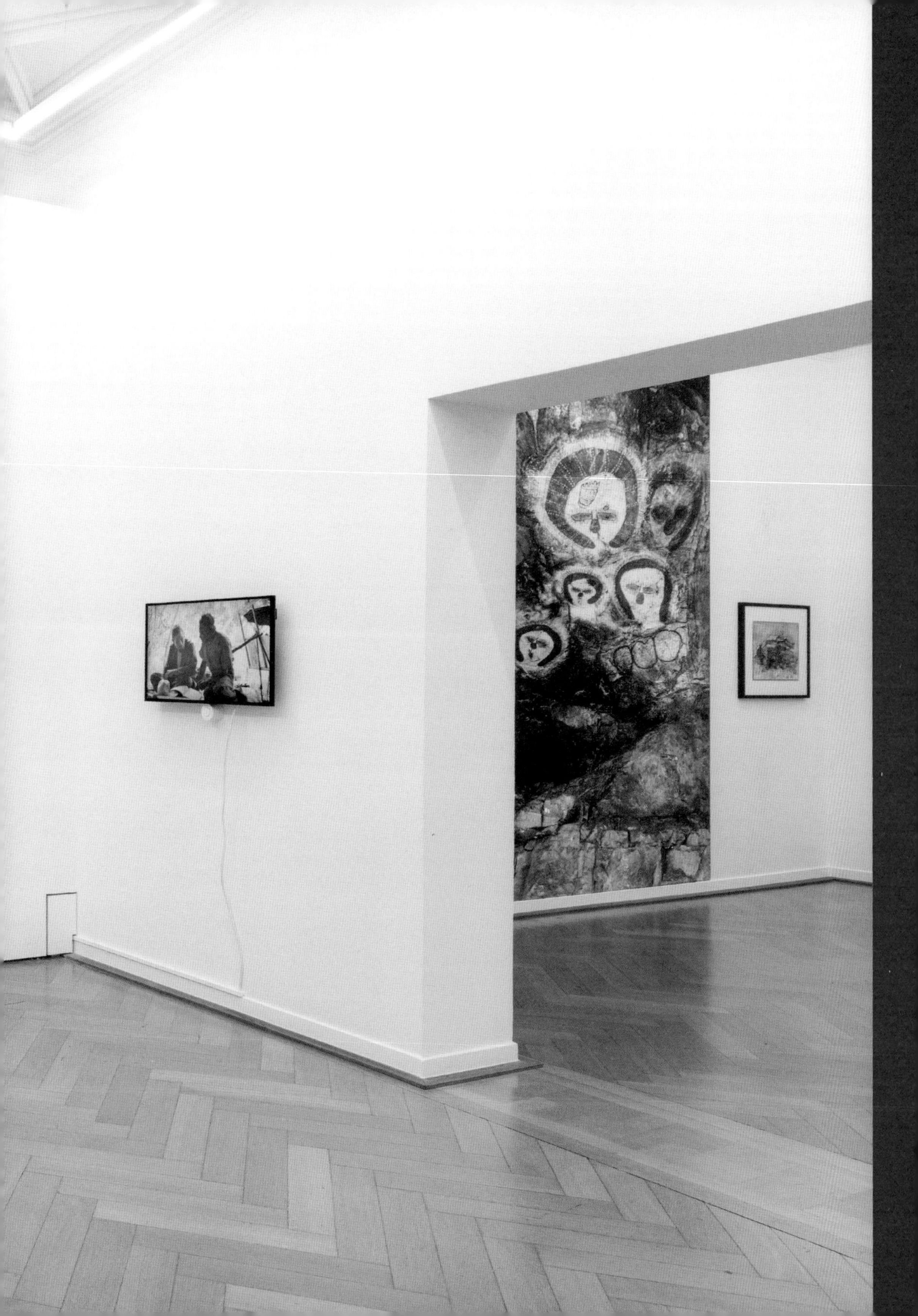

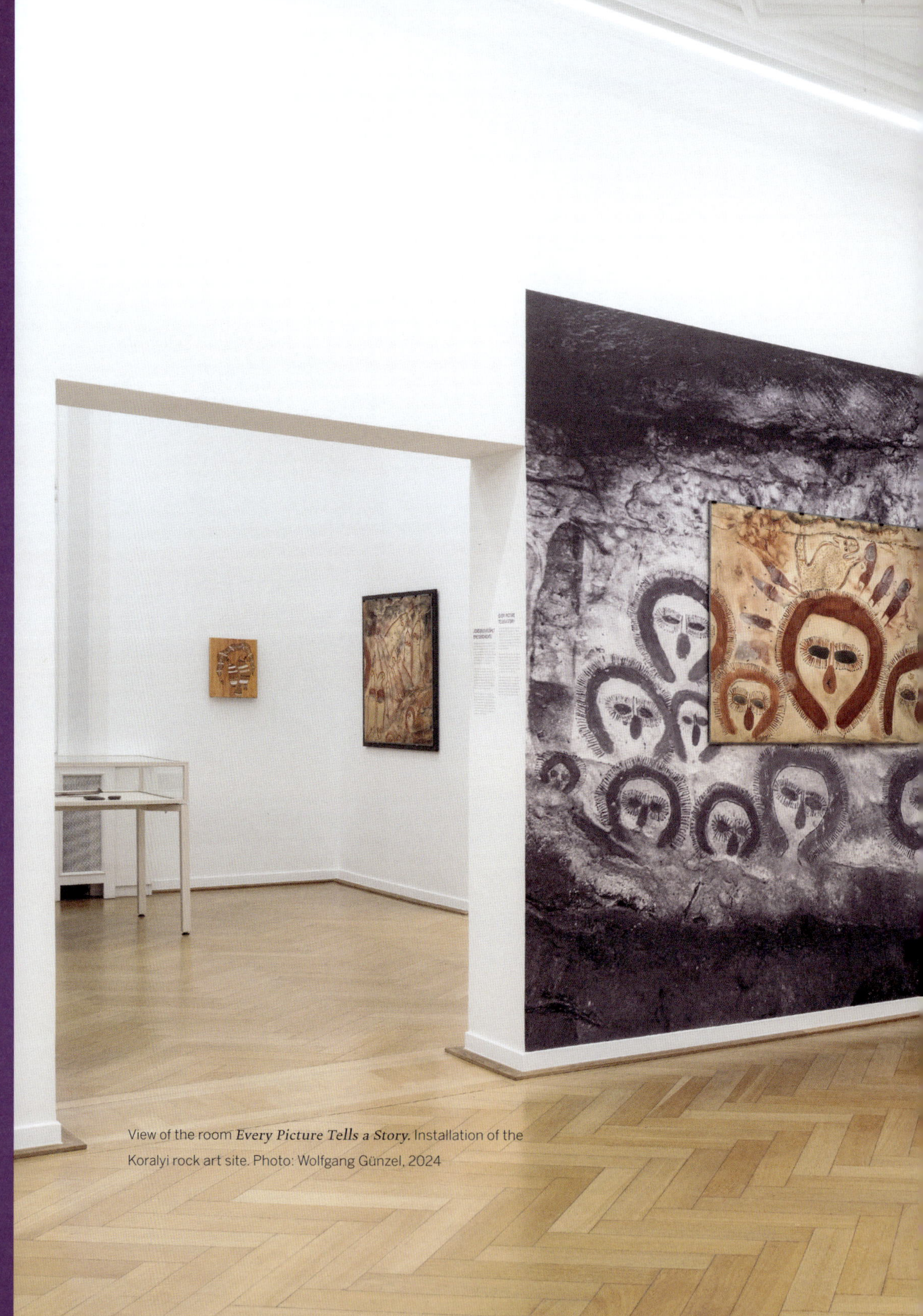

View of the room *Every Picture Tells a Story.* Installation of the Koralyi rock art site. Photo: Wolfgang Günzel, 2024

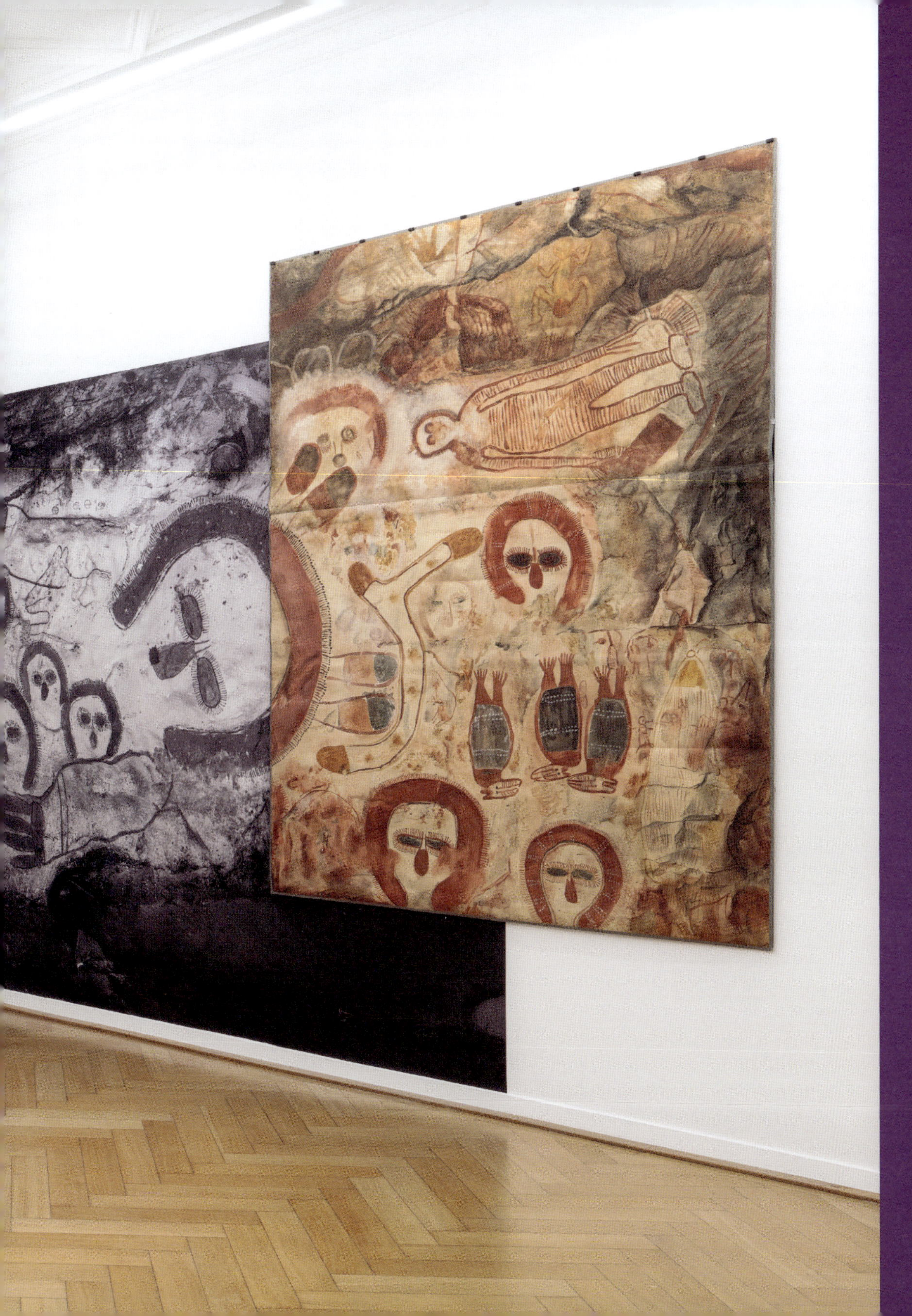

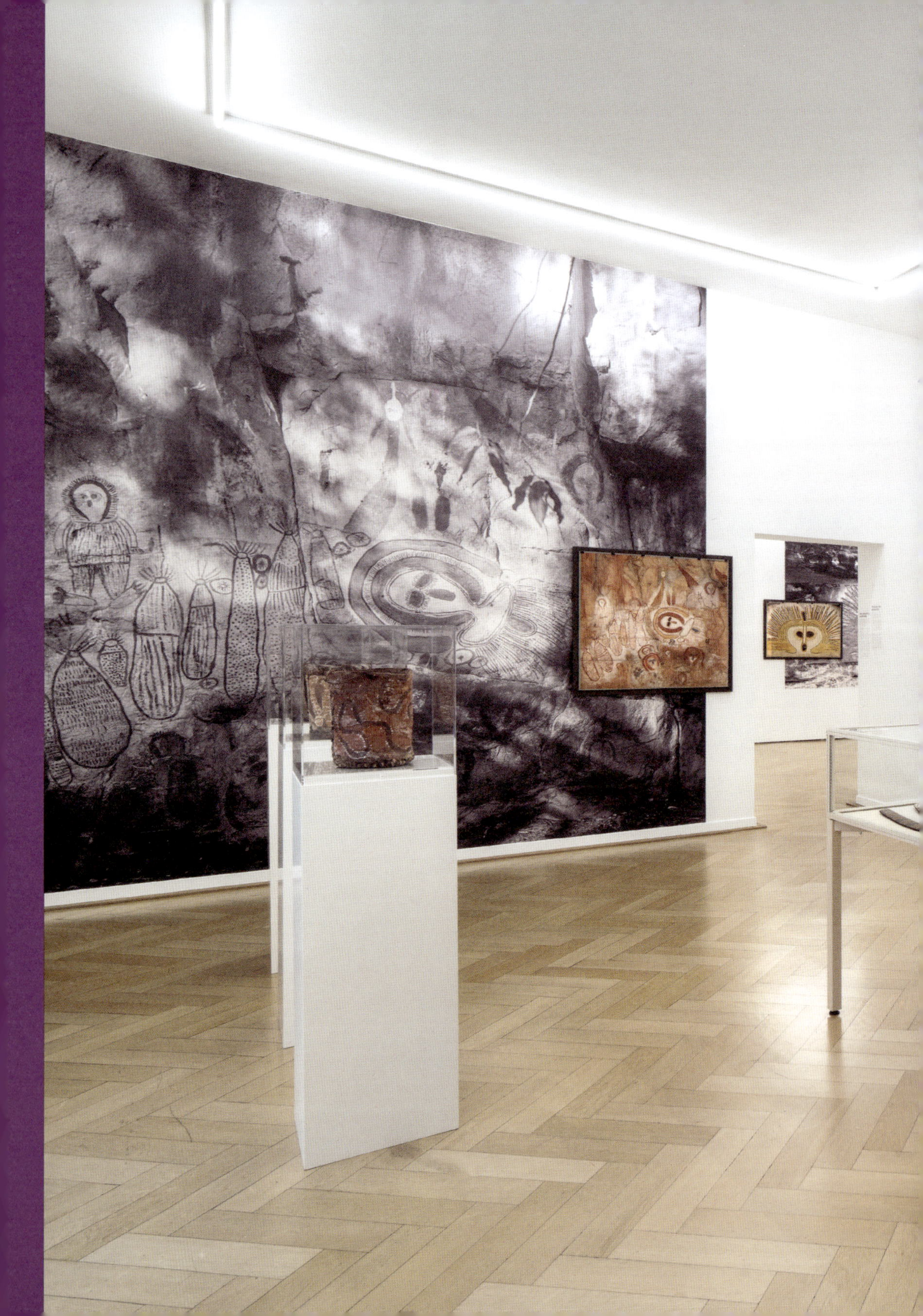

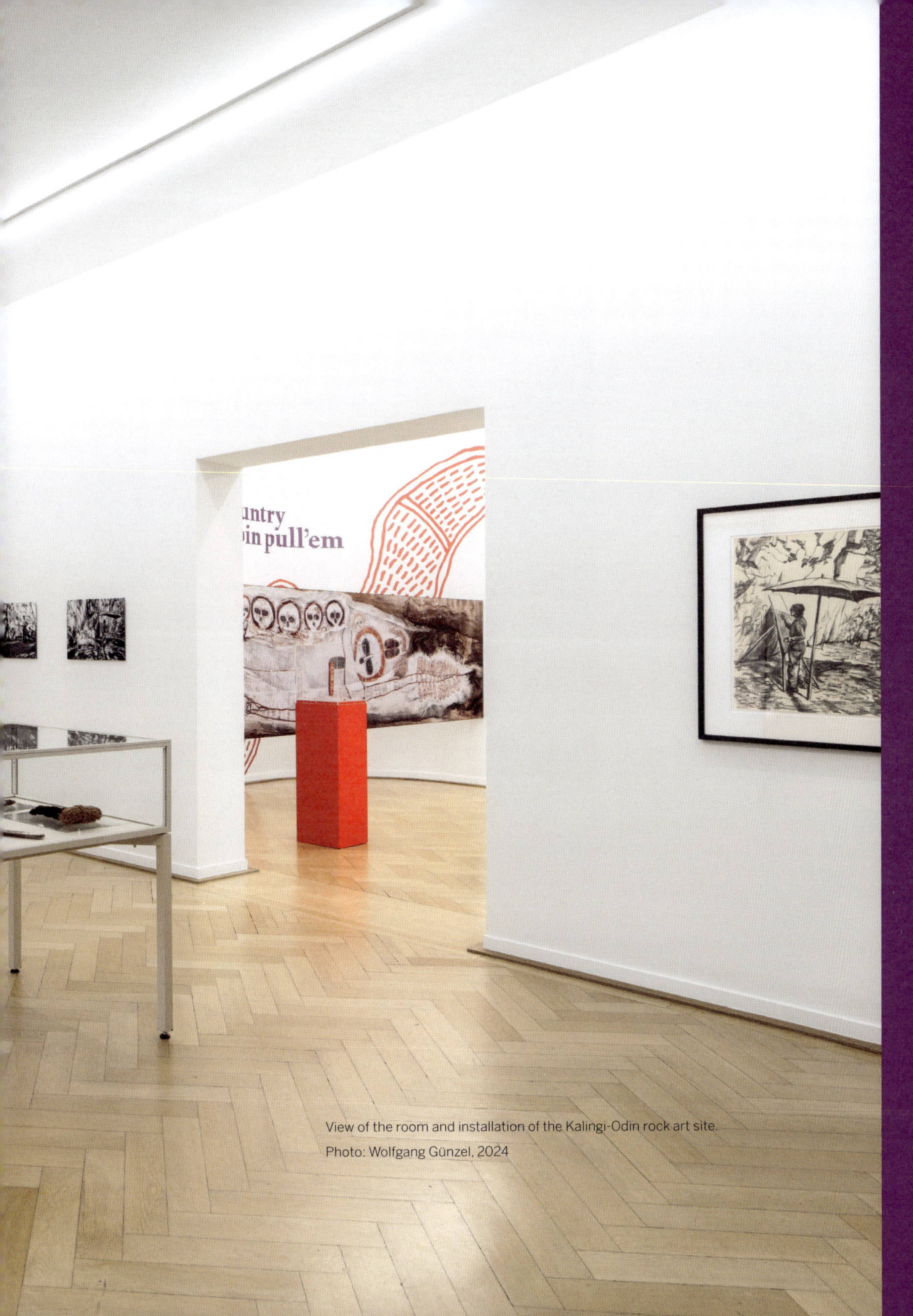

View of the room and installation of the Kalingi-Odin rock art site.
Photo: Wolfgang Günzel, 2024

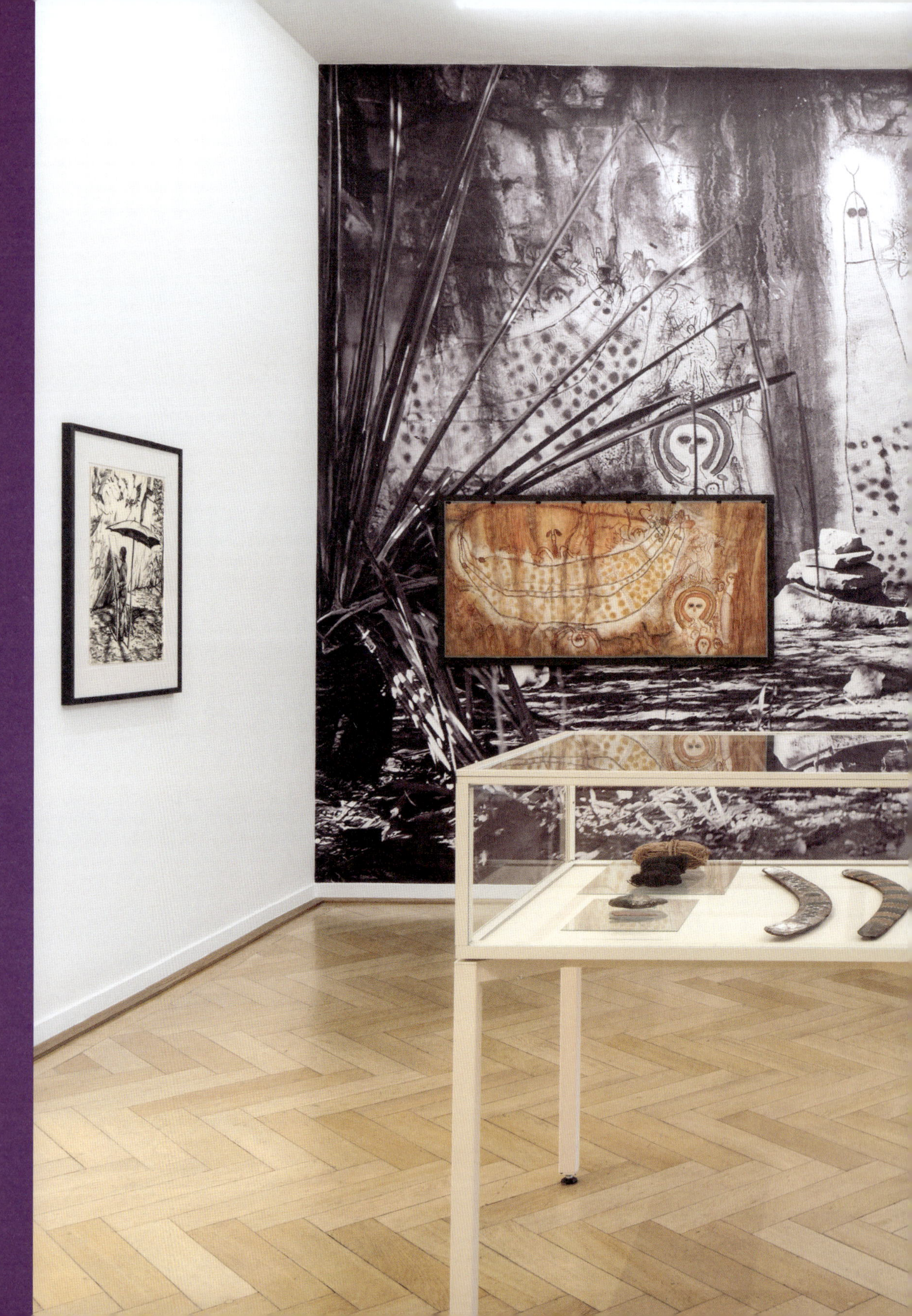

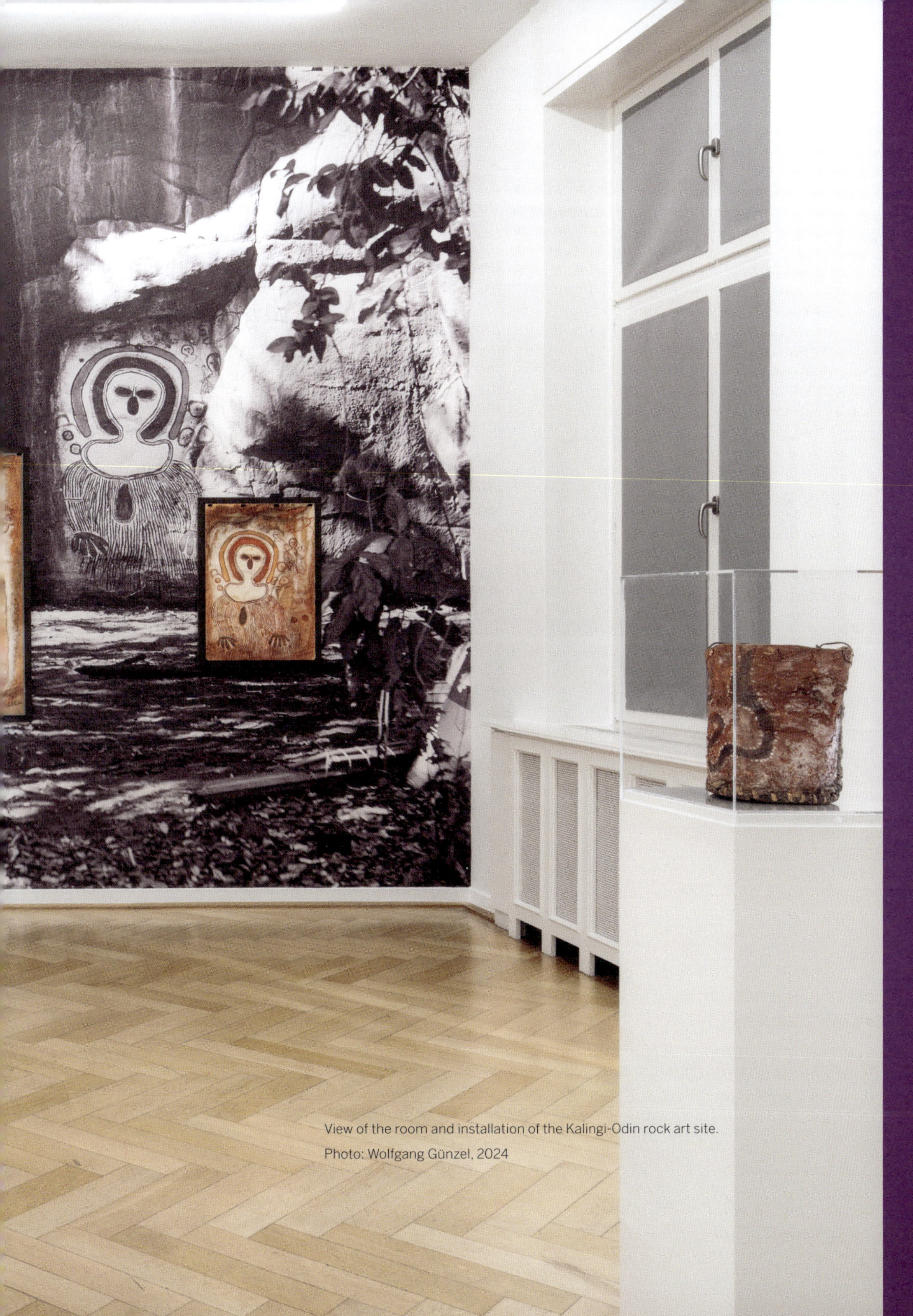

View of the room and installation of the Kalingi-Odin rock art site.
Photo: Wolfgang Günzel, 2024

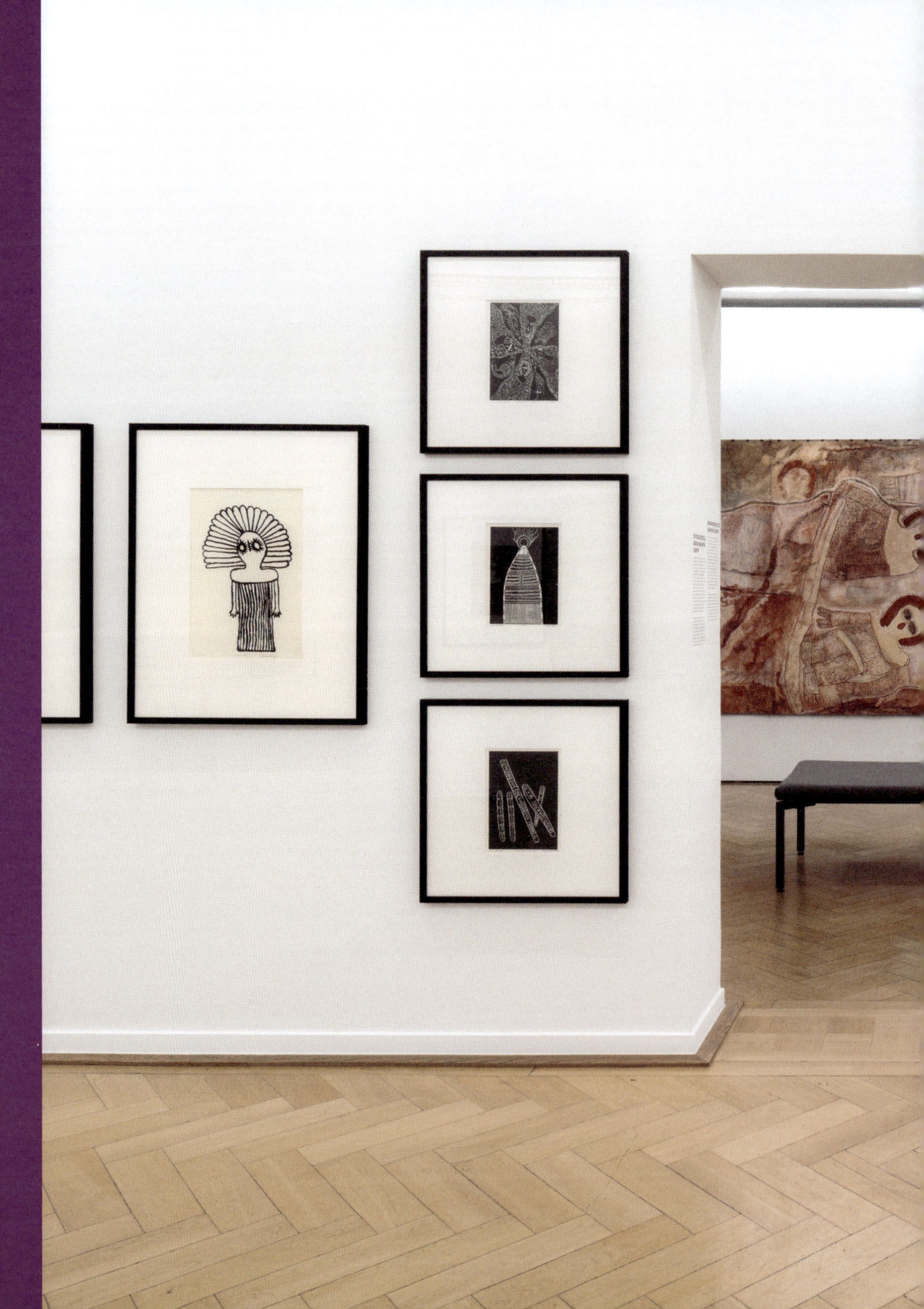

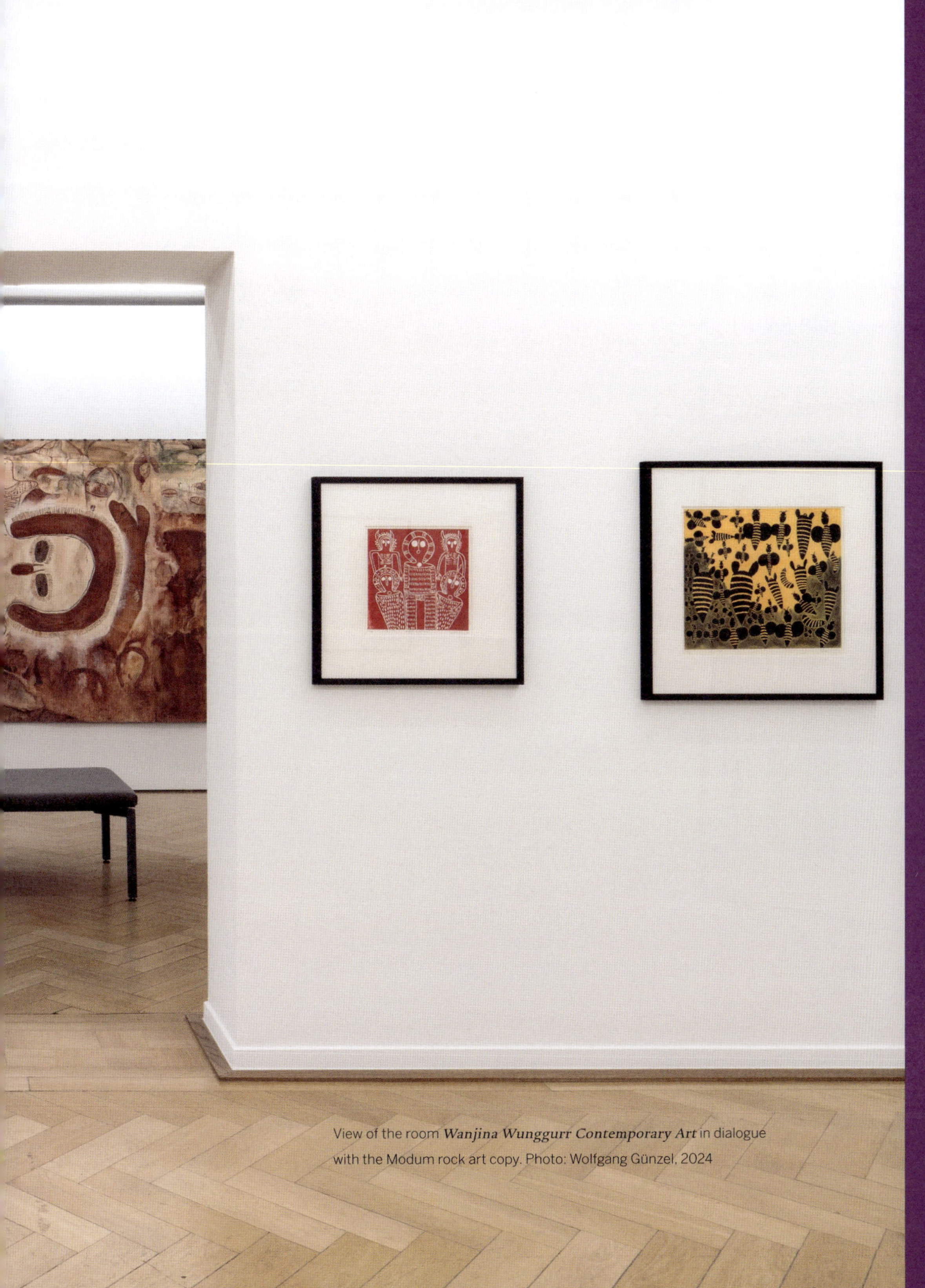

View of the room *Wanjina Wunggurr Contemporary Art* in dialogue with the Modum rock art copy. Photo: Wolfgang Günzel, 2024

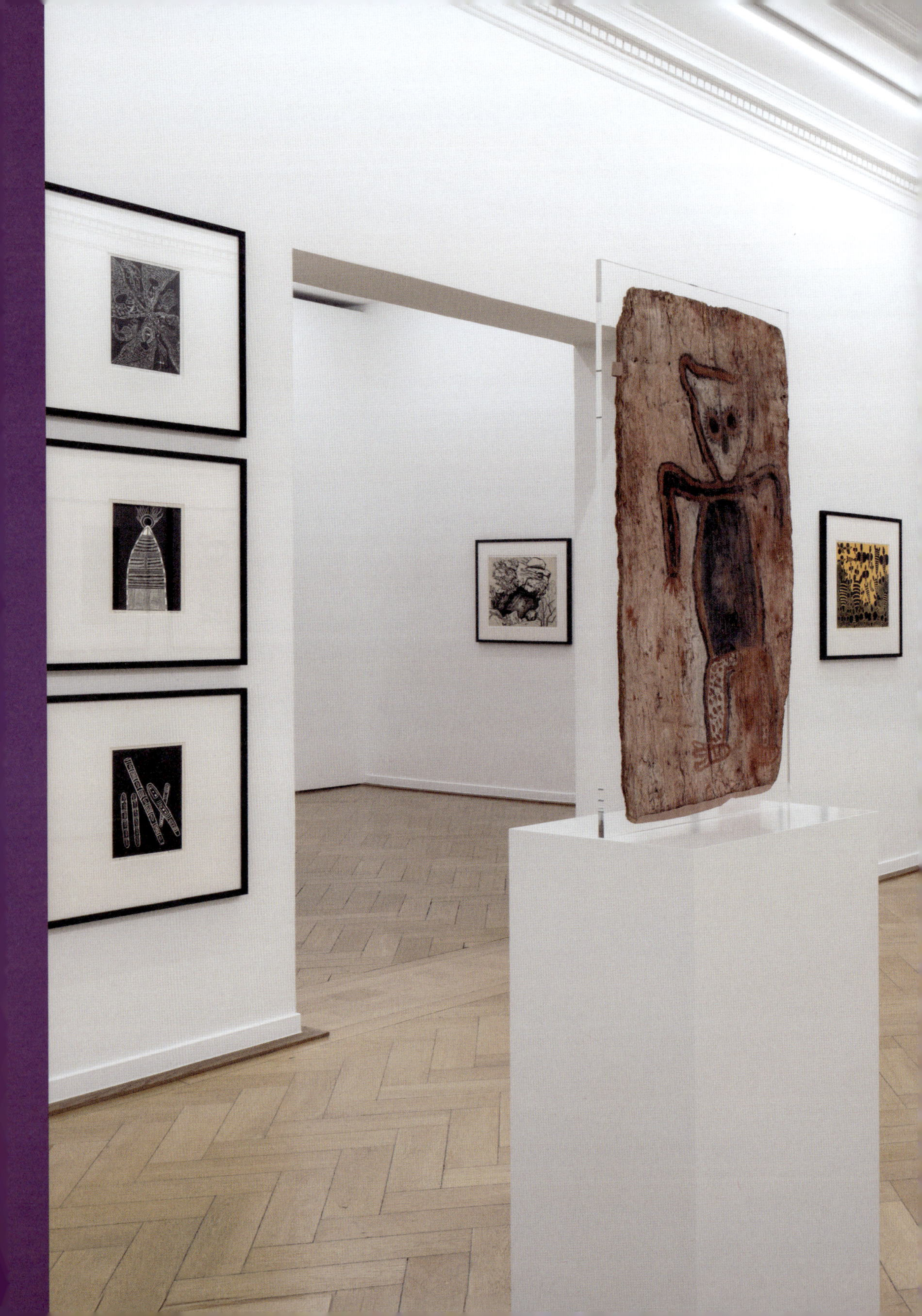

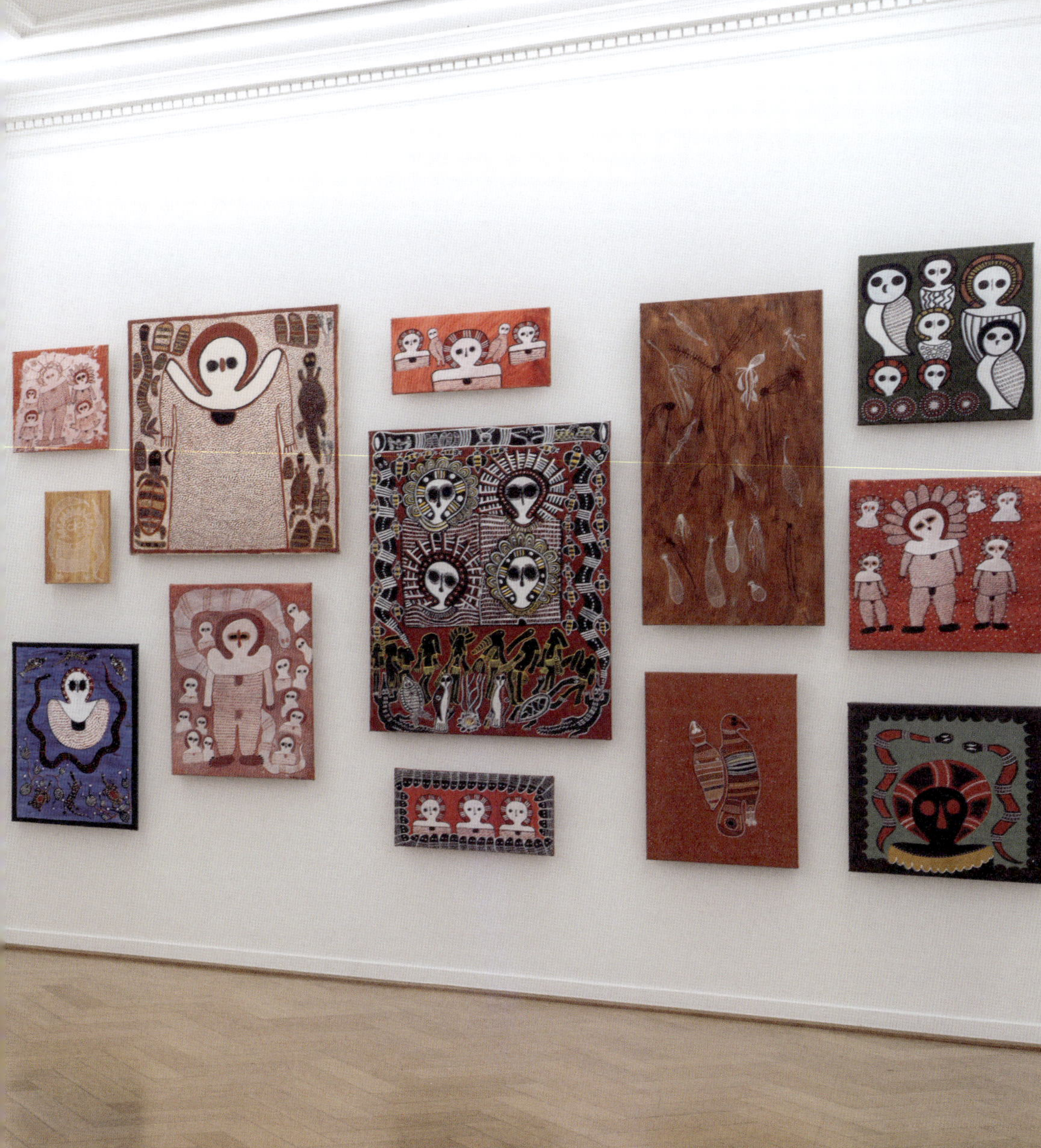

View of the room *Wanjina Wunggurr Contemporary Art.*
Photo: Wolfgang Günzel. 2024

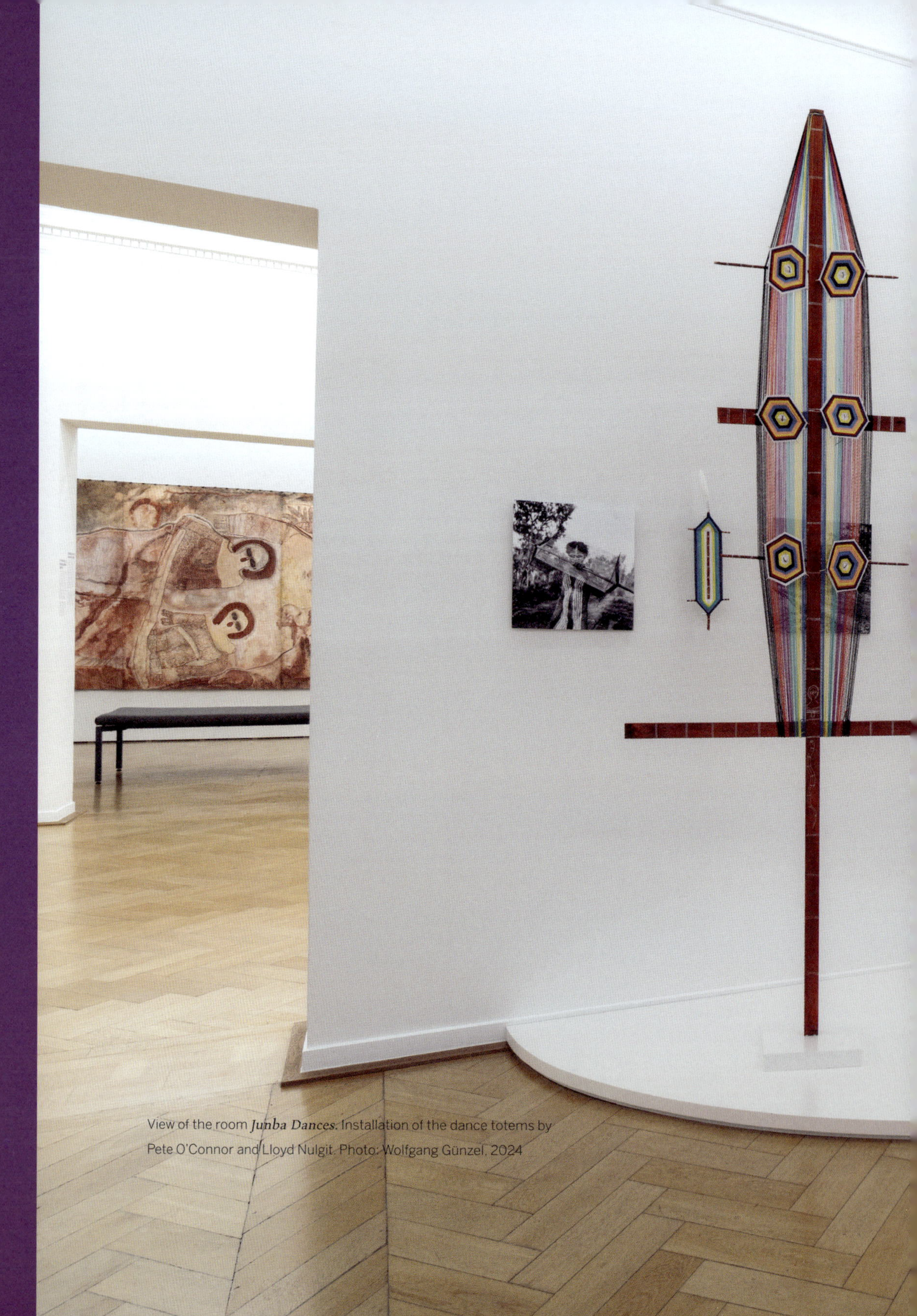

View of the room *Junba Dances*. Installation of the dance totems by
Pete O'Connor and Lloyd Nulgit. Photo: Wolfgang Günzel, 2024

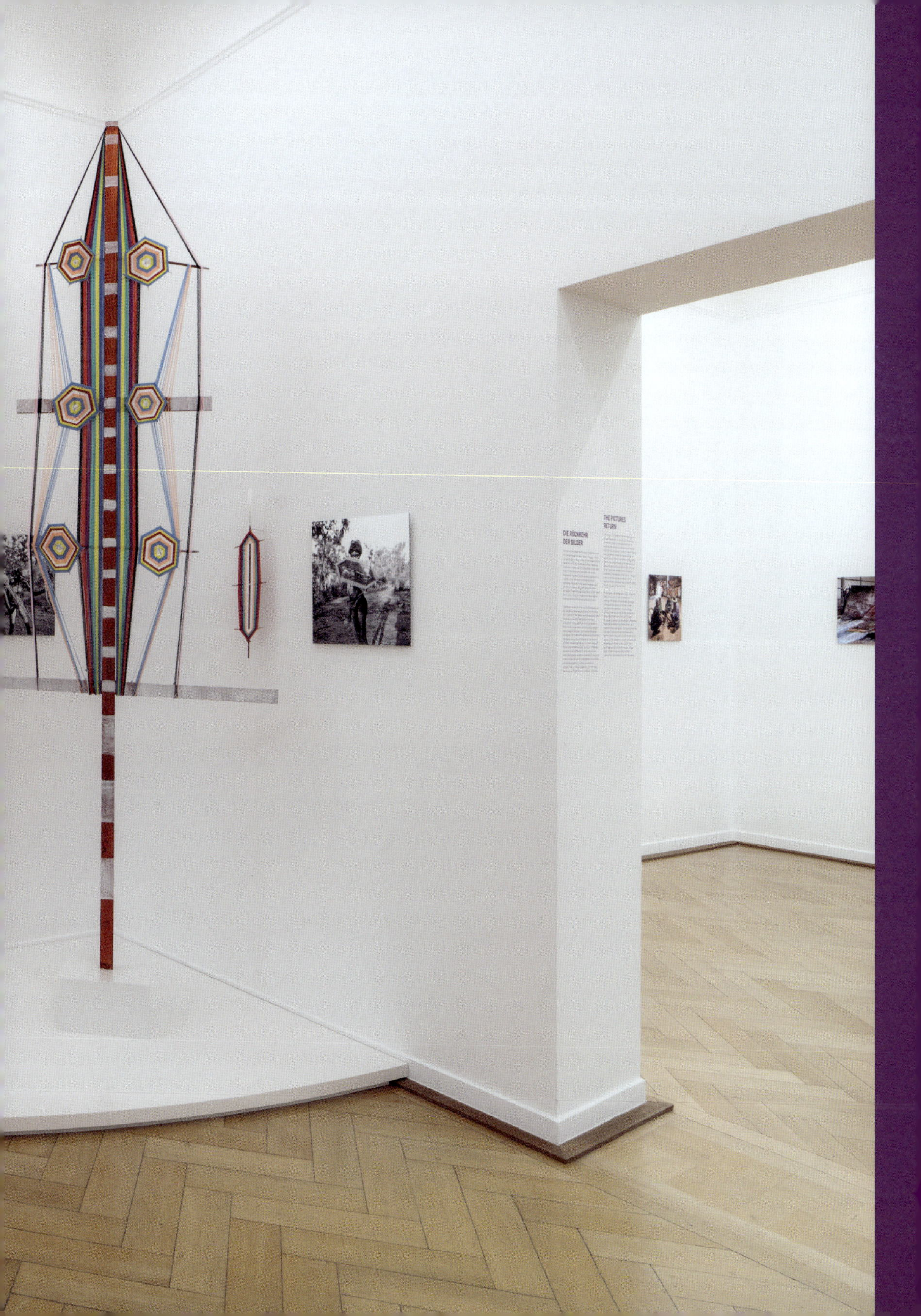
DIE RÜCKKEHR
DER BILDER
THE PICTURES
RETURN

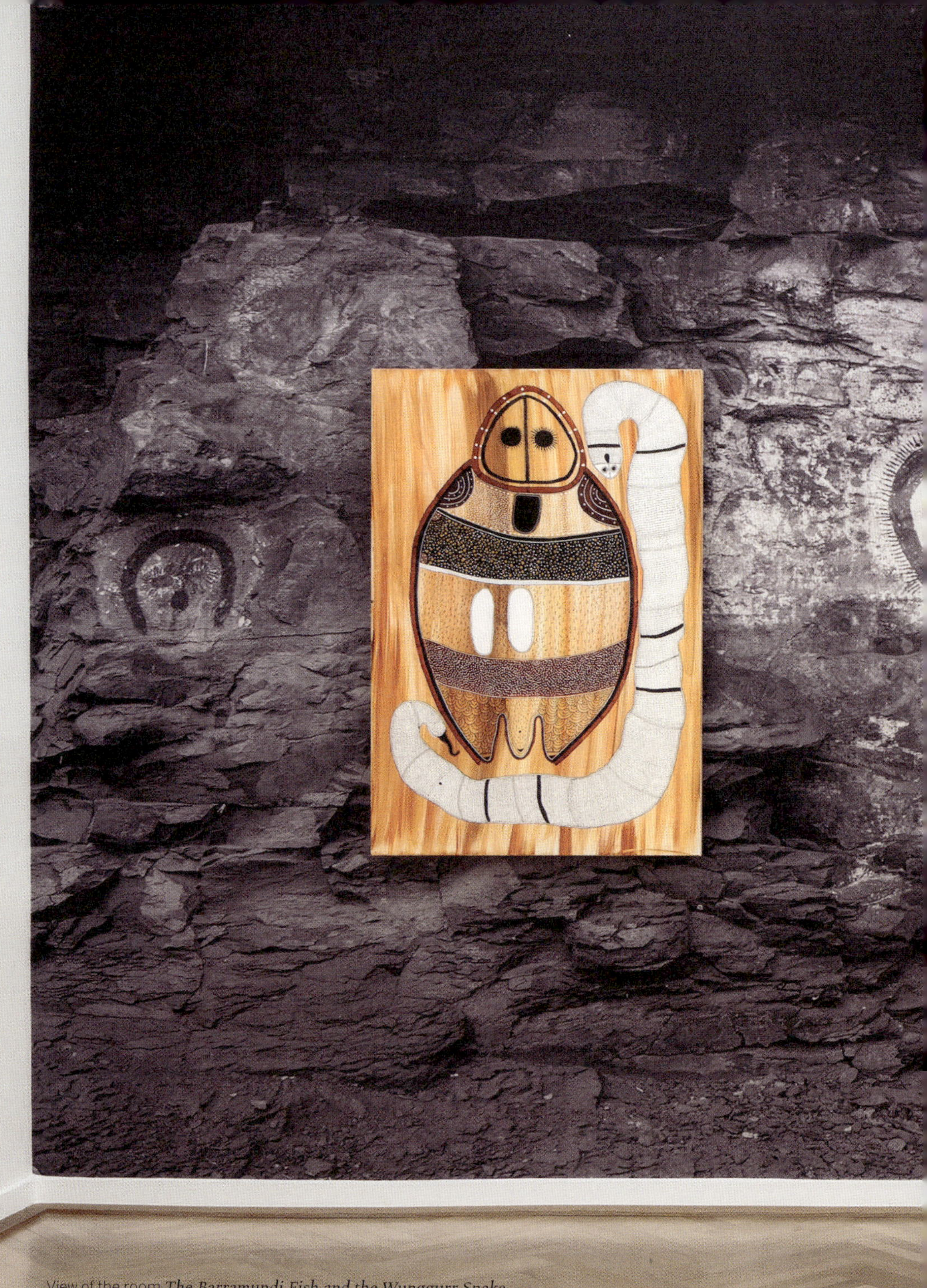

View of the room *The Barramundi Fish and the Wunggurr Snake.*
Installation of the Bind'ibi rock art site. Photo: Wolfgang Günzel, 2024

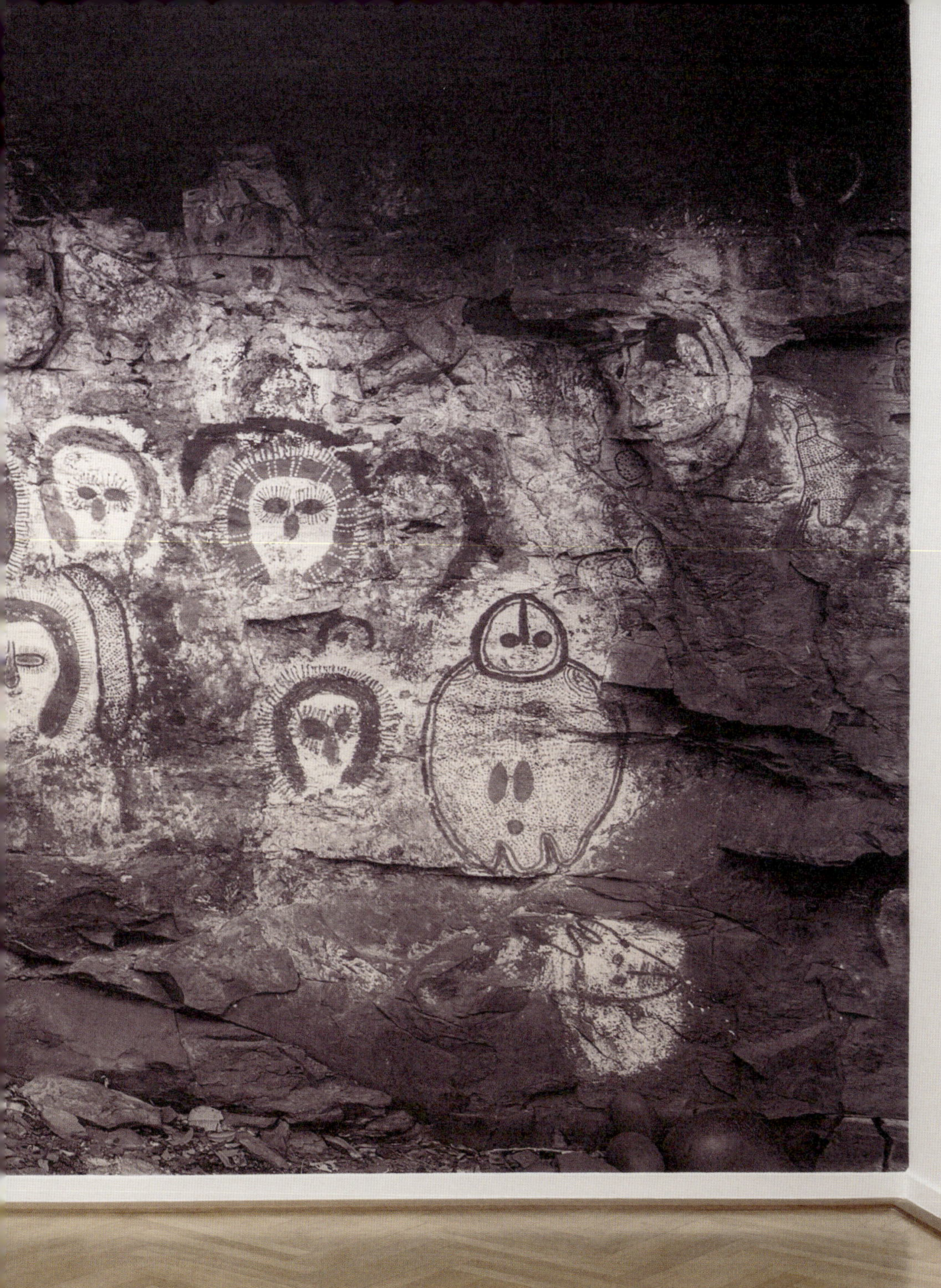

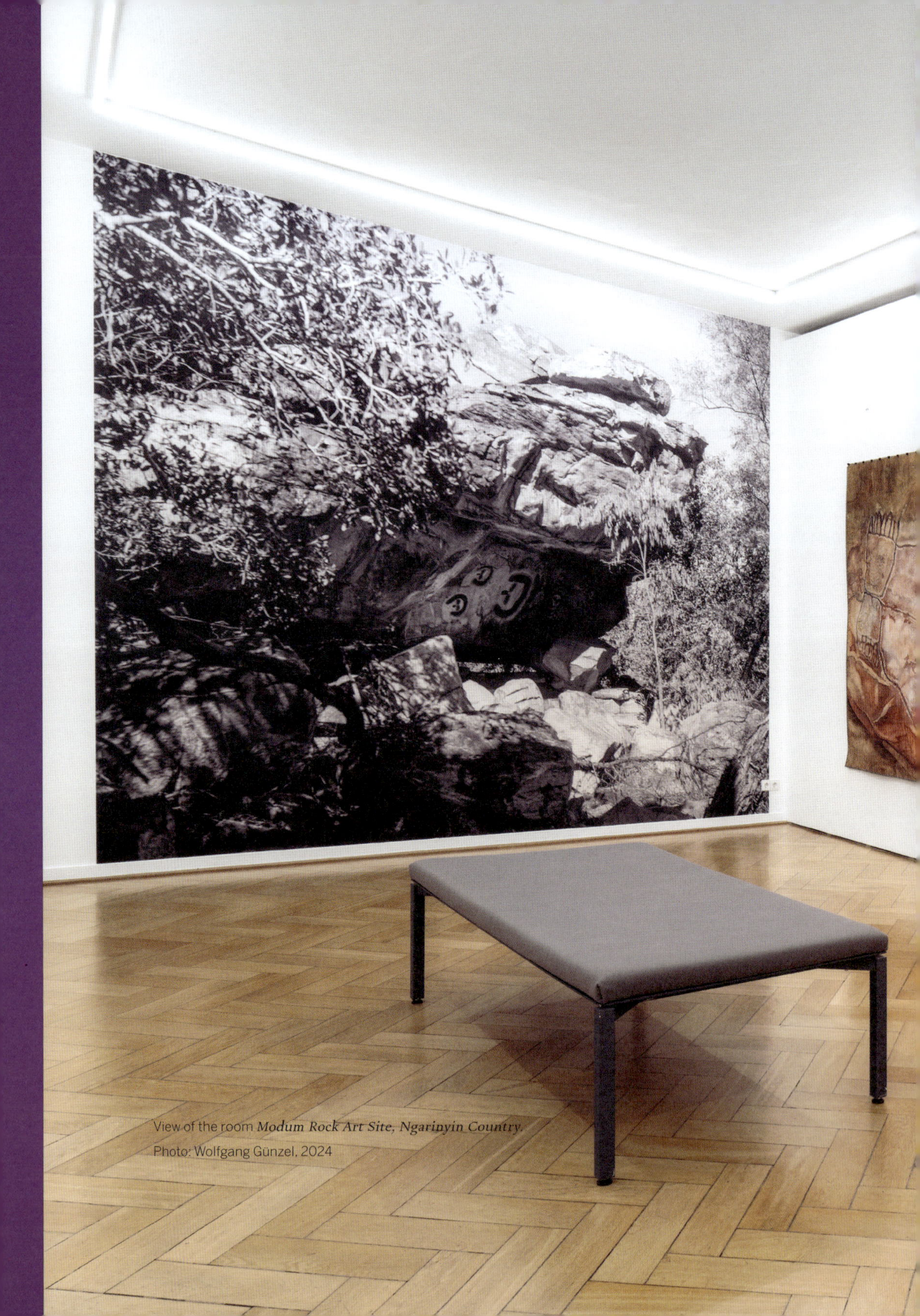

View of the room *Modum Rock Art Site, Ngarinyin Country.*
Photo: Wolfgang Günzel, 2024

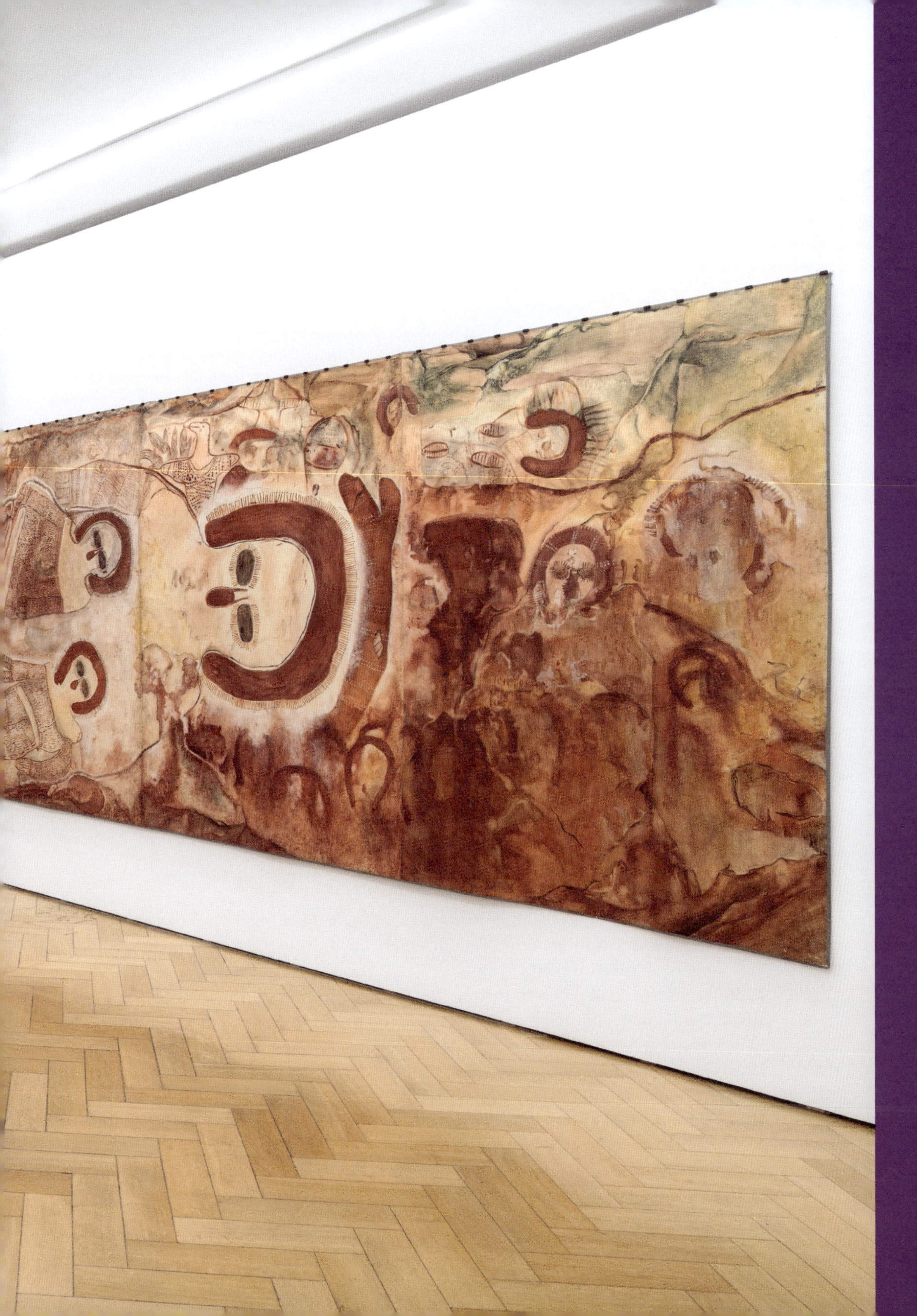

Timeline

"It is not about dates; it started from Lalai. When there was no beginning of time, it was when the world started"
Yornadaiyn Woolagoodja, 2018

For *Wanjina Wunggurr* Traditional Owners time is not linear. *Larlan* or *Lalai* is the beginning of time as evidenced by the physical presence of *Wanjina* images on the surface of rock shelters.

c. 60,000 years ago Archaeological dating of Indigenous presence in Australia.

c. 12,000 years ago Archaeological dating of *Gwion* rock art tradition in the Kimberley region.

c. 5,800 years ago Archaeological dating of *Wanjina* rock art tradition in the Kimberley region.

1770 James Cook lands on the east coast of Australia.

1838 Sir George Grey is the first European to document rock paintings in the *Wanjina Wunggurr* area.

1890–1920 The "killing times". Large numbers of the Indigenous population are killed in confrontations with settlers in the eastern Kimberley region.

1905–1969 The Aborigines Act aims to enforce assimilation. The Chief Protector of the Department of Native Affairs is given powers to place Indigenous children under 16 in state care without parental agreement (the "stolen generation").

1920 The Kunmunya Presbyterian Missionary Station is set up on Woddordda land.

1926 Munja Government Ration Station is set up on Ngarinyin Country in order to prevent the Indigenous inhabitants from hunting the land, which has been claimed by cattle farms.

1938 Frobenius Expedition to the territory of the *Wanjina Wunggurr* community.

1944 During aerial bombing in World War II, the museum building in Frankfurt is destroyed along with most of the collections from the Frobenius Expedition.

1950 The Indigenous communities of Kunmunya and Munja are resettled to Wotjulum on Yampi Sound.

1955 Rock art expedition undertaken by the Munich Völkerkundemuseum (Andreas and Katharina Lommel) on Ngarinyin land.

1956 The *Wanjina Wunggurr* community of Wotjulum is resettled to "Old Mowanjum" in Derby, which takes them beyond their ancestral land.

1967 Universal suffrage is introduced for Aboriginal Australians.

1968 The introduction of equal pay for Indigenous livestock workers in the Kimberley region leads to numerous dismissals.

1979 The *Wanjina Wunggurr* community is once more resettled, this time New Mowanjum, outside Derby.

Late 1970s Launch of the Northwest Australian Indigenous art movement at the Mowanjum Art and Culture Centre.

1992 The decision of the High Court of Australia in Mabo v. Queensland recognises the legal status of Indigenous peoples within the Commonwealth of Australia and the myth of 'Terra Nullius' is refuted.

2008 The Australian Parliament officially apologises to Aboriginal Australians for generating conditions creating the "stolen generation".

2011 Wanjina Wunggurr Prescribed Body Corporate (WWPBC) receives "Native Title" land rights for territory the size of Germany and Austria combined.

2022 As part of the research project, an archive containing the complete collections of the German expeditions to Northwest Australia in 1938 and 1955 is digitally repatriated to the *Wanjina Wunggurr* community in the form of a database.

2023 The referendum to recognise an Indigenous Voice to Parliament fails.

Timeline

Glossary of Indigenous Concepts

In the languages of the *Wanjina Wunggurr* communities of the Woddordda, Ngarinyin and Wunambal Gaambera there are different spellings for the terms listed here. There are many ways of speaking within the *Wanjina Wunggurr* communities: different languages, dialects and accents. Some of these ways of speaking have been lost. The languages of the *Wanjina Wunggurr* have found different written expressions in the post-contact context of missionaries, linguists, researchers and others. The glossary provides an overview of a selection of key terms for a better understanding of *Wanjina Wunggurr* culture.

Dambun (Ngarinyin) – Clan estate. A term indicating an area of land and/or sea to which an individual or group have particular connections. This can be a named geospatial area, ranging from a very specific place to a much broader area of land. In the past ethnologists referred to the term as a "clan estate". **Graa** (Wunambal), **Dambeem** (Woddordda).

Gaambera – Language of the Gaambera people who are today represented by the Wunambal Gaambera Aboriginal Corporation.

Gwion (Ngarinyin) – Spiritual beings and figures in rock art. **Gwiyon** (Wunambal), **Geeyorn** (Woddordda).

Larlan (Ngarinyin) – A rich body of religious narratives that concerns the core of how and when land, sea, heavens and all that is within them came into existence by the actions of Creator Beings and continue to exist. Rules for social behaviour and caring for Country are an essential component of Larlan. **Lalai** (Woddordda/Wunambal).

Junba (Ngarinyin/Wunambal) – A type of traditional song-dance performance, **Joonba** (Woddordda).

Ngarinyin – Language of the Ngarinyin people who are today represented by the Wilinggin Aboriginal Corporation.

Wanjina (Ngarinyin/Wunambal) – Anthropomorphic beings that can often be seen as rock art paintings and in contemporary art. They are regarded as the ancestors of today's Traditional Owners and are associated with the creation of the world, in particular rain bringers, and typically have no mouth. *Wandjina* (Woddordda).

Wanjina Wunggurr **community/society** – is a term which has arisen in contemporary socio-political contexts such as when asserting native title rights. The members of this society share a unique body of beliefs and practices concerning non-human sentient beings called *Wanjina* and *Wunggurr*. The *Wanjina Wunggurr* community is a single society with a defined territory whose members share a common system of Laws and customs that are unique to them and their Country.

Woddordda – Language of the Woddordda people who are today represented by the Dambimangari Aboriginal Corporation. Alternative spelling: *Worrorra*

Wodoy **and** *Jungurn* (Ngarinyin) – The two moieties of the *Wanjina Wunggurr* society, which, among other things, form the basis of the marriage system. They are represented by the two nightjar birds; the spotted nightjar (Wodoy) and the owlet nightjar (Jungurn). *Woday* **and** *Jirrin* (Wunambal), *Woodoi* **and** *Joongoon* (Woddordda).

Wunambal – Language of the Wunambal people, who are today represented by the Wunambal Gaambera Aboriginal Corporation.

Wunggurr (Ngarinyin/Wunambal) – All enduring sacred and powerful life force of central importance, often found in rock art sites, painted as a snake and associated with the power of oceans and cyclonic activities. *Woongudd* (Woddordda).

Wurnan (Ngarinyin) – A practice of binding reciprocal relationships of sharing and trade including marriage and ritual exchanges between Aboriginal people embedded in *Wanjina Wunggurr* Law. *Wunan* (Wunambal), *Woonan* (Woddordda).

Authors

Michaela Appel studied anthropology, Indology, Tibetology and Thai at the Ludwig Maximilians University in Munich and researched life cycle ceremonies on the islands of Timor in East Indonesia and Java. She was curator for South Asia, Southeast Asia, Oceania and Australia in the Museum Fünf Kontinente in Munich.

Kim Doohan is an anthropologist and human geographer working as an independent consultant utilising decolonising and participatory research methods. She has worked for more than thirty five years with senior *Wanjina Wunggurr* Traditional Owners to create private and public materials as part of the ongoing intergenerational transfer of knowledge.

Rona Gungnunda Charles is a Ngarinyin and Nyikina singer, dancer, cultural teacher/consultant, multi-disciplinary artist and researcher. As an Environment and Cultural Heritage Ranger, she serves the Law, language and cultural interests of *Wanjina Wunggurr* people as well as Nyikina people and focalises on sustainability and research collaborations.

Christina Henneke participated as a PhD student and research associate at the Frobenius Institute in a German Research Foundation (DFG) project on the German rock painting expeditions to Northwest Australia. Her research,

conducted in close cooperation with the *Wanjina Wunggurr* community, addressed issues of Indigenous agency and digital repatriation.

Matthias Claudius Hofmann is curator of the Oceania collection at the Weltkulturen Museum, Frankfurt am Main.

Isabel Kreuder is research assistant in the Oceania collection at the Weltkulturen Museum, Frankfurt am Main

Richard Kuba is an ethnologist at the Frobenius Institute in Frankfurt am Main. As head of the rock art archive he has examined, amongst other things, the reception history of prehistoric rock art and curated numerous exhibitions. Over recent years he has directed a project of the German Research Foundation (DFG) on the German rock art expeditions to Northwest Australia.

Matthew Dembalali Martin is a Ngarinyin and Wunambal Elder, singer and cultural teacher. Following his parents Maisie Jodba and Scotty Nyalgodi Martin, Matthew preserves *Junba* and *Wolungarri* songs and associated knowledge for the *Wanjina Wunggurr* peoples. He has worked with researchers and led the work to return recordings of *Junba* to his peoples and Country.

Lloyd Nulgit is a member of the *Wanjina Wunggurr* community living in Derby, Western Australia. He is a Ngarinyin man who grew up in his traditional Country and in the *Wanjina Wunggurr* culture. Lloyd had been working with the Wilinggin Aboriginal Corporation for the past fifteen years as a cultural adviser and with the Wilinggin Rangers caring for Country.

Pete O'Connor is a Woddordda man and member of the *Wanjina Wunggurr* community living at Looma in North-west Australia. Pete works as a Cultural Advisor to the Dambimangari Aboriginal Corporation. He is particularly committed to ensuring cultural continuity through *Joonba* practice, establishing respectful cultural archives for his people and caring for Country.

Martin Porr is an Australian Research Council Future Fellow and Associate Professor of Archaeology and a member of the Centre for Rock Art Research + Management at the University of Western Australia. He has published widely on Palaeolithic art and archaeology as well as theoretical and decolonizing approaches in archaeological and rock art research.

Eva Ch. Raabe studied ethnology at the University of Göttingen. From 1985 to 2019 she was the curator of the Oceania collection at the Weltkulturen Museum, Frankfurt am Main. From 2015 until her retirement in 2023 she directed the museum, first provisionally, then as its appointed director. A focus of her work was the Indigenous art of Australia and New Guinea.

John Wunargnu Rastus belongs to the *Wanjina Wunggurr* domain in the Top North Kimberley situated in Western Australia. He speaks Ngarinyin language. His clans are both Guyingarri and Galurungarri from his father's parents. He is of *Jungurn* moiety. He remotely resides in Dodnun Community on Wilinggin Country.

Anthony Redmond has worked with Ngarinyin people and their neighbours in the northern Kimberley region of Australia since 1994, in Central Australia since 2002 and in Cape York Peninsula since 2005. He is currently a Visiting Senior Research Fellow at The University of Queensland.

Sally Treloyn is Associate Professor in Ethnomusicology and Intercultural Research at the University of Melbourne. Treloyn has conducted research with Ngarinyin, Woddordda, and Wunambal *Junba* singers since the late 1990s, and has a special interest in musical systems, archives and access, and sustainability.

Leah Umbagai is a senior Woddordda woman living in the Mowanjum community near Derby, West Australia. The nationally and internationally recognised artist is committed to the preservation of the Woddordda language as well as providing cultural education and support for children and young people in her community.

Colophon

Exhibition

Country bin pull'em.
Looking back together
1.11.2024 – 31.8.2025
Weltkulturen Museum
Schaumainkai 29–37
60594 Frankfurt am Main
www.weltkulturenmuseum.de

Head curator
Matthias Claudius Hofmann

Project assistant
Isabel Kreuder

Participating persons and co-curators
Rona Gungnunda Charles,
Kim Doohan, Christina Henneke,
Richard Kuba, Lloyd Nulgit,
Pete O'Connor, Martin Porr,
Eva Ch. Raabe, Leah Umbagai

Editing
Vanessa von Gliszczynski

Exhibition design
Graphics
U9 visuelle Allianz,
Offenbach am Main

Framing and setup
Bernd Vossmerbäumer

Exhibition technology
Marcel Bode, Jan Philipp Kluck,
Jakob Nebel, Sascha Svoboda

Media design
Photo-Archives Frobenius
Institute
Jennifer Markwirth,
Peter Steigerwald

Film production
Christina Henneke, Mark Jones,
Florian Kluck-Ceyhan, Richard
Kuba, Mariangela Lanza

Restoration
Mareike Mehlis, Kristina Werner
Trainee: Chi-Chen Shen

Library and archive
Renate Lindner

Education
Julia Albrecht, Melina Angermeier,
Stephanie Endter

Press and public relations
Christina Henneke,
Julia Rajkovic-Kamara,
Christine Sturm
Trainee: Laura DiNardo

Events
Margit Zimmler

Administration
Susanne Becker, Claudia Bodens,
German Kruten, Heide Schott

Publication

This publication accompanies the
exhibition:
Country bin pull'em.
Looking back together
1.11.2024 – 31.8.2025
Weltkulturen Museum

Editors
Matthias Claudius Hofmann,
Richard Kuba, Christina Henneke,
Isabel Kreuder

Editorial team
Vanessa von Gliszczynski,
Christina Henneke,
Matthias Claudius Hofmann,
Isabel Kreuder, Richard Kuba

Design
U9 visuelle Allianz,
Offenbach am Main

Copy-editing
Vanessa von Gliszczynski,
Matthias Claudius Hofmann,
Isabel Kreuder, Renate Lindner,
Nicola Morris, Colin Shepherd

Translation
Herwig Engelmann, Nicola Morris,
Colin Shepherd, Jan Wilms

Photo-archive Frobenius
Institute
Jennifer Markwirth,
Peter Steigerwald

Photo-archive Weltkulturen Museum
Audrey Peraldi

Object- and exhibition views
Wolfgang Günzel

Our thanks to the publishers, institutions and individuals who kindly gave permission for the reproduction of photos and texts from their publications.

The images used were either made available by the lenders and copyright holders specified in the captions or come from our archives. In cases where it was not possible to identify the copyright holder correctly, legitimate claims are subject to compensation in accordance with the standard agreements.

All works, objects and photographs of the Wanjina Wunggurr people in this publication are shown with the kind permission of the relevant Traditional Owners and the three corporations that represent them: Dambimangari Aboriginal Corporation (DAC), Wilinggin Aboriginal Corporation (WAC) and Wunambal Gaambera Aboriginal Corporation (WGAC).

Project management, Kerber Verlag
Lily von Wild

General production and distribution Kerber Verlag
Rudi-Dutschke-Str 26,
10969 Berlin, Germany
+49 30 259 28 280
info@kerberverlag.com
kerberverlag.com

Kerber publications are distributed worldwide:

ACC Art Books
Sandy Lane, Old Martlesham
Woodbridge, IP12 4SD, UK
Tel. +44 1394 38 99 50
Fax +44 1394 38 99 99
uksales@accartbooks.com
accartbooks.com

Artbook | D.A.P.
75 Broad Street, Suite 630
New York, NY 10004, USA
Tel. +1 212 627 1999
Fax +1 212 627 9484
orders@dapinc.com
artbook.com

AVA Verlagsauslieferung AG
Industrie Nord 9,
5634 Merenschwand, Switzerland
Tel. +41 44 762 42 00
Fax +41 44 762 42 10
avainfo@ava.ch

Zeitfracht Medien GmbH
Distribution, Germany
+49 711 7860 2254
service.zeitfracht.de

The Deutsche Nationalbibliothek lists this publication in the Deutsche Nationalbibliografie: dnb.de.

ISBN 978-3-7356-1028-7
Country bin pull'em.
Looking back together

This book is also available in a German edition:
ISBN 978-3-7356-1026-3
Country bin pull'em.
Ein gemeinsamer Blick zurück

www.kerberverlag.com

Printed in Germany

Cooperation partners

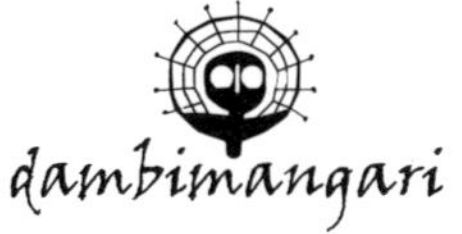 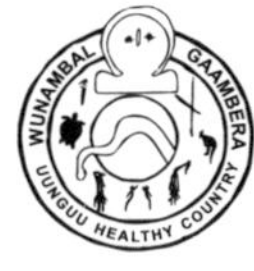 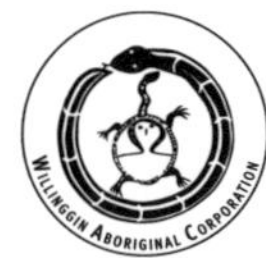

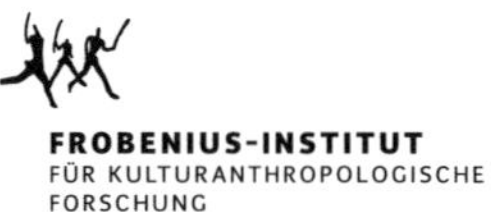 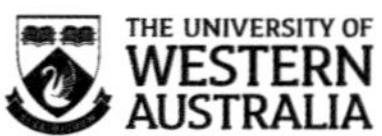

With the kind support of

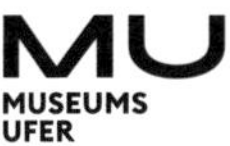 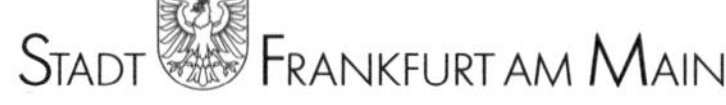